The Counter-Revolution
in Pennsylvania
1776-1790

The Counter-Revolution in Pennsylvania 1776-1790

BY

ROBERT L. BRUNHOUSE

1971

OCTAGON BOOKS

New York

Published in 1942
by the Pennsylvania Historical Commission

Reprinted 1971

by special arrangement with Robert L. Brunhouse

OCTAGON BOOKS
A DIVISION OF FARRAR, STRAUS & GIROUX, INC.
19 Union Square West
New York, N. Y. 10003

LIBRARY OF CONGRESS CATALOG CARD NUMBER: 70-120237

Printed in U.S.A. by
NOBLE OFFSET PRINTERS, INC.
NEW YORK 3, N. Y.

FOREWORD

TO THE LAYMAN, a university doctoral dissertation often appears as something to be regarded with awe. Unfortunately, because of this and other factors there are many historical studies in this category which never come to achieve the attention they deserve. Often they are not printed at all; usually, if printed, they are filed in series in the libraries to gather dust with other similar studies. This is not as it should be. Ofttimes these scholarly studies, the product of months and even years of laborious research, are well-written and valuable contributions to historical literature.

Pennsylvania history has been enriched recently by the publication and general distribution of two important studies concerned with its political development. Dr. J. Paul Selsam, now a member of the Department of History at the Pennsylvania State College, completed a few years ago, as a Princeton University dissertation, a study of the Pennsylvania Constitution of 1776 and its background. This has been published by the University of Pennsylvania Press. Dr. Philip Klein, of Franklin and Marshall College, published more recently the results of a similar intensive study of the Jacksonian era in State politics.

The Pennsylvania Historical Commission is delighted to have the opportunity to publish, under its auspices, another of these contributions to knowledge concerning the early political history of the State. It is the first volume in this field made available as a Commission publication. Doctor Brunhouse has shed new light on the political evolution of Pennsylvania during the critical years of readjustment following the American Revolution. The study will take its place with those previously mentioned, and others in preparation, as contributions toward the ultimate reconsideration of many phases of the political history of the Commonwealth.

ROSS PIER WRIGHT, *Chairman,*
Pennsylvania Historical Commission.

CONTENTS

PREFACE

THE INDIVIDUAL STATES have always been a significant factor in American history. This was especially true during the period of the Revolution and the Confederation when the states enjoyed more power than at any other time in their history. As provinces in the colonial period they were limited to a varying degree by the oversight of the English government. After 1787 their powers were curtailed by the Federal Constitution. From another viewpoint the history of the states during the Revolution and Confederation is significant. After the Declaration of Independence the Revolution came under the control of the radical element. By 1787 the radical strength had waxed and waned so that the Constitution represented a return to conservatism. Only with the detailed story of the struggle between radical and conservative forces in each state can one gain a more complete understanding of the history of the Revolution and Confederation.

The aim of this work is to describe the political changes which took place in Pennsylvania from 1776 to 1790. The rise of the revolutionary movement has been explained by Charles L. Lincoln[1]* and the conditions producing the Constitution of 1776 have been investigated by J. Paul Selsam.[2] The present work continues the story of the political fortunes and misfortunes of Pennsylvania during the existence of that Constitution. Due to overemphasis upon the early years of the Revolution, there has been a tendency to regard the radical party as dominant in the State until the overthrow of their frame of government in 1790. That was not the case. It was the conservative element that controlled the State or shared power equally with the radical group for nine years. The significant part played by the conservatives has never been adequately emphasized.[3]

The whole theme permeating the factional quarrels was that of counter-revolution. Even during the years of Radical supremacy from 1776 to 1780 the conservative element did much to embarrass the government and made two strong but unsuccessful attempts to have the Constitution revised. From 1780 to 1784 the Radicals lost their grip except in the Council of Censors where only the equal vote of each county made it possible for them to prevent alterations to the Constitution. During these years the conservatives in the assembly marched on to success, a success, as it proved, which went to their heads and brought a brief reaction. In 1784-1785 the Radicals enjoyed their last taste of power; in attempting to undo all the work of the conservatives, the Radicals overshot their mark and were repudiated at the following election. The end of the period covering the years 1786 to 1790 marked the complete triumph of conservatism and respectability which found its expression in the overthrow of the Constitution of 1776. From the days of 1774 and 1775 when the eastern oligarchy dominated the province until the adoption of the new frame of government in 1790, the State had passed through the complete curve of revolution.

* Explanatory notes for the preface and the various chapters begin on page 229.

Some interesting aspects of this study are here briefly mentioned. The conservatives never advocated the overthrow of the Radical Constitution by resort to arms. This was natural, since the strength of the conservatives lay with the property holders and the business men. In the movement for the emancipation of Negroes the strongest opposition came from the Radicals of the Scotch-Irish hinterland. After the law had been passed, the Philadelphia conservatives strenuously opposed any relaxation of its provisions. Although men like James Wilson and Robert Morris advocated more power and authority for Congress, it was the conservative party that despised Congress when it was driven from Philadelphia; and, to turn the tables completely, the Radicals professed a respect for the national legislature. In the Wyoming controversy the Radicals blamed the Republicans severely for their handling of the affair, but when the Radicals came into power they failed just as completely in solving the problem. Although the Radicals condemned the wealthy conservatives like Robert Morris for speculating in lands and public securities, it was the Radical assembly of 1784-1785 which passed the funding law; this action showed that frontier democrats were willing and eager to speculate in depreciated certificates. And lastly, it was the Radical democrats and not the conservative moneyed men who passed the first protective tariff of Pennsylvania.

The author is indebted to numerous persons for various kinds of aid in the process of the work. They are: Mr. Whitfield Bell, Jr., Mr. John Bender, Professor Arthur C. Bining, Dr. Julian P. Boyd, Mr. Barney Chesnick, Mrs. Frederic Clarke, Miss Helen Crowne, Dr. Leonidas Dodson, Miss Hartwell, Miss Anna Hewitt, Miss Laura Jordan, Dr. Philip Klein, Mr. Burton A. Konkle, Mr. Bernard Levin, Miss Jean Longacre, Mr. Charles B. Montgomery, Professor Roy F. Nichols, J. Bennett Nolan, Esq., Miss O'Connor, Col. Henry W. Shoemaker, Dr. St. George L. Sioussat, Miss Nell B. Stevens, Mr. Heinrich Suhr, Mr. Maxwell Whitemen, and Mr. Thomas Young. The staffs of the following institutions extended gracious help in making their resources available: the Historical Society of Pennsylvania, the Library Company of Philadelphia, the American Philosophical Society, the University of Pennsylvania Library, the Pennsylvania State Library, the Krauth Memorial Library of the Lutheran Theological Seminary, the Library of the Drexel Institute of Technology, the Roberts Collection of Haverford College, the Reading Room, Rare Book Room and the Manuscripts Division of the Library of Congress, the Maryland Historical Society, the York County Historical Society, the Berks County Historical Society, the Archives Division of the Department of Public Instruction at Harrisburg, and the Historical Records Survey.

ROBERT L. BRUNHOUSE.

I

The Background

Population and Communication

DURING the early years of the Revolution between 270,000 and 280,000 persons lived within the boundaries of Pennsylvania. The density was greatest in Philadelphia and vicinity, and decreased in proportion as one moved north and west. The northwestern section of the State had no white inhabitants during the period from 1775 to 1790. What effect the war had on the population is difficult to determine, but after peace came there was a steady immigration into the State. Some clue to the increase can be gained by comparing the figures on which seats in the assembly were apportioned. In 1779 there were over 54,000 taxables in the State; by 1786 the number had increased to over 66,000. This represents a gain of twenty-two per cent within a period of seven years. The latter figure indicates a total population of about 350,000 people. The first federal census of 1790 credited the State with 434,373 persons. This was a phenomenal increase in view of the emigrations to Kentucky and Canada of which contemporaries complained during the years following the close of the war.[1]

Although the great majority of the people engaged in agricultural pursuits, urban centers, especially the city of Philadelphia, were significant in the political life of the new State. According to one estimate Philadelphia increased from 28,000 souls in 1769 to over 34,000 in the first year of the war. During the British occupation its numbers decreased to 25,000, but by 1783 it was boasting over 37,000. At the end of the decade more than 42,000 persons were counted in the city and its suburbs. Compared with Philadelphia, other communities in 1790 were mere villages except for Lancaster with 3,773 inhabitants, York with about 3,000 inhabitants, and Reading with 2,225. Harrisburg could boast only 800 people, Pittsburgh 376, and Wilkes-Barre 300. In Philadelphia in 1790 about one-fifth of the people were employed in domestic and personal service, a third in trade and transportation, and over two-fifths in manufacturing and mechanical pursuits. Among the latter group carpenters, shoemakers, and tailors were the most numerous.[2]

The racial strains in the State are interesting and at the same time difficult to determine with accuracy. Most of the calculations are based on family names, a process which involves an indeterminable probability of error. Before the Revolution Franklin estimated that about one-third of the people were English Quakers, another third Germans, and the remainder a variety of races, chiefly Scotch-Irish. Most investigators agree that from some time prior to the Revolution until the last decade of the century the Germans constituted a third of the inhabitants. A recent study gives the following figures for the end of the period, based on the census of 1790:[3]

	Population	*Percentage of total*
English	149,451	35.3
Scotch	36,410	8.6
Irish: Ulster	46,571	11.0
Free State	14,818	3.5
German	140,983	33.3
Dutch	7,500	1.8
French	7,500	1.8
Swedish	3,325	.8
Unassigned	16,815	3.9
Total white population	423,373	100.0

The three important racial groups were the English, the Germans, and the Irish. From the time William Penn came into control of the land late in the seventeenth century the English swarmed into the province, not only from England, but also from other English colonies. They inhabited and dominated the original three counties of Philadelphia, Bucks, and Chester in the extreme southeastern part of the province. Among them the Quakers held a predominant place in the political affairs of the colony until the middle of the eighteenth century and with gradually diminishing force until the outbreak of the Revolution. Other religious elements in the English stock were Episcopalians, Baptists, and Methodists.[4]

The second important racial group were the Germans who immigrated in large numbers during the half century preceding the Revolution due to unfavorable religious and economic conditions in Europe. Religiously they were divided into "church people" comprising the Lutheran and Reformed persuasions, and the pietistic groups represented by Moravians, Mennonites, Schwenkfelders and similar sects, which split the Germans along religious lines and accounts in part for their lack of organization as a political force. They settled in Berks, Lancaster, and Northampton counties where they were protected from the unsettled conditions of real frontier life. Industrious, frugal, little addicted to strong drink, and unexposed to the rigors of frontier life, they reared large families and became important as the farmers of the State. Remarkably clannish in retaining their language and customs, they were conservative in outlook.[5]

Despite their numbers, the Germans carried little weight in the political scale. This was due to the fact that the wide divergence among their religious sects made organization on a racial basis difficult, if not impossible, and their failure to produce important political leaders. The only man in this period who showed any potential qualities to lead the Germans was Frederick A. Muhlenberg, but his European education and his cultural interests placed him beyond the common touch. He lacked popular appeal and entertained little respect for the mentality of his own race. As in colonial times, the Germans divided their political allegiance between the two major parties. In Philadelphia and in the Scotch-Irish rural regions, they often followed the Radicals; in other sections the conservative, propertied group fell under the leadership of the Republicans. In the early days of the Revolution in York and Lancaster counties they displayed resistance to the test oaths and militia fines, but they did not persist. From 1776 to 1790 both political parties made spasmodic, half-hearted attempts to court the entire German vote. In 1788 the Germans showed some signs of voting as an independent political unit with the sole aim of placing some of their own nationals in public office.[6]

The part played by the Germans might have been different, had they been well informed on what was taking place in the State. In 1778 the Reverend Helfenstein reported that "the most part of them cannot read English, and some don't understand it."[7] During most of the period under survey there was only one German newspaper and its circulation was confined to several hundred copies. Only occasionally did the assembly order its most important actions to be printed in German. Pamphlets and broadsides rarely appeared in that tongue and Germans complained especially that the assembly minutes were not printed in their language.[8]

The third significant racial group was the Scotch-Irish who came to the province in the later colonial period, especially during the years 1771 to 1774. The Cumberland Valley became their exclusive possession from which they pushed westward over the several mountain ranges into the untouched regions of Bedford and Westmoreland counties. Combining Presbyterianism and individualism, they settled the frontier region where their restlessness was given free vent in seeking out better lands. Other characteristics of this sturdy race were their hatred of England, a flair for politics, and their belief in education. Their ministers had much influence over them and did not scruple to combine politics with religion. When the Executive Council wanted to draw the settlers of southwestern Pennsylvania from a new State movement in the early 1780's, they sent a Presbyterian minister among the people as the most effective vehicle of propaganda. The Scotch-Irish Presbyterians became the rank and file of the Radical Constitutionalist party, so much so that the faction was sometimes referred to as the Presbyterian party. Temperance in the use of hard drink was not one of their virtues, especially in the frontier region. One divine in the backwoods finally lost his job because he opposed the drinking habits of his congregation.[9]

Not all of the Irish migrated westward, for in Philadelphia they were not insignificant. Here, however, there was a marked division among them. The Sons of Saint Tammany, organized for social purposes, contained the leaders of the Radical party and undoubtedly had an influence in political life despite the fact that they assembled only once a year for a grand picnic. A small but entirely different group of Irishmen was composed of wealthy, aristocratic merchants. They had their own organization, known as the Sons of Saint Patrick. With only one exception the members were all conservatives who in politics opposed the Radical Sons of Saint Tammany.[10]

The other racial groups in 1776 were the Welsh, French, Scotch, Catholic Irish, Dutch, Swedes, and Negroes, but they were negligible in numbers and influence. A number of Jewish families lived in Philadelphia and Lancaster.[11]

The lack of adequate communication was a significant factor in the political situation. Undoubtedly the Radicals would have experienced more success in administering the affairs of state during the early years of the war if they could have maintained closer contact with the hinterland. On the other hand, the Republicans would probably have gained more adherents in the frontier region during the decade of the 1780's had they been able to spread their views effectively beyond the urban regions.

Evidences of poor communication are numerous. At Easton magistrates were at a loss how to act in certain cases because they had not received the laws of the assembly and the resolutions of Council. In Lancaster the lack of State laws also handicapped local officials. This condition was not due to the disorganization caused by the war, for after hostilities ceased the same complaints recurred. In 1784 the populace in Carlisle was "almost in the dark" concerning the work of the Council of Censors.[12] At this time John Okeley writing from Bethlehem explained the situation:

> *Knowledge* & the proper *Circulation* thereof, I take to be the very Essence of a Republican Government—How is it, then, that the Proceedings of Assembly are rarely, if ever, communicated in the *back Parts* of the State, 'till the Session is over? Why may we not be favord with the perusal of their Minutes as regularly as we are with the weekly Papers?[13]

Some conservatives believed that the Radicals maintained their hold on the western regions because news reached that area only in small quantities and because unfavorable information was counteracted by the backwoods stump speakers. It was asserted that the Radicals opposed the establishment of a postal system through the West because they wanted to keep their constituents uninformed.[14] The two methods used by the Constitutionalists in rallying the frontier regions to their support were stump speakers like William Findley who would talk to the settlers in their own language, and the circulation of printed pamphlets.[15]

Until the middle of the 1780's all the newspapers printed in the State were issued from Philadelphia, and their circulation in the hinterland was limited and news was stale by the time it reached those parts. It was more than a decade after the opening of the Revolution until local news sheets sprung up in Carlisle, Reading, Pittsburgh, Lancaster, and York. By the end of the decade the State boasted twenty-three newspapers; over half of them were weeklies.[16] The editors found it necessary to take sides in the political warfare in order to exist. When William Spotswood tried "to steer an impartial line" in his *Pennsylvania Herald,* he found it impracticable. Rather than advocate one political party, he threw up the whole venture.[17] It should be noted, however, that most of the newspapers held their partisanship within moderate bounds. The exceptions were Francis Bailey's *Freeman's Journal* and Eleazer Oswald's *Independent Gazetteer;* the former was offensively Radical and the latter violently Republican. Two other characteristics of the news sheets should be mentioned. Political opinion was expressed not in editorial comments which were rare, but in articles written over pseudonyms. Although the public generally knew who the authors were, the modern reader has few clues by which to identify these men who in many cases were prominent public figures. During the first half dozen years covered by this study most of the newspapers mentioned political affairs only in a formal way. There was a peculiar reticence about revealing affairs taking place "behind the scenes." When such references were made, they were extremely vague and conveyed the idea that politics was a dirty, scheming business which no editor would condescend to introduce into his columns. As the period progressed, this reticent attitude disappeared and in the 1780's the press descended to unbelievable depths of repulsive muckraking.

Aside from the newspapers other methods were used to disseminate information and opinions. Broadsides were employed for emergencies and special occasions. Sometimes they were issued as an extra page of newspapers. Bills of the assembly printed for public consideration were often issued in this form; but these bills never exceeded five hundred copies and their circulation was confined largely to Philadelphia. Broadsides were supplemented by pamphlets which gave the views, often political, of a writer who had a special cause to present. Although the outstanding example was Thomas Paine, pamphleteer extraordinary, there were numerous other writers, most of them appearing under assumed names. In centers of concentrated population the public mass meeting provided another method of discussion and dissemination of views. Such gatherings were common in Philadelphia and often took place at the State House; they were held less frequently in county towns like Reading, Lancaster, and Carlisle.

General Political Conditions

The annual election of members to State and county offices took place on the second Tuesday of October. In Philadelphia voting was by wards and in the counties by townships. The sheriff was required to give public notice of election at least eight days in advance. On the Saturday preceding election day the qualified freemen assembled and chose inspectors. On election day the inspectors selected three reputable persons who, together with the sheriff, acted as judges of election and assisted the inspectors in receiving and counting the votes. Judges and electors were required to take oaths for the faithful performance of their duties. Some disputed elections centered around the omission of this formality. The judges of election were required to open the polling place "at some time between the hours of ten in the morning and two in the afternoon."[18] If an elector was suspected of not qualifying, the judge or inspector was empowered to take the oath of the elector that he met the requirements. After closing the polls, the election officials cast up the return within two days, and one of them presented it at a meeting of the judges of election of the several districts at the court house, where the returns for the whole county were tabulated and within twelve days submitted to the President and Council. After it was found that the assembly was tardy in convening because the members had no formal confirmation of their election, the law required the judge of election to send official notification to each successful candidate.[19]

The procedure described obtained without change until 1785 when some alterations were made and the whole election process was more clearly defined. The constable was required to post notice of election in at least six places within the ward or township. County commissioners were required to furnish a list of taxables to be used by election officials as a guide to determine the eligibility of electors who presented themselves. By this new law voters were required to vote within the districts in which they resided. Polls were to be opened between ten and two o'clock and to be closed at seven o'clock except in Philadelphia where the closing time was extended one hour. A year later the assembly declared that election officials had been too precise on the point of closing and required that thereafter the polls should remain open until every elector present had the opportunity to cast his vote. The 1785 act granted eight shillings four pence per day to each election official, but in 1787 this provision was repealed as unnecessary. Regulations for the casting of ballots were specifically stated in the 1785 act. The voter was to write his choice for assemblymen and councillor on one slip of paper, fold it so that only the names of the offices were visible, and place the ballot in the ballot box in view of the judge of election. The choice for sheriffs and coroners was to be placed on another slip of paper and the names of commissioners on a third. Any voter convicted of receiving bribes was subject to a maximum fine of fifty pounds and six months in prison; one convicted of offering bribes could be fined and imprisoned at the discretion of the court.[20]

Two innovations in election procedure were planned in 1777 and 1778 to determine whether a convention should be called to reconsider the Constitution of 1776. The unique method outlined by the assembly in June, 1777, was due to unsettled conditions caused by the British invasion. At the election of inspectors the freemen were asked to choose a commissioner. His duty was to go to the residence of each qualified freeman or to take some other opportunity of meeting him, and ask him whether he desired a convention to be called. The freeman would then give his answer in writing, which the commissioner would place in a bag or box for that purpose. These ballots would be returned to the sheriff who would cast up the votes on each side of the question and report the result to the assembly. The only guarantee of a fair election was the oath required of the commissioner not to influence any voter and not to open or read any ballot until he assisted the sheriff in casting up the returns. In 1778 the assembly planned another vote on the same question but along more conventional lines. At this election there were to be two boxes. The voters would indicate on a ticket whether or not they wished a convention and deposit their ballots in one box. In the other box they were instructed to place their ballots for members to the convention. If the vote for a convention prevailed, then the second box would be opened and the six highest candidates would be declared the delegates from that county.[21]

According to the Constitution of 1776 the franchise was possessed by every freeman who had resided in the State for one year and had paid taxes during that time, and by sons of freeholders who had not paid taxes but who could vote on age. Actually the franchise was restricted by test oaths imposed by the Convention of 1776 and later by the assembly. Only freeholders, however, had the privilege of voting for justices of the peace. Twice the number of these magistrates was elected and the Council chose half of them to whom they issued commissions. It became a fixed custom for Council to select those men who had received the largest number of votes. During the period from 1776 to 1790 Chester, Bristol, and Lancaster enjoyed the status of boroughs with the right to elect burgesses and constables. After the Revolution Reading, Carlisle, and other towns were incorporated. The city of Philadelphia lost its independence with the Revolution and was governed by resolutions of Council and laws of the assembly. It elected only wardens and street commissioners who had insignificant duties. At the close of the period Philadelphia was incorporated and governed by a council and a board of aldermen.

The problems arising at the polling places can be illustrated by a brief glance at the causes of the disputed elections. At Lancaster borough in 1778 the main contention was that the ballot boxes had been stuffed. The inspectors had asked few of the electors to show their certificate of having taken the oath of allegiance, and some of the election clerks performed their duties without being sworn. In the following year, at York, a United States deputy commissary of purchases used angry and threatening language at the first district voting place, intruded himself upon the district judges assembled at the court house to make out the county returns, and dictated to them how to make out their return. The voting of the militia and of soldiers from the continental line caused serious trouble. In Philadelphia County in 1781 the militia had tickets thrust into their hands, and were not allowed to alter them or consult with friends. In military array, the officers standing with drawn swords, each member of the militia stepped up, deposited his ballot, and returned to the ranks. In 1783 in the city of Philadelphia Wayne's soldiers were accused of over-awing election officials and of crowding the polling place so that citizens had no opportunity to vote.[22]

The other disputed elections were caused by minor differences. In Northumberland County in 1783 the judges of the four districts could not agree and sent in a double return. In Chester County it was asserted that minors and non-jurors had voted. In the following year in Lancaster "hot work" at the election produced stuffed ballot boxes. Technicalities gave rise to disputes in Bedford County in 1786 where the returns from the second district were refused because they did not arrive on time and where one of the inspectors was discovered not to be a freeholder. In the following year, at Bedford, the seat of an assemblyman was contested because the judges of election refused to count a ticket which contained the vote for councillor and for assemblymen, but which the voter had failed to cut before depositing. By ignoring this ballot two candidates tied for a seat in the assembly. In Philadelphia County in 1788 it was charged that men who had not resided in the State for a year and had paid a trifling poor tax only two or three days before the election were allowed to vote. This catalog of troubles lists only the isolated cases of contested elections. In all other counties the elections were held in an orderly manner. Considering that this covers a period of fourteen years, in the earlier part of which the State was waging a war against an external foe; that political passions flamed to white heat on numerous occasions; that the people were passing from one political system to another; and that many of the disputed elections involved trivial technicalities, it is an excellent record of orderly government. Certainly it belies the older conception that the period of the Confederation was marked by confusion and disorder.[23]

Candidates for public office were chosen by the caucus system. The freemen of a ward or township gathered at a private house or tavern and agreed on the ticket to be run at the following election. Often this took place on the Saturday preceding election day when the freemen assembled to choose inspectors of election. This system did not please some extreme democrats. "When candidates are all put up together in a county ticket," one writer explained, "they are to be considered the favorites of a junto; when every district sends a man that man may be considered the real representative of such a number of the freemen of that district, chosen by them for properties they know him to be possessed of."[24] Another complainant decried "the rougish way" of electing members to the assembly and other offices. The tickets were planned in "clandestine conventicles" by six, eight, twelve or perhaps a few more cunning politicians, he said, and on election day these tickets were distributed by the leaders and their henchmen to the unwary populace.[25] Practical politicians realized that domination of the caucus was the key to their success. Meeting previous to the caucus, they agreed on a ticket and then convinced the caucus to adopt it. After the Federal Constitution of 1787 began to operate, the political parties of the State were forced to adopt the convention system for choosing candidates to the national house of representatives. Since Congressmen and presidential electors were voted for on a state-wide basis and not by districts, the old caucus would not answer. The Republicans, for example, sent delegates from each county to Lancaster in 1788 where the party slate was agreed upon.[26]

Although political parties were not officially recognized by the State government, they formed the warp and woof of political life at this time. In 1777 the Whig Society, representing the Radical group, had a semblance of organization in Philadelphia and maintained a committee of correspondence with the counties in the hinterland. Two years later the same men called themselves the Constitutional Society and published a platform of principles. The opposing faction had already taken the form of the Republican Society. At best these organizations were only loose, nebulous affairs and should not be confused with the highly organized political machines of the present time. As we approach the end of the period, there was a greater tendency to consider these party organizations as permanent structures. In the latter part of the 1780's other political groups threatened the two-party system which became common after the adoption of the Constitution in 1776. The mechanics were urged to form an organization in order to place some of their own men in assembly to promote the interests of the laborers. At the same time the recently arrived Irish immigrants banded together under the label of "The Lately Adopted Sons." This group was wooed by both of the major parties.[27]

Rise of the Revolutionary Movement

When the first news of the action of Boston in resisting the so-called Intolerable Acts reached Pennsylvania, the government of the province was in the hands of conservative elements. John Penn, as governor, represented the intrenched interests and privileges of the proprietary family which had economic as well as political interests in the colony. The assembly of 1773-1774 was dominated by the conservatives resulting from a coalition of the Quaker, German, and commercial powers, headed by Joseph Galloway. When Paul Revere arrived in Philadelphia in May, 1774, the leaders of the "popular" party resorted to a clever arrangement by which they persuaded John Dickinson to lend his presence to their meetings, and were thus able to crystallize public sentiment in favor of some moderate action sympathetic to Boston. A committee of correspondence was created. Already, however, the Quakers displayed a distaste for any radical measures. The refusal of Governor Penn to summon the assembly to deal with the new situation provided the extremists with an excuse to call popular mass meetings and to encourage the formation of local committees of correspondence. Assured that the Germans and the back-country would support the popular cause, the leaders advocating action against England issued a call for a convention to meet in Philadelphia in July, 1774. At this meeting men like Dickinson, William Smith, and James Wilson, all later branded as tories because they would not follow through the movement which they fathered, were still in control of the revolutionary action. The July meeting resulted in a declaration in favor of calling a congress of all the states to consider in what manner the colonies should oppose English aggression.[28]

The provincial assembly now came into the picture. Due to Indian trouble on the frontier, Governor Penn was forced to summon the assembly which soon turned its attention to the larger question of the coercive methods used by the mother country against the colonies. It quickly approved the idea of a continental congress and appointed seven delegates representing the respectable, commercial interests of the province.

The assembly was moving with current affairs but as events proved it did not move fast enough to keep up with the increasing pace of the radical element. When it elected delegates to the first Congress, it did not include Dickinson and Wilson, which action was resented by the extremists. In the assembly Speaker Galloway still held the upper hand and counseled the most pacific means in order to induce Britain to redress American grievances. The first blow to his power came in October when Wilson was elected to the assembly and was thus in a position to dispute the Speaker's mild program.

Gradually the breach broadened between the ultra-conservatives led by Galloway and the moderates represented by Dickinson and Wilson. When the first Continental Congress assembled in Philadelphia the extremists from Massachusetts and Virginia were irked at the slow pace with which Pennsylvania was taking decided measures. However, after Congress adopted a plan to stop importation of British goods, the assembly under Dickinson's influence approved this plan. This marked the end of the ultra-conservatives under Galloway; henceforth the Revolution in the colony entered its second phase as it came under the direction of moderates who demanded some action against England. The new assembly elected in the fall of 1774 appointed delegates to the second Continental Congress, which included Dickinson and Mifflin, both now leading the popular movement. The election of Edward Biddle as Speaker of the new assembly was a small revolution, for Biddle came from Berks County; this was a harbinger of the loss of power for the three eastern counties which traditionally controlled the assembly and the politics of the colony.

Another phase of the revolutionary movement took the form of the creation of committees of correspondence. This gave an opportunity of expression to many men who did not enjoy the restricted franchise. These committees were significant in the formulation of public opinion and gradually undermined the constituted authority in the province. Already the Quakers had withdrawn from the popular movement and their condemnation of these committees marked the Quakers as one of the bulwarks against extremism. By the early part of 1775 several political groups were discernible. The tories were composed of the proprietary and crown interests with the passive sympathy of the Quakers. The whigs were made up of various elements, all agreeing on the one objective of opposition to England. Within this revolutionary party were two district groups. The moderates, comprising the propertied and commercial interests who were now dominant in the committees, were at this time leading the revolutionary movement; they advocated opposition to England, in fact, almost any type of opposition short of independence. The other faction, which might be termed the violent or the ultra-radical party, was abetted by the radical spirits in Congress and hoped for independence and continued war with the mother country.

During the year 1775 the assembly continued to keep its hand on the revolutionary movement. The delegates chosen to Congress represented the moderate faction. Robert Morris, Thomas Willing, and Andrew Allen were closely allied with the old order of things. John Dickinson drew up the instructions for the delegates, which indicated the moderates' repugnance to any action savoring of independence or of a change in the form of provincial government. Events of 1775 showed that these moderates, in turn, were not moving fast enough for radicals who gained converts because of the open military conflict which roused the people against Great Britain, and who were strengthened in their own faith by revolutionaries of the type of John Adams, then attending Congress in Philadelphia.

The difference between the moderates and the radicals came to a head in the summer of 1776. The violent party realized that the assembly would advance no further, and looked to a convention to change the form of government of the province. This raised a storm of protest. To pacify the radicals and to retain control of affairs the assembly belatedly enlarged its membership by the addition of seventeen seats, of which thirteen went to the back-counties. Although the radical group had urged such action, it was not successful in dominating the assembly because the new arrangement continued to preserve control in the hands of the eastern oligarchy even though that control was based on only two votes. On May 1, 1776, when the election of the additional assemblymen took place, the radicals received an overwhelming defeat in the city; in the rural regions, however, they were more successful.

During this time sentiment for independence was growing in Congress. But the Pennsylvania delegates were expressly bound by their instructions not to vote for independence and the assembly refused to alter its position on this head. Thus the radicals in the province and the radicals in Congress had common cause and agreed that the only way to solve the problem was by overthrowing the provincial government of Pennsylvania. Thereupon Congress in May recommended to the colonies to set up new governments if the old forms did not respond to the new situation of affairs. In effect Congress invited the Pennsylvania extremists to throw the old proprietary government overboard. With all their strength the moderates opposed this action; in Congress Wilson did all he could to counter-act this proposal which would open the gates of radicalism with unpredictable results. The revolutionary movement thus advanced another step; the influence of the moderates waned and they were cast aside as being too cautious.

Preparatory to electing members to a convention to frame a new constitution for Pennsylvania, the radicals arranged that they should have control of the convention. In a final effort to preserve its authority the assembly modified its position on independence; it no longer prohibited the delegates from voting for that action but it did not specifically enjoin them to do so. This gesture was so obviously half-hearted that the whig members withdrew gradually from the assembly and that body quietly went out of existence for want of a quorum. In the meantime the county committees sent delegates to the provincial conference which met at Philadelphia on June 18 and elected Thomas McKean presiding officer.[29] In this extra-legal conference each county was granted one vote, another indication of the increasing strength of the back-counties in provincial affairs. The important work of this conference was to guarantee the radical element control of the constitutional convention. This was easily effected by changing the qualifications of electors. The fifty pound property restriction was wiped away, and the suffrage was bestowed on every associator who had arrived at the age of twenty-one, had resided in the colony at least one year, and had paid or had been assessed for any provincial or county taxes. In addition, judges or inspectors of election could require of each voter an oath denying allegiance to the king and a sworn promise not to hinder the establishment of a free government. Members elected to the convention would be required to declare their belief in God, Jesus Christ, and the divine inspiration of the scriptures. These regulations constituted the first real step in the overthrow of the provincial government.

The Constitutional Convention was in session from July to September, 1776.[30] When the Declaration of Independence was voted on in Congress on July 2, Franklin, Wilson, and Morton were for it, Willing and Humphreys opposed it, and Dickinson and Morris were present, but did not vote.[31] One of the first acts of the Convention was to oust the delegates who did not vote for the Declaration, except Morris, and to replace them with others who were favorable to independence. This action of the Convention was indicative of the new situation; the assembly had ceased to function and the Convention took over its legislative and appointive powers.

The composition of the Convention showed that the old order had passed. The members constituted a mediocre body to frame a Constitution for the State. Franklin was the only man who had any experience along that line. The other members were for the most part strangers to the theory or practice of government. "They were mostly honest well-meaning Country men, who are employed; but intirely unacquainted with such high matters" as were entrusted to their hands, was the comment of the Reverend Francis Allison.[32] According to the popular theory, honest, industrious men with little education could evolve a simple, democratic form of government more likely to preserve the rights of man. The radicals would not trust the educated lawyer or the wealthy merchant. Their smooth manners and apparent logic might turn out to be only a shield for convenient interpretations and other ruses to keep the people out of power and to advance themselves to high places more overbearing than the proprietary government under the Penns. In the Convention men like Wilson, Morris, and Dickinson do not appear, but in their stead were Franklin, Timothy Matlack, James Cannon, and George Bryan.[33]

Although the Convention was recognized by Congress and exercised legislative and executive powers, its important work was the framing of the Constitution of 1776 which reflected the prevailing democratic thought of the period.

According to the new instrument the legislative branch of government consisted of a unicameral assembly. In this respect the framers followed a practice in use in the colony for three-quarters of a century. They were two theoretical checks on the assembly. Bills introduced in a session were to be printed for public consideration and not passed upon until the succeeding session. Only in the case of measures of sudden necessity was this injunction to be waived. In actual practice this check proved to be worthless. Newspapers and handbills had a very small circulation outside of Philadelphia; there was no absolute method of determining public reaction to a bill; and the dominant party in the house could rush through any piece of legislation on the plea that it was an emergency measure. Representation in the assembly was based tentatively on the equal voice of every county, each sending six delegates to the house. After two years a census of taxables was to be taken and thereafter representation would be proportioned on that basis, and a new census and reapportionment would take place every seven years. Qualifications of electors were similar to those laid down by the provincial conference; every freeman of the age of twenty-one, resident in the State for at least one year and having paid public taxes was granted the franchise. There was no property qualification for assemblymen but they were allowed to serve a maximum of four years in seven. On taking office each assemblyman was required to take two oaths; that he would do nothing prejudicial to the Constitution and that he acknowledged belief in one God and the divine inspiration of the Bible.

The supreme power of the assembly becomes more evident when the provisions for the executive branch are understood. Distrustful of a governor, the framers created a plural executive, called the Supreme Executive Council, composed of one member from the City of Philadelphia and each county to serve for a three-year term. One-third of the members were replaced annually so as to train more men for public service and to avert "the danger of Establishing an inconvenient Aristocracy."[34] At the head of the Council were the president and vice-president, elected jointly by the Council and assembly. Five members of Council constituted a quorum. The president's powers were closely merged with those of Council of which he was a member. Council could appoint all officers not elected by the people or the assembly, grant pardons under certain limitation, try State officers impeached by the assembly, and call the legislature in special session. Its chief function was to see that the laws were faithfully executed. The lack of a veto on legislation and the division of authority and responsibility among twelve or more councillors constituted the significant weaknesses in this organization.

The judges of the Supreme Court were appointed by Council for a term of seven years with no restriction on reappointment. This was a marked departure from former times when judges held office during good behavior. To make the judiciary independent the assembly was enjoined to vote the judges fixed salaries. The legislature was given power to establish a system of inferior courts throughout the State.

The most unique aspect of the new frame was the provision for criticism and amendment of the Constitution. A Council of Censors, composed of two members elected from each county, was to meet every seven years. Their task was to determine whether the Constitution had been preserved inviolate, whether the assembly and executive Council had performed their duties or had assumed unwarranted powers, whether the taxes had been levied and collected fairly, and whether the laws had been executed. After investigation the Censors could pass public censures, order impeachments, and recommend laws which the assembly should repeal. If the Constitution needed alterations, the Censors could propose amendments and call a convention to consider them. This was the only method of altering the Constitution. Equal representation of each county in the Council of Censors gave the western regions a predominance far beyond their respective population, and guaranteed the Radicals the control of the State.[35] No alterations were ever made to the frame of 1776.

Scarcely had the Convention proclaimed the Constitution the law of the land, when the voices of dissent cried out. This opposition continued in one form or another for fourteen years. In this struggle the party lines had already been drawn before the adoption of the Constitution. The former "violent" party which had originally demanded independence from England was now in control of the State. The moderates, men of property and respectability who had led the revolutionary movement to the point of independence and then lost control, looked with horror on the new situation. Henceforth, their aim was to gain control of the State and to turn rampant democracy into more conservative channels. It required fourteen years to achieve this end. During that time they formed the opposition to the radical democratic faction and became known variously as conservatives, Republicans, or more accurately, Anti-Constitutionalists. The democratic group, whose political welfare depended on the existence of the new frame of government, were termed Radicals or Constitutionalists. The tory and Quaker element gave their moral support to the Republicans, and this had a damaging effect on that faction during the years of actual war because it was easy for the Radicals to howl down their opponents by branding them as tories and traitors.

Immediate opposition to the Constitution took two forms: criticism of the Radicals who now rode in the saddle, and objection to many of the political principles embodied in the frame of government. In the new order men of unknown parts and obscure background like Timothy Matlack and George Bryan, rose to prominence. This was unbearable to the social and commercial aristocracy which had ruled the State from time immemorial. The social overthrow was accompanied by the increasing political importance of the lower classes. The Scotch-Irish and Germans had formerly been looked down upon because they were recent immigrants, possessed of little or no property, deficient in formal education, and lacking in the urban sophistication of aristocratic Philadelphia. This new element not only possessed the suffrage but was also coming into public office. Conversely, the wealthy Quakers and the office holders under the proprietary government were excluded from the polling place and from offices of public trust by the restrictions imposed by the test oaths. The "leather aprons"[36] triumphed over scions of wealth and culture.

The political principles of the new Constitution also drew the fire of the Republicans. Although they believed in democracy of a mild type, they lost no time in pointing out that the Constitution had not been submitted to the people for a vote of approval. The most persistent criticism was the lack of checks on the unicameral legislature. There was no upper house to apply brakes to extreme legislation. There was no veto power vested in the Executive Council or in the judiciary system. Events of the coming years adequately proved that these criticisms were well founded.

Another factor which roused the ire of the conservatives was the series of oaths required of all voters and office-holders by the Constitution and the Convention. On September 26 the Convention declared that all voters in the fall elections would be required to take an oath to uphold the new frame of government.[37] In addition, officers of government were required to take an oath declaring their belief in one God and the divine inspiration of the scriptures. These arrangements not only annoyed men of rigid religious scruples, but bound those men to refrain from working for changes in the Constitution. At least this was the interpretation which they chose to place on the oaths. The plan of a septennial Council of Censors also evoked criticism because it did not provide a method for immediate change of the Constitution; furthermore, the equal vote of each county in the Council of Censors gave the rural counties control and thus precluded any possibility of amendment.

Conceived in days of strife, the Constitution of 1776 was introduced to a people already heated over divergent political ideologies. The Constitution became the center of the political warfare which filled the annals of Pennsylvania for the ensuing fourteen years. That story will now be followed in detail.

II

The Rise of the Radicals (1776-1778)

THE RADICALS of the Convention achieved a double-edged victory in the ordinance of September 26 designed to insure them success at the polls in the fall, and in the Constitution framed to guarantee them supremacy in governing the State. Their plans were well laid and the machinery well calculated to operate in their favor. They were masters of the Commonwealth and they intended to remain in control.

The Political Revolution in Progress

The first concerted attack against the new instrument of government was the attempt of the Republicans to prevent it from going into operation, and then to rewrite it along the lines of conservative thought entertained by men like Rush, Morris, and Wilson. The fact that these men were not inclined to revolutionary activities precluded the idea of their overturning the new government by force. They realized, however, that if they accepted the oath prescribed on September 26, they would be bound hand and foot against making any changes. Thereupon they planned to ignore the oath. As early as October 8 the Anti-Constitutionalists of the town of Carlisle, in Cumberland County, held a popular meeting at the court house where they agreed without dissent not to take the oath on election day. In Philadelphia, newspaper writers suggested similar action which culminated in a meeting at the hall of the Philosophical Society on October 17. John Bayard was placed in the chair, and a four-hour debate ensued on framing a plan of opposition to the new government. Thirty-two resolutions were adopted condemning various actions of the Convention and certain parts of the Constitution. Then they explained their plan. To leave the door open for amendments they agreed that as voters they would not take the oath laid down by the September ordinance but would substitute in its place a general oath of faithfulness to the State. The assemblymen chosen at the coming election should not take the oath provided by the new Constitution but an oath professing faith in God, Jesus Christ and the Holy Trinity, and acknowledging the divine inspiration of the Bible; also the general oath of allegiance to the State, and a declaration to do nothing which would lessen the rights of the people.[1]

So far the plan was devised to leave voters and assemblymen morally free to advocate changes in the new frame of government. Other provisions adopted at this meeting revealed the ulterior purpose of the Republicans. They declared that the assembly should have full power to make amendments to the Constitution. When the proposed changes were made, the house would then adjourn while the people at large discussed the revisions; then the house would reassemble and incorporate the changes in the Constitution. To prevent the Radical government from going into full operation until alterations could be made, the Republicans agreed not to elect members of the Executive Council on November 5. These plans were printed and distributed among the people. Four days later another meeting was called, this time in the State House Yard, where about fifteen hundred people assembled to debate the new plans. Thomas McKean and John Dickinson spoke against the Constitution, while the work of the Convention was defended by its chief actors, James Cannon, Timothy Matlack, Dr. James Young, and James Smith of York County. When the sun set on October 21 no decision had been reached and the meeting adjourned. On the following day the meeting agreed to a few changes in the original proposals, the most important being a rejection of any oath for voters; and then appointed committees to visit each county to seek concurrence in the work of the city conservatives.[2]

Obviously the back-counties would not acquiesce in such a program. In short order the committee of correspondence in Cumberland County reported that most of the township representatives were satisfied with the oath prescribed by the Convention as well as with the Constitution as a whole. Three members of the committee did not agree with the report but their side of the story never appeared in the public prints. One of these conservatives circulated fifteen copies of the appeal from the city to various parts of Cumberland County. A meeting in Chester County agreed unanimously to disregard the Philadelphia Republicans and asserted that the new government of the State should be put into operation at once. The county committee of Berks was presided over by the conservative Mark Bird, with the result that they approved the action of the city conservatives in declining to take the oath, but agreed unanimously that inspectors of election should tender an oath of allegiance to the State to suspected persons.[3]

In the interim, in Philadelphia the Radicals did not rest on their oars. In newspaper articles they answered attacks on their new government and counseled the faithful to keep to the Constitution as the only safe political creed. One writer branded the conservatives as the "cautious and well-meaning party," and praised the oath as "a mighty stumbling block in the way of our gentry."[4] Another declared that the conservatives opposed the Constitution because it deprived them of public office; "they will not be governed by leather aprons."[5]

With election only three days in the future the Republican leaders assembled at the Philosophical Hall to complete their plans. To spike the accusations brought against them by their enemies and to put down the wild rumors then in circulation, they issued a statement defining their position. Emphatically they explained that the assembly which would make the proposed changes in the Constitution would not be the same group to carry them into effect, for the Republicans planned to order the assembly to dissolve itself after the revisions were adopted and to call a new election. Furthermore, certain fundamental principles they accepted whole-heartedly, such as liberty of conscience, freedom of the press, trial by jury, annual elections, division and rotation of office. They absolutely denied that they were connected with the tories or aiming to restore the proprietaries or trying to establish a house of lords. They made clear their attachment to the cause of independence. Referring to the danger of the radical Constitution going into effect unaltered, they warned, "We are now on the brink of a precipice."[6] At the same meeting the Republicans agreed on their ticket of assemblymen to be elected for the city.[7]

The election on November 5 gave encouragement to the Republicans, but not victory. They were triumphant in the city where George Clymer, Robert Morris, Samuel Morris, Jr., John Bayard, and Michael Shubart received seats in the assembly. These men, together with Joseph Parker, who received the votes of both parties, composed the Republican ticket agreed upon three days before the election. At the city election the oath was not required. In Philadelphia County Robert Knox, John Dickinson, George Gray, and Thomas Potts, all conservatives, as well as Isaac Hughes and Frederick Antes, received the majority of votes. In these two electoral regions the Republicans were also successful in preventing the election of members of the Executive Council.[8]

Beyond the urban region the Radicals offset any hope which the Republicans might have had of success for their plan. The exception was Bedford County where a full conservative delegation was returned. Although the general committee of Berks County had adopted the plans of the city Republicans, they were out-maneuvered at the polls by the Radicals.[9] In Cumberland County, George Stevenson had predicted the day before the election, that the Radicals would win. How many persons in the town of Carlisle were qualified to vote is not known, but Stevenson did not expect more than twenty votes from that community because the inspector was a man who would swallow the oath "if there were as many

Fish-Hooks in it as thire [sic] are Letters;" this excluded the non-juror vote.[10] The temper of the county is revealed in another incident. James Brown, a member of the Convention, was accused of spreading a report that John Harris, a member of the same body, had joined with lawyers like George Ross and James Smith and with "great men" like George Clymer and Owen Biddle in leading the people into slavery. The county committee asserted that the slander was published to influence the people against Harris in the election. Whatever the cause, Harris failed at the polls.[11]

It was asserted by the Republicans, and never denied by the opposition, that of the fifty thousand voters eligible to cast their ballot under normal conditions not more than two thousand went to the polls in November due to the detested oath.[12]

Conducted under these conditions, the election did not promise a peaceful political future. When the assembly convened late in November several constitutional issues were in the air. Some members had been elected by voters who had not taken the oath provided by the September ordinance; in other districts large numbers of people refrained from voting because of the oath. Was the body of men in Philadelphia a legally constituted assembly? Another question involved the oath to be taken by the representatives. Conservative members absolutely refused to take it as it stood in the Constitution because it would prevent them from working for amendments. If at least a majority of the assemblymen would not take the oath, could that body procede to business and legislate in the name of the people?[13]

As the legislators arrived in Philadelphia late in November, a compromise was attempted. The Radicals possessed a large number of seats but the Republicans held sufficient votes to block a quorum. The Republicans attempted to make the most of their bargaining power by entering into an agreement with the Radicals. The conservatives would agree to choose a speaker and to cooperate in passing acts of an emergency nature for the defense of the State. On the other hand, the Radicals were to agree to call a Convention to meet in January to revise the Constitution, and to dissolve the assembly the day before the Convention met. This plan, however, never materialized. After the assembly organized and John Jacobs was elected Speaker, the Radicals changed their mind and, according to their enemies, broke the agreement. At the time the general public was ignorant of the proposed plan.[14]

On the qualification of members a more successful compromise was effected. On the first official day of the new house twenty-four members took the oath as directed by the Constitution and a like number took the oath with reservations which did not prohibit them from seeking amendments. The official journal of the house simply stated that the members qualified for their seats but gave no inkling of the two different oaths administered.[15]

Failing to come to terms with the Radicals, the leading Republicans still had in their possession a negative weapon in the form of passive resistance. They boycotted the new government in the hope that they might keep it from functioning. A few like John Dickinson, Robert Morris, and others withdrew from the assembly. The whole delegation of six members from Bedford County, all ardent conservatives, left in a group.[16] Doubtless more of the twenty-four who took the qualified oath would have withdrawn had it not been for the urgent need of legislation to prosecute the war.

The Radicals pressed on to strengthen their hold on the government. In February, 1777, the assembly declared the seats of the absent members from Philadelphia City and County vacant and ordered a new election. Since the Executive Council could not function because the same districts had refused to elect Councillors in November, the voters also were asked to choose persons to fill those places. The Radicals gained by this action, for three of the new assemblymen and one of the Councillors were men who had been run in November but had suffered defeat. Their most notable acquisition was George Bryan who became Councillor from the City. The next move of the Radicals was to inaugurate the whole machinery of government by putting the Council into operation and by electing executive officers of the State. Early in March Thomas Wharton, Jr., was elected President of the Council and George Bryan Vice-President. On the following day they were inaugurated with elaborate ceremonies. The ardent Constitutionalist, Timothy Matlack, became Secretary to the Council.[17] The Radicals finally had control of both branches of government, an objective they had sought for almost a year. On the other hand, the Republicans were reduced mainly to the role of spectators on the sidelines. Power had slipped completely from their hands.

While the political factions fumed over their differences, the war with Great Britain moved in upon the arena. In the summer of 1776 State associators had been sent to New Jersey, and on their return in August the flying camp had been organized to furnish man power to Washington's rank and file. The Council of Safety, acting in an administrative capacity until the Executive Council came into existence in the spring of 1777, was now busily occupied with war problems arising from the need for more troops and the necessity of fortifications along the river. Soon after the election in November, 1776, the warning came that Howe's forces were on their way to Philadelphia. Hurried conferences were held between the congressional Board of War and the State Council of Safety to raise men for the defense of the city against the British.[18] Doubtless many conservatives at this time felt like Richard Peters who was quoted as saying that the Convention had "produced a sickly Constitution, not worth defending." [19] Whether they felt this way or not, they came out to fight.

As the month of November passed, the threat of invasion increased. Congress made an urgent request for all the associators from the city and four adjacent counties, believing that the preservation of Pennsylvania as well as of New Jersey depended on the success of this requisition. Due to his influence over the associators, Congress ordered General Mifflin to remain in Philadelphia to rouse the men to arms, and incidentally to keep an eye on the assembly and the Council of Safety to see that they carried out the vital requisition.[20] "In the afternoon I waited on the Committee of Safety," Mifflin explained to Washington on November 26, "and with much success addressed *their* passions. The Assembly are to meet this morning. Their lesson is prepared by the Committee of Safety and some of their leading members, who say matters will now go on well."[21]

Without a militia law on the statute books the State had much trouble to induce the men to come out and fight. Although the Council of Safety had sent urgent calls to the various counties, the response was so unsatisfactory that two weeks later Congress made special pleas to the State authorities to call again on the laggard counties. In the city a meeting of "Real Whigs," with the Radical Jonathan B. Smith in the chair, resolved that all men between the ages of sixteen and fifty should be ordered under arms except conscientious objectors who should pay fines. In the face of unfavorable returns from the counties the assembly appointed a delegation of fourteen men, the majority of whom were Radicals, to accompany General Mifflin in a tour of the adjacent counties to stimulate the war fever.[22]

During this crisis the assembly enlarged the Council of Safety which was the only executive power in the State. The action was undoubtedly a bid for united political support, for four of the seven new members were well known conservatives, Andrew Caldwell, Thomas FitzSimons, Joseph Marsh, and George Campbell, and only one, Jonathan B. Smith, was an ardent Radical. The assembly could not make a quorum from the middle of December until the middle of January because of the activity of various members in the militia.[23]

In haste Congress fled from Philadelphia to Baltimore. The obvious cause was the approach of the enemy; at one time the British were only seventeen miles from the city. But there were other reasons to contribute to the panic which "seized the nerves of some members" of the national legislature. The dilatory mobilization of the State associators and the considerable number of disaffected in the city caused great uneasiness. Fear of the disaffected was not idle gossip because the Quakers, of significant numbers and economically of great importance, constituted an unknown factor. The day after Congress decided to remove, Marshall noted that the Friends made little preparation to leave the city, for they were satisfied that if General Howe should come, their goods and property would be safe.[24] A week later their meeting of sufferings had the temerity to issue the following statement to fellow communicants:

> Thus we may, with Christian fortitude and firmness, withstand and refuse to submit to the arbitrary injunctions and ordinances of men, who assume to themselves the power of compelling others, either in person or by other assistance, to join in carrying on war, and in prescribing modes of determining concerning our religious principles, by imposing tests not warranted by the precepts of Christ, or the laws of Christ, or the laws of the happy Constitution under which we and others long enjoyed tranquillity and peace.[25]

Howe's proclamation of November 30 had the effect of removing some doubtful characters from the scene. Among the tories who fled to the British banners were Joseph Galloway, former Speaker of the provincial assembly and later a member of Congress; John Allen, former member of the city committee of inspection; his more famous brother, Andrew Allen, who had also been a member of Congress and of the committee of safety; and another brother, William Allen, who had resigned from the continental army.

In the military action which took place as the year expired, leading Republicans adequately proved that they were as ardent in fighting for the American cause as the Radicals. John Cadwalader was brigadier general of the associators, and Samuel Miles, brigadier of the State troops. John Nixon was colonel of the third battalion of associators; Samuel Meredith, a major. The aristocratic City Light Horse, dubbed the "silk stocking brigade," engaged in actual fighting as well as in displaying their fine trappings. The roster of this troop in 1776-1777 reads like a "Who's Who" of Republican respectability. It included Samuel Morris, John Dunlap, William Hall, Samuel Penrose, Levi Hollingsworth, George Campbell, John Mease, James and Samuel Caldwell, and Alexander Nesbitt.[26]

The Radical assembly turned its attention to Congress where the Pennsylvania delegates had been faithful in their attendance until the desperate military situation of December, 1776, drove the national body to Baltimore. From then until March few of the Pennsylvania delegates attended except James Smith and James Wilson. Early in February the assembly went into the task of electing new delegates. Morris informed Wilson that the latter was not slated for reelection due to his opposition to the Radicals.[27] On February 5 the assembly chose Benjamin Franklin, William Moore, Daniel Roberdeau, Jonathan B. Smith, all Radicals of one degree or another; and Robert Morris, the only conservative. Moore declined due to personal affairs. When it was rumored in Congress that Morris would not accept his reappointment, Rush hastily pled with him: "For God's Sake do not desert" Congress.[28]

Several weeks after the first election the house found it necessary to elect two more State delegates to Congress; one to fill Moore's seat, and another to be added to the delegation. Already Wilson was resigned to the slight tendered by his exclusion. "I retire without disgust," was his comment.[29] When the house held its second election George Clymer and James Wilson were the successful candidates. "What in the name of Wonder, has induced the Assembly to reappoint me?" Wilson asked Morris.[30] On resuming his seat he explained that he hoped to be able to bring some order out of the confusion that existed in the State. The way in which the threatened British invasion played into the hands of the Radicals annoyed him. "The very critical situation of public affairs," he observed, "is of much advantage to the assembly and their friends." [31] From March until September he and his fellow conservatives, Clymer and Morris, and the Radical Jonathan B. Smith, were in constant attendance at Congress. Living in Philadelphia, Wilson was able to take part in national deliberations and at the same time keep his eye on the state political situation.

One policy which Pennsylvania followed constantly during the whole period from 1776 to 1789 was the desire to keep Congress in Philadelphia. Hardly had the national legislature fled to Baltimore when a movement was on foot to return. Early in 1777 Benjamin Harrison informed Morris, who remained in Philadelphia with two other Congressmen to carry on public work, that he wanted to return, but he understood that the New England delegates opposed the plan. "If so, we *go not,*" he concluded, for "they Rule [Congress] as absolutely as the Grand Turk do[e]s in his own Dominions." [32] At the same time Morris as well as Rush were attempting to persuade Congress to return. Among other reasons Rush believed that the absence of the national body from Philadelphia would depreciate the paper money. In addition, he predicted that the return would have the same favorable effect on national politics as Washington's recent successes at Trenton and Princeton had in the military sphere. On February 8 a resolution to return was kept from a vote by the opposition of one state. Rush asked Morris to write more letters urging Congress to change its mind. The recalcitrant state was doubtless North Carolina represented by Thomas Burke who later in the month threatened to withdraw if the question of removal were put to a vote. On February 27 sufficient votes were marshalled to make the return to the Quaker City possible.[33]

Another problem which Rush and Morris wrestled with in Congress was their desire to increase the interest rate on loan office certificates from four to six per cent. While Congress was still in Baltimore, Morris wrote from Philadelphia urging a higher rate of interest to attract specie from the coffers of money holders. During the month of February several heated debates took place on the subject. The first vote resulted in a tie. Wilson also championed the increased interest rate as the only way to draw out money. Three million dollars, he said, was at the command of the "usurers" in Pennsylvania, but only six per cent would call it forth. Another vote, and again a tie. "We are all in confusion," cried Rush. "Nothing can save us but a reconsideration of that question." [34] That seven members representing five dissenting states could block this measure which was supported by seventeen members representing two thirds of the national population stirred his anger. This unjust mode of representation would ruin the continent. "We shall attempt the important question again . . . If we fail we are undone." [35] Finally at the end of February the advocates of the higher interest rate won their point by gaining the votes of Connecticut and Georgia.[36]

The credit of continental paper money became a problem, for this currency was not universally accepted. As early as October, 1776, some members of Congress believed that the Quakers in Philadelphia had determined to refuse it. During the crisis in December General Putnam who was then in command in the city issued a severe order against everyone who would not receive the paper currency. On the solicitation of Congress the Council of Safety laid down regulations to sustain the national credit. In quick order the assembly legalized Council's action and declared all State and continental paper money legal tender.[37]

Despite the precautions, depreciation of continental paper money was widespread. To protect themselves even good whigs were forced to acquiesce in the practice. Mennonite farmers in Lancaster County refused to sell their provisions except for hard cash; when it was not forthcoming, they carried their articles home rather than accept paper money. As prices soared, the country people became exasperated and threatened not to bring provisions to the Philadelphia market.[38]

With the failure of legislation to prop the declining credit of continental paper, the next step was an attempt to regulate the price of commodities. Four New England states took the first action in this direction when they sent delegates to Providence late in 1776. For days Congress debated whether it would recommend the proceedings of this price-fixing convention to the other states. The delegates from Pennsylvania disapproved the convention but for reasons that varied with political tenets. The Radical James Smith believed that if Congress recommended price-fixing, such action would interfere with the police power of each state; this is one of numerous occasions when Radical particularistic doctrine based on inviolability of police power raised its head. Rush and Wilson likewise opposed congressional sanction because their conservative philosophy insisted that any attempt to regulate prices was bound to fail. Congress took no action on the New England experiment, but asked five of the middle states to send delegates to York, Pennsylvania, to confer on the regulation of prices of labor, manufactures and internal produce. At York the states could not agree and the conference was a failure.[39]

The Conservative Opposition

While these changes were taking place in the economic realm, argument over the Constitution agitated State political life. The six representatives from Bedford County had left the assembly, went home and called a meeting in an appeal to their constituents. To justify their withdrawal they cited the various methods by which the representatives had been elected and the two forms of oath taken by the assemblymen. The test oath had excluded many electors from voting, they pointed out; yet the house continued to sit in defiance of the known sense of the people. Asserting that they had been expressly instructed to alter the Constitution, the Bedford members had refused to take their seats on any other conditions. They prepared a remonstrance in which they denied the authority of the assembly and called for a convention. This document was sent to the various townships for signatures. But a group of Radicals in the eastern district of the county thought otherwise and spoke their mind. Such a remonstrance, they declared, "tends directly to blow up discord" when all should be united. Reciting the conventional arguments in favor of the Constitution, they concluded that the present perilous days when "the drums beat to arms" were no time to quibble over forms of government. As a parting shot they accused the six assemblymen of unfaithfulness; they had been elected but had no intention of taking their seats.[40] When the Philadelphia press took up the affair, three of the Bedford conservatives pointed to James Cannon as one of their attackers. At once they proceeded to embarrass him by relating how he had written to the back-country to stir up the Radicals with admonitions that his name was to be kept secret. Cannon's reply was no masterpiece of rebuttal. When a Radical petition from Bedford calling for the election of new county representatives was read in the assembly, seventy copies of the Constitution were ordered distributed in that region. Perhaps the good people of Bedford would be converted to Radical ideology if they perused the Constitution.[41]

If the Radical leaders hoped to discredit the conservatives in Bedford, the Republicans were reconnoitering in Cumberland County. In March,

James Wilson in Carlisle complained that the assembly was establishing its power by taking advantage of the cooperation given by the conservatives who remained in the assembly in order to legislate for the defense of the State. It was high time to rouse the opposition; and Wilson believed there was sufficient discontent with the assembly to organize the Anti-Constitutionalists. In Carlisle a declaration was in the process of signing which voiced this opposition in phraseology strikingly similar to Wilson's letter. The "Arbitrary and Unreasonable Oath" was roundly condemned, and a demand was made for a vote on the Constitution without this restriction.[42]

Scarcely had the Executive Council come into being when the whole issue of the Constitution blossomed forth with renewed vigor in the Philadelphia press. Old arguments were resurrected flanked by additional facts. "Phocion," thought to be John Dickinson, issued a blistering attack on the Radical regime. The paucity of voters at the elections in November and in February, the broken secret agreement at the opening of the assembly, and the several violations of the Constitution, stirred him to demand the election of members to a new convention, unfettered by test oaths.[43] "Hampden" covered similar ground with sharp barbs: "Our Assembly is an *omnipotent* body." "We must lie low before them, and kiss the dust of their feet."[44] Replies were not wanting. One accused Phocion of "ambition" and the "thirst of power" which could be gratified only if he headed everything.[45] Thomas Paine was of the opinion that "the whole matter is more personal than political;" that it was a case of "sour grapes" with those men who had not been chosen to the Convention. Although admitting that the Constitution had defects, he predicted that its excellent features would be the pride of ages to come.[46]

In order to counteract sentiment against the administration, the Whig Society attempted to strengthen Radical support through press and petition. It issued an address moderate in tone but unmistakable in aim. Willing to accept amendments to the Constitution when the majority of the people should think them necessary, the Society deplored attempts at immediate revision. They deprecated changes which would produce "the dreadful experiment of a violent dissolution of the present bond of our society."[47] A paper was circulated in the city, doubtless a product of the same organization, asking subscribers to agree to uphold the government as it was then administered. In April the Society constituted a committee of five prominent Radicals to correspond with other individuals and societies that were interested in preserving "our common liberties."[48]

Something was brewing in Republican quarters. Just what it was is difficult to determine. Perhaps these men were simply groping about to strike on a plan to neutralize the government which the Radicals had established.

It is certain that they were talking and consulting among themselves. Matthias Slough reported from Philadelphia that although all men of property concurred in the opposition, "few have as yet Ventured to appear Publickly on the Stage, but I believe the time is not far Distant when the whole of them will appear . . ." Morris, Clymer, Wilson and others were "in the Plot," by which Slough probably meant that they hoped that the lawyers would boycott the government.[49] At the same time Sharp Delaney urged Wayne to return from the army in order to throw his weight into the scale of conservatism.[50]

The result of this agitation was a concerted demand by the conservatives for a new convention. In this objective they were aided by current military events. Before discussing the new offensive, it should be noted that the demand of the Republicans for a revision of the Constitution had gone through an interesting evolution. Before and immediately after the election of November, 1776, they claimed that the assembly had the right to make alterations in the form of government. In effect, they planned that the assembly should act as a new convention. After the election, but before the returns from the back-counties had come to the city, the conservatives drew up instructions to their representatives in the assembly. They continued to work on the theory that the house could tamper with the frame of government; in fact, they ordered a new Constitution which would adhere to the pre-Revolutionary form except for the regal and proprietary powers.[51]

After the assembly met and the Republicans discovered that they did not have control of that body, they shifted their ground completely. Asserting that the assembly did not truly represent the people of the State because its members had been elected by a small percentage of the electors who had taken the oath, the conservatives now demanded a newly elected convention to alter the frame of government.[52]

In the spring of 1777 the Republican demand for a convention was aided by the turn which military affairs had taken. After two short sessions the house adjourned on March 21 with plans to reassemble in May. In April, however, the State was threatened with invasion by the British army. All was confusion. Not only was the assembly not in session but the Executive Council was paralyzed by the lack of a number of members who had left Philadelphia. Dissatisfaction with the Constitution, the passive attitude of the conservatives, and the uncertainty of military maneuvers brought all action to a standstill. Large quantities of provisions and other articles stored in the city were in danger of falling into the hands of the enemy. Washington had urged Congress to have the supplies removed and Congress agreed, but when it turned to the State there was no executive authority to carry out the task. In Congress, Duer moved to appoint a committee to confer with President Wharton, the members of the State Board of War, and the members of Council who were in town at the time. After several conferences Congress took official notice of the situation and in veiled terms threatened to intervene in the internal government of the State. ". . . It is the indispensible duty of Congress," the national body declared, "to watch over all matters [in Pennsylvania], the neglect of which may, in its consequences, deeply affect the welfare of the United States, till such times as the legislative and executive authorities of the Commonwealth of Pennsylvania can resume the exercise of their different functions."[53] In addition, Congress practically ordered the President and the various State officials who could be assembled to take necessary measures to protect the State, and appealed to the people of the State to submit cheerfully "to the exertion of an authority which is indispensably essential . . ."[54] At once the Republicans cried, "We told you so," pointed to the Constitution as too inadequate in a time of crisis, and professed regret that Congress was obliged to interfere in the state "in order to save it from anarchy and ruin."[55] Since Duer was a conservative and associated with important Pennsylvania Republicans, the Constitutionalists pounced upon him for urging Congress to interfere in the internal affairs of the State. The Radicals viewed the whole incident as a Republican plot to embarrass and discredit their administration.[56]

With the threat of invasion the Anti-Constitutionalists temporarily suspended their agitation for a Convention and urged everyone to join in the common defense of the State. But not for long. When the immediate danger had passed, the conservatives turned the recent crisis to their own advantage. They were quick to point out the inability of the Radicals to carry on the government. They complained of the lack of courts in which tories could be punished, the increased cost of living, and the general languor in the face of another threatened invasion. The core of the trouble, they insisted, was the Constitution. To secure the whole-hearted cooperation of all the inhabitants, it would be necessary to call a convention to alter that instrument. Forty-two conservatives, including prominent men like Benjamin Rush, Robert Morris, Thomas FitzSimons, James Wilson, Sharp Delaney, and George Ross, asked the President of the Council and the State Board of War for concurrence in a new plan. As soon as the assembly should meet, it should be asked to recommend the election of members to a convention. Until this took place the assembly and the Council were to continue to exercise all authority for the safety of the State but as soon as the convention met it would assume all administrative powers. The Board of War which contained a majority of conservatives endorsed the request and made its statement public under the signature of its chairman, Richard Bache.[57]

Reiterating the weaknesses of the Constitution, the Republicans launched an effective propaganda in favor of calling a convention. Memorials and newspaper articles were the general media used for pressing their point. Not only did the city conservatives circulate a petition for signatures but eight leading Republicans addressed all parts of the State exhorting the people to petition the assembly for a convention. A memorial in German was printed for distribution among that nationality.[58] A host of pamphleteers forwarded the crusade, the ablest being Benjamin Rush whose "Observations" gave a clear statement of the case against the Radicals. In York a mass meeting was held at the court house where the Philadelphia memorial calling for a convention was approved.[59] Benjamin Rush and Richard Peters tried their best to induce Anthony Wayne to leave the army and come home to rescue his state which had "lifted a knife to her own throat." If he could not come, certainly he could lend his moral support by encouraging his Chester County friends to concur in the plan for constitutional revision.[60] One writer in the *Journal* stated the views of the conservatives calmly when he explained that the Republicans did not insist on a convention at once but that they wanted the assembly to promise to call a convention at some definite date in the future. In the interim the opposition would support the Radical government in matters of common defense, would cooperate in executing the militia law, and would continue to suppress tories and traitors. Furthermore, they approved a mild test law like the one then under consideration.[61]

The Radicals relied mainly on organization to counteract the new challenge to their control. As early as April the Whig Society had appointed a committee of prominent Constitutionalists to correspond with others of similar political leanings. Several weeks later Charles Willson Peale, as chairman of the Society, issued several addresses answering the proposal of their opponents. It was pointed out that the demand for revision was entirely the work of a few men from the city, that the times were too critical to tamper with the form of government, and that the Constitution should be granted a longer period of trial before it should be changed. The main argument of these addresses turned on the point that it would be wiser for the assembly to gather the sense of the people as to whether they desired a convention before actually calling one. Several Radical memorials were presented to the assembly, declaring unflinching support of the Constitution as it stood.[62]

The result was a compromise. The Radicals were in a dilemma. Obviously the government under their direction was not able to cope with the perilous situation of the times. The threat of Congress to interfere in State affairs was also a blow to their regime. And the listlessness of various groups in the face of the invading enemy was a patent fact. The

Radicals were forced to do something to save their political face. Acting on a representation from the Executive Council, the assembly voted to ask the people to indicate whether they wished a convention to reconsider the Constitution. This resolution provided that in October each district would choose a reputable freeholder to be known as a commissioner. He would go from house to house and collect the written yea or nay of every qualified voter. Before November 10 each county sheriff was required to report the returns to the next assembly. Only those electors who had taken the oath of allegiance could participate in the plebiscite.[63]

The Radicals pinned their hopes on stirring up sufficient agitation against a convention so as to nip the Republicans' proposal in the bud. In announcing the resolution the assembly sent copies of the Constitution in English and in German to the various counties. This was accompanied by a general address to the public which pointed out that the assembly had received more memorials in favor of the Constitution than against it, and which indirectly asked for vindication of the Radical philosophy.[64] The assembly then adjourned until September.

Securing this one step toward their goal, the Republicans declared a truce and indicated that they would support the government until the issue over the Constitution was settled. They pledged entire concurrence in matters of public safety and indicated they had suspended their opposition to the government.[65] But they did not let their cause die while waiting for a favorable plebiscite from the voters. Especially in the back-country the Republican flame burst out on occasion. In Lancaster John Hubley was vexed "to see capaling so much in voke." He had understood that the compromise had effected a union of the contending parties, but he was disturbed to learn that the conservatives in Philadelphia were planning to employ the presses in order "to keep up a continual heat."[66] Many Republicans took the I-told-you-so attitude by casting doubt on the legality of all acts passed by the assembly and by asserting that nothing could be settled until the vote for calling a convention had been taken. In August Christopher Marshall noted in his diary how he overheard one James Webb, a mason, state that the assembly had been "voted in by a parcel of soldiery and apprentice boys; therefore, their laws were not worth regarding." Marshall also noted the opposition of the conservatives in Lancaster to the formation of the Civil Society for assisting the present form of government.[67] In York County Archibald McClean had his troubles in counter-acting the Republican propaganda of George Ross. When visiting his iron works in York County, Ross took the opportunity to enlighten the people on current politics. According to the compromise, he explained, nothing done under the existing government was to have effect except the acts to repel the enemy and nothing further was to be done until a convention should be called. McClean reported that "divers men of Weight here have imbibed" of Ross's doctrines. Radical propaganda could have been better organized, for in York County where there was a persistent opposition only ninety-six copies of the Constitution in German, two hundred and forty copies in English, and fifty copies of the laws had been forwarded by the assembly; these were not received until early in September.[68]

Faced with the oath to support the Constitution, which they were unwilling to take, and at the same time desiring to embarrass the Radicals who were attempting to put their governmental machinery into operation, prominent Republicans boycotted the new regime by refusing to serve in public offices to which they were appointed or elected. In the fall of 1776 a number of assemblymen had left their seats in the house. Early in 1777 at least one writer in the public press suggested that the people of Philadelphia should demand the resignation of all its representatives in the assembly.[69]

Several posts in the State militia, a military organization never held in high esteem by the Republicans, were refused. In March, 1777, Sharp Delaney was offered the lieutenancy of Philadelphia with the rank of Colonel Commandant, "so that you see I may have been at head of the militia of our State but declined it—for reasons I know will be pleasing to you . . ."[70] Council appointed John Cadwalader and Samuel Meredith, both conservatives, brigadier generals of the militia but it was announced that they refused to accept the posts. Cadwalader felt that freedom and happiness had fled from Pennsylvania and he betook himself into temporary exile.[71]

More important than the posts in the militia were the administrative offices in each county, such as lieutenant, sub-lieutenant, sheriff, and prothonotary. They were in effect the strings which bound each local unit of the State to the administrative head in Philadelphia. They were the agents of the Executive Council. When these posts were refused by appointees, it proved a great hindrance to the government in its desperate attempt to assemble the forces of the State. News traveled slowly to Philadelphia; weeks passed before the Council learned that a lieutenant or prothonotary refused to act, and more weeks before a successor could be appointed and commissioned. In April, 1777, Ephraim Blaine refused the lieutenancy of Cumberland County because of the differences prevailing there over the Constitution and of the ill-judged appointment of some of the sub-lieutenants. About the same time Jacob Morgan declined the same post for Philadelphia. In Bedford County Council was forced to appoint successors to Richard Brown and Abraham Cable who refused to perform their duties as sub-lieutenants until a vote was taken to call a convention. William Ross of Lancaster County declined his appointment. Refusal to take the oath of allegiance to the State was tantamount to declining an office as was the case of James Pollock who was superseded in Westmoreland County in April, 1778. Lukewarm Republicans sometimes found that the resentment and strong feeling of people in their county made it more comfortable for them to give up their posts. In May, Hugh Davison of Bedford County begged to resign as sub-lieutenant because he could not afford to gain the ill will of the local inhabitants.[72]

This boycott on local office holding was not confined to lieutenancies and sub-lieutenancies. George Campbell, a serious and conscientious Republican, put the facts squarely up to Council in March, 1777. He would accept the office of prothonotary of Philadelphia County only if he was not required to take the oath to support the Constitution, "not choosing to tie down my conduct to the support of what I do not totally approve." He was willing to take an oath to support the United States and to renounce the British king; yea, even an oath to the government of Pennsylvania, if the six words "as Established by the late Constitution," would be omitted.[73] In June Benjamin Jacob declined a similar office in Chester County. County sheriffs opposed to the radical regime also boycotted it by resignations. This happened in Philadelphia and York counties in 1777. The same thing occurred in the case of some justices of the peace. In August the inhabitants of two townships in Northampton County complained that Robert Traill and Henry Fullert had declined taking the oaths to qualify them as magistrates and that the people experienced great inconveniences from the lack of these officials. Magistrates were necessary to aid in collecting the substitute money for the militia; when the posts were declined and continued unfilled, the militia organization in that vicinity received a set-back.[74]

The boycott was applied by other office holders. Late in 1777, in Philadelphia County, James Stroud refused to serve as a commissioner to seize the personal estates of traitors. Daniel Heister, appointed to a similar post, left the State without indicating whether he would serve or not; many months later he made his resignation known. As late as August, 1778, the clerk of the courts in Berks County declined to accept his appointment. Some local officials tried to carry water on both shoulders. A case in point was that of Richard McAllister, lieutenant of York County in 1777. Passive in his post because he was not reconciled to the Constitution, he feared that any activity on his part would have at least an indirect effect in finally establishing the new government. A local Radical leader complained of McAllister's inattention in arranging the militia but at the same time was convinced that the inert official had the common defense at heart.[75]

One of the most conspicuous cases of refusal to accept an office under the new Constitution was that of Joseph Reed. In the spring of 1777 the Council elected Reed to the post of Chief Justice of the Supreme Court. For four months he considered the offer before giving his final decision. These were the months when the political situation was wholly uncertain. The conservatives were marshaling their forces; the Radicals were embarrassed by the ineffective functioning of their government; and attempts were made to find some common ground between the two groups for a basis of compromise. A month after the offer had been made, Reed pled that military necessity and the movement of the enemy prevented him from leaving the army at that time. Two months later, on June 23, he declined the office. He offered two reasons for his action. He could not approve of certain parts of the Constitution; and he did not relish the idea that militia officers and members of the assembly did not take the same oath as other persons. Later Reed was accused of opportunism. Whatever his real reasons for refusing the judgeship, it cannot be denied that a year and a half later he took an entirely different attitude toward the Constitution. In the fall of 1778 he became President of Pennsylvania.[76]

The man who filled the seat of Chief Justice was Thomas McKean. Since the late days of 1776 when he was in the Republican camp and spoke publicly against the Constitution, he experienced a change of heart. The cause of this change was the attractive offer of first place in the judicial system. The fact that the invitation was tendered "in the politest manner" made a great impression on McKean although his friends differed as to whether he should accept it. He decided to take the post in order to prevent the least suspicion that he was against any government except one which he might frame himself and to avoid the charge that he wanted to embroil the State and increase disaffection to the government. These were the reasons which he expressed privately to a friend. His later actions indicate that it was the power and prestige of the office that caused him to receive it from the hands of the enemy. Although he supported the Constitutionalist faction, he was never an ultra-Radical at heart.[77]

Debating the merits of the Constitution in the newspaper columns or waxing hot on its leveling principles over the tavern cups provided only a safety valve for the pent up passions of the Republicans. The resignation of local offices and the refusal to take the qualifying oath kept the conservatives beyond the pale of active participation in the government. In one direction, however, they did make a definite effort to hold their ground. In at least six counties they refused to give up the county records and papers to their Radical successors. They asserted that since the final establishment of the Constitution was not certain and that a Convention would surely be called to make amendments, they would retain possession of the county records until the contest over the Constitution was settled.

In the middle and frontier regions the State authorities had experienced trouble in gaining possession of the local records. In Cumberland County Agnew refused to deliver the papers of the prothonotary's office to his successor, Creigh. Agnew was acting on the unofficial advice of the local Republican leaders. One of them, John Montgomery, informed his friend James Wilson of the incident and asked, "will you advise [us] to Submit our neck to the Yoak like [an] ass, I trust not . . ." [78] Agnew resorted to petty arguments to justify his actions and eventually the new appointee appealed to Council for help. In Westmoreland County the Council had a harder problem to solve. Michael Hoofnagle had been a deputy prothonotary under the former government. The Radicals appointed Archbald Lochry to the post but he was helpless without the records. Hoofnagle had come East, was reported to have secreted the records somewhere in Lancaster, and then joined the continental line. Council appealed to General Washington to order Hoofnagle to appear before the authorities in Philadelphia. A month later Council ordered a search of dwellings in Lancaster. But seven months passed and Lochry still held his post without benefit of the records. At last Council ordered the arrest and seizure of the unyielding Hoofnagle.[79]

The situation in Bedford County was peculiar. Thomas Smith, a leader of the conservatives in that region, held the offices of prothonotary, register of wills, recorder of deeds and clerk of the orphans' court. When his successor, Robert Galbraith, was appointed in the fall of 1777, Smith refused to turn over the records on the ground that a constitutional convention was about to be called. The conservative adherents of Smith were sufficiently strong to make Galbraith advise Council to "dispose" of him other than by arresting and jailing him in Bedford where he would probably be rescued. At length Justice Bryan issued an order for the arrest of Smith but it took almost three months until it was carried over the mountains and served. Thereupon Smith capitulated and surrendered the records. In Chester County it was necessary for Council to authorize Caleb Davis, the new prothonotary, to enter and search his predecessor's dwelling in order to recover the official records. There was also some trouble in Philadelphia over the books of the clerk of orphans' court. By October, 1777, the new prothonotary and clerk of Northampton County had not yet succeeded in procuring the records from the evasive Mr. Gordon.[80]

With the change in government which accompanied the Revolution and the overthrow of British authority, and the confusion due to raising men to repel armed invasion, the courts of the State did not open their doors until 1777. When the Radicals planned to set the wheels of justice in motion, they found that the conservatives were determined to do everything to embarrass them.

Many of the lawyers were naturally conservative. They thought that if they refused to practice under the new government they would eventually bring the Constitutionalists to their knees, and hence carry their demands for a new convention. Early in 1777 Matthias Slough explained to a friend that some of the leading Philadelphia Republicans "Wish and hope that the Gentlemen of the Bar will agree not to act under the present Government . . ." [81] It was openly asserted in the newspapers that the lawyers had refused to accept office under the Constitution. At the end of the same year after a semblance of judicial administration had been established by the Radicals, Edward Burd refused to go to Reading "because the Constitution was not settled;" and he learned that "some Strangers are running away with all the Business." [82] A few months later William Lyon wrote from Carlisle that there was only one lawyer there who practiced under the new frame of government. In Berks County there was not a single attorney who carried on business. The conservative Jasper Yeates admitted that he did not go near the Justices, "nor do I think I shall until I cannot help it. In my Idea there is little Law amongst us." [83]

With the lawyers observing a form of passive resistance, and the county officials resigning or refusing to hand over the records to their successors, the Radicals faced one of the crucial tests of their regime. On the opening of the courts depended their success or failure with the people at large. In begging John Morris to act as State prosecutor at the approaching sessions at Lancaster and Reading, Council observed: "Should these courts pass without proceedings, the disreputation of such a lapse would hurt Government considerably." [84]

After a considerable delay the Radicals succeeded in opening the courts. In April, 1777, John Montgomery reported of Cumberland County: ". . . we shall have a blessd Set of Justices in this County," who plan to hold a Court in a few days. "The Town will be full and Stink[in]g with yellow w[h]iges." He voiced the apprehension of the conservatives when he added: "I am afraid if they once are alowd to Open the Courts, it will be over with us . . ." [85] In Lancaster in August a three day session of the county court was held and concluded to the satisfaction of the Radicals who made special note that "the greatest good order" prevailed, that a "respectable" grand jury attended, and that the court adjourned "with great decorum." John Hubley felt that this victory of the new administration should be brought to the attention of the public through the newspapers. This well betrays the anxiety of the Radicals. The ignorance of the newly appointed local officials appeared in the frank confessions of Archibald McClean of York County, who explained that as for the approaching court session he was at a loss to know what measures to take due to his inexperience; furthermore, he had no one to advise him whether it was prudent or not to open the session. He asked Council to send Colonel Morris to the first session, if only as a spectator, so that McClean could "learn Experience therefrom." McClean's path sprouted more thorns. The precept to summon juries was issued but went unserved for want of an officer to execute it; and the county sheriff did not appear when he was needed. After four months McClean proudly reported that a court of general quarter sessions had been held, notwithstanding the opposition of many of the inhabitants.

By May, 1778, court sessions at York had been securely established. In other counties the courts had gotten under way by the close of 1777. Near the end of October the courts at Bedford had been opened without opposition, despite the Indian disturbances. A month later the court at Sunbury was ready for business, which the Radicals looked upon with pleasure. In Cumberland County the session "went on middling well" at first, and by early 1778 the courts were in full swing. At the same time the sessions in Berks County were retarded because James Read was holding the three officers of prothonotary, assemblyman, and executive Councillor, although he insisted that he had found a way to remove the impediments so that the business of the court could be put in good train. By the end of September the lawyers under the old government were readmitted to the courts in the order of their original rank. By 1778 the Radicals had succeeded in re-establishing the judicial system under their own control.[86]

Problems of the Radical Administration

Since the Constitutionalists had the upper hand in the control of the State, they faced the task of administering the government. This was a huge undertaking in view of the passive opposition of a significant part of the population, the problem of supplying men and money for the war, and the lack of experience of many of the Radicals in the actual work of government. The political factor played its part in the handling of these problems. After all, it was the success of the Radicals in managing the government which would determine whether they could retain their hold on the voting population.

With the war raging on every side, the militia assumed unusual importance. In 1776 Pennsylvania provided for its common defense through the formation of associators who were the ardent whigs of the time. This method was wholly voluntary, for the men were not bound by any laws of the State. Wholesale desertions occurred and need for a legalized system was evident. At a meeting of the "real Whigs," presided over by Jonathan B. Smith, held in Philadelphia in December, the Council of Safety was requested to require every man between the ages of sixteen and fifty to be ordered under arms except conscientious objectors who were to pay a fine based on property assessment. The Council took no action but referred the matter to the assembly.[87]

The first assembly under the new Constitution finally took up the problem of defense and placed the militia on a compulsory basis. The people were divided into districts, each to furnish a battalion of six hundred forty men. Sub-lieutenants commanded the district battalion, and the county lieutenant commanded the forces of his county. The assembly decided that its own members should not be exempted from militia service. The votes for exemption were scattered largely among the representatives from the back-counties. By a similar majority militia officers were not required to take any oath to qualify them for their commissions.[88]

The new government experienced considerable difficulty in putting the militia law into effective operation. Radicals argued that it was a piece of legislation necessary for the common defense; but conservatives had no taste for any acts of the assembly. Only by constant urging did the people gradually accept the law. In the spring of 1777 when it was necessary to call out the armed forces, Congress sent General Mifflin to inspirit the people to action. He was not only popular and influential with the people but he was a conservative. At the same time John Armstrong, in Cumberland County, bent his efforts to convince the people of the wisdom of accepting the militia law; by the end of April he thought he had accomplished his aim. The Radicals experienced various difficulties in executing the laws. Magistrates refused to take the oath of office or to perform their duties, and the press of business in Philadelphia delayed the Council in issuing commissions for militia officers. To speed up the work Council appointed additional sub-lieutenants, and wrote strong letters to others exhorting them to collect the fines for neglect of duty.[89]

The operation of the militia law was far from flawless. In actual service the militiamen gave a poor account of themselves. Even President Wharton, moderate Constitutionalist that he was, admitted that "The base conduct of our militia gives me much pain." [90] He hoped that the assembly would fill the State battalions in the continental army so that it would not be necessary to call out the militia. The political divisions in the State constituted one of the drawbacks. Republicans were not eager to fight for a Constitution which would keep the Radicals in power. A more important factor was the defect in the law. The practice of allowing substitutes had vicious ramifications. Late in 1777 Congress asked that this practice should be abolished and suggested fines for persons who refused to respond to the call. General Wayne also opposed the plan of substitutes and asked President Wharton to induce the assembly to abolish it. Wayne did not have too much faith in the militia anyway, for he thought that the salvation of the State depended on filling up the continental line.

The question of fines also produced problems. Local constables were not eager to collect the money, and in York it was reported that they would rather go to jail than undertake the unwelcome task. In other cases local petty politics bore hard on those who served an arduous tour of duty. Acting on a public order, James Maxwell of Cumberland County took volunteers to join Washington's troops. But these men were not credited with this service because they had not acted according to the strict letter of the law. The fact that Maxwell and his volunteers were conservatives was scarcely a good reason why they should have been fined by the Radical county officials.[91]

Since the militia law was the product of the Radical legislature, and as it was essentially democratic in its philosophy, the Radicals supported and defended it in preference to the continental army. While serving with General Washington, Joseph Reed, not yet publicly identified with the Radicals, sympathized with this view. From camp he wrote that the militia system was good; its defects came largely from the want of competent persons to execute it. He warned against listening to the complaints of continental officers, for they thought it fashionable to scoff at the raw levies raised for State defense.[92]

The test oaths imposed by the Radicals continued to cause friction. Always averse to oaths of any kind, the Quakers, in December, 1776, had declared their outright opposition to them. Already out of favor with the Radicals, the Quakers by this official statement put their head in the noose for later troubles with the ultra-revolutionary party. In March, 1777, a more pointed political affront was administered to the dominant party. Nine members of the newly appointed Navy Board of the State flatly refused to take the oath tendered by the Council, although they declared they were willing to take an oath of allegiance to the United States. The Navy Board proceeded with its work and the Radicals never forced the issue.[93]

As part of the militia law the assembly included a test oath in the act of June, 1777. The obvious aim was to separate the sheep from the goats, to mark off the insolent tories from the sincere patriots. The act provided that all white male inhabitants of the State were to take the oath of allegiance before July 1, except in the western counties of Bedford and Westmoreland where the time was extended to August. The oath renounced fidelity to George III, pledged allegiance to Pennsylvania as an independent State, and promise to expose to a justice of the peace all traitorous conspiracies against the United States. The disabilities of the non-juror were numerous. He could not vote or hold public office, serve on juries, sue for debts, buy, sell or transfer real estate, and he was liable to be disarmed by the county lieutenant. By July 3 it was announced that about thirty-six hundred persons in Philadelphia had taken the new oath within the previous ten days. In the back-country it was another story. In the town and neighborhood of Carlisle, in Cumberland County, the people had "not yet falen in to take the oath of fidelity save a very few" [94] by July 7. In Lancaster John Hubley predicted to Council: "you will hear a loud cry against this *Tiranical* Oath, that it was intended for naught but to hinder substantial, good disposed People to ellect or be ellected; depriving them of the rights of Freemen, &c." [95] In the same county the Radical agitation to form a Civil Society to forward the present government by requiring every member to take the oath or leave the State met "great opposition from a Junto, who call themselves Moderate men." [96] As late as October, Archibald McClean, in York County, reported that not one quarter of the inhabitants had taken nor would take the oath. Although they spurned the test, they were friendly to the common cause. McClean thought that if the abjuration of the king had been omitted, it might have been more palatable.[97]

Despite the opposition to the oath, the disabilities were applied to non-jurors. When arms were needed for the militia to repel invasion, they were seized from those who had not taken the oath. Legal disqualifications handicapped non-jurors in unusual ways. Council, however, informed county lieutenants not to extend the execution of the law beyond the words of the statute. When local authorities in Northumberland County imprisoned two men because they refused to take the test, Council ordered them released unless there were grounds for suspecting them as spies. In a letter to local officials in Lancaster County, Council revealed its policy. The tories could be made serviceable in many respects. They should be allowed to continue to plow land, raise corn, fatten cattle, make leather, set up salt works, and engage in other economic activities. If the disaffected were restrained, Council warned, no salt would be produced. These non-jurors doubtless derived many unmerited advantages from their enterprises, admitted the state authorities, "but let us take all the goods we can [get] out of them." [98] George Bryan recognized the peculiar religious tenets of the pietistic sects when he suggested that local officials should act with all tolerance toward the Moravians and Schwenkfelders who refused to take the oath.[99]

The Quakers continued to arouse suspicions in the minds of ardent Whigs. Events of the fourth of July, 1777, illustrate the attitude toward this sect. According to the custom of celebrating an event of importance, everyone was expected to illuminate the windows of his house. Council realized that religious scruples would prevent the Quakers from participating in the festivities, and recommended moderation toward them. To keep the happy spirits of the celebrators within range, the magistrates had orders to be alert and to put an end to festivities by eleven o'clock at night. Another order provided that two hundred soldiers would patrol the streets. Despite the precautions Council was "willing to give the idea of rejoicing its swing. The spirits of the whigs must be kept up." [100] Because the Quakers did not illuminate their windows, some hotheads engaged in petty acts of property damage on a number of houses. Within a few weeks the resentment against Quakers was to break out with redoubled harshness. [101]

As the military situation became more tense and the threat of invasion constantly alarmed Philadelphia, action was taken against men suspected of disaffection or considered capable of giving news to the enemy. Acting on a report of the Board of War, Congress asked Council to apprehend former officers of the Crown and to send them into the back-country or to take their parole. Forthwith Council seized John Penn, former Governor of the colony, and Benjamin Chew, former Chief Justice and Councillor. When both men refused to sign a parole of any kind, Council asked Congress to have them removed from the State. This Congress did. But on the following day Penn and Chew faced about and decided to give their parole. This occasioned a spirited and lengthy debate in Congress. The Radicals insisted on exiling the prisoners to Virginia while the conservatives wanted to give the prisoners a chance to pledge their word. At last the order to send the suspected men to Virginia was superseded and the Board of War was ordered to take their parole. Another blow to the Radicals was that this action was taken deliberately without first receiving the concurrence of the State Council. A few weeks later, however, when the pressure of events pointed to immediate danger from the British, Congress ordered the Board of War to move Penn and Chew out of Pennsylvania.[102]

At the same time that Penn and Chew were ordered out of the State, the national legislature turned attention to the Quakers. John Adams, William Duer, and Richard Henry Lee outlined to Congress, with little definite proof, the notorious disaffection of certain wealthy Quakers. They cited the declaration of December 20 as a seditious publication. Congress asked the State Council to arrest eleven Friends who were listed by name; they included members of the Pemberton, Drinker, and Fisher families, as well as Thomas Wharton, Sr., a cousin of President Wharton. In addition, Congress broadened the order to include all persons who were suspected of gross disaffection, and ordered seizure of the records of the

Quaker meetings of sufferings. Within a few days Council summoned David Rittenhouse, William Bradford, Sharp Delaney, and Charles Peale to aid in compiling a list of persons dangerous to the State. A committee of twenty-five was appointed, including Radicals like James Claypoole, Charles Peale, and James Cannon, to arrest suspects.[103]

Some ill feeling developed between Congress and the State Council over the policy to be pursued against the Quakers. After seizing members of the sect and reporting that only a few were willing to give assurances of model future behavior, Vice-President Bryan asked Congress whether it would approve sending the remainder to Virginia. Before receiving the papers which had been seized in possession of the Quakers—papers which do not appear incriminating—Congress approved Bryan's suggestion. Then President Wharton inquired whether those who would take the oath of allegiance to the State should not be relieved of exile. Congress also approved this policy. By this time the Quakers had been aroused and pled for a hearing to clear themselves of the charges. Congress told Council to conduct the hearing; Council took the attitude that the whole affair was under the direction of Congress, and on the plea of urgent business excused itself and asked Congress to hold the hearing. This provoked further debate in the national legislature with the resulting brusque order that all prisoners who would not take the oath should be packed off to Virginia. Both public bodies wanted to avoid the risk of a public hearing where the Quakers would further air their complaints and profess their neutrality.[104]

To complicate matters, the Quakers applied to Chief Justice McKean for benefits of writs of habeas corpus. Although the writs were granted and served on the custodians of the prisoners already on their way southward, they were ignored. In a hurried Sunday session the assembly approved the action of Council in deporting the prisoners. In the afternoon of the same day a committee was ordered to draft a bill to suspend for a time the writ of habeas corpus and to give Council sweeping powers to arrest and imprison suspects and to seize their papers. With record speed it was rushed through the parliamentary formalities and was enacted within forty-eight hours after the committee had been appointed. Thus the last legal defense of the exiles was removed. McKean vigorously defended his action in issuing the writs. In December, 1777, a letter from one of the prisoners, Owen Jones, Jr., to three men in Lancaster was intercepted and interpreted as a plot to depreciate the continental currency. The Board of War thereupon moved the Quakers from Staunton to Winchester and ordered Jones into close confinement. The exiles were not released until the middle of 1778.[105]

The petitions from the Quakers and their friends kept the case of the exiles constantly before Council and Congress. Late in January, 1778, Congress determined to release them if they would subscribe to the oath or affirmation of allegiance to Pennsylvania, or take a special oath which Congress prepared for the occasion. By the special oath the prisoners were asked to acknowledge that they were subjects of the independent state of Pennsylvania. But the Quakers would subscribe to nothing of the sort. Time dragged on and it was not until April that Council determined that when the prisoners should return from Virginia they should be set free.[106]

In March the State authorities became anxious for the return of Penn and Chew. Council explained to Congress that "the dangerous example which their longer continuance in banishment may afford on future occasions, has already given some uneasiness to some good friends" of independence, and requested that the two former Crown officials might be returned to the authority of the State.[141] But Congress was unwilling to comply without being assured that the State would take precautions to prevent the prisoners from doing mischief. Not until May did Congress liberate the men and then not in a way to suit Council. In the meantime the assembly included in the new test act a section requiring all former Crown officers who had not renounced their commissions to take the oath of allegiance within a month or forfeit all of their property or be considered enemies of the State.[107]

September was an especially dark month for the fortunes of the conservative forces. For unannounced reasons the Radical assembly declared James Wilson and George Clymer superseded as delegates to Congress. Since J. B. Smith had already resigned to accept the more attractive post of prothonotary of Philadelphia City and County, the house elected Joseph Reed, William Clingan, and Samuel Duffield to fill the vacant seats. Reed had not deserted the consevative camp but he was evidently on good terms with the Radicals. Clingan was described by Gouverneur Morris as "of the true Eastern Stamp and Clay," that is, a Radical. Duffield never attended Congress.[108]

In other ways the Radicals reinforced their power. When the British threatened Philadelphia in September, the Radicals saw an opportunity to strengthen their hold on the government. They not only gave the President and Council sweeping powers to apprehend suspicious characters, but fearing that the next assembly might not be able to meet, they provided for an emergency executive power to guide the State until the crisis was over. More important from the political viewpoint however was the way they continued to ignore the opposition party. The crowning blow came with the action of September 16. On the morning of that day a committee of the assembly was appointed to draft a resolution postponing the vote calling a convention. In the afternoon the house adopted the measure. The reasons given were that it was impossible to carry out the voting procedure prescribed by the action of June 17 because part of the State was in the hands of the enemy and because many of the electors were on the march to repel the invader. Technically the vote was only suspended and not rescinded, but the Republicans knew that they had been defeated once again in their attempt to throw off the Radical Constitution. Hastily the assembly adjourned to Lancaster where it decided that during the invasion it was necessary to exercise military authority in the State until the meeting of the next assembly. In all its hurry it found time to increase the salary of Vice-President Bryan from five hundred to a thousand pounds. After creating an emergency Council of Safety, the assembly went out of existence.[109]

All of these measures would have been accepted by the people who realized that in times of danger strong power is necessary, but the Radicals committed the fatal blunder of all new political groups on first tasting power; they would not recognize the opposition. And the opposition would not give full cooperation to a government and a Constitution they could not stomach. If the Radicals would have added leading Republicans like Morris and Wilson to their councils, a different story might be told.

As the British soldiers headed toward Philadelphia by way of the Chesapeake Bay, Congress found it necessary once again to leave the city. This time the members decided not to leave the State but to go into the hinterland. The reason for this action was the fact that tories of the State would cooperate with the British and thus weaken the American cause. On September 18, John Adams noted in his diary: "We are yet in Philadelphia, that mass of cowardice and Toryism." [110] On the 27th Congress held its first sessions in Lancaster, but found it more suitable to move to York where the business of the nation was carried on during the British occupation of Philadelphia. The government of the State was located at Lancaster. Not until July, 1778, did Congress and the State government return to Philadelphia.[111]

Just before the election of October, 1777, some members of Congress put their heads together in an effort to heal the breach between the two political factions in Pennsylvania. Public and private rumor asserted that the distracted condition of the State, caused by the British invasion, would prevent a quorum of the assembly just at the time when vigorous measures were necessary to put down the disaffected and to collect men and money for the national cause. Furthermore, according to the June resolution the time for voting on whether a convention should be held was approaching. This group of Congressmen reasoned that the best substitute for a nonexistent legislature would be a convention which could "lay down a system to be executed by Committees of that Body, dispers'd thro' the State," and enact laws to meet the emergency of the times. This method, it was believed, would provide for the safety of the State better than by the interference of Congress, until the convention could appoint a legislative body. Such a system might also "prove a healing measure to our unhappy Divisions." Immediately the State authorities took alarm at the suggestion and it was dropped at once by the originators.[112]

With the British in possession of Philadelphia and American troops in the surrounding territory, the election of October, 1777, was held under trying circumstances. This was particularly true of the southeastern part of the State. Several days before the election, Secretary Matlack warned the sub-lieutenants of Philadelphia County to take every care in carrying out the election so as to preserve "the succession of the legislative body." He suggested also that the local officials should stir up the voters "to a proper conduct" in the choice of assemblymen and county officers. What he meant by "proper conduct " might be open to debate, but certainly he hoped that the people would elect good Constitutionalists. If regular inspectors of elections were lacking, Matlack was of opinion that that fact should not prevent the electors from voting. Roberdeau, who was in the town of York as Pennsylvania delegate to Congress, bent his efforts toward holding the election in York County. In Lancaster the event took place "with great order and sobriety," according to Marshall. But the number of voters was small even among those persons who had qualified by taking the oath. No election was held in the city of Philadelphia due to the British occupation. In the rest of the State the voters cast their ballots under favorable conditions.[113] The new assembly was predominantly Radical. The city of Philadelphia could send no representatives, and at the first session the delegations from Philadelphia and Bucks counties did not appear. Sixteen members did not enter the house until late in November and early in December. Nine more came during the first two months of 1778, and the remainder straggled in from March to August. The personnel of the membership was of low calibre. Over half of the members were inexperienced in government under the Constitution of 1776. Only thirty-one men were reelected from the old assembly; in practically every case they were Radicals. No outstanding leaders appeared. Robert Whitehill, James McLene, and John Bayard were the only luminaries among the satellites. On November 20, James McLene was elected Speaker because John Bayard, who held that position in the former house, did not appear. The general understanding became evident in February when McLene resigned and urged the election of Bayard who was thereupon reinstated.[114]

Wharton and Bryan were reelected to the first and second offices of government. Wharton had been a moderate Constitutionalist and with his death in May, 1778, one of the last brakes against Radicalism was removed. With the Radical Bryan at the head of the executive branch, the Constitutionalist faction could desire little more. When a special election was held in July to fill Wharton's seat, Joseph Reed received eighty-four votes and Robert Morris two.[115]

To meet the emergency against threatened British invasion and the fear of tories in October, 1777, the assembly augmented the Executive Council by the inclusion of nine additional men to whom they granted very broad powers. The nine were all Radicals of whom the most outstanding were John Bayard, Jonathan Sergeant, Jonathan B. Smith, James Cannon, and David Rittenhouse. The new body was known as the Council of Safety and had full authority to search for traitors, to seize provisions for the army, and to regulate prices.[116]

One of the first actions of the Council of Safety was a campaign against the disaffected. Commissioners for each county were appointed to seize persons and property of men who joined or aided the British army. When the assembly was finally able to secure a quorum and proceed to business, it suggested that the temporary Council of Safety should be dissolved. This President Wharton did by proclamation of December 4.[117]

Jealous of the sovereign rights of the State, the Radicals were quick to resent interference by outsiders in the affairs of the Commonwealth. This trait was illustrated in the incident of the British convoy at Lancaster in January, 1778, which involved meddling by Congressman Gouverneur Morris, delegate from New York and a friend of the Pennsylvania conservatives. General Washington had granted a pass to a convoy of British soldiers to transport clothing to British prisoners in Pennsylvania. When several of the English officers bought some victuals at an inn in Lancaster, they offered to pay in specie. But because of a State law, Council compelled the innkeeper to make out a new bill at an exorbitant rate, payable in paper money. John Harvey and Gouverneur Morris were present. Morris believed that the assembly never thought of such a situation when it passed the law and claimed that these British officers were not subject to State legislation. Thereupon he wrote a protest to Council. Council complained to Congress, where the incident was introduced, on the ground that the wagons of the convoy contained counterfeit money intended to be circulated in Pennsylvania. Although the activity of Harvey and Morris was kept out of the debate in Congress, the incident left a sting in the memory of leading Radicals of Pennsylvania who were quick to resurrect the story later when they brought a series of accusations against Morris.[118]

Danger to the internal police power of the State was quickly detected by the Radicals. In September, 1778, the assembly repealed an earlier law which gave General Washington the right to impress wagons and horses in case of emergency. Certainly the Commander-in-Chief did not abuse this power, but the assembly declared that it had "from experience proved inconvenient and prejudicial" to the citizens. Henceforth impressment would be allowed only on warrant from Council. The State delegates to Congress remonstrated that too many horses and wagons had been requisitioned, thus throwing an over-proportion of that burden on the State.[119]

Some of the men appointed by Congress in the quartermaster's service irritated the Radicals by not cooperating with the State administration. The most flagrant case was a by-product of the opposition to the oath of allegiance; this controversy centered about Robert Lettis Hooper, a deputy quartermaster general acting under Congress in northeastern Pennsylvania. Local Radical officials in Easton claimed that Hooper not only refused to take the test of allegiance but discouraged the inhabitants of Northampton County from taking it, a fact "too general and too glaring to deny."[120] In October, 1777, the Council of Safety complained to the continental Board of War about Hooper and John Biddle who also was in the quartermaster's line. Both men were under the direction of Thomas Mifflin who headed the quartermaster service at this time. Mifflin defended Hooper as an excellent officer and cited his meritorious work in removing the stores from Philadelphia and in securing forage supplies during the last three months of the campaign. Mifflin also had high praise for John Biddle who had recently resigned, "being tired out with the Clamours of his Enemies." The complaints against his department Mifflin asserted were "grounded solely on a suspected Detestation, in some of my Assistants," to the government of the Radicals.[121]

Later when the State delegates in Congress were asked for evidence against Hooper, they had none to present because more pressing business in Council relegated the Hooper affair to the background. General as they were, Council finally listed the charges. In addition to refusing to take the oath, he had granted passes, an authority that did not come under his office. In the portrait drawn by Council, Hooper was nothing more than a tory.[122]

The whole affair degenerated to personal animosities. Hooper took spectacular means of displaying his contempt for several State officials. Some of the information forwarded to the Council of Safety against Hooper had been furnished by Jonathan D. Sergeant. When Sergeant attended court sessions at Reading, Hooper was on hand to give him a severe beating. After this affray Sergeant found it wiser not to complete his testimony against his assailant. Other facts had been supplied by

Jacob Arndt, "the oldest and most infirm of the late Council of Safety," who was insulted and threatened by Hooper. In a letter which was freely handed about, Hooper recounted his triumphs and boasted that his horsewhipping activities would not cease until he had treated every member of Council in the same way.[123] This made President Wharton's blood boil. Admitting that Hooper would have a physical superiority over him, he added, "But I have something in me that will not suffer me to be silent." [124] Eventually Hooper was arrested and Chief Justice McKean gave a piece of his mind concerning Hooper's conduct. With the tide going against him, Hooper took another tack and tried to excuse his manhandling of Sergeant and Arndt on the ground that they attempted to ruin his reputation. He admitted that he had written to Gouverneur Morris about his victims in derogatory terms. The whole affair faded into the past but was not forgotten. Like many similar incidents growing out of the political differences, it reposed in the Radical treasure chest of complaints for future use. In a joint memorial, Council and assembly asked Congress not to appoint officers who had not taken the oath.[125]

The Radicals forged ahead with a stronger act. The law of April 1, 1778, extended to June 1 the time for taking the oath of allegiance. It provided that men in professions and trades could not carry on their business unless they had complied with the law. This act stirred up much opposition. Certain religious groups like the Moravians were conscientiously opposed to the abjuration of the British King; and some were jailed for refusing to take the oath. In Northampton County an official reported that not a tenth of the disaffected had taken the oath nor did they ever intend to do so. In visiting three back-counties Alexander McDowell heard loud complaints by Quakers and Mennonists against the oath because they interpreted it as an obligation to fight. Many said they would affirm to be faithful to the State but to affirm more would be persecution. Some "sensible whigs," according to McDowell, favored an oath suited to the sentiments of these people, for it would increase the friends of the State and reduce discontent.[128]

The act of September, 1778, extended the scope of the test law. In the future, delegates to Congress would be required to take the oath; and no one would be allowed to vote at elections unless he could produce a certificate proving that he had taken the oath before June 1, 1778. A month later a newspaper writer asserted that not one-fifth of the male inhabitants over the age of eighteen had taken the oath before June 1, and Republicans complained that due to the invasion the people of Philadelphia had only two months within which to take the test. On the other hand, conservatives gloried in a court decision declaring that men in the continental army were exempted from the oath but retained all the privileges of citizenship.[129]

After the British evacuated Philadelphia, the cry against tories, suspects, and disaffected was raised higher than ever. Hundreds of men including well-known Quakers had remained in the city during the British occupation. Beyond the vicinity of the city were the American soldiers who had spent a miserable winter at Valley Forge, the farmers whose provisions were seized, if not by the Americans then by the British, and the refugees who had left the city at the approach of the British. The forays made by English soldiers into the open country to kidnap Americans intensified the patriotic feeling.[130]

As early as February, 1778, the *Packet* printed a fervant plea addressed to the legislature; the estates of all disaffected should be seized so as to encourage the friends of the State. Before the city was evacuated, Council appointed forty-three commissioners to hunt down traitors. Benjamin Towne performed the miracle of publishing his newspaper in Philadelphia while it was in American hands, continued his trade under British auspices, and then reverted to the American cause after the British had left. In his columns appeared a hint to all tories who had taken an active part with the enemy during their stay in Philadelphia; they should lower their heads and not stare down their betters with angry faces. The day is close, they were warned, when they would answer for their impertinence. Another writer cried out for punishment of the tories. On July 17 an association was formed to seek out tories. The numerous signers of this association contained representatives of both political factions. Doubtless the level-headed Radicals believed with John Armstrong that although lenity towards one's enemies was a virtuous ideal, "a few Examples ought to be made of the more attrocious" cases.[131] In a jocular vein Peale suggested that tories should be designated by having the first story of their houses painted black. Wrath of the Radicals also fell on the Quakers. Samuel Adams was furious on hearing that Quakers and tories circulated rumors that Gerard did not come in the capacity of a French public minister but only as a private agent. And the newspapers launched a series of attacks on them for their address to the assembly on oaths. Another report that they had bought much merchandise at a very low price from the departing English and then resold it at high profit did not endear them to the Radicals.[132]

The crusade against traitors took official form when within a period of five weeks proclamations attached the taint of treason to a hundred thirty-nine persons who were laborers, shopkeepers, and artisans. Demands were made in Council for a more general seizure of tory property but the executive body declined to act beyond the provisions of the law and allowed the courts to take up the cases in regular order.[133]

While the Radicals defended the sovereignty of the State against encroachment and crusaded against tories, a more difficult task faced the administration as paper money continued to depreciate and prices soared. They applied the obvious panacea of price regulation to the disjointed financial system. The first step in this direction was an ordinance by the Council of Safety late in 1777, followed by a law to prevent forestalling. A more stringent measure to legalize definite prices had already been under discussion in the assembly. In December, 1777, a test vote on such a bill found only four members opposed. When the bill was brought up four months later, twenty-one members unsuccessfully opposed considering it, and on April 1, it became law. This act ordered all imported goods to be sold at an advance of not more than twenty-five per cent over prime cost. Local magistrates were given power to determine the price of goods sold in public places. In the interim Congress acted on the report of the proceedings of a convention of the northern and middle states, and asked the states to suspend price-fixing legislation until the southern states could report some action. Accordingly, the Pennsylvania assembly in May suspended the April law, stating that it would be injurious to the people to lower prices when neighboring states were selling at the prevailing inflated rate. Eleven assemblymen held to their principles and voted against the suspension but in vain. Eight others reversed their votes as given on April 1.[134]

As continental paper money depreciated and the State needed funds to meet the extraordinary expenses of carrying on the war, the assembly ordered an issue of 200,000 pounds in bills of credit. The old provincial money ceased to exist after the assembly provided methods for exchanging it for the new emission. Persons who had taken the oath of allegiance were granted an additional three months to exchange the old paper.[135]

In the summer of 1778 the question of embargo on export of foodstuffs raised the old Radical particularistic doctrine. When Congress asked the State to embargo foodstuffs, Council, even though it considered the measure prudent, entered a formal protest on its records. Although it issued a proclamation in line with the request, Council pointed out that it was not to be considered a precedent; Congress did not have power to restrain the trade of a State. The assembly ratified the embargo for an additional six weeks but gave Council the right to revoke it at any time in the interim.[136]

During the first two years of control of the government the Radicals had been able to ward off attempts to have the Constitution revised, thanks to the British invasion. They were also in a favorable position to capitalize on the wartime hysteria in order to discredit their conservative opponents. The death of President Wharton marked the disappearance of the last moderate man who had significant influence in the Radical circle. Thereafter the party was under the leadership of George Bryan and Joseph Reed who carried out their principles of democracy to a logical, if not satisfactory conclusion. The years of 1776 to 1778 marked the rise of the Radicals; the years of 1778 to 1780 witnessed their triumph.

III

Triumph of Radicalism (1778-1780)

FINDING their stride and strengthening their hold on the government during the period from 1776 to 1778, the Radicals marched forward toward their democratic ideals. Two landmarks of the old regime were slated for demolition. The University symbolized intrenched conservatism and the ownership of vast tracts of land by the Penn family constituted a feudal vestige of older days. The economic upheaval occasioned by the war produced the more immediate problems of inflation and profiteering. In control of the assembly the Radicals visualized an easy solution by legislation. This failing, extra-legal committees supported by the mob attempted to dispense democratic justice. Before the Radicals reached this point of supremacy, they came face to face with the renewed opposition of the conservatives who insisted upon a revision of the Constitution. Gradually sinking beneath the wave of democratic hysteria, the Republicans made one final attempt to inject their ideas into the frame of government.

Revision of the Constitution Defeated

For the first time since the fall of 1776 the conservatives began to feel their strength as they made some gains in the assembly. This was caused by a reaction to the inefficient rule of the Radicals whose administration floundered during the stress of invasion and failed to produce the necessary men and taxes. War always favored Radical politics; but when the State was no longer the scene of actual military operations, the cold logic of the Republicans counter-acted to some extent the emotional appeal of Radical upstarts.

The conservatives launched a concerted campaign to diminish the rising power of the Constitutionalists. Out of office, the Republicans resorted to the normal tactics of attacking the record of the previous assembly. The assumption of powers beyond mere defense measures and the use of the oath to keep the Radicals in power formed the stock-in-trade for the attack by the Republicans. They also advanced the charge that the assembly had been extravagant in the use of public money. Deliberately ignoring depreciation, conservatives pointed to the enormous increase in the salaries of the judges and the failure of the assembly to settle its accounts which involved millions of dollars.[1] The activity of a conservative like Jasper Yeates was typical of renewed hope. "I have been doing little for these ten days past, but electioneering," he wrote on October 10. In his opinion the numerous violations of the Constitution by the assembly created uneasiness and disgust among the people at large in Lancaster County. The Republicans would be successful if there were divisions in the outlying districts of the county. "In the city of Philadelphia and other counties, every nerve will be strained to effect a change of men and measures." [2]

To answer the charges brought against them, the Radicals resorted to the ever useful cry of "Tory, Tory." They warned the public that at a pre-election meeting in Philadelphia County "noted tories and neutrals" shared with "honest whigs" the task of forming a ticket. Throughout the State the tories were maneuvering themselves into position to capture seats in the assembly. If such an event takes place, "what will become of our glorious Independence," asked one writer.[3] The Radicals called for the re-election of present members of the house because they had stood by their posts and furthered the Revolution.[4]

Although the Republicans made considerable gains in the election, they were not victorious. Their capture of less than one-third of the seats in the house was small in itself but constituted a significant invasion of the overwhelming Radical power in the assembly of 1777-1778. Robert Morris, Thomas Mifflin, George Clymer, and Samuel Meredith formed part of the new delegation from the city, and became the leaders of the conservative minority. Bedford County returned Dougherty, Woods, and Thomas Smith, who had walked out of the house in the session of 1776-1777. Republicans also made gains in the counties of York and Cumberland. At first sight of the returns they were overjoyed with the outlook and optimistically asserted that a majority of the members were "sincerely & warmly disposed to rescue their country from tyranny & contempt." [5] Joseph Reed, elected to the house but soon to become a Councillor and then President, believed that the assembly contained a considerable majority of real whigs, some new converts to independence, and a few inveterate but concealed tories. The Republican gain in the new house was remarkable. Either they had "strained every nerve" as Burd predicted or they allowed many persons to vote who had not taken the oath before June 1.[6]

Evidence that the Republicans fought tooth and nail to make every possible gain appeared in the numerous contested election returns. At the bottom of most of the trouble was the irritating question of the oath. In Berks County the Republicans who controlled the election officials were charged with negligence in allowing everyone to vote who presented a certificate of having taken the oath, whether the oath had been taken before or after June 1. Whatever the violations of election procedure, the Republicans gained three staunch conservatives from that county and the contested return was never investigated. In the town of Lancaster there were similar charges that few certificates of oath were demanded by the inspectors from the voters, that some election officials were admitted to their duties without being sworn, and that the ballot box had been stuffed. In Northumberland County a double set of returns involved two seats in the house and about forty votes. The assembly accepted the return which gave the seats to moderate Republicans.[7]

More serious election disputes occurred in Chester and York counties. The oath was the contentious point in the Chester election. By a vote of almost two to one the house determined first that any person who took the oath after June 1 was not entitled to vote in the succeeding election. At once the Republicans attempted to void the whole election in order to call a new one, but they were unsuccessful as the house adopted the return which gave the seats to the Radicals. There was also other local trouble in Chester County. A group of assessors and a commissioner "illegally elected" took the oath of office and sat in defiance of those whose election had been accepted by the Council. Council found it necessary to command the legally elected group to assume their duties. The oath also was one of the disputed points in the York County election. In February the assembly finally determined to confirm the sitting members who composed the conservative ticket. The election of the Councillor from York also aroused bitter feeling. John Ewing, a moderate, had occupied his seat for several months before Council decided that George Eichelberger had aroused so much clamor and terror at the election as to influence the judges and inspectors. Therefore, by a vote of eight to one, Ewing was unseated and James Thompson declared duly elected.[8]

When a quorum finally assembled ten days after the meeting date, some of the Republicans objected to taking the oath as prescribed for assemblymen by the Constitution, arguing that it precluded them from learning the sentiments of the people on calling a convention. On the next day it was unanimously agreed that every member should take the prescribed oath but previously he might add a proviso allowing him full liberty in regard to a convention and the right to participate in such a meeting. Forty-one members, one-half of whom had sat in the previous assembly, took the oath as it stood in the Constitution. Twenty-four members, of whom all but one had not attended the assembly of 1777-1778, added the reservation. Thus they openly declared their dissatisfaction with the Radical Constitution and came to Philadelphia with the definite purpose of effecting some alteration. The geographical distribution of these avowed conservatives indicates where revolt against the Radicals was brewing. Four were from the city of Philadelphia, one from Philadelphia County, three from York, four from Cumberland, two from Berks, six from Bedford, and one each from Northampton and Westmoreland.[9]

After the new house had organized and John Bayard again filled the Speaker's chair, delegates to Congress were elected. The new men like the old were predominately Radical. They were Daniel Roberdeau, William Clingan, John Armstrong, William Shippen the elder, Samuel J. Atlee, James Searle, and Edward Biddle. All were true Radicals of various shades except Edward Biddle who appears to have been the only concession the Radicals allowed to the conservative minority. Biddle, however, refused to serve in such a delegation. Representing the interests of the continental line, Colonel Stewart confided to Anthony Wayne his disappointment at the new delegation, "a real set of Caitiffs," in his opinion. His chagrin was increased by the rumor that Duffield would replace Biddle.[10] From the votes available it is evident that both political factions in the house put up their own list of candidates for delegates and voted for them on strictly party lines.[11]

The instructions to the delegates revealed Radical outlook on continental affairs. Although the power and honor of the United States were to be maintained, the due importance of the State was to be "cautiously" upheld. Credit of the paper money should be restored. The assembly wanted immediate notice of the adoption of the Articles of Confederation so that it could settle the boundary disputes pending with Virginia and Connecticut. If the Articles would not soon be confirmed, then the delegates were given a free hand to enter into further foreign alliances. In March, 1779, Biddle, Roberdeau, and Clingan were replaced by Frederick Muhlenberg, Henry Wynkoop, and James McLene.[12]

Following the meeting of the assembly, the next problem was to elect the President and Vice-President. Back in May, 1778, Thomas Wharton died in office while the government had temporarily moved to Lancaster. George Bryan as Vice-President headed the Council during the remainder of the unfinished term. At the October elections, Joseph Reed had been elected to the assembly from the city of Philadelphia. But Reed had also been elected a Councillor. Near the end of November he resigned his post in the assembly in order to retain his seat in Council. On December 1 the assembly and the Council met jointly and elected Reed President and Bryan Vice-President. The charge was later made that Reed had played a clever game of politic maneuvering. Not only did he run for a seat in both the assembly and the Council but he had cultivated the support of both political factions. The fact that he waited six weeks after the election to resign the seat in the assembly was imputed to his desire to see which house offered him the best chance for advancement. Aside from this contemporary speculation, it is probable that there was some understanding that the Republicans would unite with the Radicals in electing Reed President, and that the assembly would agree to call a convention.[13]

Reed's administration was ushered in with elaborate festivities. Gerard and Miralles, the foreign representatives in the United States, attended the official proclamation. A banquet was the occasion for patriotic toasts and Gerard was overcome by the "manifestation of sensibility and delight" at every allusion to France or to the French King. In his inaugural speech Reed declared that the happiness of the people of the State would be his object and the Constitution and laws the rule of his conduct. Thus Reed formally deserted the Republicans and became a bulwark of the Radical party.[14]

If the assembly and Council agreed unanimously in elevating Reed to the high office, this view was not shared universally. Although Anthony Wayne congratulated him on his new honor, doubtless with the hopes of disposing Reed favorably toward the continental line, and Thomas Cushing of Massachusetts repeated similar sentiments, with a reminder of the importance of the fishing privileges to the New England States, Anti-Constitutionalists found other expressions in regard to Reed. Some said that the office of President had been offered to several distinguished men before the election but that they refused because they would aid in bringing tyranny to the State. Others berated Reed for deserting to the Radicals and accepting the office when he was known to oppose the Constitution.[15]

Due to Reed's resignation from the assembly, a special election was held in Philadelphia to fill the seat. By a vote reported to be four to one, Hollingshead, a Radical, was elected. A conservative tried to explain this result by saying that the Republicans were satisfied with the assembly resolves to call a convention and that they were generally satisfied with the character of Hollingshead.[16]

Looking forward to an early revision of the Constitution, the conservatives in the assembly had been careful to take a modification of the oath of office which would leave them free to work for a convention. Except for a few alterations, men like Benjamin Rush expected the restoration of the old government of the State "under which Pennsylvania became the first spot, not only in America, but upon the Surface of the earth."[17] Late in November the assembly adopted plans to call a convention. On March 25, 1779, voters all over the State were to cast two ballots; in one box a ticket for or against a convention, and in another, the votes for members of the convention. If the majority of votes prevailed for a convention, then the second box would be opened and the six highest candidates from the city and each county would be declared duly elected members of the convention. The assembly also determined the questions which the convention would discuss. Should there be a second house? If so, how should it be administered? If there should be no second house, should any provision be made for the review of laws? There were also the questions of whether the Council of Censors should be abolished and whether the judges should be made more independent by having fixed salaries. The work of the convention was to be received and adopted by the people as the Constitution of the State.[18]

At once the Radicals cried out against the action of the assembly. They realized that the Constitution was the bulwark of their power, and that if it were changed in any essential points they would lose their grip on the government. They defended their frame of government and the actions of the former Convention which gave it birth. But they advanced few arguments to support their position except that the assembly's action was displeasing to them. Some writers did point out that the election would cost the public a good deal of money, or that the assembly had no right to meddle with the Constitution.[19] From Sadsbury, Lancaster County, Andrew Boyd declared that the assembly resolution "is very offensive to us in this part of the County for various reasons, which we think very obvious, and [we] mean to oppose it. . . ." He thought that the city Radicals should "act in consert with us." [20] Cumberland and York counties were also displeased with the measure, according to the Radical Robert Whitehill.[21]

To negative the work of their enemies, the Radicals did not rely wholly on newspaper propaganda. They resorted to an old method which had often proved effective, that is, the use of petitions to the assembly to rescind its resolves. In these remonstrances one seeks in vain for good solid arguments against the call for a convention. The general line of reasoning was that designing persons sought to destroy the Constitution in order to introduce anarchy, that the assemblymen had disregarded their oaths to protect the Constitution, that the frame of government had already provided a Council of Censors to initiate any movement for reform, and that the oath of allegiance taken by the people required them to defend the Constitution.[22]

Confident of success the Republicans displayed only occasional activity to counteract the zeal of the Radicals. A number of newspaper articles set forth the conservative view. They charged the opponents of the convention with being office holders or those who expected office. "Cursed *Mammon,*" private interest and the thirst for power were the sole motivating principles of the Radicals. Another argument was that the assembly was simply paying back an old debt to the citizens by carrying out the vote which had been postponed by the British invasion in 1777. One writer asserted that the total of Radical activity in the country consisted of several new catch-phrases: all who favored a convention were branded tories, and the proposed second branch of the legislature was dubbed a house of lords. The Germans in particular were considered susceptible to these arguments. Personal attacks were also made on President Reed for joining the Constitutional faction.

A contributor to the *Packet* explained succinctly that the Radicals feared a change in the Constitution because it would mean the loss of their power. "But they will hereafter find, they have been deceived." With prophetic insight he warned:

> When the wealthy men become a majority in the Assembly, they may imitate the present rulers of the state in violating the Constitution and vote themselves as perpetual as the rump Parliament of England. The party that now bears sway will then curse their present leaders, and wish in vain for a Convention to alter and amend the Constitution.[23]

Considering the fact that it was mid-winter and that settlements in the rural regions were scattered, the Radicals made an excellent showing in flooding the house with memorials. On one day, February 18, petitions carrying over four hundred signatures from the hinterland were presented to the assembly. Other remonstrances continued to pour in. It was asserted that fourteen thousand persons thus voiced their disapproval of the assembly's resolves. The Radicals pointed with pride to these figures. The question remains, however, how many of the signatures were genuine. The Radicals had correspondence societies in the back-counties, and it was common knowledge that signatures could be quickly manufactured by two or three persons at a tavern table.[24] This fact the Republicans were not slow to point out. County lieutenants and sub-lieutenants, assessors and collectors, they asserted, peddled the petitions and kept the scheme from those who were opposed to the Constitution.

> . . . were you not told, [the conservatives reminded the people] when the petitions were presented to you, that the opposition to the Constitution arose, and was supported only by a junto of gentlemen in Philadelphia, who wished to trample upon the farmers and mechanics, to establish a wicked Aristocracy, and to introduce a house of Lords, hoping to become members of it? . . . Was not this doctrine preached to you from the pulpits? . . .[25]

Whatever the origin of the petitions, they had their effect. On February 27, exactly three months after the original resolves had been passed, the assembly turned about face and rescinded its action to take a plebiscite on calling a convention. Of the fifty-four members voting, only seven resisted the sweep of the tide. They were the unbending conservatives—Robert Morris, Thomas Mifflin, Samuel Meredith, George Clymer, from the city; and Bernard Dougherty, Thomas Smith, and George Woods from

Bedford County. In dissenting from the vote these men roundly condemned the Constitution and questioned the validity of the petitions. Later they declared that some members of the house voted to rescind the resolution in the honest belief that a majority of their constituents had signed the petitions.[26]

Little comment was made on the action of the assembly. In one newspaper article the writer demanded of President Reed that if he had assumed office for the purpose of calling a convention, he should resign. Gunning Bedford, Jr., expressed grim humor in the situation when he wrote: "We are determined to have no convention—our last one made such a damned bad constitution, we are afraid to trust another." [27] The important fact remained that the Republicans had lost their last chance to alter the frame of government. Radicalism was riding high.

Personalities Under Fire

With Congress located in Philadelphia it was inevitable that disputes over national questions would be injected into the political affairs of Pennsylvania. Prominent among the national political quarrels was the controversy which waxed hot and furious between Arthur Lee and Silas Deane. Although the crux of the debate centered on the question whether the supplies furnished by Beaumarchais before the alliance were a gift from the king of France or comprised a loan to the United States, this question was soon swamped by numerous less important ramifications and obscured by prolix articles of political flapdoodle. Deane had been privy to many of the transactions and maintained that they were of a purely commercial nature. The ever suspicious Lee maintained an opposite stand and suggested that Deane and Beaumarchais were simply trying to feather their financial nests. After being torn into factions by the controversy, Congress eventually dismissed both Deane and Lee.

In Pennsylvania the controversy served to aggravate the breach between the two political factions. The Radicals championed Lee while the Republicans maintained Deane's honor. The controversy took the form of a barrage of newspaper articles from both camps. Although most of the articles were printed over pseudonyms, a sufficient number have been identified to show that Thomas Paine, Arthur Lee, Richard Henry Lee, William Lee, and Timothy Matlack upheld the Virginia family, while Silas Deane, Robert Morris, Matthew Clarkson, Robert Treat Paine, William Duer, and Gouverneur Morris manned the opposition in whole or in part.[28]

Aside from thrashing out the general question at issue, other phases bearing more closely on State politics appeared in the newspaper warfare. Paine attacked Robert Morris for his business associations with Deane and suggested that State assemblies should investigate such activities by all former and present delegates to Congress, with the Pennsylvania legislature taking the lead. Morris boldly replied that on becoming a delegate he did not forfeit any of his rights to private business and included a strong defense of Deane's character. Referring to Deane's financial accounts, Paine took occasion to laud the State Constitution. The provision for a Council of Censors to inspect the expenditures of public moneys and to call defaulters to account appealed to him as one of the best features of the frame of government. He thought that Congress should adopt the same idea. Friends of Morris believed that he had given a good account of himself; Thomas Mifflin thought that Paine "fell a victim to his own stroke."[29] They did not realize that in a few months Morris would be answering before a public committee on similar charges of illegal business transactions.

In line with the other Radicals Joseph Reed vigorously upheld the Lees. He was forced to work more covertly however due to his position as President of the State. Deane later asserted that on the occasion of a public celebration at the city tavern in February, 1779, Reed warned him to desert his old associates, Morris, Deane, and Wilson, if he ever expected the Pennsylvania delegates in Congress to vote for his cause. Deane replied that so long as the State was run by the Radicals he did not expect or wish for the votes of its delegates. Although Reed communicated with Deane later, it was in tones of icy formality tinged with sarcasm. Evidently Reed realized that his attempt to separate Deane from the Republicans was fruitless. Reed also had attacked Gouverneur Morris on the ground of supporting Deane from interested motives. Morris deemed the charge ridiculous, insisted on Deane's right to be heard by Congress, and told Reed that he would be willing to have his own commercial transactions with Deane probed to the bottom at any time.[30]

It is possible that Gouverneur Morris came into the picture on another occasion in connection with the New England fisheries. The writer under the name of "Americanus," supposed to be Gouverneur Morris, suggested that in the negotiations with the British, the Americans should not insist on the right to the fisheries; moreover, the United States could not expect France to prolong the war for this one insignificant factor. This was a defiant thrust at the friends of the Radicals from New England. Thomas Paine and "Tiberius Gracchus" (perhaps a pseudonym of Timothy Matlack, Secretary to the Council) rushed forth to reply by asserting that Morris was trying to exclude the United States from the fisheries. Matlack also resurrected the old charge that Gouverneur Morris and William Duer were officiously intermeddling in State politics. Jonathan Sergeant, the attorney general, was unusually obnoxious to the Republicans. Hooper had manhandled him at Reading; Colonel White had ordered his mulatto servant to horsewhip him at Lancaster, and Whitehead Humphreys had threatened to cut off his ears. In the press Matlack boldly defended Sergeant and attributed the attacks to the chagrin of the Republicans at not being able to call a convention to revise the Constitution. Matthew Clarkson became involved in the Lee-Deane affair but his part was minor.[31]

The Radical interests in Pennsylvania were concerned in the fate of the Lees. When Congress voted on recalling Arthur Lee, the three staunch Radicals of the Pennsylvania delegation, Armstrong, Shippen, and Searle, teamed with Samuel Adams, Lovell, and Holten of Massachusetts in opposing this blow to their political brother. The moderate Pennsylvania delegates, Atlee, Muhlenberg, and Wynkoop, supported the conservative side led by Jay, Duane, and Gouverneur Morris of New York. Richard Henry Lee explained that Arthur's recall made the whigs of the State uneasy, for they considered it "as coming too near to sacrificing one of themselves and their good and able friend." [32] A few weeks later, on the vote to recall Arthur's brother, William, only Muhlenberg and Wynkoop cast their ballots for this action. Two days later Wynkoop gave his support to the Radicals.[33] When the assembly elected new delegates to Congress in November, 1779, Samuel J. Atlee and Henry Wynkoop were passed over. "It seems the General Assemblies resent the treatment of Doctor Arthur Lee by Congress," was Thomas McKean's explanation; S. J. Atlee had told him "this was the cause in Pennsylvania." [34] This was undoubtedly the case, for the Radicals got full control of the house in the fall elections. The whole Lee-Deane affair was an important factor in raising the political tension in the State.

More fat was thrown on the fire by an indiscreet expression made by Peale to some gentlemen at the Coffee House in July when the investigation of Morris by a popular committee was in progress. He explained that Silas Deane had offered Paine a bribe not to write against him. Soon Peale was faced by James Wilson and John Nixon with a demand for an explanation. Peale sent them to Paine who later "explained" the situation in the newspapers in vague and unsatisfactory generalities. By this and other activities Peale exposed himself to attack from the opposite party. He was assaulted in the street, and afterwards went about accompanied with his strong ash cane, "Hercules." [35]

In the meantime Paine was carving out the curious angles of his career. Realizing his need of money and hoping to divert him from further attacks on Morris and the commercial relations with France, the French minister, Gerard, proposed to enlist his journalistic services in the cause of the alliance but Paine would not cooperate. In September the author of "Common Sense" plagued Council for some form of income and reminded the members how at Reed's request he undertook the defense of the Constitution. It was the assembly, however, and not the Council which cared for Paine by electing him their clerk. Radicals considered him satisfactory on this post and some hoped that he might get a better position in the land office. To add honor to substance the newly created University conferred on him the master's degree on July 4, 1780. Paine's last attack upon the Republicans came when Deane wrote letters from abroad to prominent men in the United States, in which he showed strong sympathy for the British cause. After these letters had been published in the newspapers, Paine publicly branded him a traitor.[36]

Radical philosophy opposed cities as the seat of public assemblies. Although there was some sentiment in Congress during 1779 to move from Philadelphia, no definite action was taken. Congressmen complained loudly of the high price of necessities in Philadelphia. The Pennsylvania delegates were for the most part favorable to removal. Searle, for example, thought that Trenton would be suitable. Some members were considering the possibility of Bethlehem but the local conditions there were unsatisfactory for the seat of Congress. Agitation for removal was always present but several years passed before it blossomed into fruition.[37]

Reed and the Radicals continued to be highly sensitive to any slights offered by continental army officers to State officials. Two incidents occurred at this time which illustrate this feeling. Both events involved Chief Justice McKean who took a particular satisfaction in putting the army officers in their place.

In the fall of 1778 Count Pulaski had incurred a debt for the support of his legion. He thought the charge unreasonable and refused to pay it. When the sheriff of Philadelphia County attempted to serve a writ on him, he resisted. McKean at once ordered Pulaski to submit to the magistrate, and Congress passed resolves condemning opposition to civil magistrates by continental officers. Pulaski continued to rouse the ire of Reed. Five months later the President of the State was complaining to the Board of War about the indiscriminate foraging by the Count's legion. The War Office thereupon reminded Pulaski that it was necessary for foreign officers to divest themselves of European ideas while in America.[38]

Another case was that of Brigadier General William Thompson of the State continental line. This fifty-three year old Irishman had already publicly opposed the Constitution. Captured early in the war, he was forced to wait several years to be exchanged. For this reason he felt that Congress had not treated him well, in fact, had "used him *damned rascally*," as he termed it. His particular grievance lay against Thomas McKean, who was a member of Congress at this time. When the two met in a tavern, and Thompson accused the Chief Justice of using his influence against him in Congress, McKean's answer was interpreted as an insult, and the two came to blows. At once Reed and Council intruded themselves upon the affair to uphold the dignity of McKean despite the fact that he was not involved as Chief Justice of the State but as a member of Congress. When the national legislature investigated the affair and determined that Thompson was guilty of misconduct, Gouverneur Morris voted in favor of the General. Reed interpreted Morris' action as a slight on Pennsylvania and treasured it for a future reckoning with that New York Republican.[39] Reed's attitude was displayed in other cases. In June he instructed Bartram Galbraith to treat the men in the continental service with respect, "But we do not expect or desire you to receive any insults from any, even the greatest of them . . ." [40] In August Reed learned that a continental officer had been involved in an affray involving one of the agents for confiscated estates; at once he suggested that some notice other than the ordinary course of justice would be taken of the offender.[41]

Chief Justice McKean became the subject of criticism from the Radical camp. He was serving in the unique capacity of Chief Justice of Pennsylvania and delegate in Congress from Delaware. By an odd twist of circumstance his plurality of office-holding was supported by the Republicans and condemned by the Constitutionalists. The conservatives maintained the right of a man to hold more than one public position. Thus they were logically bound to defend McKean's situation. By a vote of twelve to forty-two the Radicals in the assembly declared that the Constitution did not allow McKean to exercise his dual functions. But the Chief Justice ignored the vote and went on his way unchallenged except for some blistering newspaper attacks.[42]

If there was one man who monopolized the spotlight of public attention, that man was Benedict Arnold. By accident or design everything he did poured oil on the political fire and increased the gulf between the Constitutionalists and the conservatives. The hatred the Radicals entertained toward him is almost unbelievable. If they distrusted Deane, they loathed Arnold. Determined on his public disgrace, Reed and Council formulated a series of charges against him. Before listing the formal counts against Arnold, it it necessary to understand how his social behavior intensified the hatred of the democrats. As an officer of the continental forces he was haughty, overbearing and commanding; thus he exemplified the worst traits for which the Radicals detested that group of men. He represented the military power which the ardent whigs had always feared might overshadow the civil power of the State. In addition, he affected an aristocratic air and entertained with lavish and ostentatious display. These faults might have been forgotten had Arnold not committed the unpardonable blunder of fraternizing with a social clique of noted tories and disaffected persons. "Will you not think it extraordinary," Reed reported to Nathanael Greene, "that General Arnold made a public entertainment the night before last, of which not only tory ladies, but the wives and daughters of persons proscribed by the State, and now with the enemy at New York, formed a considerable number? The fact is literally true." [43] To crown it all he courted and married Peggy Shippen, daughter of a man who by the most generous interpretation could be classed only as neutral if not actually sympathetic to the British cause.

Examined individually, the charges against Arnold do not appear serious. The small indiscretions, however, accumulated with increasing momentum when the emotions of the Radicals were already strained by their exasperating struggle against the external enemy as well as against the stubborn internal opposition of Republicans, Quakers, and tories. In the first place, he was charged with having given permission to a vessel owned by Robert Shewell who was considered by many as disaffected, to come from the enemy into an American port. This permission was granted without the knowledge of the State authorities or of General Washington. Arnold had a commercial interest in the vessel but whether before or after he gave the permission is difficult to determine. On another count Arnold was charged with having closed the stores of Philadelphia on taking over the city after the British withdrew, and of seizing the opportunity to make large purchases to his own advantage. This was a shallow charge, for Congress had already granted power for such a stoppage of business, and Arnold's purchasing was not substantiated in the ensuing trial. Personalities as well as the old conflict between the militia and the continental army flared up in another accusation. When the local militia was serving in the city after the withdrawal of the British, Timothy Matlack's son acting in the local forces as an orderly sergeant was required by one of Arnold's aids-de-camp to summon a barber. This wounded the pride of the Matlacks as well as the proud spirit of the militia. Father Matlack, then holding the reputable post of secretary to Council, complained to Arnold who replied that when a citizen becomes a soldier the rules of the army prevail. The Radicals were inflamed at this callous disregard for the independent spirit of the militia which they considered the only true military backbone of the Commonwealth. It should be noted that the influential Matlack represented the State as well as Radicalism in the ensuing court-martial of Arnold.[44]

At the time when the delicate question of who had rightful possession to the prize sloop *Active* was threatening the relations between the State and Congress, Arnold became an interested contestant in the controversy. It is sufficient to explain that the prize involving some ninety-three thousand pounds was claimed by Gideon Olmsted and associates on the one hand and by the State of Pennsylvania on the other. A Pennsylvania jury determined that one quarter of the money should go to Olmsted and the remainder to the State. Dissatisfied, Olmsted appealed to Congress where a committee sitting as a court of admiralty reversed the award and ordered the whole sum to go to Olmsted. But Pennsylvania refused to yield. To complicate the situation which was already fraying the nerves of Congress and the State officials, Arnold purchased a share of the claims held by his fellow-countryman, Olmsted, and used his influence in Congress to forward the claim against Pennsylvania.[45] This action inflamed the Radicals and well illustrates the State-rights attitude of that group. Incidentally, it should be noted that later in the year James Wilson became counsel for Olmsted in his claim before Congress, an action far from pleasing to the Radicals.[46]

Other charges against Arnold included his use of wagons, impressed from citizens for urgent public service, for his own private purposes. In another case the sensitive Council complained that Arnold had granted passes to persons to go within the enemy's lines despite the fact that Congress had given the officials of each state the exclusive power to recommend persons for such passes. Finally, Council asserted that Arnold had acted too favorably toward the disaffected to the prejudice of faithful whigs.[47]

If the Radical Council aimed at the public disgrace of Arnold, they received satisfaction, but only after straining relations with Congress to the breaking point. During Arnold's absence from the city the Council adopted and printed the charges for general circulation, addressed a copy to the governor of every state with the request that they should be laid before each state legislature. Council transmitted the charges to Congress. Reed ordered the Pennsylvania delegates to call for a vote in Congress on every question which might affect "the Authority or Reputation of this Council, & more especially in the Case of Gen. Arnold." [48] Although Arnold had a number of friends in Congress, their support was due largely to the fact that he was pitted against the Radicals of Pennsylvania. The New York delegates were favorable to him because they expected to employ him as commander-in-chief against Vermont. His speculations, however, were generally detested.[49] Sharp letters passed between Council and the investigating committee on the subject. Congress at length determined that only four of the charges were triable by court-martial. Meanwhile Radical heat increased. On the night of March 24 Council held a conference with a committee of the assembly. The result was a series of resolutions declaring that the relations between the State and congress had come to a critical pass because former complaints to the national body "had been either wholly neglected, or so treated that it would have been more honorable and advantageous to the State, to have submitted silently . . ." [50] These resolutions were sent to Congress with a request for a conference.

The conservatives in Congress were incensed over this action by the State. After such accusations had been published against that body, they asked, should Congress meekly confer with the State authorities? Gouverneur Morris, leading the conservative faction, declared that no conference should take place until Pennsylvania made reparation. Meriwether Smith added, "No Sir, let us . . . vindicate our conduct first, to the World, before we talk of conference." [51] Penn and Drayton agreed. Their resentment was directed more at Reed than at the assembly. John Penn and Meriwether Smith unsuccessfully attempted to limit the conference to the assembly and ignore Council. After Henry Laurens pointed out that party spirit infected the whole debate, Congress agreed to grant a conference with the joint representatives of the assembly and the Council.[52]

At the meeting the Radicals opened their Pandora's box and let forth all the carefully hoarded complaints which they held against Congress. It was an opening of old sores. The activity of Gouverneur Morris and John Harvey in the affair of the British convoy at Lancaster in January, 1778, headed the list. Then followed a number of instances in which Congress had ignored complaints made by the Council. The whole episode of Hooper was revived with virulence; the demand of Secretary Thomson for a residence and the many-sided story of the Arnold affair were the highlights among numerous petty accusations. No record of the meeting has been preserved, but it appears that the Radicals felt better after they had aired their grievances, for the dove of compromise descended on the men and a truce was declared. They decided to recommend to their respective bodies a set of resolutions declaring the restoration of happy relations, and that Congress and the State held each other in mutual high respect. Reed and his cohorts grudgingly surrendered on some of the charges against Arnold while Congress ordered Washington to submit four of the charges to a military court.[53]

After long delay Arnold was tried and the Radicals enjoyed their belated victory. He was found guilty of violating an article of war while his use of public wagons for private ends was deemed imprudent. He was sentenced to receive a reprimand from Washington. Knowing that they had achieved their end and that public reaction might turn in favor of Arnold, Reed in the name of Council requested Congress to suspend the reprimand which Congress refused to do. In the tone of citation rather than censure Washington delivered the reprimand. The Radicals had their triumph.[54]

In spreading their net for Arnold, the Council caught Matthew Clarkson, aid-de-camp to Arnold. In order to investigate the charge that Clarkson had issued a pass to Miss Levy to go to the enemy's lines, contrary to a resolution of Congress and after Council had refused such permission, Council summoned him to appear before them. When he refused to comply and sent a letter couched in disrespectful terms to Council, Reed complained to Congress. After some debate that body determined that Clarkson should have attended Council, and for the indecent language in his letter he was reprimanded by the President of Congress. After Clarkson left the house one of the members with a malicious sense of humor moved that a brevet commission of Major should be bestowed on the errant aid-de-camp; this motion, of course, was withdrawn. This was another attempt of the Radicals to protect the civil power against military domination.[55]

Radicalism Unleashed

The severe criticism of personalities served as propaganda to inflame the emotions of the populace for an explosion. The rise of the mob element among the Radicals was a gradual process. First, certain leaders demanded that the assembly should take action against engrossers. Then a popular committee instituted a public court in which to hear individual cases; and, finally, the lowest element armed with guns and clubs attempted to drive leading Republicans out of the city.

The core of the trouble was economic. The lower classes knew only one thing, that the cost of living had increased. The paper money issued by Congress and by the State had depreciated. Prices rose and sometimes foodstuffs became scarce.[56] It was natural and easy to point the accusing finger at the men of wealth and business like Robert Morris and Levi Hollingsworth. The Radicals also saw in these merchants men of a political faith which was unsympathetic to the new democratic form of government.

Agitation against the merchants began late in 1778. Action had been requested against engrossers and speculators. Prompted by a petition from several relatively unimportant men, Council appointed nine Radicals to inquire throughout the city of Philadelphia about the monopolizing of flour. Except for an inflammatory newspaper article suggesting that the mob might rise against the forestallers and break open their supplies, the subject lay dormant for five months.[57]

Unimportant at the time but portending discontent against the merchants was a strike by the sailors in January, 1779. One hundred fifty seamen banded together and decided to force the importers to raise their wages by unrigging some outward-bound vessels and by driving off the workmen. On complaint from the merchants, Council speedily ordered the justices of the peace to call on General Arnold for troops to put down the riot. Soon the malcontents landed in jail and the episode was closed.[58]

The next incident to arouse attention involved the merchant Levi Hollingsworth who had sold a quantity of flour to an agent acting under Maryland law. Within a few weeks the people took up the cry that Hollingsworth had applied to his own use flour that had been sent into the city for the State prisoners. The mob seized Hollingsworth among others and congregated in front of the Coffee House, desiring revenge and avoiding cool reflection. A sensible official persuaded the mob to allow Hollingsworth to be placed in jail where the authorities thought him safe from further harm. Six weeks later when flour was scarce in Philadelphia, Secretary Matlack asked Hollingsworth then at Head of Elk, whether he would send a supply to the city. Such an act, Matlack reminded him, might remove the unfavorable impression which the Radicals had formed of his conduct.[59]

Another discontented group was the militia which always formed the backbone of Radical strength. A list of grievances, drawn up by the Philadelphia militia artillery early in May, indicated their train of thought. The principal complaint was leveled against the men who stayed at home and did not fight. This was a veiled reference to the conservatives like Morris to whom the war meant profitable trade and to the speculators who drove hard bargains in paper money and provisions. Other accusations were forthcoming. The assembly had not placed the militia on a respectable footing (another reference to the powerful conservative minority led by Morris), the whole organization was viewed in the most disrespectful light, and the few fines that were enacted were artfully evaded. Then the militiamen unwittingly criticized the first Radical assembly by pointing out that in the summer of 1777 the hiring of substitutes had enabled the disaffected to remain at home and amass fortunes. True it was that in the last session heavy fines had been imposed, but the middle and poor classes continued to bear the burden, either by leaving their families starve while they fought or by remaining at home and being ruined by fines. To avoid this situation they demanded a law which would assess the fines in proportion to a man's estate or leave it to the faithful members of the militia to compel every able-bodied man to join them; to leave so many disaffected at home would create a situation "worse than making us prisoners of War." [60]

Portents of a storm surcharged the atmosphere of the city. After the regular meeting of the Constitutional Society on May 22, a number of citizens led by Christopher Marshall issued a call for a general mass meeting on the 25th. Quakers privately voiced their dread of a mob rising to hunt down forestallers. These fears were not unfounded. Two days later commotion was rife; leaderless bands paraded the streets seeking some method to vent their resentment on speculators. "What will be the issue God knows," exclaimed one witness.[61] Preparatory to the town meeting on the 25th, Christopher Marshall, behind the scenes, had asked the city magistrates as well as President Reed "to be out of the way, if possible, on this day."[62]

At the meeting the Radical Roberdeau acting as chairman struck the keynote when he explained that prices must be reduced if the depreciation of paper money was to be halted. Monopolizers and forestallers, as he viewed the situation, had really been laying a tax on the people for the last six months. He had no doubt that combinations had been formed to raise prices. The meeting then adopted resolves to reduce the price of goods and provisions, to support the currency and to reform abuses. Two committees were appointed to carry out these aims. A group of twenty-six formed a committee of inspection to determine what price articles should sell for, and a smaller committee of more prominent Radicals was ordered to wait on Robert Morris to inquire into his dealings in flour.[63]

These conditions were inflamed by an address of Congress coming a few days later. On May 26 President Reed, Speaker Bayard, and Councillor James Smith presented a petition to Congress requesting alleviation from the economic distress. The national body offered little comfort except to suggest that the states must help themselves, that there had been too much complaining and not sufficient investigation of abuses and that the trouble lay with greedy merchants who monopolized the necessities of life.[64]

Several other incidents indicated the temper of the times. Two days after the price-regulating committee had been formed, Roberdeau complained that Joseph Dean had joined with some other men in buying a parcel of molasses contrary to their own resolutions. A number of the committee requested that he should be expelled from their body "in order to pacify the minds of the public, who were irritated."[65] Tories supplied another objective for the Radicals. On May 29 at a meeting at the German school house a committee of twelve was chosen to sit three days a week as a court to receive evidence against persons suspected of disaffection. More important was the action of the city militia artillery which addressed the local price-fixing committee. Speculators were still rampant, the soldiers declared. Something more poignant and striking must be done to bring them to reason. "We have arms in our hands and know the use of them;" "nor will we lay them down till this is accomplished." They demanded a proportional reduction of prices, and suggested that if the committee found itself inadequate to the task, *"our drums shall beat to arms."*[66] In the meantime the committee on prices was attempting the impossible task of regulating and reducing the cost of necessities.

Contemporary comment on the committees varied with the political persuasion of the observer. Meriwether Smith believed the committees were instituted for the worst purposes. He cited Gerard as saying that they were the tools of designing men, not friends to the French alliance, who wished for an ultra-democratic government the better to enable them to gain their ends. William Bradford, of course, as chairman of the Constitutional Society, justified all the work of the committees. President Reed was generally pleased with the situation. Republicans supposed, probably correctly, that Reed and the Council were secretly supporting the irregular procedures. Reed later denied that he originated or conducted these popular meetings which he characterized as "the effusions of honest but intemperate zeal" and "the angry relique" of the Lee-Deane quarrel.[67]

A more spectacular episode stemming from this same movement involved Robert Morris, the French Government, the State of Pennsylvania and Congress. Because of his activity in all kinds of business transactions, his wealth and social prestige, and his known opposition to the State Constitution, Robert Morris was the prime objective of the Radicals. He was called before the special committee for examination. He found it better not to appear and he and the committee carried on most of their transactions in writing. After seizing the flour from Morris, the investigators learned that the cargo he was accused of engrossing as a private venture was really flour bought for the supply of the French fleet. On this revelation the committee was nonplussed and rather hastily dropped the affair. But it was not at an end. Gerard, the French minister, fully supported Morris' actions and complained to Congress of the interference with the supply of the French forces in America. A committee of Congress found the whole thing embarrassing and gave an odd report. They cleared Holker, French consul, of all charges made against him in the Radical newspapers; they learned that the State authorities had already returned the flour and they declared that the city price-fixing body was not an official organization. In other words, Congress made its peace with the French and the Radicals went unscathed.[68]

Conservatives viewed these proceedings with helpless amazement. Some thought the country would soon be overrun by committees to the entire subversion of government. Others regarded Pennsylvania as without law, "for every man who takes a club in his hand to town meetings (which, by-the-by, have been very frequent of late) undertakes to be governor." As much as James Read detested the State Constitution, he considered it better than "the present mob government." [69] John Jay reported that it was the policy of the Constitutionalists to deprecate every man "who refused to draw in their harness." [70]

After the first flush of dominance, the committee on price regulation met resistance. The tanners, curriers, and cordwainers declared that they would not be bound by the regulated prices of their commodities until a general regulation of all other commodity prices took place by common consent. The committee found it desirable to call another mass meeting at the end of July. To guarantee a sympathetic audience it was ordered at first that only those who could produce their certificates of having taken the oath would be admitted, but several days before the meeting this restriction was lifted. At the meeting held on July 27 in the State House yard it was decided that the committee should be enlarged to one hundred and twenty members to be chosen at a general election. The work of the present committee was approved with few persons dissenting. At this meeting, however, prominent conservatives like James Wilson, Sharp Delaney, and Benjamin Rush appeared in order to oppose further price regulation. But when John Cadwalader attempted to speak he was interrupted by about a hundred men armed with clubs who had marched with fife and drum and located themselves near the stage. Even after taking a vote of the whole body which Chairman Roberdeau declared was in favor of Cadwalader's speaking, the hoodlums continued their interference. The conservatives withdrew in a body to the College yard where they held their own meeting. At this gathering at which Robert Morris presided several resolutions were passed stating the Republican position. They denounced the interruption of Cadwalader as a violation of liberty of speech; agreed to vote for the committee of one hundred twenty and to support them in keeping down prices; and defended Holker and Morris in the recent flour fracas.[71]

When the elephantine committee was elected by popular vote on August 2, the Radicals received an overwhelming victory. Andrew Caldwell, Thomas FitzSimons, John Shee, and Francis Hopkinson were the only outstanding conservatives to be included. The unsuccessful ticket was swamped by a vote of almost ten to one. Oddly enough the French Alliance threatened to become an important issue in this election. On election day the conservatives issued a broadside reminding the people of the threat to free speech when Cadwalader was not allowed to speak at the meeting. "Change both Men and Measures," warned the Republicans, "or Ruin inevitably awaits us. The late public Insult offered to the French Nation, through their Officer in this City, sufficiently warrants this Caution." [72] To nullify this charge the Independent Constitutionalist ticket carried the arms of the alliance. Soon after the election the new committee sent a long-winded letter to Gerard on the advantages of the French Alliance and congratulated him on d'Estaing's victory over Byron. It was in effect an indirect apology for the excesses of the former committee which had attacked Morris on his work of supplying flour to the French forces. Gerard replied in general and elegant terms as only a Frenchman would. The Radicals had made their gesture to France but they were not unconvinced that the whole cry of danger to the alliance was only a smoke screen for Republicans interested in the West India trade.[73]

The attempt to regulate prices by popular action was not confined to the city. Christopher Marshall, who had been instrumental in the work in Philadelphia, went to Lancaster where he had a hand in similar action. This time he was not so reticent and acted as chairman of a number of the Lancaster meetings. The formula was much the same: a committee was appointed and enlarged; the scale of prices was patterned on that of the city; resolutions against tories and speculators were adopted; and early in their proceedings they detected one of the committee violating the agreements. Nor was the movement without opposition. Conservatives and Radicals, both presumably of the lowest classes of society, paraded, taunted each other, and finally came to blows. The zealous Marshall continued to write circular letters and distribute newspapers to forward his ideas of price regulation. Similar meetings were called in other counties including Chester, Philadelphia, Berks, York, and the Paxton district of Lancaster. At the same time Marshall was supplying plans for the use of a committee in Northumberland.[74]

In Philadelphia the Radicals had been aroused to the point where anything might happen. Late in July the inevitable took place. Whitehead Humphreys, writing under an assumed name as was the custom, published an article in Towne's *Evening Post* which inflamed the Radicals. The fact that the printer was considered a tory did not help the situation. Dragging Towne before their society, the Radicals extracted a confession that Humphreys was author of the offending article. Aiming to seize the author, two of the society, followed by the mob, went to Humphreys' house. Edward Langworthy, delegate elect to Congress from Georgia, was at this time rooming in the residence; he believed that the mob attack was also intended for him. Threats and counter-threats ensued. Humphreys had been absent at the time, but on returning and finding that his sister had been handled roughly, he armed himself and defied the assailants who tried to intimidate him by bringing up a small file of armed soldiers from the continental guard. Humphreys held his ground and the mob dispersed without further incident. Irritated by the use of continental troops in this riotous proceeding, Langworthy appealed to Congress for protection and indicated that the Radicals planned in a day or two to seize Drayton, Gouverneur Morris, Deane, and himself. Although McLene from Pennsylvania tried to defeat the motion to investigate the incident, Congress referred the facts concerning the continental troops to the Board of War. Colonel Bull and Charles Peale, who had been accused of leading the mob, presented a weak justification of their conduct. The whole affair blew over but it was a significant portent of things to come.[75]

The committee headed by William Henry continued on its work of checking inflation. They aimed to solve the problem by regulating the retail price of articles and by decreasing the amount of paper money in circulation. The task was difficult. "The universal cry is, 'Stop the emissions'," the committee explained to the people. But immediate funds were needed to defray the expenses of government. Taxation was too slow and loans at exorbitant rates of interest were repulsive to the lower classes. "Yet money *must* be had, *that the emissions may be stopt.*" [76] Some of the members of the committee put their heads together and produced the Citizens' Plan. By this method Congress was requested to issue no more paper after September 30; committeemen were to make a house-to-house canvass for subscriptions of money for the government for a three-year period; the subscribers' taxes during that period would cancel their loans. The committee included the prominent Radicals Daniel Roberdeau, William Bradford, William Henry, Thomas Paine, Dr. James Hutchinson, David Rittenhouse, and Owen Biddle. At a later mass meeting the plan was adopted with practically no dissenting voices. Enthusiastic over the newly concocted panacea, the committee submitted it to Council for approval with the suggestion that it might be adopted by the other states. Council gave its blessing to the plan.[77]

Protests against the price-fixing activities of the committee grew louder. When Caldwell tried to describe the futility of regulation at one meeting, his voice was drowned by the tumult of a band of ruffians. The shoemakers had already determined to ignore the fixed prices unless their wages were raised. Early in September eighty merchants, of whom twenty-six were members of the Republican Society, sent a vigorous protest to the Council. They attacked the action of the committee as an invasion of property rights when a trader was compelled to accept less for his goods than he could otherwise obtain. An arbitrary scale of prices was impossible when the economic situation fluctuated from day to day. The whole system, they continued, would discourage domestic trade as well as foreign imports. "Like him who owned the goose which laid golden eggs," the merchants warned, "you will cut off the source of all farther supplies, and like him too, when you repent, you will repent in vain." [78]

The merchants' protest fell on deaf ears. The Radicals were furious at their own failure to solve the money problem. They had stirred up the mob and the mob would not be satisfied until it found a scapegoat for the economic ills of society. Morris had deftly slipped through their hands; the attack on Humphreys had resulted in a fiasco with a sting administered by Langworthy. The extra-legal committee functioned without marked success; prices continued to soar and paper money slipped to new lows. The stiffening of the test act in September was small consolation to an infuriated populace. James Wilson increased his unpopularity by defending Robert Morris and other men of more torified complexion.

Monday, October 4, 1779, was the highwater mark of Radical democracy in Pennsylvania during the revolutionary period. For some time previous to that eventful day the Radicals had been laying plans to seize the women and children of all who had gone over to the enemy, put them on a boat and ship them to New York. More level-headed men like Peale and Dr. Hutchinson disapproved the plan but they could not dissuade the zealots. Handbills appeared calling the militia to meet at Byrne's tavern on the commons. At this meeting the aim changed to driving out the leading Republicans, some of them about to stand for election to the assembly in a week. The natural leaders of the Radicals protested in vain, especially to the many Germans in the militia "who only looked straight forward, regardless of Consequences." [79]

Realizing the danger, the threatened Republicans met with arms and were protected by the City Light Horse, the aristocratic "silk-stocking brigade." Thinking the danger past, the Light Troop went home to dinner at noon. Meanwhile the mob started on its mission by seizing Sims, Story, and John Drinker. After allowing Drinker to eat his dinner, they paraded the three men through the streets, beating the rogue's march. Then they set out for James Wilson who had applied to the assembly for protection but found the mob upon him before any aid arrived. Wilson and a group of well-known Republicans gathered at his home where they barred the doors and awaited with arms. Soon came the mob, reinforced by the militia and accompanied by two field pieces. The infuriated group stopped before Wilson's house. Angry words and threats soon led to firing; the door was broken in and the invaders reached the stairway. Several persons were killed and many wounded. At this serious juncture President Reed and the Light Horse troop galloped up to the rescue. Order was gradually restored as some of the militiamen were sent to prison. Next day when the Germans of Philadelphia County learned that several of their countrymen had been killed, the militia advanced toward the city for revenge. Exerting all of his parleying ability, Reed persuaded them to turn back.[80]

It required several days for the hot heads to cool. The assembly assured Council of its concurrence in all measures to quiet the commotions. The ostentatious funeral for those who had been killed did not aid in allaying the ferment. James Wilson went into hiding for a time while Robert

Morris urged him to escape to New Jersey until matters were in better train. The militiamen were released from prison on bail and Reed persuaded the discontented Radicals to draw up their grievances and send them to the assembly. To make matters worse Reed became sick. In addition Chief Justice McKean who was holding court at Lancaster displayed a peculiar reluctance to come to the city at Reed's request. The assembly quickly approved the manner in which the President had handled the riot.[81]

The Radicals realized that they had overstepped their mark. A writer in one of the newspapers gave an account of the episode from the Constitutionalist viewpoint but regretted the whole affair. A number of officers of the city militia addressed Reed with praise for his part in quelling the rioters; but they admitted the mistaken zeal of one faction and the equal imprudence of the other. Reed continued the role of mediator and peacemaker. To the assembly he explained away the incident "as the casual overflowings of liberty," and wisely asked for an act of oblivion which was granted.[82]

Two days after this Fort Wilson riot the rabble, still thirsting for a victim, attacked General Arnold in the streets of Philadelphia. He was cordially hated by the Radicals and doubtless only his military character had preserved him from earlier insults. On this occasion he brandished his pistols and scared off his assailants. At once he applied to Congress for a personal body guard of twenty men and an officer, and insinuated that the State authorities did not have it in their power to protect him. Congress took umbrage at this statement, and told him to apply to Pennsylvania for aid. There the matter dropped. It demonstrates how careful Congress was at this time not to become involved, even remotely, in the State political situation.[83]

The State Revolution Completed

The fury against engrossers, tories, and well-to-do Republicans in general presaged only one result at the October elections. The returns showed a complete Radical victory in the assembly. It could not have been otherwise. The Republicans had been driven underground. With John Bayard in the Speaker's chair, Thomas Paine holding the clerkship, Reed and Moore unanimously re-elected to the first and second administrative offices, the Constitutionalists had absolute control of the government. The assembly did not even contain a Republican minority as in 1778-1779. The only important change during the ensuing year was the admission of George Bryan to the position of a Justice of the Supreme Court. His place in the assembly was filled by the election of Dr. James Hutchinson, prominent Radical, in May, 1780.[84]

This was the first assembly since the Revolution in which the representation was apportioned on the basis of taxables rather than on the equality of each county which had been the prevailing rule since the Constitutional Convention of 1776. By the new method the eastern counties gained at the expense of the frontier region. Philadelphia City and County, for example, gained two additional seats; Chester, Lancaster, and York counties a total of nine additional seats; while Bedford, Northumberland, and Westmoreland lost a total of ten seats. The new arrangement gave a preponderance to the City and the four counties of Philadelphia, Chester, Lancaster, and York; in the earlier assemblies this group held two-fifths of the seats; now they held three-fifths. Although the Radical leaders in Philadelphia feared that the western counties would not submit to their decreased representation, the election was held without untoward results.[85]

Satisfied with the record of most of the State delegates to Congress, the assembly reduced the number to five, and re-elected all except S. J. Atlee and Henry Wynkoop who were omitted because of their votes on the Lee-Deane affair in Congress. In June, 1780, the house decided to add two more delegates and then chose Jared Ingersoll and Timothy Matlack.[86]

To the Radicals the most obnoxious citadel of conservatism scarcely touched by the new democratic spirit was the College of Philadelphia. Provost William Smith had labored a quarter of a century to develop the institution into one of the best in the English colonies. But he had been identified with the conservative spirit. A Scot by birth, *protégé* of the proprietary interests, he took the side of the Penns in political disputes in the 1760's. This was natural, for the Penns had always fostered the College. At the time of the Revolution the whole board of trustees was conservative, some members later going over to the British.[87]

As the Revolution progressed, events did not augur well for the institution. The trustees were slow to take the oath to the new government, while three of them were outright tories. Furthermore, the institution was dominated by the Episcopalians while the new democratic government was infused with a strong Presbyterian spirit. In 1778 two acts indicated the growing resentment against the College. Early in that year the trustees were deprived of all power for a limited time; a later act provided that trustees, provost, and teachers of any college or academy would be required to take the oath before they could continue in their professions. This was intended mainly for the College. Before the summer of 1778 twelve of the trustees, the provost, and all the professors had taken the oath.[88]

Feeling their strength, the Radicals launched their attack early in 1779. In February the assembly appointed a committee to investigate the conditions at the College; the resulting report interpreted the facts to suit Radical purposes. At the same time Provost Smith's conduct during the Revolution was explained in the newspapers in a most unfavorable light. During the summer when the matter rested due to the adjournment of the assembly, the State authorities became bolder. As if to prevent any disturbance, the trustees decided that the ensuing commencement should be held privately; and in an attempt to remedy some of the glaring charges brought against the institution, the trustees elected new members to fill the seats of those who had gone over to the enemy or had resigned. The commencement scheduled to be held on July 5 was postponed on notice from President Reed that Council was in the midst of discussing the whole state of the College. Faced with the inevitable, the trustees asked Council to settle the question "in a legal way." [89]

The final blow fell late in 1779. The assembly appointed a new committee to complete the inquiry into conditions of the College. Lacking the signatures of Hartley and Chambers, the two conservative members of the committee, the report explained that several of the trustees had joined the British, that the funds were inadequate, that several trustees were disqualified by the test act of June, 1777, and that the original broad plan of equal privileges to all denominations had not been adhered to. The Radicals admitted the political aspect of their motives when the report declared that the College had shown "an Evident Hostility to the present Government and Constitution of this State, and in divers Particulars, Enmity to the common Cause." [90] James Wilson and William Lewis, two eminent lawyers, were chosen to present the case for the College, and the assembly went through the formality of hearing the arguments pro and con. The Republicans attempted several methods to stave off assembly action. They asked that the opinion of the judges of the Supreme Court should be requested before a committee was appointed to report a bill altering the charter; then they demanded that the committee which had reported against the institution should present the evidence on which they based their report. But legal forms and reasoning were to no avail. The Radicals brought forth their thirty-three votes to outmatch the sixteen in the minority. In vain did the conservatives denounce the party spirit which actuated the Radicals because some of the trustees had sought alterations in the State Constitution.[91]

The act of November abolished the College under its old leaders and created a new institution known as the University of the State of Pennsylvania. Technically the old charter was not voided; the amendments and alterations were so sweeping that actually it amounted to revocation. Reconstructed on a broad basis so as to give all important religious denominations representation on the board of trustees, the new institution really became an organ of the Presbyterians and a stronghold of the Radicals. John Ewing was elected Provost, David Rittenhouse Vice-Provost, and George Bryan Treasurer. Scarcely had the University been organized when wire-puller Christopher Marshall was using his influence with Robert Whitehill and Dr. Ewing to have James Cannon and James Davidson return and again become tutors. Cannon had gone to South Carolina where he was unsuccessfully attempting to convert David Ramsay to Radical democracy.[92]

The second great objective of the Constitutionalists was to wipe away the landed holdings of the Penn proprietors who already had been stripped of all governing power in the State. The problem was to give legal form to the confiscation of the public lands and the abolition of the quit rents. The two political parties in the State agreed that a settlement should be made. The conservatives pressed for an arrangement based on justice and the good name of the State. They feared that too drastic action might give a blow to property rights in general.[93]

The Radicals moved with unusual caution toward the divesting act. For more than eight months the question was before the assembly at one time or another. In March, 1779, the case for and against the proprietaries was heard by the assembly. Ross, Wilson, Tilghman, and Chew appeared on behalf of the Penns while Attorney General Sergeant represented the State. Ross argued that the holdings of William Penn and his descendants were purely of the nature of private property. Sergeant and the Radicals contended that Penn had obtained the land from the Crown and had administered it in trust for the adventurers; therefore, the proprietor and his successors were but the people's trustees. In addition, so much land in the hands of any one person, the Radicals continued, was dangerous to the liberties of the State.[94]

It was a foregone conclusion that the Penns would lose their holdings of a public nature. The question to be settled was how much recompense the State would allow them. In September a grand committee of the assembly was put to work on the problem and within a few days a bill was framed. When it was proposed to give John Penn a chance to lay before the house a statement of annual income from quit rents as well as other figures on the financial aspects of his case, only fourteen staunch Republicans were willing to concur. After ordering the bill to be printed for consideration on September 23, it was carried over to the next session which contained no important conservative members. In the new assembly in November a test vote showed forty for the act and only seven opposed. At length it passed, and the Radicals added one more feather to their triumph.[95]

The divesting act was surprisingly liberal, especially as the product of a Constitutionalist assembly. This was doubtless due to the fact that John Penn had given no opposition during the early Revolutionary days and because the Radicals employed their best legal talent, men like Bryan and Sergeant, to frame the measure. The act provided that all rights to the soil and arrears of purchase money devolved on the Commonwealth, and it completely abolished the collection of quit rents. In return for their loss the Penns were allowed to retain their personal estates and were granted one hundred thirty thousand pounds sterling to be paid after the end of the war.[96]

City Radicals of the stripe of Bryan, Peale, and Paine turned their attention to the abolition of Negro slavery in Pennsylvania. This object was particularly close to George Bryan's heart. Soon after becoming Vice-President Bryan and Council suggested an emancipation measure to the assembly in 1777 and 1778. This stirred up resentment in assembly, not on the issue itself, but on the point of how far Council should go in submitting heads of bills to the house. It is possible, of course, that the significant conservative minority in the 1778-1779 session fostered the conflict in order to embarrass Bryan. There is little evidence that the emancipation question assumed an important political aspect. When the Radicals had complete control of the house in 1779-1780, Bryan determined to put through his measure. The first recorded vote of the new session was on the question whether the bill should be engrossed for a third reading and published for consideration. Only eight members voted against the measure; two of these members were reported opposed to the bill because it did not provide complete freedom for blacks born after the bill took effect.[97]

As the bill progressed toward passage, more opposition developed. The opposition did not come from the enemies of the Radicals. For a few years prior to the Revolution the Quakers had been using strong measures to force their slaveholding members to free their charges. Other tory elements were cowed during the Radical year of 1779 and could not have offered much opposition had they wished. The opposition came from the Radicals themselves, and centered in certain Presbyterian strongholds in the back-counties. "In the meantime, it is irksome to find, that these few opposers of the bill should generally be members of the Presbyterian churches, which are otherwise remarkable for their zeal and for their exertions in the cause of freedom," remarked an anonymous newspaper open letter to an unnamed clergyman.[98] The arguments offered against the bill were largely religious, buttressed by numerous quotations from the Bible in defense of slavery which had the ring of Calvinist theology.[99] At least eight slaveholders voted on the bill. Of these three voted for the bill; two against it; and another, Meason, who later registered eight slaves, voted at first for the bill but reversed his vote on the final roll call. When the second vote occurred on the bill in February, 1779, the opposition had increased its votes from eight to eighteen, six of whom had changed their minds in the intervening months. The final vote on the bill on March 1, 1780, showed thirty-four persons in favor and twenty-one opposed to it. Ten of the minority had voted for the measure on the two earlier roll calls.[100] Material is not at hand to determine whether the growing opposition developed because the bill was considered too liberal or too conservative. It is probable there was a fusion of both elements. But the point remains that much of the opposition came from the Radicals themselves. The act did not provide for immediate abolition of slavery but for the gradual emancipation of Negroes. Every colored person in servitude at the time the act was passed continued in that state during the remainder of his natural life; Negroes born after the passage of the act became free when they reached the age of twenty-eight. The act has the earmarks of a compromise measure.[101]

One result of the emancipation act was to intensify the situation in southwestern Pennsylvania. The Virginia settlers who had brought their Negroes with them when they migrated to this region found the act an additional grievance as they learned that they were no longer under the jurisdiction of Virginia. Incensed by the act and the new boundary line, numerous slaveholding families sold their land claims and returned to the South.[102]

If the gradual abolition of slavery was a humanitarian indulgence of the Radical followers of Bryan, the support of the militia was an absolute necessity for the maintenance of the whole Constitutionalist party. The vital link between the central government in Philadelphia and the militia organization scattered over the State where the county lieutenants and their assistants, the sub-lieutenants. These offices were filled by the Council with the inevitable political aspects in mind. The lieutenants were thus the local henchmen of the Radical leaders in Philadelphia. To strike at this organization, the Republicans late in 1778 moved to abolish the office of sub-lieutenant with the argument that it was needless and expensive. Unsuccessful, they then tried to prevent these officers from sitting in the assembly on the ground that such plural office-holding violated the Constitution and allowed lieutenants to vote on settling their own accounts. By a party vote the Radicals killed this suggestion.[103]

President Reed realized the importance of the militia to the party. The attempt to remove the sub-lieutenants he viewed as only a prelude to laying aside the whole militia law. Although he admitted that the failure of the frontier militia was due to the neglect and misconduct of "our own officers," he laid heavy blame on the Republicans who did all in their power to distract and censure the people occupying the fringes of civilization. Radicalism and patriotism were the grounds of his entreaties to militia officers to induce their men to turn out. If these men "are Lovers of this Government & Constitution they will shew it by their submission to its Laws & a chearful Discharge of their Duty. . . ." [104]

With the assembly completely in their control in 1779-1780, the Radicals labored over the task of amending the militia laws. The votes disclose that the Radicals were not of one mind in the business. In general the urban Radicals were outvoted on practically every measure by the counties. The house exempted its members from militia duty, would not consent to change training days from Monday to Saturday, insisted on retaining the policy of allowing substitutes, and defeated a provision to fine a man whose substitute deserted. Although the city Radicals supported the idea that fines should be proportioned to a man's wealth, the back-country defeated the measure.[105]

Failures of the Radical Regime

Conditions in the economic realm went from bad to worse. The Radicals were at their wit's end. They had tried tender laws and popular regulation of prices without success. The enthusiasm attending the birth of the Citizens' Plan evaporated into thin air as paper money continued to fall. Congress was considering a recommendation to the states to repeal their tender laws. This would constitute a blow to the Radicals. In the winter of 1779-1780 John Armstrong reported that at Carlisle prices continued to increase; paper money was refused and in some instances barter was introduced. Although grain was scarce, he understood that stills were going at top speed. Like a true Radical he insisted that legal regulation of prices was the only key to recovery. Despite the unsuccessful attempts to regulate prices, Congress persisted in that philosophy. It called on the states to establish price limitation by law. Congress also revived the idea of an interstate convention for the same purpose. Delegates from various states were to meet at Philadelphia. The assembly gave its approval to the plan and the Radicals looked forward to it with hope. The conservatives had no taste for the idea. "The real Statesmen among us," explained Rush about the proposed convention, "expect nothing from it—but the final dissolution of our money." The Radicals, he continued, "expect to see all the miracles of transubstantiation, & all the mysteries of alchemy performed in an instant upon the currency. . . . The folly & madness of mankind used to distress me—But I have learned to hear & to talk of errors in Government with composure." [106] Representatives from only six states attended the convention in Philadelphia in the early months of 1780; it adjourned without proceeding to business because commissioners from New York and Virginia never appeared.[107]

The question of the tender laws once more came to the front. In March, 1780, Congress adopted McKean's motion asking the states to repeal the legal tender quality of continental money. The next day in the State assembly the question was raised whether a clause to suspend the tender laws on continental money should be included in a current money bill. The urban Radicals favored the repeal while the rock-ribbed back-countrymen held to their principles. The division was a tie; the casting vote of Speaker Bayard enabled the anti-tender group to carry the day. A similar question came up two days later when the city Radicals lost by six votes. When Congress finally legalized the depreciated value of its own emissions at a rate of forty to one, it was a hard blow to the rural Radicals. While men like Rush hoped that this action would restore the vigor of 1775, Christopher Marshall and his friends in Lancaster consulted on framing a petition to ask the assembly to rescind the forty-to-one proposition. Philadelphia merchants and traders formally asked the house to abolish the tender laws. By the end of May the Radicals accepted the inevitable and the suspension of the legal tender of national currency was carried by a two-to-one vote. In the ten weeks elapsing since the first vote ten back-country members of the strongest Radical bent changed their minds and voted for this bill. Without public office and silenced by the mob, Robert Morris looked on the financial situation and confided to a friend: ". . . in this redundancy of paper circulation, after all the feverish palliations of restrictions, regulations, limitations, etc., are found ineffectual, they will be universally condemned, cool taxation will take place, and common sense . . . take place in the minds of the people. Then, and not till then, will our finances be put in the train that they ought to be." [108]

Not until 1780 were the Radicals able to issue a State paper currency that gained considerable acceptance. In March, the assembly authorized an issue of 100,000 pounds in interest-bearing treasury notes as part of the new plan of Congress to establish a sound currency. It was believed that the merchants in the city would accept the new paper. Small tradesmen and the common people were at first shy of it; hence it did not obtain so wide a circulation in small business as had been hoped. In Cumberland County the new money was reported to be gradually gaining ground among the populace. President Reed stood aloof from other Radicals when he wished that the new money would not be made legal tender, for he did not believe that coercive measures created public confidence.[109]

In the other endeavors to solve the complex economic situation, the Radical regime made little headway. In the fall of 1779 the house issued further regulations to prevent forestalling after laboring over the bill for three weeks. Six months later, however, the assembly reversed its whole policy and repealed all laws directed against monopolizing. One of the problems hampering the financial situation was the uncertainty of the value of loan office certificates and the numerous certificates issued by quartermaster and commissary departments of the army for property turned to the use of the United States. The assembly demanded some action by Congress to clarify the value of these credits widely distributed among the people. In May, 1780, the assembly chose a committee headed by Peale to confer with Council and Congress on the subject. As a result Congress agreed to an official scale of depreciation for the loan office certificates; the scale progressed to a ratio of forty to one; and the payment of the principal and interest was promised. In order to assist official purchasers to buy supplies for the army, an embargo was laid on exports at various times. It did not solve the problem and it created further ill feeling. The merchants in particular were opposed to this restriction on trade. The Radicals themselves differed on the proper policy to follow. In August, 1779, when Congress decided to lift embargoes on all interstate trade, the Pennsylvania delegates divided in their vote. McKean and Armstrong wanted to end the restriction on foreign trade in October but Congress decided on January.

Whenever the opportunity offered, Reed pointed out duplicity on the part of Republican sympathizers. In September, Reed explained that on the assurances of Gouverneur Morris to Council that there was an abundance of flour, permission was given to export one thousand barrels. It then developed that flour was very scarce when Washington called for supplies. Reed also blamed the situation on the inability of farmers to thresh or market their wheat at this time, on the practices of "our speculators," and on some merchants who thwarted every measure to check depreciation of paper money. The embargo in Pennsylvania was ineffective because Delaware had no similar restrictions; hence flour could be shipped to that state from which it could be exported to foreign destinations. Reed complained to Congress about this situation. The national legislature resolved against exports from any states, and specifically asked Delaware to lay an embargo on all provisions.[111]

Full blame for failure to meet the requisitions of Congress cannot be placed entirely at the door of the Radicals. The demands made by Congress were very heavy. The first requisition which came in January, 1777, called on the states for as much money as they found it convenient to pay. Like other states, Pennsylvania ignored this demand. Late in 1777, the sum of $620,000 was quotaed on the State. In 1779 three heavy requisitions were made, due to the declining credit of continental paper money. In January the State was called on for $1,900,000; in May for

$5,700,000; and in October for $2,300,000 monthly for eight months, which was later extended for another seven months. When the paper money system sagged from its own weight, Congress turned to requisitions of specific supplies. In December, 1779, Pennsylvania was levied for 50,000 barrels of flour due before the following April. In February, 1780, came the first of two great demands of supplies. At that time Congress called on the State for 40,000 barrels of flour, 200,000 bushels of corn, and large quantities of salt, hay, and rum. The inability of the State Government to meet this demand led to hard feelings and strong words between President Reed and the continental officers. In September of the same year a levy was made on the State for fifteen hundred head of cattle. But in November came the last and largest demands for supplies. Beef, pork, rum, flour, and salt amounting to over $700,000, in addition to $273,000 in money was quotaed on the state.[112]

As time went on, the State became increasingly paralyzed in complying with the national demands. By the early part of 1780, Pennsylvania had paid over $6,000,000 in money or about half of what was demanded of it. This was about the same ratio paid by the rest of the states. As for specific supplies, the State did very little in 1780; so little that the next year the State turned the whole problem over to Robert Morris to solve. The method of raising the money to meet these continental demands was by direct taxes quotaed upon the counties. Four districts were required to furnish fifty-seven per cent of the whole State tax; they were Philadelphia City and the counties of Philadelphia, Chester, and Lancaster. At first the tax was laid largely on property. Later, duties were placed on single freemen, Negro slaves, horses and cattle, ready money, plate, carriages, mills, forges, distilleries, trades, and occupations.[113]

After conferences between a committee of Congress and the State assembly and the Council, President Huntingdon of Congress informed the committee at headquarters, that the State had adopted measures "as seem to promise, and if duly executed cannot fail, of Success in procuring speedy supplies." [114] But the committee at headquarters was faced with another entreaty from Washington for flour, and Pennsylvania was considered the logical source of supply. Although the committee made a desperate plea to Reed for flour, it asked Congress to intervene to second its application. Relations between the committee and Reed became increasingly strained because Reed ignored the various demands and appeals for supplies, wagons and soldiers. Reed protested to Congress against the accusations by the committee; and Congress found it best to declare that the committee at camp had been too harsh on Reed.[115] The petty quibbling and personal recriminations brushed aside, the fact remained that the national situation was critical and that the Radical administration failed to produce results in supplying the needs of the army. This fact was patent to contemporaries as the following train of events discloses.

With the breakdown in the ability of the State to furnish men and provisions for the continental army, a new movement was set on foot to take care of the critical situation. A meeting of prominent citizens was held in the Coffee House on June 8, 1780, when it was resolved to raise money by subscriptions for bounties to fill up the continental line. Nine days later another meeting was called in which the first plan was altered. By the new proposal, it was agreed to raise three hundred thousand pounds in real money; this sum would form the capital of a bank which would supply and transport three million rations and three hundred hogsheads of rum to the army.

In a short time the money was raised by about ninety subscribers. Although the subscription list was headed by Joseph Reed and contained names of other Radicals, the bank was dominated by the conservative Republicans. Over a quarter of the money was offered by twenty-one men who had been publicly listed as members of the Republican Society in 1779; and many more subscribers like William Bingham, Richard Peters, Samuel Meredith, Henry Hill, Thomas Willing, and Charles Thomson were sympathetic with Republican aims. The center of the institution was made up of the outstanding merchants and moneyed men of the city. The inspectors of the bank were Robert Morris, John M. Nesbitt, Samuel Miles, Cadwalader Morris, and Blair McClenaghan, all conservatives in political life except McClenaghan who was a mild Radical, but definitely allied with the merchant class. The directors, John Nixon and George Clymer, and the factor, Tench Francis, also represented conservative respectibility. Congress gladly grasped at the idea and pledged the national faith to reimburse the subscribers. On the day the subscription was opened, Morris, who was considered the head of the association, and others dispatched five hundred barrels of flour to the army. Three days later the amount of the subscription had reached 270,000 pounds hard money and the enthusiastic *Journal* believed that over twice the sum could be raised if needed. From the earliest days there was some feeling that the action by the merchants was taken to embarrass the Radical government of the State.[116] Whether this was the case or not, officials of the national government began to look to the bank as the only hope in solving the problem of feeding the army. As provisions were needed, Tench Francis drew on the directors for money with which he bought flour, beef, pork, sugar, coffee, and salt. These provisions he stored and from time to time forwarded them to the army. The money was collected from the subscribers in ten per cent instalments, the last three being requested before the end of November before bad roads made it impossible to send supplies to the army.[117] The continental line had been saved, but not by the regime of Reed and Bryan.

During the years 1778 to 1780 the Radicals had control of the government of Pennsylvania. In the latter part of the period they had undisputed supremacy. The conservatives had been defeated in their attempt to revise the Constitution. The newspaper warfare intensified the hatred between the two parties and roused the rabble to acts of violence which the Radical government had difficulty in controlling. The vital stumbling block of the Radical regime, however, was not the sound and fury of the mob but the inability to solve the financial and economic problems of the day. The Constitutionalists failed; and the Republican merchants stepped forth to show what money and financial credit could do. That they succeeded where the Radicals had failed was obvious to everyone; that the public would turn to them for guidance and leadership was inevitable.

IV

THE CONSERVATIVES EMERGE (1780-1782)

THE TASK of administering the government of the State was too much for the Radical revolutionary faction which had held the reins of leadership for four years. The leaders had exhausted their ingenuity and whatever ability they possessed to solve the stupendous puzzle of drawing forth the resources of the State to carry on the war. They had nothing new to dangle before the people. In a sense their program had been carried out. They had set up a democratic Constitution, had dispossessed the Penns of their control over the State, had driven the conservatives from the University, had waged their fight against Arnold, and had proscribed tories. The popular committees of the summer of 1779 reflected no glory on the Radical regime; the inability to collect taxes and to keep down high prices did not enhance their popularity. Then came the beginning of 1780 when the army was in desperate straits. But it was the conservative merchants who came to the rescue after the State had failed. Weary of war with its high taxes, seizure of property, inflation of money, and demands for men, the people tired of an administration which could promise no relief from the hardships.

The Political Revolt of October, 1780

No great issues were debated as a preliminary to the election in October. Two incidents occurred which could have had an adverse effect on Republican political fortunes. The first was news of Arnold's treason which reached Philadelphia on September 27. The Radicals were vindicated in their earlier prosecution of this man; in triumph they staged a parade vilifying Arnold and his deed. Unable to lay hands on the traitor, the Radical Council seized David Franks, William Hamilton, James Seagroves, William Constable, and Major David Solebury Franks, all of whom were suspected of having connections with Arnold or with the British. They were eventually released, under varying conditions, except David Franks and William Hamilton who were ordered out of the State. Early in October Reed issued a proclamation declaring ten persons traitors, with Arnold heading the list, for having joined the British. Just how far Mrs. Arnold had been involved in the designs of her husband could not be learned conclusively, but opinion branded her as an accomplice and since the Shippen family of which she was a member was not in the good graces of the Constitutionalists, her case was hopeless. By the end of the month Council ordered her to leave the State. Although the popular party attempted to make capital of Arnold's treason in order to discredit men like James Wilson and others who had had any acquaintance with the man, they did not succeed. Arnold was so generally disliked by everyone that even this appeal was too much for the voters to swallow.[1]

Closely connected with the Arnold treason and the elections was a violent newspaper attack on James Wilson. Obviously intended to draw votes away from the conservatives, the writer painted a lurid picture of the ranking member of the conservative faction. Wilson's opposition to the present government and his "Tory Toleration" were heinous crimes. Moreover, he was the director of the "violent party," and at his house guests "intermixed with chosen strangers" partook of his dinners and hatched sedition against the State.[2] Wilson's reply revealed the attitude of the Republicans. Admitting that he never approved of the Constitution, he made clear that he always worked within peaceful, legal means to revise it. But the issue of the Constitution was shelved temporarily. "No endeavours," he stated positively, "have been lately made to change the Constitution: Nothing of that kind, that I know, is now intended." [3]

Aside from the attack against Wilson, Radical election ardor had cooled. In September the assembly made strenuous efforts to have copies of its proceedings printed, ostensibly to be used by the homeward-bound members who could point out the achievements and efforts of the house during the past year in governing the Commonwealth. Another measure had potential political implications. When the financial machinery of the State fell into hopeless confusion, the assembly appointed President Reed, Speaker Bayard, and Treasurer Rittenhouse, all Radicals, as a traveling commission to tour the counties and investigate local economic conditions. If this was an indication that the Radicals intended to do something about the tax situation, it had little effect on the voters. During the two weeks preceding election day these three men had visited Northampton and Berks counties. Whether they electioneered in the cause of Radicalism is not known; one of the significant Republican gains came from Berks County in the ensuing election.[4]

The election was a minor revolution. The people turned against their old representatives and installed new men in the seats of the assembly. Sixty per cent of the members were new men, and a majority of these new members were Republicans. In Philadelphia the Radical guard led by Charles Peale and Dr. Hutchinson gave way to leading conservatives, men of respectability, like Robert Morris, Samuel C. Morris, Sharp Delaney, and Frederick Muhlenburg. This victory was won in the city by a vote of three to one. In Philadelphia County John Bayard, Speaker of the House, and other Radicals were swept away in favor of the conservative George Gray and Henry Hill. Similarly, Lancaster County replaced over half of its delegation with Republicans. Berks returned industrial men like Ege and Patton, Mifflin and Bird. The frontier counties made fewer changes. The outcome of the election was a cause of surprise to both factions. The Republicans had no idea that they would capture so many seats.[5]

The new assembly was organized on the basis of a Republican majority. Actually the two factions were almost balanced, but a considerable number of representatives from the back-counties, Radicals for the most part, did not appear until after business was under way. In the meantime the Republicans had undisputed control. Muhlenberg was so acceptable to both factions that he was unanimously elected speaker.[6]

Although Reed retained his office as President of the Council, he showed no signs of weakening his opposition to his political enemies. The unanimous vote given by the combined assembly and Council for his election may have been an evidence of compromise extended by the conservatives to the Constitutionalists. William Moore, a moderate Radical became Vice-President by a large majority. On the occasion of the inauguration Reed gave an address not aimed to allay party feeling. The internal divisions of the State, he asserted, were fomented by strangers. In his opinion the martyr's halo was already visible over his head, for governing now called for the sacrifice of present popularity; although he had given up a lucrative practice to serve the public, his present salary was insufficient to his needs. The ascendancy of the Republicans was a bitter pill for Reed. Henceforth he whined continually of the ineffective work of the legislative branch on items he considered vital. In his eyes the new system was a concerted attempt to neglect or overrun everything accomplished in the past two years; he predicted that all would end in confusion.[7]

The election of delegates to Congress reflected the turn away from rampant Radicalism. None of the old delegates received reappointment. Ingersoll, Armstrong, and Matlack gave way to a more conservative delegation. The choice of both factions fell on Joseph Montgomery, a moderate Constitutionalist. Samuel J. Atlee and probably Henry Wynkoop belonged in the same category while George Clymer and Thomas Smith were decided conservatives. The ultra Radicals, Ingersoll, Hutchinson and Sergeant, lost however only by a narrow margin.[8] Friends of this group bewailed the change. "They have displaced every Whig, but the President," was Arthur Lee's complaint.[9]

Although the conservatives attempted no fundamental changes in the system of government, they did attempt with varying success to incorporate some of their ideas into the legislative program. Of the large issues, the alteration of the Constitution was dormant and did not come to the surface during the year. If the Republicans had a definite platform they did not announce it. Having been in the opposition for four years and then coming unexpectedly into prominence, they were caught unaware without a definite program. There was always the possibility that they could not count on the house to accept their proposals, for the two factions were almost perfectly balanced and a few absentees might defeat the conservative measures. Morris and his immediate followers did not have a majority of the votes but the conservative strength increased as the year progressed and Morris loomed into the limelight as financial pilot of the State and nation. Only about half the measures for which Morris and his close associates voted were carried. The significant group of members who stood in the middle of the road shifted from one political camp to the other as the winds of popular opinion or local prejudice directed them.

Struggles over the Problem of Defense

Aside from domestic issues, the new assembly faced vexatious questions relating to the continental welfare. In working out the details of supplying men and money for national defense, the Republicans made an effort to inject some of their principles into the measures. One of the first problems was to bring a competent force into the field. President Reed pointed out to the house the new continental military arrangement of September by which the State was to furnish almost three thousand men. Both factions agreed to the bill except on one point. If a deserter were reenlisted for the war, should he be as acceptable as a new recruit? The Republicans strenuously opposed such a suggestion on the ground that deserters should be punished or military discipline would suffer. But the Radicals, especially those from the frontier counties where men were scarce, thought that in the army a man was a man whether he had deserted or not. By a margin of five votes the Radicals won their point. Other provisions of the bill were in accord with past Radical practice and the Republicans made no effort to change them. By this act the counties were quotaed on a proportional basis. Philadelphia City and County were responsible for a third of the total number of recruits while several of the frontier counties were called on for only two to four per cent of the whole quota. The people were classed on a dual basis of taxables and property holdings; each class was required to furnish an able-bodied recruit or pay a fine of fifteen pounds specie.[10]

If raising men for the continental line was important, it was vitally urgent that the men in the ranks should be satisfied. With perseverance the army officers struggled to have the soldiers' pay adjusted and settled. In September the Radical assembly showed a willingness to go into the problem, and the officers were encouraged, but no concrete results materialized. Colonels Johnston and Humpton and Lieutenant Colonel Harmar remained in Philadelphia until the new house assembled. When the Republicans carried the city in the October elections these officers were overjoyed to see their friends come into power. Their hope was not unfounded, for a bill to settle the soldiers' pay was rushed through the house with relative speed. The opposition came from the Radicals, "the yellow Whigs," who always entertained a constant dread that the army would rise to dominate the civil affairs of the State. Willing to grant the soldiers some settlement for their pay, the Radicals preferred to keep it at a minimum. That part of the bill providing for the sale of confiscated estates to meet the demands of the army was savagely attacked in the newspapers. With dogged insistence the Radicals attempted to deduct an estimated fifty thousand pounds expended by the State for clothing and other articles for the soldiers. In the face of these attacks the army officers thought their case was on the road to defeat. In a last desperate effort Anthony Wayne made an impassioned appeal to Reed, apparently in the hope that the President could sway sufficient members of his party to approve the measure. But it is doubtful if Wayne's letter had any effect on the final vote. The officers were inexperienced in the art of lobbying and had become too alarmed by the newspaper attacks. By a decisive vote the bill became law, thereby promising to the soldiers their pay for the past three years reduced to specie. The Republicans had taken care of the army.[11]

Although the assembly had provided for the soldiers, the measure came too late. It would take months until it could be put into operation. The enlistment of many of the troops expired on the first of January. Two weeks before that date General Wayne confessed to a fellow officer: "I certainly wish the Ides of Jan[uar]y was come & past—I am not superstious, but can't help cherishing disagreeable Ideas about that period." If he could only assure the soldiers a grant of "solid landed property" which could be converted into specie, he was confident it would "restore Content & fidelity," but "on the Contrary we have everything to fear from their Defection."[12]

On the first day of the new year came revolt. With the hope of reenlisting the seven months men for the war, Reed sent a supply of hard cash to camp for that purpose. A number of soldiers were reenlisted and they spent their bounties on liquor. The old grievances of arrears of pay and lack of adequate food and clothing came to the surface. The men who were enlisted to serve for the war, and many of them had fought for years under the most trying conditions, did not relish the sight of the seven months men receiving fat bounties while they went unpaid. These ills were aired through the camp where a general holiday mood prevailed. At night some of the sober troops joined the intoxicated ones and disorder broke out. Not only were the officers unable to discipline the men, but the troops seized arms and took affairs into their own hands. In the confusion several officers were killed and four or five wounded. Through a committee of sergeants the soldiers presented their complaints. Many thought the State was taking advantage of them over the term of enlistment, for it was not always clear whether they had signed up for three years or for the war. Arrears of pay and deficiency in clothing also irked the men. At once Congress appointed a committee to treat with the soldiers but Reed kept the committee in the background and carried on most of the negotiations himself. He patched up a settlement with the soldiers by practically capitulating to their demands.[13]

To raise money necessary to meet the emergency, Reed committed a blunder. He directed Vice-President Moore to set on foot a subscription loan among the Philadelphia merchants for fifteen to twenty thousand pounds. After a week when only fourteen hundred pounds had been collected, Reed issued a sharp rebuke to the merchants and threatened to place an embargo on the port if the funds were not forthcoming. The port was closed for a day or two; several important merchants subscribed. Reed then withdrew his request with considerable ill grace and in a sulky spirit unpropitious of a better understanding with the mercantile class. General William Irvine urged the immediate call of the assembly, "as the spirit of party seems to be revived." [14] But Reed and Council staved off this suggestion and only went so far as to request the members to be prompt when the session assembled on February 6. After the house made a quorum on the 12th, Reed referred to the mutiny only in vague terms. The attacks on his handling of the affair continued and in June he asked for a blanket approval of his actions. A committee headed by Robert Morris vindicated Reed, but in guarded language and in terms of cold formality, while the army officers, Wayne, Butler, and Stewart, were cited for equal zeal in bringing the soldiers back to their duty.[15]

The numerous difficulties of reforming the line and the exasperating troubles of moving it to the South in the summer of 1781 cannot be detailed here. It is sufficient to note that in September when the assembly strengthened the recruiting law, it introduced two changes which bear the earmarks of Republican handiwork. Fines on delinquent classes were placed at the disposal of Council for procuring recruits instead of in the hands of local officials. Anyone apprehending a deserter from the State line was exempted from the next two tours of militia duty.[16] Thus the

Republicans stressed centralization of administrative activity and favored the State line at the expense of the militia.

The militia furnished the rank and file of the Radical party. This organization was particularly dear to the heart of President Reed. He never overlooked an opportunity to plead for its maintenance. When the assembly convened in February, he pointed out that the militia must be relied on temporarily while the broken State line was in process of rehabilitation; therefore, no innovations should be made which might enfeeble the home guard. On numerous occasions later in the year he pleaded with the assembly to strengthen the militia law. The house considered the question several times but came to no final action. This grieved Reed who believed that the "avarice and indolence" of the American people would prevent them from keeping up a permanent military force necessary for the defense of the country; as a result "we must give up the contest or cherish the militia." [17] Not only did the house ignore Reed's pleas but it considered measures which militia enthusiasts regarded as a direct blow to the organization. In December, 1780, the attempt to abolish the office of sub-lieutenant was lost by only eight votes. At the same time an effort was made to exempt from militia duty certain classes furnishing recruits for the continental line. This point was won in June, 1781. Irvine observed to Wayne that "in several places the Monied & luke warm are beginning to procure Men—not the Classes, but individuals under that clause which exempts from Militia duty during the term of enlistment—this goes down hard with *people* who are fond of *Militia*." [18] And then in September the assembly exempted anyone from two tours of militia duty, who might apprehend a deserter from the State line.[19]

Providing adequate defense for the settlers in the frontier region did not give much concern to the assembly despite Reed's strong recommendations on this head and the numerous urgent petitions from the stricken sections. In the bill to complete the quota of the federal army there was a provision to detach some two hundred fifty men from the soldiers enlisted for the Pennsylvania line and place them under the control of Council who would direct them in protecting the frontiers. This measure was deleted before the act was passed, probably due to the exertions of the federal-minded Republicans. The house adopted a more logical solution by making a separate temporary provision.[20]

The Rise of Robert Morris

One of the fundamental aims of the conservative merchant group was a sound monetary system. This was impossible so long as the fluctuating continental and state paper money circulated freely. Although the Republicans made little headway in other changes in the State during their first year of resurgence, Robert Morris was able to wipe out the worthless paper money and to place the State on a specie basis. The process, however, was a painful one.

The continental paper money continued to fall to new lows. In November the exchange was eighty to one. The decreasing value was attributed to various causes such as the conversion of large quantities of paper into specie by tories lately exiled from the State, or the unfavorable balance of American trade; and with greater truth some people realized that the condition was due to the lack of well-established funds to sink the bills of credit.[21]

In the face of the steadily declining value of continental paper, the merchants and traders agreed to measures to peg its value. A meeting was held at the suggestion of the assembly, at which Frederick Muhlenberg temporarily presided and John Bayard became chairman. The resulting resolves fixed the exchange of continental paper to specie at seventy-five to one, and set up an association to enforce the agreement. This was a coalition movement between the two political factions; the committee of thirteen to put the agreement into writing contained about an equal number of members from both parties. Undoubtedly the Republicans cooperated in order to satisfy public opinion and to avert an outbreak of popular committees in which they would have no control, as was the case in the summer of 1779. The association attempted to bind the merchants by the threat of social disapproval. At least one case of violation was reported. But at once some of the merchants used subtler tactics; they raised their prices in specie so that the actual exchange was about one hundred to one.[22]

The troublesome continental paper money went out of existence with a dramatic gesture. By February 7 it had sunk to a hundred fifteen to one. To clear the situation for payment of debts contracted between 1777 and 1781, the assembly established a legal progressive scale of depreciation, ending in February, 1781, with the rate at seventy-five to one, and then authorized Council to declare the official exchange at periodic intervals. The real exchange was far below the official exchange, for on the day the act was passed continental paper was worth only one hundred thirty-five to one. Late in February the New Jersey officials set the exchange at one hundred fifty. This action forced the Pennsylvania Council to lower the rate to one hundred seventy-five. At once the paper sank to fantastic depths of depreciation and suddenly went out of existence.[23] Gold and silver were forced into use. With all restrictions on export trade removed, a lucrative trade in flour opened up with Havana, and "the Mexican dollars flowed in by thousands." [24]

The action by Council in lowering the exchange to one hundred seventy-five became the subject of newspaper controversy. As soon as Pelatiah Webster opposed Council's action, several pseudonymous writers sprang to a spirited defense of Reed with the counter-accusation that the depreciation had been engineered by the disaffected. In true Republican fashion "Walsingham" attributed the fall of continental paper to its excess quantity and to the various Radical expedients such as the laws regulating the prices of goods, the embargo and the provision allowing Council to alter the exchange. Reed found a laundatory defender in "Impartial" who described the conservatives as ". . . the pestilent spirit, which . . . hath long actuated and now maddens this *junto,* to overturn the *democracy* of our constitution, and to blast the *president* and every other *exalted character* of this state which abets it."[25] Whatever were the arguments, it remained a fact that the disappearance of the continental money was a definite boon to Morris and his group who wanted to stabilize the financial system.

While continental paper money sank to worthlessness, the assembly struggled over the fate of the paper money issued by the State. In December the one hundred thousand pound emission authorized by the Radicals early in 1780 was declared legal tender with mild penalties for the first offense and with imprisonment and forfeiture of half of the accused's real estate for the second offense. The earlier State paper issues were given up as hopeless; in February, only six die-hard Radicals opposed the act which repealed the legal tender quality of the early State emissions. In this measure Morris' crusade for the abolition of all tender laws and penalties marked its first milestone. But late in March when the house prepared a new emission of State paper, Morris and his followers could marshal only twenty votes against legal tender provisions. His doctrine was having effect, however, for in this act the penalty was reduced to simple forfeiture of the goods offered for sale. Gradually the public press began to support him in the struggle against legal tender.[26]

In its fall the continental paper money had dragged down the new State emission. As early as January it had fallen to four to one. In an effort to bolster its credit the assembly called for the immediate sale of State Island on which it was funded. In view of the falling State paper Reed was in a quandary. Although he was in favor of asking the people to accept it at their own valuation, the rest of the Council opposed such action on the ground that it would sanctify a depreciation in face of the assembly act. Past experience had also taught them that a general agreement among merchants and the public would not be respected. So Reed issued a proclamation asking the people to accept the money at face value until the assembly could convene and determine otherwise. At this time

State paper was worth six to one. Flaunting Reed's proclamation, the merchants gathered at the Coffee House and after some hesitation agreed to circulate the new money but decided to let everyone fix his own rate of exchange. At a subsequent meeting held at the State House the angered Radicals violently accused the disaffected of depreciating the money. In an attempt to bring the merchants to terms, they agreed to receive the new currency at face value as the law directed and planned to ask the assembly to invest Council with power to drive out of the State all who should not do likewise. Feeling was so strong that in his proclamation Reed cautioned the Radicals against perpetrating another Fort Wilson riot.[27]

When the house reassembled, Morris took advantage of the situation to press for the abolition of all tender laws. Although he had been elected by Congress to manage the finances of the nation, he delayed taking the oath so that he could retain his seat in the assembly for this purpose. A test vote showed forty members for repeal and only eleven opposed, the latter representing the country districts. About to win victory in his fight to place State finances on a strictly specie basis, Morris suffered one minor defeat. At this time the house was considering a tax bill in which a clause provided that all persons who had taken the oath of allegiance and had performed their militia duty or provided a substitute (in other words, all patriotic whigs) would be allowed to pay half of their tax in the new State paper, while all other persons would be required to pay the full amount in specie. By a margin of five votes the Republicans were unable to defeat this measure which they claimed would tend to depreciate the State paper. Thus the Radicals aimed to "allay the present ferment and jealousy of the whigs, who have long laboured with the legislature but in vain, to establish some criterion by which the *friends* and the *enemies* may be *legally* distinguished." [28] In June the assembly abolished the legal tender quality of all State and continental paper money. Thus Morris and his Republican followers had achieved their first significant victory. By July the State was beginning to recover from the purge of depreciated money. Public and private credit picked up, and by August the new State emission had risen almost to two to one.[29]

Typical of the Republican opposition to Radical plans to meet the financial problems of the State was the disregard of the Searle mission. In the middle of 1780 the Constitutionalist assembly had arranged for a commissioner to go to Europe to borrow two hundred thousand pounds for a period of ten years. In July Council appointed James Searle, then a Pennsylvania delegate to Congress, to carry out the negotiations. Little is known about the man except that he was a small Philadelphia merchant and an active patriot with Radical principles.[30]

The new assembly of 1780-1781 gave no encouragement to this attempt to float a State loan in Europe. In fact, there are suggestions that Robert Morris working through Franklin thwarted the whole business. As soon as Searle landed in France in September, 1780, he sought out Franklin and soon began a tactless chatter about the suspicious activities of Silas Deane. Franklin and Morris agreed that State loans were not advisable so long as Congress was seeking financial help from European lenders. Hence the Radical emissary made no progress in France. John Adams in Amsterdam vaguely promised Reed that he would do what he could for Searle. But when Searle arrived in the Netherlands, Adams was pessimistic. Reed pressed the assembly to support Searle. Since the Republicans had the upper hand they suggested that he should be recalled. This aroused Reed who broadly hinted that Morris had plotted to defeat Searle's endeavors in Europe. Searle faced unfavorable odds from another source. While he was authorized to offer only five per cent for money, Congress was dangling six per cent before European money lenders. The fact that Congress would not guarantee the proposed loan constituted the greatest handicap to his endeavors. Although he was not at once recalled and Reed continued to hope month after month that the mission might be successful, it was doomed to failure. When Searle finally returned, he was a broken man. His efforts had been fruitless, his wife had died, and his personal business was on the way to ruin. For years he pressed the assembly to reimburse him for the expenses of his European trip, but so long as the Republicans were in power they ignored his pleas.[31]

A restriction which the Republican merchants were eager to see lifted was the embargo which had been laid to insure the fulfillment of the specific requisitions made by Congress on the State. The failure of the embargo was due to Delaware's refusal to adopt similar measures. For this reason the assembly early in its first session approached Congress on the question of lifting the embargo. Asserting that the restraint was justified only in years of scarcity and pointing out that the ability of the State to furnish its quota of specific supplies depended "materially on the freedom of trade," the assembly modified the embargo so as to allow the export of flour if the exporter would sell one-third of his cargo to the State. The merchants opposed this remaining restriction because the State paid for its flour in depreciated money. Moreover, Delaware continued to thwart Pennsylvania's efforts. So in June the last restriction on exports was removed. Thus the Republican mercantile group scored another victory.[32]

In its extreme need for money to carry on the war, the State had at its disposal the arrearages due on lands. Since 1776 there had been no land office for collecting this money. In April, 1781, the assembly authorized an emission of paper money not to exceed five hundred thousand pounds, to be funded by these arrearages and to be redeemed over a period of five years. This was followed by an act establishing a land office where the money was to be collected in quarterly installments over a period of four years. Thus any person could complete the legal and financial steps necessary for full title to land; there was no provision, however, for the further taking up of land. A typical Republican action was the appointment of the officers of the land office by the assembly and not by Council.[33]

Two financial innovations appeared during this year. To procure funds to repay a loan contracted by the former assembly, a small specific duty, the first during the Revolutionary history of the State, was levied on spirituous liquors, wines, sugar, coffee, tea, and one per cent on the declared value of all other goods. When Congress had asked all the states for power to levy a five per cent duty on all imports, the assembly responded quickly with the desired grant and gave the national government the right to appoint the collectors. This impost never went into effect because all the states did not agree to it.[34]

While Morris was fighting in the assembly for a complete change in the currency situation in the State, Congress had elected him superintendent of finances for the nation. This was the result of a general consensus that he was the only man who by the use of his enormous private credit could stabilize national finances. At the same time his influence was increasing. In Congress various other officers were elected who were considered to be Morris' choice. The assembly gave him full control of a large fund with instructions to carry out the details of furnishing the specific supplies demanded by Congress. In this task he pledged to use his private credit. When he accepted the office of financier general he received from Congress the privilege of continuing his own private trading activities. Later this gave rise to ugly rumors that he took advantage of his official position for personal gain.[35]

By 1781 the nation in general was swinging over toward conservatism and respectability. Congress had to admit defeat in its efforts to bolster up the national finances. So it laid upon Morris' shoulders the mantle of "a pecuniary dictator," to use Reed's phrase. That he had ability, money at hand, and private credit for more, even his enemies admitted. Reed thought it but just to acknowledge the real benefit from Morris' handling of finances, but he severely criticized the manner in which Morris could manipulate the currency, issue his own notes, and carry on private trade on the side. The rising power of Morris in the national side of affairs doomed the Radicals to expect no political preferment from him. They attributed to him the appointment of the new minister of foreign affairs, Robert Livingston of New York, and General Schuyler in the War Department. Reed had been proposed as a candidate for the military post but he could not compete with the growing power of Morris. To his friend, General Greene, Reed confided: "I say nothing of the whole appointments wearing so much the appearance of cabal, when at the same time you consider that Mr. Gouverneur Morris is the Financier's assistant, and censorious people say his director." [36] In this drift toward conservatism, which was taking place in 1781 Reed saw public affairs turning in favor of "British interests." In a few years he expected to see the national as well as the State power in the hands of the tories. He was not altogether incorrect. The same idea was voiced by the Radical journalist "Censor" who claimed that the tories were attempting to overthrow the Constitution, restore the proprietaries, and get power into their own hands.[37]

Factional Quibbling

Political animosity infected the air of Philadelphia. It cropped out in the most unexpected places. Social life was not exempt, for in December a warning appeared in a newspaper that no one but active patriots should presume to participate in the dancing assembly. Some of the hot-heads could not walk the streets without coming to active blows. Whitehead Humphreys, whose house the Radical mob had attacked in July, 1779, lost no love on Timothy Matlack, the doughty Secretary of Council. Humphreys vented his spleen by publishing a handbill of rhymed verse in which he painted Matlack most unflatteringly as an ill-bred social upstart, a rabble rouser, and a traitor to the Quakers. On New Year's day Humphreys and Matlack met on Market Street and instead of exchanging greetings they resorted to harsh words, and finally blows. Although the affair was patched up within a few weeks, it indicated the tension of the time.[38]

Although the newspaper warfare during the year was waged mainly over financial questions, there were several spasmodic outbreaks of a more personal nature. Not daring to attack Robert Morris, the Radical pamphleteers aimed to embarrass some of his fellow conservatives whom they considered as outsiders. They painted James Duane and Gouverneur Morris, both New Yorkers, as tory wolves in sheep's clothing. Duane had to face the old charges that he cooperated with Galloway, opposed the expeditions to Detroit and Nova Scotia, and was in league with Silas Deane and Benedict Arnold. Similar attacks were made on Gouverneur Morris; the old Lee-Deane controvery continued to provide the Radicals with columns of slanderous articles. Duane and Mòrris replied in such a manner that the contest ended in a tie. These replies sometimes pricked the Radicals, as when Reed made a special effort to convince Morris that he had had nothing to do with the Arnold expedition to Canada in 1778. Neither Morris nor Duane was injured in the muckraking. Duane justified himself before the New York legislature while Morris was securely intrenched as chief assistant to Robert Morris.[39]

There were several echoes of Arnold's treason. The most noticeable result was the trial of James Mease and his deputy William West. When Arnold had been in charge of Philadelphia after the British evacuation, Mease and West, acting for the quartermaster's department, broke open stores and seized goods apparently for the use of the army. On Arnold's desertion to the British the Radicals sought scapegoats among his associates. They brought charges against Mease and West for having cooperated with Arnold in carrying off the goods for their personal emolument. There was a political angle to the prosecution, for Mease was an Irishman, had been a partner with Caldwell in the shipping business, became clothier-general of the army in 1777, associated with the conservative Sons of St. Patrick, and was a member of the Republican Party. West, deputy under Mease, was the son of Irish parents and likewise a member of the Sons of St. Patrick. Their poltical affiliations, as well as their associations with Arnold, made both men a perfect target despite the fact that the Radicals were defending the property stolen from at least one noted Quaker tory who at the time of the prosecution was still languishing in jail because he refused to recognize the Revolution.[40]

Occasionally Council and the Supreme Court came into conflict as happened this year in the case of Joseph Griswold. It was a repetition of the use of habeas corpus proceedings which occurred in 1778 over the Quakers exiled to Virginia. Council arrested and imprisoned Griswold on suspicion of treason. Issuing a writ of habeas corpus without consulting the executive body, Justice McKean released Griswold on bail. This action provoked Reed and the Council who complained to the assembly for safeguards against such action. In this particular case Reed contended that the Chief Justice did not give them a fair opportunity to explain the case before the prisoner was released. Although McKean maintained the full operation of the habeas corpus safeguards, Council immediately ordered the rearrest of Griswold.[41]

Another newspaper outbreak was the resumption of discussion over McKean's plurality of office. Several writers attacked the Chief Justice for occupying his judicial chair in Pennsylvania and at the same time holding a seat in Congress from Delaware. The 23rd section of the Constitution specifically declared that no judge of the Supreme Court shall sit as a member of Congress. McKean's defenders resorted to the subterfuge that he was not violating the Constitution because he was not sitting in Congress from Pennsylvania. The controversy waxed hot for several weeks and then petered out. McKean replied to the attacks, asserting that Jonathan Dickinson Sergeant and William Clajon were his anonymous accusers. Though Clajon denied the charge, Sergeant never did. McKean was not in the middle stream of Radicalism at this time. As time passed, he grew more conservative.[42]

An unfortunate injection of politics into education marked the commencement at the University on July 4. It was logical that the new Radical administration of the institution should confer an honorary degree on Attorney General Bradford who a few months earlier had been appointed to that office. But it was petty animosity that prevented young T. W. Murray from receiving his degree. Dr. Ewing, Radical Presbyterian Provost, had warned all graduating students that if they delivered parts of their orations to which he objected they would not receive their diplomas. Murray resented the idea and boldly delivered his address in full. The trouble centered over a short paragraph in which he followed a condemnation of Arnold's treason, a sentiment shared by all, with an expression of pity for Andre's fate. Dr. Ewing carried out his threat, and Murray left the exercises without the coveted diploma.[43]

Despite the abolition act of 1780, new aspects of the slavery controversy appeared. Although some petitions reached the house praying for a repeal of the act, most of the requests were from individuals seeking a special extension of time in order to register their slaves. In the earlier part of the year a test vote indicated that the house was willing to grant such an extension, but it took no formal action. Two proposals for a relaxation of the abolition act were defeated. The first was an attempt to repeal the provision directing the trial of slaves; and the second was a proposition to require a longer term of service from those Negroes whose masters had failed to register them. Although the votes on these measures did not follow party lines strictly, the conservatives from Philadelphia City and County generally opposed every attempt to modify the law, while numerous groups of Scotch-Irish Radicals from the back-counties consistently favored relaxation. In deference to the refugees from South Carolina the assembly allowed them to retain their slaves while residing in Pennsylvania. On the other hand, Reed's suggestion that masters in southwestern Pennsylvania should be allowed additional time to register their slaves received no encouragement from the assembly.[44]

In this session the Republicans inaugurated a program of starving out the judges, which became a bone of contention for several years to come. As early as November, Justice McKean had asked the house for depreciation pay for the judicial branch, but no action was taken. In the following month a tentative salary scale was adopted for the various officers of State. These salaries, although appearing large, were paid in depreciated paper money. But in 1781 the conservatives showed their full intentions when they proposed a bill to settle salaries for three years. Reductions of pay for all offices held by Radicals was the aim of the bill. The remuneration for the President, the Chief Justice, and the third and fourth justices was cut the most. The salary of Matlack, Secretary of Council, was also set at a figure which Radicals claimed was so low as to force him out of office. Bryan, leader of the Radicals and now on the Supreme Court bench, became furious at the proposed bill. The December scale "might have done," he admitted to one of his associates, but this new bill was monstrous. His wrath fell on Jacks, Hoge, and Steinmetz, the assembly committee which slashed the salaries. In the house Lowery had moved to make no provision for the seat Bryan held. "Why I cannot say," complained Bryan. "I never had any dispute with him." Although the proposed bill did not come up for a final vote, the Radicals fully understood the intention of the conservatives.[45]

During this year when the Republicans were steadily gaining influence, there were indications of leniency toward tories which the Radicals resented. In the house the representations of Moses Roberts and Job Hughes, accused of treasonable activities, were referred to the committee of grievances instead of being summarily dismissed, as was the wish of the Radicals. In the case of two merchants, Daniel Rundle, and Matthias Aspen, who had been declared traitors by one of Reed's proclamations, the house granted them an additional nine months in which to appear for their trial. The roll call disclosed eight Radicals opposed to this measure. At the same time the assembly by a special act returned to Mrs. Ferguson her paternal estates which had been automatically confiscated when her husband was proscribed as a traitor. These actions irked the Radical Council and gave ground for accusations that the Republicans were committed to a policy of favoring tories.[46]

Conservative Gains Maintained

The election of 1781 presented no new or startling issues. This might have been due to the fact that leadership in both parties was not definitely settled. The Radicals could no longer rely on Joseph Reed, their standard bearer, because his three years of service disqualified him for re-election. The Republicans considered both Thomas Mifflin and John Dickinson for President; it seems that they could not unite on one of the two men.[47]

Aside from the usual plea that the voters should elect men of education and property, the only important Republican issue was that of the test laws. Shortly before the election Pelatiah Webster issued a vigorous attack on the test acts. This taunted the Radicals like the snap of a whip and set the pace for later attack and counter-attack on the subject. On reading Webster's articles, the Constitutionalists declared that the Republicans were meditating a secret blow at the Constitution, that they had formed a secret alliance with the tories, and that the aim of abolishing the test laws was to allow the tories to vote which would provide an entering wedge in leading the State back to British tyranny. Republicans were taunted with the reminder that as soon as they were elected to public office, they quickly swallowed their scruples and took the oath so that they could accept the office. Conservatives were forced to hear of their former associations with Arnold and more especially with Deane. Quakers likewise were not exempt from general criticism. Radicals threw out the warning that their followers should be on guard. At the same time John Morgan and Benjamin Rush revived their feud with Dr. Shippen, after it had lain dormant for months. They accused Reed of having offered Shippen a way out of his embarrassments in the Hospital department by promising him the chair in anatomy at the University. To even the score Radicals attempted to embarrass Morris in details of national finance.[48]

It was natural that the Radicals should condemn the past year's record of the assembly. They accused the Republicans of deliberately continuing the embargo after the effects were seen to be harmful, and the merchants of conniving with the house to retain the one-third flour arrangement in order to benefit the mercantile class. The downfall of paper money in April, 1781, was ascribed to the assembly's emission of five hundred thousand pounds. The Radicals realized that the Republicans had reproached their predecessors with unnecessary taxation and for that reason adopted a paper money issue in order to keep the financial machine in order.[49]

The political complexion of the assembly, when it met in the fall of 1781, is very interesting. It took eighteen days to assemble a quorum. When a bare fifty met on November 8, the delicate division between the two factions was manifest. The balloting for a Speaker resulted in a tie between Muhlenberg, the representative of the Republicans, and Joseph M'Lene, the candidate of the Radicals. The next day Muhlenberg was successful.[50] The balance of power rested in the hands of those few members who appeared in the house at spasmodic intervals. The close division is shown also by the fact that in over one-third of the recorded votes of this session the successful side won by the slender majority of three or less votes. It should be noted, however, that the members voted more consistently in party groups during this session than in the previous year.

By almost unanimous consent William Moore, former Vice-President and moderate Constitutionalist who was not distasteful to the Republicans, was chosen President. For the second office there was a division of thirty-eight votes for James Potter and twenty-eight for James Ewing. Potter was an outstanding Constitutionalist.[51]

The activity of the 1781-1782 session was concentrated on several important issues. One of the most time-consuming was the contested election in Philadelphia County. The affair roots back to September when public officials feared that Clinton would suddenly swoop down on the city. Congress asked both Pennsylvania and New Jersey to call out three thousand men. Accordingly, Council summoned several classes of militia from Philadelphia and the six eastern counties, to rendezvous at Newtown. The first suggestion of any political problem growing out of the mobilization was the action of the assembly on September 29 when it asked a committee to consider the dangers that might attend the absence of the whole militia out of the State or out of their respective counties at the time of the coming election. A committee report was made on October 1 but on the following day the house adjourned without taking further action. On the 2nd, however, when Boudinot in Congress moved to disband the militia if the State executives thought it advisable, the motion was lost. Three days later Joseph Montgomery, delegate from Pennsylvania, made the same motion for which Massachusetts, New Jersey, New York and Pennsylvania, Maryland and Virginia voted in the affirmative, but this too was lost. On October 3 Council sent the Lancaster County militia home due to lack of arms. Next day Council ordered General Lacey to furlough his men so that they could attend the election on the following Tuesday. On election day, October 9, the Lancaster County militia was ordered discharged; on the 12th the same orders were given to Lacey's militia at Newtown with the special thanks of Council to the men for responding to the call to arms. On October 13 John Bayard, elected from Philadelphia County, took his seat in the Council. These facts form the background of the disputed election.[52]

Behind this official record was the more important element of the manner in which the militia voted in Philadelphia County. Jonathan D. Sergeant went to Newtown where he induced one of General Lacey's subordinates to call a general meeting of the militia officers at the general's headquarters on the Sunday evening preceding election Tuesday. Several dozen officers as well as General Lacey attended when Sergeant produced a slate of candidates, declaring it to be the list previously agreed on by the electors at Neff's Tavern. Next day the officers signed a written agreement to support the ticket. The clerks of the different companies then proceeded to make copies of the ticket for their men. On election day these tickets were distributed to the men who were under military orders to march to the election ground. Little if any opportunity was given the men to alter the tickets. It was later asserted that one of the colonels, on learning that some of his men were dissatisfied with the ticket, indicated that anyone who refused to vote was a tory and would be whipped. Under strict and formal military discipline the men drew up at the election ground, left their ranks one by one and gave in their tickets. Only after this procedure was completed were they granted their furloughs.[53]

The election came up in both the assembly and the Council. It was first taken up in the assembly when a petition carrying over fifteen hundred signatures protested against the action of General Lacey who was accused of carrying out the whole scheme. The examination of witnesses and conferring of committees lasted until the following April. On almost every ballot on phases of the question the house divided by a close vote, the Republicans favoring the petitioners and the Radicals supporting the election as it was held. After a month the sitting members from Philadelphia County were disqualified from further voting on the subject. In December the conservatives tried to set a closing date for the evidence, but the house refused. In the meantime more serious business was neglected by the legislature. By March the assembly finally authorized the taking of further evidence by a committee. The committee was composed of Whitehill, a Radical, and Dougherty and Maclay, both conservatives. For a week after the committee reported, the house continued to argue and debate. Early in April the final issue came to a head after much hair-splitting; by a vote of thirty-two to eighteen the Radicals managed to declare that the charges against the election were unsupported.[54]

It can be seriously questioned whether the Republicans actually wanted to set aside the election for assemblymen despite their votes for that purpose. Of the nine members from Philadelphia County, two did not appear until near the end of the session; Joseph McLene and George Smith were Constitutionalists, and the remaining five were Republicans. It is probable that the conservatives wished only to embarrass their political foes as much as possible. The Republicans were passing the bills that they wanted; a new election might have proved a boomerang. Moreover, council had already confirmed John Bayard in his seat, the point which really seems to have been the main issue.

If the Republicans aimed to keep John Bayard from the Presidency by casting doubt on his election, they succeeded. At first very reluctantly Council considered the question of the eligibility of Bayard to his seat; from the end of December until the middle of March Council went into the case spasmodically. After hearing witnesses from both sides the executive body attacked the problem in an interesting way. By sifting out a few charges, most of them relatively insignificant, they agreed that they were probably supported by the evidence. When the question came up whether these charges should be submitted to the Supreme Court for opinion on points of law, Council split five to five over the issue. Ewing, Pentecost, Van Campen, and Byers, all mild Radicals, insisted that the charges should not be considered separately because that would not give a clear picture of the election. They thereupon withdrew from the proceedings. When the judges of the Supreme Court were called on for their opinion on the various charges, Bryan and McKean reported in effect that the election should not be declared irregular. With the appearance of Piper in the Council the Radicals had six members against the five protesting ones. When Council began to vote on each individual charge, the protesting group left. The rump went through the formality of declaring that each charge individually did not tend to invalidate the election. Bayard was secure in his seat. Although Bayard had absented himself from all sessions in which the election was discussed, General Lacey flagrantly continued to cast his vote through the whole affair.[55]

The result was that the election was whitewashed by both Council and assembly. From the evidence available it appears that the election was very irregular. Despite the whitewashing, the Radicals suffered in popular esteem; though Radical writers defended the election in an apologetic tone, they never gloried in it.

After the house had assembled one of the early tasks was to choose delegates to Congress. The question arose whether Pennsylvania delegates who had served two years out of five though not successively were eligible for re-election. This was obviously aimed at George Clymer who had served in Congress in 1776-1777 and 1780-1781. The Radicals thought that they might eliminate Clymer on this issue, but Republicans prevented the question from coming to a vote. The house then proceeded to re-elect all of the delegates who had served in Congress during the preceding year. Friends of Joseph Reed "pressed" him to go to Congress but he withdrew his name from nomination. After retiring from the Presidency, Reed failed to secure a permanent public post due mainly to the increasing wave against Radicalism and the waxing power of Robert Morris. Reed became a bitter, disappointed man.[56]

When the news of Cornwallis' surrender arrived in Philadelphia, on Wednesday, October 24, the rough Radicals, "a set of people who have no name," as Hiltzheimer characterized them, directed their enthusiasm into channels of vandalism. There was general celebration in the city but any house where the windows were not illuminated was certain of attack. Window smashing, furniture breaking, and Quaker baiting ensued for a few hours during the night. There were combustibles for another Fort Wilson riot but the Quakers took no defensive measures, and one of the last acts of mob violence passed off without serious repercussions.[57]

Finance under the Republicans

Soon after the house assembled, it was confronted with the Congressional requisition for 1782. Pennsylvania's quota was $1,120,794. The Radicals, especially those from the frontier regions, tried to provide for only one-half of the quota called for, and to let the other half as a problem for a future session. This would have devastated Morris' plans of national finance, and the Republicans made a valiant effort to provide for the whole requisition. On the issue the vote was tied; Speaker Muhlenberg's casting vote gave the Morris group victory. There was much debate over the way the tax should be levied. The Republican view was voiced by a writer in the *Journal* who stated that Philadelphia citizens complained of the tax on trade, professions and merchandise; this method had been introduced when commerce was considered a bane of the State and merchants were thought to be vultures; he objected to this mode because it threw an unjust proportion of the burden on Philadelphia and was calculated to destroy the harmony that should exist between farmers and merchants.[58]

In solving the taxation problem in the 1781-1782 session the Republicans met with varying success in having their program adopted by the assembly. When the house reassembled in February, 1782, petitions showered in, especially from Chester and Philadelphia counties, complaining that the tax quotas assigned to them were far too great. The whole question of the quotas was re-opened and after long debate the urban Republicans had to surrender to the hinterland. A Constitutionalist committee was ordered to report the quota scale used in the 1781 requisition. Philadelphia City and County were again saddled with one-third of the total sum to be raised. The Republicans won a slight concession, for section one of the bill stated that the quotas listed would be subject to future correction by the assembly in the light of a property census. The Republicans won another concession by having the tax collected in gold and silver with jurors no longer enjoying the privilege of paying half in paper money as in the 1781 levy. In another direction the Republicans won a distinct victory. At the beginning of 1782 the house began to construct a new system to centralize the collection of taxes. It created the office of comptroller-general with very broad powers and appointed John Nicholson to that station. This was part of Morris' plan to apply good business methods to State finance. But Morris was not completely successful, for he failed to put through his policy in regard to the payment of tax arrearages. Thirteen conservatives aligned with the frontier Radicals in determining that former uncollected taxes might be paid with depreciated State and continental paper at the rate of seventy-five to one.[59]

The Republicans took keen delight in embarrassing the Radical Council especially in matters of finance. This was illustrated when immediate funds for frontier defense were necessary in the spring of 1782. The expiring session of the assembly told Council to go ahead and contract a loan for thirty thousand pounds. The monied men, it will be remembered, were the Republican mercantile group. After a month Council had not succeeded in making the loan. In despair Council summoned six assemblymen who happened to be in the city and asked whether a special session would be advisable. These six men were Republicans and they advised against such a move. But two days later Council called a special session. The committee of ways and means swiftly negotiated a loan from the Bank for frontier defense. In the dry, formal record of this proceeding it is not difficult to sense the malicious satisfaction which the conservatives enjoyed in their little triumph.[60]

The committee of ways and means probed further into State finances and discovered various problems. On learning that there would be a shortage of some five thousand pounds at the end of the year, the committee decided to raise the sum not from additional taxes on landed and personal property which they thought was loaded to the limit but by levies on non-residents, beer, billiard tables, and additional duties on liquor licenses, carriages, and wines. At the same time the committee deplored the neglect in tax collection and suggested that the Council should see that the laws were enforced. By the first of October the total tax deficiency amounted to over 3,300,000 pounds continental money, 84,700 pounds State money, and 19,600 pounds specie. The arrearages were largest in the frontier counties where the quotas had been small. The eastern counties which bore the brunt of the tax burden showed a good record in meeting their public obligations. The suggestion that the Radical Council should enforce tax collection was a veiled implication that the executive had favored the western Constitutionalists. As early as April the assembly noted the deficiencies in the frontier counties and slyly determined that when collected they might be used for frontier defense. Stirred by the indirect reprimand from the assembly, the Council went through the form of calling on tax collectors to exert themselves and to show favoritism to no delinquent. A series of mysterious robberies of tax collectors in 1782 did not ease the situation of the treasury. While on the state of finances, the house called on Timothy Matlack, Secretary of Council, to turn over to the treasury more speedily the public moneys that came into his hands. This was the beginning of another grudge-taking episode which marked the activities of the assembly during the following session.[61]

The public debt of the United States had complicated the taxation problem. When army officials bought and seized supplies or requisitioned wagons for the use of the continental troops, they gave in return certificates which were promises to pay in the future, based entirely on the good faith of the national government. The breakdown in the financial system of the states and the United States as well as the inability to collect taxes made it impossible for Congress to pay off these debts. In his struggle for a sound financial system, Morris fought vigorously against the popular demand that these certificates should be accepted in payment of continental taxes. In this he was only partly successful.[62]

Appeals were made to the assembly that some action should be taken on these certificates. Deputy quartermasters asked the house not to press the holders of these certificates for taxes until they were liquidated. If Morris would not allow the taxes to be paid at least in part with these certificates, wrote Philip Marsteller to George Bryan, "I really dread the Consequence, for it is very Grieveous to any Man to have his property Sold for Taxes when at the same time the Public is indebted to him a much larger sum, and [he] can obtain no part thereof . . ."[63] On advice from Morris, however, the assembly decided to take no immediate action respecting the certificates. He asked them to delay in hope that the five per cent impost would be adopted. Three months later the assembly approved the impost proposal and lamented that other states neglected to adopt it.[64]

An equally important part of the public debt was in the form of loan office certificates which bore six per cent interest. For some time France had been furnishing the money to pay the interest on these obligations; but when the war ceased, France withdrew her aid. Congress had no fund on which to draw for continuance of these payments. At once the public creditors in Philadelphia petitioned the assembly and Congress to devise some means to pay the interest money.[65]

In commenting on one of these petitions to Congress, Morris took the opportunity to explain his ideas on national taxation. The five per cent impost, even if accepted by all of the states, would not be sufficient to meet the total debt of the nation. He then reminded Congress of his earlier proposal of a land tax of one dollar on every hundred acres, a poll tax of one dollar on each freeman and male slave, and an excise on all spirituous liquors. On the same day a committee composed of Osgood, Clark, and Arthur Lee reported that Morris' plan was "too exceptionable." The committee admitted it might be necessary to resort to his plan later but at the present time they believed that the certificates should be received in payment of deficient taxes. About the same time the public creditors of the State urged the assembly to do something about their plight. In response the assembly framed a petition to Congress.[66]

One of the cardinal points in the program of the conservatives was a charter for the Bank of North America. As the assembly was waiting for a quorum at the beginning of November, twenty-three leading men, mainly merchants from Philadelphia, met at the City Tavern, organized the Bank, elected directors, and arranged to press for incorporation by Congress and the various states. The directors were Thomas Willing, Thomas Fitz-Simons, J. M. Nesbitt, James Wilson, Henry Hill, Samuel Osgood, Cad-walader Morris, Andrew Caldwell, Samuel Ingles, Samuel Meredith, William Bingham, and Timothy Matlack. A few days later Willing was elected President and Tench Francis Cashier.[67] Hill and Meredith were members of the assembly; Osgood was a delegate in Congress from Massachusetts; and Matlack was Secretary to Council.

The Bank obtained its first triumph in Congress. By the end of December a committee had reported in favor of immediate incorporation. There were several reasons prompting this suggestion. It was believed that the Bank could not operate without an act of incorporation from Congress. Furthermore, it was obvious that the State assembly could take no action until it met in March; it was feared that in the meantime the national finances would suffer without a Bank.

Two days later Congress clothed the institution with legality and asked the states to pass similar laws. On January 7, 1782, the Bank began active operations.[68]

The conservatives then planned for the incorporation of the Bank by the assembly. Early in February Thomas Willing sent to Council a petition addressed to the assembly and requested that it should be laid before that body. Within four days after the petition had been received, a bill of incorporation had been prepared and had gone through the first reading. The struggle over the Bank centered not so much over the actual incorporation, for that was taken for granted, but over certain powers to be granted to the institution. An attempt to limit the charter to seven years instead of "forever" was defeated by the Republicans by an overwhelming vote. The Radicals then made an attempt to grant the assembly power to amend or repeal the charter in 1789. In the ensuing week the Radicals won over eleven of their wayward brethren but not enough to bring victory on this point. Fearing the monopolistic feature of the Bank, the Radicals tried to strike out the provision of land from the types of property that the institution would be allowed to hold up to the value of ten million dollars. Again they were defeated. Thomas Willing was particularly obnoxious to the Constitutionalists because of his actions when the British had occupied Philadelphia. They branded him as *"the man"* who had deserted the country in its direst need. To load him with honors, they claimed in characteristic rhetoric, is "a discouragment to the whigs, is a wound to the cause of patriotism, and is trampling on the blood of those heroes and martyrs, who have fallen in the defense of our liberty." [69] But the conservatives preferred to forget the distinction between tories and "heroes and martyrs," and by an overwhelming vote confirmed Willing as President and the twelve men as directors of the Bank.[70] The Constitutionalists realized they had been defeated on a vital issue; and Arthur Lee privately damned the "torified" city of Philadelphia with increasing vigor.[71] The incorporation of the Bank was the outstanding achievement during the period of Republican resurgence.

The Voice of the West

One of the thorniest problems confronting the State authorities was the settlement of the boundary line with Virginia. Around this problem clustered numerous irritations: the Virginia adherents versus the Pennsylvania adherents, a new state movement, payment of taxes, land claims, frontier defense, the cry for erection of new counties, and the application of the emancipation act.[72]

Protection of the frontier in southwestern Pennsylvania, either defensively or offensively, was weak due to the lack of cooperation between the Pennsylvania faction and the Virginia adherents. The former claimed privileges because of their loyalty; the other group called for exemptions on account of their transfer. When Council demanded that every voter should take the oath of allegiance to Pennsylvania before exercising the franchise, a great cry went up and both camps declared for voting without the oath. Because of slow communication, a pro-slavery attitude, and a claim for special treatment, the Virginia settlers did not register their slaves in accordance with the emancipation act. If the act had been enforced, all their slaves would have gone free at once. These two problems of citizenship and registration of slaves were solved by an act of assembly. The legislature declared that any settler, on producing proof of having sworn allegiance to Virginia, would to all intents and purposes be considered a free citizen of Pennsylvania. The act of gradual abolition was mitigated by extending time of registration of slaves in western Pennsylvania. This was an unusual concession, for many petitions had been sent to the assembly from the older part of the State requesting further time to register slaves; in these cases the house took no measures to relax the act.[73]

The vote to allow the later registration of slaves in Washington and Westmoreland Counties presents a problem. Of the eighteen who voted against the measure, five had in the assembly of 1780-1781 voted for an extension of time to be applied to the whole State. Carnahan, the only representative present from Westmoreland County when the 1782 vote was taken opposed an extension of time. Of the remaining eleven members, seven were Constitutionalists and four were Republicans. On the other hand, the Philadelphia conservatives who had stood stiffly against any relaxation of the abolition measure in 1780-1781 now fully supported this special privilege for the two western counties. In all, eleven members who had sat in the 1780-1781 house reversed their votes in the 1782 assembly; five decided to oppose late registration and six decided to support it. The strange thing is that the Philadelphia conservatives suddenly championed this special privilege for the two western counties, and yet they did not propose it for the rest of the State. No material has come to light to show the reasons for this change of attitude. Another fact might supply the answer. Within a year after this act was passed, several Philadelphia conservatives, Robert Morris, James Wilson, and Levi Hollingsworth were already dickering in Kentucky lands, then under control of Virginia. It is possible there was a direct connection between the extension of registration of slaves passed for the benefit of Virginia settlers in Pennsylvania and the interests of the Philadelphia speculators in Kentucky lands.[74]

The lack of specie in the western counties aroused the people against the new taxes levied in hard cash in line with Robert Morris' new financial plans. Dorsey Pentecost, Councillor in 1781-1782, it was said, actively encouraged these discontents and fostered the idea of a new state independent of both Pennsylvania and Virginia. Other leaders of the new movement were Benjamin Johnson, Thomas Smallman, and James Innes. In the East it was rumored that Johnson had British connections, and was planning to lead his followers into the Indian territory where he would establish an independent community. It seems that this movement was deeply rooted in the lust for land. Although punitive expeditions into the Indian country had not been successful in keeping the savages from scalping activities, President Moore in December, 1781, suggested that the organization of such an expedition might divert the people from their new state idea. The movement for independence was especially serious to Pennsylvania authorities not only because it threatened the loss of some of the western territory but because it was believed that Johnson's emigration scheme was but a ruse to lead these innocent land-hungry settlers under the protection of the British at Detroit. In the summer of 1782 at the prompting of leaders from the western part of the State, Council and assembly consulted with General Washington and with Congress on plans to send three punitive expeditions to the Indian Country, one from Westmoreland, one from Northumberland, and one from the Genesee country. At the last moment, however, Washington declined the proposal on learning that the British had withdrawn all their parties from the frontier region. During this period Pennsylvania decided not to run the permanent boundary line between Pennsylvania and Virginia because of the expense. The two states agreed to run a temporary line. Council appointed commissioners to meet with similar commissioners from Virginia for the purpose. But the Reverend James Madison, the Virginia agent, delayed on various pretexts which confirmed Pennsylvanians in the belief that he was acting in conjunction with the Virginia adherents in the west. When Archibald McClean, the Pennsylvania appointee, determined to survey the line himself, he was halted by the pro-Virginia element, and was forced to give up the attempt.[75]

The formation of new counties was temporarily halted by the war. However, before the conflict came to an end, the assembly admitted Washington County in 1781, in the extreme southwestern part of the State. Numerous requests were presented to the house for division of counties during the ensuing three years. In 1782 the people north of the Tuscarora Mountains asked for a division from Cumberland County, pointing out the great distance from the county seat at Carlisle, the lack of roads thither, and the geographical convenience of the Juniata River. Neighboring townships in Bedford and Northumberland counties asked to be included in the proposed county. The people of the central part of Cumberland county opposed these maneuvers. Although an assembly committee reported a bill to divide the County, the matter dropped. Two years later the southern end of Cumberland County was cut off and became Franklin County with Chambersburg as the county seat. In 1783 other sections of the state agitated for individual status. People in the upper part of Chester County, the lower part of Berks, and the upper part of Philadelphia, asked for a new county with the county town at Pottstown. Naturally this was opposed by the counties which would be diminished. Although no action was taken at this time, Montgomery County was created late the following year, being cut off from Philadelphia County. In the western section of the State, the southern part of Westmoreland County desired a separate existence. A bill providing for the division was presented for consideration late in 1782. Christopher Hayes explained to President Moore that such action would ruin the old county and make it an easy prey for the enemy because the majority of the people that would be left were in forts and blockhouses and scarcely able to support themselves. Evidently these arguments had their weight, for it was not until a year later that Fayette County was created.[76]

The most pressing agitation came from the regions in the middle of the State. The people of the upper part of Lancaster County and the adjoining region of Berks asked for a separate administrative existence. Berks County opposed the move. John Harris, founder of Harrisburg, actuated by zeal to develop his community, was the leading spirit back of the agitation. He proposed to lay out two hundred lots of a quarter of an acre each, to reserve twenty for himself, and to rent or sell the rest. He would convey all streets and a square of four acres to the State, if the new county seat would be located at Harrisburg. In March, 1784, an assembly committee reported favorably. They declared that a division of Lancaster County was necessary, and that fixing the county seat at Harris' Ferry would benefit the commerce of the State; they also advised the house to accept the proposals by Harris. Reporting on the topographical and natural advantages of the proposed county seat, Rittenhouse and Hutchins added their approval. The people in and around Middletown were alarmed, for they feared that if the new county seat were fixed at Harris' Ferry, the whole trade of the back part of the county on the river would be carried from the ferry point directly by the way of Reading and hence would hurt Middletown and Lancaster. Thus they favored Middletown for the county seat. So the matter rested until the following year when Dauphin County was created and John Harris won his victory.[77]

It was inevitable that there should be an attempt to move the capital of the State westward. Such suggestions met with short shrift from the dominant Republicans. In April a petition, doubtless emanating from some back-county Constitutionalists, was received by the house praying for a removal of the government from Philadelphia. Although no action was taken, it was a prelude of a more concerted attempt to be made several years later.[78]

Defense of the frontier regions continued to be a problem, due to constant Indian attacks. Unable to till the soil or reap the fruits of their labors, the settlers suffered from economic distress. The assembly made one gesture toward them. It passed an act providing that the settlers who had been driven from their lands by the savages were to be exonerated from part of their taxes, at the discretion of the local county commissioners. The vote on part of this bill discloses a division largely on sectional lines. The back-counties of Cumberland, Berks, Northampton, Bedford, Northumberland, Westmoreland, and Washington voted unanimously in favor of the act; and the Constitutionalists from the eastern counties supported them. The opposition came from conservatives scattered through the eastern counties. There were two interesting exceptions; Delaney and Hill from Philadelphia consistently supported the frontier regions.[79]

Trade, Religion, and Politics

Other questions more directly resulting from the war plagued the assembly. The illicit trade with the British excited the cupidity of at least some of the merchants. The Republicans continued to tantalize the judges by refusing them fixed salaries. The fighting Quakers discovered that patriotism did not insure them meeting houses in which to hold religious services. And the conservatives learned that the impending peace treaty could prove embarrassing.

The Philadelphia merchants could not resist the temptation to carry on a commerce in British goods, especially if the trade might be covered by getting the merchandise from one of the neutral isles. St. Eustatius was the great *entrepôt* for this trade, but its capture late in 1781 by the British put an end to this island commercially. La Luzerne, the French Minister, did everything to discourage this trade which aided the English; he used his prestige, which was not insignificant, to get Congress and the various State legislatures to prohibit the illicit traffic. The Pennsylvania law, he found, was evaded by the laxness of Delaware. Pennsylvania shipped principally wheat to the neutral islands and received in exchange British cloth. Unable to stand by while seeing other men gaining enormous profits, the Philadelphia merchants in spite of the law hazarded importing some English cargoes into Philadelphia; some shipments got by but others were caught and confiscated "despite the efforts of a considerable party." [80] The merchants then presented a memorial to the house asking for the legalization of this trade.

When the mercantile interests found that they could not open trade with the British, they took another tack and tried to have it closed equally in all the states. Finally, the house passed a law definitely prohibiting this foreign trade in British goods. To carry out its plan the house then made a plea to New Jersey and Delaware to pass similar restrictive legislation.[81]

Another channel of trade sprang up which excited the wrath of the Radicals, the trade in British goods from New York. The increasing lack of hard money during the summer of 1782 was attributed to this traffic which was said to drain the money out of the State into British hands in New York City. Finally, the house determined to suppress all commercial intercourse with enemies of the United States. One of the notorious channels of the illegal trade from New York was through the store maintained at Lancaster which supplied the British prisoners there with clothing. Mr. Taylor, the storekeeper, plied a lucrative business by selling large amounts of goods to the inhabitants and by sending the hard cash to New York. By June Council took official notice of the situation and ordered an investigation. In the summer of 1782 Council ordered the British goods seized. Members of the Hubley family and Christian Wirtz, local Republicans, had been interested in this trade. The implication of these men was duly advertised by the Radicals in their news sheet.[82]

One of the burning issues of the 1781-1782 session was that of the judges' salaries. In December, 1780, the house adopted a temporary scale;

in the meantime paper money wrought havoc with all fixed salaries. But the house bedeviled the judges by doing nothing for them. At the end of the 1780-1781 session, the assembly refused to take any action and shifted the responsibility to the next session. Finally, in December, 1781, the house debated a bill granting the salary of the judges at a greatly reduced scale. The theory was that the money would be paid in specie or its equivalent. But the only money the State had available was the recent issue of State paper which circulated at a depreciation. In desperation McKean appealed to the house not to vote on the bill until all of the judges could give their side of the question. This was ignored, and the bill became law by a vote of thirty-nine to fifteen, the minority being the Radical old guard which was helpless in this struggle. Two parts of the bill are interesting. It provided for the salaries for only one year "and until the same shall be afterwards altered by the legislature." The additional rub was an *ex post facto* arrangement whereby the new salaries were to begin as of the former June 22, the day on which legal tender on all paper money was repealed and specie came into general use. The majority explained their action by asserting that no one ever believed that the former high salaries were to be paid in specie. The act also provided for the salaries of other governmental officials. When President Moore's salary was lowered from fifteen hundred to twelve hundred and fifty pounds, only thirteen Radicals came to his defense. This would indicate that he did not have the full support of the Radical faction and could count on no help from the Republicans. At the same time McKean's salary had been increased by a hundred pounds.[83]

The judiciary and executive branches made vain efforts to protest the measure. Bryan and McKean called Atlee to the city late in December to confer on some action. In March McKean asked the house for depreciation pay prior to June 22, 1781. Characteristically the letter was referred to the city members to report next session. In the meantime the committee was to confer with the judges on the matter. Judge Atlee hoped that "the conference, if we can keep our tempers, will be productive of some good for us." [84] There the matter rested. Nor did Council sit idly by. On April 16 President Moore informed the house in a blasting message that the legislature had usurped the powers of the executive branch. His first example was of the unconstitutional method of destroying the independence of the judges by altering their salaries. Interestingly enough, he did not contend that the independence of the executive branch was in jeopardy because of the changing salary scales. By a close vote the Republicans branded Moore's charge as improper and groundless. On September 21, Moore complained to the assembly that the President's salary was insufficient to maintain the dignity of that office. But the Republicans made no move to alter any of the salaries; undoubtedly they gloated with joy over their enemies' discomfiture.[85]

Finally, in 1784 the assembly settled fixed salaries upon the judges by restoring the scale of 1777. The Chief Justice was granted one thousand pounds a year, an increase of one hundred pounds over his former salary; and the assistant judges received five hundred pounds which constituted an increase and at the same time placed them on an equal footing. The Republicans took this action to silence the ever recurring charge that they tried to starve out the judges and violated the injunction of the Constitution to keep the judiciary independent. At this time the conservatives were attempting to call a convention to alter the Constitution; thus by wiping out one of their past wrongs, they deprived the Radicals of an effective argument against them. With the death of Justice Evans of the Supreme Court, the Republicans had a chance to place one of their own men in the vacancy. Council chose Jacob Rush, brother of the Republican Benjamin Rush, but instead of making him fourth justice, they ignored George Bryan and placed Rush above him in the third seat. This action increased the resentment of the Radicals.[86]

Another struggle between the Council and assembly was over the three offices of auctioneer, one for the city of Philadelphia, one for the Northern Liberties, and one for Southwark. In the fall of 1780 when John Bayard was without political office, Reed and the Radical Council gave him the best office in their gift. They made him auctioneer for the city. The fees attached to the office made it the envy of all other office holders. According to an act of November, 1779, the fees consisted of five per cent on all sales. In 1781 it was rumored that this measure provided a handsome income for the auctioneer, and newspaper writers brought this fact to the attention of the public. When the house assembled in the fall of 1781, it was understood that the Republicans intended to take the power of appointment out of the hands of Council, where the former act lodged it, and appoint new men. A number of petitions filed into the house from hopeful applicants. One of these petitions gives some indication of the income of the office. Thomas Pryor proposed to farm the office from the State for three years; for this privilege he was willing to pay the State sums varying from two thousand to three thousand dollars a year. Republicans insisted that some of the auctioneers' profits should go into the public treasury. The house considered Pryor's proposal seriously enough to appoint a committee to confer with Council on it. In February the merchants of the city suggested to the house that the auctioneer's five-per-cent commission should be reduced.[87]

In discussing the bill the reduction of the fees was a foregone conclusion. The more important item involved the attempt of the Republicans to take the power of appointment away from Council. At first this seemed possible by the casting vote of Speaker Muhlenberg, but on the final issue the Republicans lost by seven votes. A few losses by absences and the shifting of several members brought defeat. The conservatives complained that Council might claim the right of appointing the auctioneers, and that Council had allowed Bayard to hold the two offices of auctioneer and Councillor simultaneously. As an anti-climax to the affair Bayard announced late in the summer of 1782 that he would not serve in Council during the following year because of the press of private affairs and "because citizens have thought it incompatible with my other appointment" as auctioneer. Naturally he preferred to retain the more lucrative position. The bill which finally passed the house reduced the fees drastically, and in addition provided that one per cent of the gross receipts should go into the State treasury to pay civil salaries.[88]

An interesting question of religion and politics cropped up at this time. It involved the Quakers who at the outset of the Revolution had split into two groups. One faction retained the old principles of non-resistance and nominal neutrality and the other surrendered to the war fever and shouldered guns in defense of the country. The latter were disowned by the original body and became known as "fighting Quakers." In 1781 the revolting group formed themselves into a body called the Free Quakers. They were without meeting houses, cemeteries, or schools because the orthodox group would not surrender any church properties to them.

The Free Quakers took their complaints to the assembly. Late in 1781 they petitioned the house and implied that the orthodox Quakers had acted as tories. This began the war of petitions which continued at irregular intervals for several years. Early in September, 1782, the assembly appointed a committee to examine the case. A spirited debate between the two Quaker factions was held before the assembly committee. The house refused to take any action. The Free Quakers then asked the assembly for a law defining their rights. Again the house took no action. Aside from general consideration of not interfering with internal disputes of religious organizations, it is logical to assume that the Republicans did not care to decide the issue. Conservatives as well as Radicals belonged to the disowned group; furthermore, a decision in favor of the Free Quakers would have been a direct blow to the orthodox group which had provided the Republicans with respectable connections and financial backing. At this time the Republicans were also actively at work to bring Timothy Matlack, one of the most ardent of the Free Quakers, into public disgrace.[89]

As a parting shot before the elections in the fall of 1781 the Constitutionalists claimed that the Republicans were planning to restore the proprietary estates and to bring back the Penns. This charge was again leveled by "Censor" in his barrage of articles at the beginning of 1782. When the peace negotiations were under way, it was feared that England might insist on the return of the Penn estates. The Constitutionalists were at once on their guard. The Radical Council then reissued resolutions adopted by the assembly in 1778 which outlined the only satisfactory basis on which the nation could come to peace terms with England. This was a maneuver to force the Republican house, already accused of harboring desires for peace at any price, to make a forthright declaration to the public. On August 23 the house adopted a committee report to the effect that power of making war and peace was vested exclusively in Congress, that a separate peace would be a "flagrant insult" to France, and that the war should be continued until Britain would grant a safe and honorable peace. By way of amendment another resolution was offered, probably by Wilkinson of Bucks County, declaring that the restoration of the proprietary family was incompatible to the future peace of the State. This resolution had already caused heat when it had been introduced into the committee. The Constitutionalists accused the Republicans of hedging on this proposition because at heart they were secretly hoping for the return of the Penns and for the restoration of confiscated property. Whatever the Republicans may have thought on the issue, they decided it was wise to adopt a clear-cut statement; on the following day the resolution disclaiming restoration of the proprietaries and of confiscated estates was passed.[90]

This period from 1780 to 1782 marked the emergence of the conservative forces. Their policy had changed from that of the earlier days. Postponing the attempt to alter the Constitution, they saw an opportunity to gain their ends by less drastic action. Increasing their power in the assembly, the Republicans sought to work within the Constitution to establish their aims. It was undoubtedly the work of Robert Morris in reorganizing the finances of the state which made their emergence possible. From 1780 to 1782 the conservatives acted cautiously but did not neglect to make the most of every opportunity. Could they continue to hold the confidence of the people for another two years?

V

Conservatives Ride to Power (1782-1784)

The PERIOD from 1782 to 1784 marked the rise of the conservatives to a place of influence and power which they had not enjoyed since the Constitution of 1776 had gone into effect. The return of John Dickinson to Pennsylvania political life in the role of President of Council indicated how far the pendulum had swung away from the rampant Radicalism of 1779. Although the Republicans had control of the assembly from 1782 to 1784, they effected no major changes in the form or organization of the government. For them the period was essentially one of preparation. From 1780 to 1782 they had discovered themselves; from 1782 to 1784 they consolidated their forces.

The Election of 1782 and its Sequel

In any election campaign the classical strategy of the minority is to attack the past record of the party in power. The election of 1782 was no exception in this regard, for the Constitutionalists laid a long list of sins at the door of their opponents. If taxes had been too heavy and numerous sources of public income were untapped, why did the Republicans saddle the State with a debt of six hundred thousand pounds specie at a rate of six per cent interest? Robert Morris had been given control of the new emission of paper money but it was an open secret that he had speculated with it. Ignoring the fact that the peace-time revenue of the State was only fifty thousand pounds, the Republicans had insisted on levying the federal quota of over eight times that sum. Other states had cut down the congressional requisition to fit the peoples' pockets. For fear of losing votes among frontier members of the assembly, the eastern Republicans did not raise the question of tax arrearages because those arrearages were heaviest in the back-counties. If the Bank were a necessary evil, there was no reason why it should be a monopoly controlled by "doubtful political characters." The Republicans had squandered time and money on the disputed Philadelphia County election and came to no decisive conclusion. "These are your œconomists of the public time, your guardians of public treasure." More serious were the plots attributed to the conservatives. Not only had they not settled the salaries of the judges but they planned to remove Bryan from the bench. They harbored the hope of bringing back the Penn family, of restoring confiscated estates to the tories, and perhaps even of returning the State to the British Crown.

The Constitutionalists carefully described the type of candidates who should receive the votes of the public. They should be men who always championed the true American cause, not slackers who hid during troubled times and emerged in "the summer of prosperity" to seek public office; men who had fair moral character and believed in the eventual punishment of guilt; men neither of dire poverty who would be open to temptation nor possessors of great wealth who were ignorant of the sufferings of the poor. Too many country members who had come to Philadelphia with robust democratic ideas had been fêted and dined by the Republican aristocrats until their principles had been "absolutely washed away by good liquor." [1]

Disregarding these charges, the conservatives reissued the arguments which had stood them in good stead in the past. They wanted to see the public creditors cared for; the proper way to do this was to have the assembly put pressure on Congress to pay the interest and to create a sinking fund for discharging the principal; Republicans turned a deaf ear to the Radical proposal that the State should assume the burden. In proposing tax reforms the conservatives appealed directly to the propertied class. Freeholders should be exonerated from heavy contributions; the increasing burdens on real estate depressed the whole economic situation of the State. Public office-holders should come from the upper socio-economic levels. The desirable candidate should own sufficient property to place him above the reach of corruption; his education should be such as to give him "generous, dignified sentiments" and divert him from the sole thought of salary; his knowledge of foreign affairs should be competent because the European nations would soon clamor for commercial treaties with the United States. Particularly for the Executive Council the Republicans recommended men of liberal education, engaging manners, and substantial fortunes.[2]

Personalities as well as policies played a part in the compaign. Joseph Reed's actions in the early years of the Revolution were brought forth in so embarrassing a light that he found it necessary to issue a public denial of accusations that he had intended to abandon the cause. Speaker Muhlenberg was the target for the severest personal attacks. The Radicals asserted that he dominated the assembly, interrupted the debates when he found it to the interest of his party, exceeded his privilege of naming committees, abused his former Radical friends who had elected him delegate to Congress, and that he used his power as Speaker to threaten Germans who disagreed with him. Republican apologists came to his defense. The Constitutionalists made every effort to hold the Scotch-Irish vote, and to draw as many of the Germans as possible away from the influence of the conservatives under Muhlenberg. At every opportunity Republicans threw out compliments to the Germans in order to retain their vote.[3]

The election of 1782 again gave the Republicans a majority in the house. As in the assembly of the previous year they had strong opposition but succeeded on crucial matters in bringing some of the rural members over to their side. The new house showed a smaller turnover in members, for two-thirds had served in the previous assembly; in the sessions of 1780-1782 the turnover had averaged half or more. Philadelphia City and County remained the stronghold of Republicanism.

This election was unusually significant for the conservatives because they made an important breach in the Radical Council by the election of John Dickinson from Philadelphia County. And on November 7 Dickinson was elected President over James Potter, the Radical choice, by a vote of forty-one to thirty-two. By a margin of only five votes James Ewing became Vice-President for which office Potter was also a candidate.[4] The return of Dickinson to Pennsylvania politics indicated that at least in the urban areas the cry of "Tory" and "deserter" was losing its hold on the people.

The real contest of the election centered in Chester County. To retain as much power as possible, the Radicals put up Thomas McKean for Council with the understanding that once he was in that body he would be elected President. His seven year term as judge was approaching an end; in Council he could bring about the appointment of Joseph Reed to the bench. Reed had been without political preferment for a year and he and his Radicals keenly felt the mortification. If the plan had materialized, the Radicals would have headed the executive and judicial branches of government. But the scheme failed when McKean was defeated for Councillor; and the luckless Reed complained bitterly of his ill-treatment.[5] Arthur Lee was active in supporting the Radicals while he was in Philadelphia as a member of Congress from Virginia. Immediately the Republicans raised the cry of interference of strangers in domestic politics.[6]

With the Republicans again in control of the assembly, with Muhlenberg reinstated in the Speaker's chair and with the conservative Dickinson at the head of the Executive Council, the Constitutionalists could do nothing but vent their wrath on their opponents. Shortly after the election Reed and Sergeant made public speeches which the Republicans interpreted as a threat to use armed force if necessary to preserve the test laws and the

Constitution. Failing to obtain the second office in the state, Potter received testimonials of loyalty from various groups of militia. In his replies he characterized his enemies with strong language, which produced the accusation that he too was attempting to stir up civil war.[7]

The election of delegates to Congress showed that the Republicans meant business and intended to drive through their conservative program. In November Thomas Mifflin, Thomas FitzSimons, James Wilson, John Montgomery, and Richard Peters were chosen. All were first-line Republicans, representing the commercial and land-speculating interests. Above all, the delegation was "respectable." The Republicans wished their new members to attend without delay because the State was unrepresented. Others considered by the Republicans for seats in Congress were William Bingham, Cadwalader Morris, and James Moore. When it was learned that John Montgomery had lost his seat in the assembly, Republicans desided to send him to Congress. Of the Radical candidates it is known only that Jared Ingersoll was nominated by Daniel C. Clymer; it is doubtful whether he really had a chance of winning a seat.[8]

Defeated in the assembly and now tasting defeat in the Council, the Constitutionalists realized that power was slipping from their hands. The wiser heads foresaw that with the end of the war and the return of peace their political structure would tumble. In desperation they resorted to a vitriolic newspaper crusade against individual Republicans. The press rarely sank to lower depths of coarse abuse than during the winter of 1782-1783.

John Dickinson became the prime target of attack. Of the various articles written against him the most stinging came from the pen of "Valerius."[9] Just who the real author was has never been satisfactorily determined. Contemporaries generally pointed to Joseph Reed, but it is very unlikely that he was the author. Dickinson was attacked on his attitude during the early days of the Revolution. Authors came forth to Dickinson's defense but they could not match the vitriolic pen of "Valerius." Dickinson replied publicly in a series of newspaper articles, but in a tone that savored of the apologetic and did not quiet his foes.[10]

Exhausting himself on the President, "Valerius" turned on other members of the Republican faction. He saw in John Montgomery a life of "dependent servility;" he had lost re-election to the assembly because he vilified his colleagues. James Wilson was also classed as a slave to party interests, and as a man who was holding an office under the King of France when he was proposed as delegate to Congress in 1782.[11] Muhlenberg was attacked because he rose to political prominence through the Radical party and then deserted it and endeavored to inflame the Germans against the Radicals.[12]

These attacks boomeranged on the Radicals in such a way that they emerged from the conflict with no increased prestige. Their own political past was exhumed by the Republican journalists and brought under the spotlight. The Radicals were reminded that their leaders, McKean, Reed, and Bayard, had originally opposed the State Constitution. Perhaps because he was thought to be the author of the "Valerius" articles, former President Reed was the subject of violent newspaper attacks. His actions from 1775 to 1778 were examined by his enemies. His alleged communications with the British in 1777-1778 were described as suggesting that he contemplated treason at that time.[13] It developed into a pamphlet warfare between Reed and John Cadwalader that became so bitter and inconclusive that succeeding generations revived it as late as the 1860's. The intensity of feeling at the time was displayed by the assiduity with which the interested parties plagued their friends for depositions of their recollections of happenings six and seven years before.[14] Harsh epithets were employed. Republicans called Radicals "the pale-faced faction," the "secret junto," and the skunk association.[15] Some of the articles descended to such depths as to approach the obscene.[16] Persons outside of the State were amazed at the lengths to which the defamers went. From France, Franklin wrote to a friend that "I am afraid to lend any of them [American newspapers] here, till I have examined and laid aside such as would disgrace us." [17]

This newspaper warfare was only the smoke that hid the real fire. Both parties were actually waging a fight for control of the Council of Censors which in turn would determine the fate of the Constitution. With the election of October scarcely over, leaders were casting about for candidates for Censors.[18] Benjamin Rush understood that the Radicals had resorted to the pre-Revolution method of setting up committees of correspondence in the interior counties in order to keep in touch with a grand committee in Philadelphia. "The Object of their Schemes at present," he explained, "is the next election." [19]

Stimulated doubtless by the "Valerius" articles and similar rumors of the Radicals, Colonel John Rodgers of one of the battalions of the Lancaster County militia took alarm at the Republican "complexion of the present House of Assembly" and called a meeting of all the colonels to determine whether the Constitution and the liberty of the State were at stake. When the militia officers assembled, Rodgers informed them that he had heard Dickinson had opposed independence in 1776 as well as the State Constitution. The other officers did not share Rodgers' alarm and a vote showed that they approved the election of Dickinson as President and of Wilson and Montgomery as members of Congress; they also decided that the State Constitution was safe as far as the assembly was concerned. If this was a Radical attempt to array the militia against the Republican administration, it failed miserably.[20]

An interesting by-product of the wrangling between the two party factions occurred when Eleazer Oswald, editor of the Republican *Independent Gazetteer,* came into conflict with Judge McKean of the State Supreme Court. At the election of 1782 Colonel Thomas Procter of the Continental line took offense at inspector John Kling who was so "scrupulous" in demanding to see Procter's certificate of having taken the oath. The next day Procter met Kling and gave him a beating. Haled into court, Procter was fined eighty pounds. McKean then informed him that the army men held their heads too high and that he would teach them how to behave. Oswald published an account of the trial in which he complained of the high fine and of McKean's attitude toward army men. Then Oswald was called before the court on the charge of libel but that did not prevent him from printing an account of his experience before the irate McKean. When a grand jury repeatedly returned the Oswald bill *ignoramus,* the judge's wrath mounted. Even Attorney General Bradford could not browbeat the jury into submission. The affair degenerated into a newspaper warfare between Justices McKean and Bryan on the one side and Francis Hopkinson, Judge of the Admiralty Court and Republican wit of the period, on the other side.[21]

The antagonisms engendered by party wrangling in the public prints were bound to stir up action. The Republicans in particular were stung to the quick by the "Valerius" articles. They were in control of the assembly and they turned their vengeance on two Radicals, Cessne, a member of assembly, and Timothy Matlack, Secretary to the Council. When George Woods, Republican of Bedford County, charged his fellow-member Charles Cessne with fraud in the public service during the war, the other Republicans eagerly took up the case. Without overworking themselves in investigating the affair, the Republicans had him expelled from the assembly for "notorious frauds and other enormous crimes," and instructed the Attorney General to prosecute him. The little evidence on the case is from the Republican sources but it leaves the impression that political spite was at the bottom of the affair.[22]

Bigger game for the Republicans was Timothy Matlack. As Secretary to Council he received the fees from marriage and tavern licenses. Just before the election the Republicans found it convenient to suggest that Matlack had been deficient in paying the money over to the State treasurer. After the assembly got under way, the charges were advanced. When the Radicals opposed hasty action against their old friend, the house went ahead and passed a censure on Matlack but postponed it for three months until the committee reported. Although the charge appears to have been a technicality, Matlack had little to stand on and no friends on whom to rely. The house unanimously declared him unworthy of public trust or confidence. When John Armstrong, Jr., succeeded him as Secretary to Council, the conservatives had filled one more State position with a Republican.[23]

Trouble on the Frontier Fringe

As soon as the Virginians in the southwestern part of the State learned that they were included within the bounds of Pennsylvania and that their new master intended to extend its laws to them, they determined to take action. As frontiersmen they were reluctant to come under any jurisdiction, and during the war they had avoided taxes and requisitions because of the undefined boundary.[24]

As the year 1782 drew to a close State officials in Philadelphia learned of ominous proceedings in the land west of the Youghiogheny River. By beat of drum, it was reported, five thousand men, good marksmen, had declared an independent state which they christened Transylvania. They were crossing the Ohio River and settling on the unpurchased Indian lands. Dorsey Pentecost, a Councillor from Washington County, was one of the leading spirits in the new state movement. On receipt of the news the Indiana and Vandalia land companies were also stirred to activity.[25]

The State authorities did not delay taking action to stem the new movement. After listening to the recital of the Reverend David Jones on the happenings in Washington County, the assembly quickly ordered preparation of a bill decreeing a traitor's death for anyone forwarding the secession movement. Within two weeks the bill became law. In addition to dangling the noose before the malcontents, the assembly took another line of attack which it entered only on its private journals. It empowered Council to appoint one or two secret agents to wean the western people from their seditious idea. Council ordered the distribution of two hundred copies of the anti-sedition law and of the law providing for the use of western lands to pay off the soldiers.[26]

Council chose the Reverend James Finley to convert the malcontents to a sense of loyalty to Pennsylvania. This Presbyterian divine spent six weeks in his quiet work of propaganda, utilizing to the utmost his prestige as a minister of the gospel. He found the people between the Youghiogheny and Monongahela rivers as well as most of the inhabitants of Washington County infected with the new state idea. The anti-sedition act and the act for the sale of lands in that territory had intimidated the populace; "even ye Ringleaders were for eating in their words & putting a new face upon their conduct." But the people were hushed, not convinced. Without disclosing the purpose of his mission, Finley preached from the pulpits, sent out letters to be circulated from hand to hand, and talked with numerous individuals. As opportunity offered, he explained the rightful claims of Pennsylvania to the land, the debts incurred in protecting the frontier and in paying off the Penn proprietors, and the allocation of the land to pay off the soldiers. Then he warned of the heavy administrative expenses incumbent on any new state. "And why should such a Nursling attempt to desert ye parent before it can stand alone; & while, if it were a State must appear contemptible & without weight in the scale of Empire?" A grievance Finley could not successfully refute was the demand for taxes in specie when hard cash was rare or unknown in the frontier region. This was also a cause of complaint against the law regulating the sale of land; the people did not have the hard money to pay the price. In his report to President Dickinson, Finley suggested that taxes should be collected in flour or wheat which could be shipped to New Orleans and sold.[27] Just what effect the six weeks' educational campaign of the Presbyterian minister had on the minds of the ambitious westerners is one of the intangibles difficult to measure. It is true, however, that after this time the new state movement subsided.

Probably more important than Finley's mission in cooling the ardor of the frontiersmen was the action of Congress on their proposal. In a petition said to contain two thousand signatures, they complained of Pennsylvania's anti-sedition law, and asked outright for admission into the union as an independent state. Reluctant to interfere in local affairs and realizing the ramifications such an event might have on problems like Vermont, not one member of Congress lifted his voice in regard to the petition. Snubbed by Congress and threatened by Pennsylvania, the people in the west temporarily laid aside their dreams of an independent existence.[28]

When the Revolution had broken out, the Wyoming controversy between Connecticut settlers and Pennsylvania land claimants on the upper waters of the northern Susquehanna Valley was already an old sore. During the early years of the war the agitation had slumbered, only waiting a favorable opportunity to blaze forth. Congress asked Pennsylvania and Connecticut to preserve the *status quo* in the region so as not to weaken the American cause against England. When the problem of frontier defense became acute and Congress in 1778 decided to send troops to Wyoming, neither state offered objection.[29]

The Radicals were just as eager as the Republicans to settle the controversy in favor of Pennsylvania. In 1779 the Radical assembly, at the solicitation of Council, asked Connecticut to agree to settle the issue according to the method prescribed by the Articles of Confederation. President Reed took a more aggressive step by stopping supplies from reaching the post at Wyoming, and for this he was duly rebuked by a congressional committee. So long as the continental forces were stationed at Wyoming, the controversy was held in check.[30]

Pennsylvania was quick to call for a settlement of the dispute on the basis of the ninth article of Confederation. Only twelve days after the Articles had been proclaimed in effect, the assembly ordered Council to apply for a settlement. President Reed had sponsored this idea but the State delegates in Congress reported that the time was improper. In the last days of Reed's administration just after the surrender of Cornwallis, Council ordered the State delegates to bring up the matter in Congress.[31]

Almost a year was consumed by delays, until a special court was set up under the auspices of Congress and began to hear the case. During this time continental troops continued to occupy the post at Wyoming and Council urged Washington not to withdraw them. At the trial Wilson and Reed, ironical as it might appear, were working together in stating the Pennsylvania claim. Wilson was interested financially in the lands under dispute. The result of the trial was the so-called "Trenton decree" by which the court declared that the jurisdiction of the land belonged to Pennsylvania.[32]

Although the Trenton decree settled the problem of jurisdiction, it said nothing about the private right of soil in the Wyoming region. This vexing question was a burning issue for the next half dozen years and had political implications. Soon after the trial the Connecticut settlers petitioned the assembly to grant them the right to their holdings. A joint committee of the house and Council, representing both political factions, reported a plan which appeared to promise peace. The Pennsylvania claimants, dominated by land-speculating Republicans, were gradually gaining the upper hand in the policy to be pursued. On the withdrawal of continental troops, two companies of State frontier rangers were sent to occupy the post at Wyoming, which gave the Pennsylvania claimants a decided advantage. The plan of settlement turned out to be a demand that the Connecticut settlers should surrender their possessions and receive land grants in the unsettled western part of the State. In attempting to drive off the Yankees, Alexander Patterson, most aggressive of the Pennsylvania claimants, encountered resistance which he painted in the most alarming colors to the sympathetic assembly. Thereupon the house repealed its conciliatory acts and went so far as to consider a plan to use military force if the Yankees would not submit to "compromise." [33]

The proceedings of the assembly in the session of 1783-1784 revealed the political aspects of the Wyoming controversy in a clearer light. In an attempt to induce the Connecticut settlers to accept lands in the western part of the State, the assembly granted three hundred acres to each of a dozen persons. The Constitutionalists opposed this measure, beneficial as it appeared on the surface, because it would lead to ultimate victory for the Pennsylvania land claimants in the disputed region.[34]

More important was the question whether the garrison of State troops should be removed from the Wyoming region. The Republicans insisted that an armed force was necessary to provide protection against the Indians. The real design was to provide a military force to sustain the Pennsylvania claimants in their efforts to take possession of lands on which the Yankees had been seated for years. Dominated by the State landholders' interests, Council urged the retention of troops until the end of 1784, but a sufficient number of assemblymen disliked the business and ordered the troops withdrawn by June 1. Thus a number of nominal Republicans who probably had no financial stakes in the Wyoming business would no longer support the Philadelphia leaders in an affair that was fast becoming notorious.[35]

On other aspects of the agitation the Republicans closed their ranks and displayed a united front. When the Council of Censors demanded of the house various papers and reports relating to the controversy, the request was flatly refused. Despite the opposition offered by the Radicals, the Republicans whitewashed or suppressed complaints against the activity of the Pennsylvania claimants and in particularly the notorious acts of their leader, Alexander Patterson. A committee reported that the complaints against Patterson could be rectified through the regular channels of the courts and voted to postpone further consideration of the affair.[36]

The national aspect of the Wyoming problem emerged when the Yankee settlers petitioned Congress for a court to try the question of the private right of soil. Wilson and Bradford were appointed by Council to represent the State. However, the Connecticut claimants did not present themselves at the stated time, and finally Pennsylvania suppressed the question in Congress by pointing out that the Wyoming settlers were not a state and hence could not qualify for a court according to the provision in article nine of the Confederation. Thus in Congress the interests of the Pennsylvania land claimants won and the Wyoming question never again came before the national body.[37]

In the assembly the Northampton representatives were commissioned to investigate conditions in Wyoming and they returned a report favorable to the Yankee settlers. At once the State land claimants threw their shadow over Stroud, one of the Northampton assemblymen, who was accused of abetting the Wyoming settlers' claims while he was on the examining committee. In the meantime the sufferings of the Wyoming settlers from the cruelty of Patterson's minions and the ravages of the flood-driven Susquehanna began to change public opinion in favor of the former Connecticut men. John Boyd, Councillor from Northumberland County, and John Armstrong, Jr., the latter against the protests of John Dickinson, were sent by Council to Wyoming to calm affairs. Both of these commissioners were fully in the interests of the Pennsylvania claimants and succeeded only in aggravating the situation. As foreseen by Dickinson, Armstrong became especially obnoxious to the Connecticut settlers; soon Council ordered him to return.[38]

Finance and Trade

Although the name of Robert Morris carried great weight in Pennsylvania and other states, he was not immune from attack. When the political factions were airing their petty hostilities in Pennsylvania, a larger battle was taking place in Congress. Morris had toiled at the thankless task of building up the credit of the United States. Suddenly in January, 1782, he published his letter of resignation as financier general. This was probably designed to put pressure on Congress to adopt his plans of centralized finance. Although Wilson and Hamilton supported him, his enemies led by Lee and Bland condemned his resignation because they realized that his name and credit were indispensable to the nation, and that his withdrawal would produce adverse effects on public credit at home and abroad. The attacks on Morris were re-echoed in the Pennsylvania press where he was accused of almost everything from speculating in loan office certificates to stirring up the soldiers at Newburgh. The Radicals knew full-well that he held a high hand in Congress and in the State. Although they respected the prestige of his name and looked forward to the financial wizardry which he was expected to perform, they feared his power and his conservative philosophy.[39]

The financial problems of the State and the nation were closely interrelated; the core of the trouble was the large outstanding domestic debt owing to private citizens in the form of certificates issued by the loan office and the departments of the army during the War. Republicans and Radicals readily agreed that this debt should be paid, but differed on the mehtod. The Radicals wanted the State to take the initiative in liquidating the claims; the Republicans supported Morris in his attempt to nationalize the whole financial structure.

Pennsylvania was deeply interested in loan office certificates, in fact to the extent of one-third of the total amount issued. In the fall of 1782 the problem became critical when the public learned that France was unwilling to continue loans to the United States to pay the interest on these certificates. Pressure had already been exerted, for in the summer of 1782 a group of influential merchants representing both political factions had twice petitioned the assembly and Congress for payment of interest and for a sinking fund to provide for the principal. The assembly in turn laid the matter before Congress with the veiled threat that if some national provision were not made, the State would be forced to assume the federal debt owing to Pennsylvania citizens. This was simply another method by which the Republican assembly utilized the popular clamor in order to support Morris, the bank, and a national revenue system. For several months Congress seriously considered what answer could be given to Pennsylvania. As the current session of the State assembly drew to a close, Congress sent Rutledge, Madison, and Hamilton to ask the State not to make separate provision for the creditors until all hope of the impost system had to be abandoned.[40]

The core of Morris' plan to secure an independent revenue for Congress was the five-per-cent impost plan of 1781. The only state which withheld its assent to this plan was cantankerous Rhode Island. A definite effort was made to convert that state to the federal viewpoint. The Republicans found an able champion in that curious mixture of a man, Thomas Paine, who made a trip to Providence where he used his pen unsuccessfully in the Rhode Island press. In desperation Congress commissioned three of its members to make a personal appeal to the recalcitrant state. Paine, always fertile with ideas, at once proposed to Morris a face-saving compromise for Rhode Island. Just as the commissioners were about to set out, news came that Virginia had withdrawn its assent to the impost plan. This gave a final blow to the first attempt of the Republicans to set up an independent source of revenue for Congress. Some of the Radicals in Pennsylvania gloried in Rhode Island's action. They thought that the five-per-cent duty would prove "a stab to our Republican system," that it would operate with unusual severity on the commercial states, and that it would destroy state sovereignty. This was in line with Radical philosophy which taught that the states should always be on the alert to detect measures that would diminish their individual rights. In the meantime the State Assembly had reconvened at the beginning of 1783 and continued to press Congress for an answer to its earlier memorials.[41]

While the answer to Pennsylvania was being considered, the Morris adherents in Congress, led by Hamilton, FitzSimons, and Wilson, advocated a new plan for federal funds to pay off national debts. Hamilton and Wilson wanted to open the doors of Congress to the public when the financial situation was under discussion. They did not succeed on this point. Madison took the opportunity to jot down some observations on this action which are enlightening:

> The Pa delegates said privately that they had brought themselves into a critical situation by dissuading their Constituents from separate provision for creditors of

U. S. within Pena hoping that Congs wd adopt a general provision, & they wished their constituents to see the prospect themselves & to witness the conduct of their Delegates. Perhaps the true reason was that it was expected the presence of public creditors numerous & weighty in Philada wd have an influence & that it wd be well for the public to come more fully to the knowledge of public finances.[42]

The debate over the new revenue plan comprising an impost and supplementary funds continued in Congress for weeks.[43]

Without the prospect of immediate help from Congress the Republicans in the assembly were forced to carry out their program of separate State provision for public creditors. When the tax bill for this purpose was debated, they attempted to have the county quotas reapportioned so that Philadelphia City and County would no longer be saddled with one-third of the total taxation burden of the State. But the other counties were perfectly satisfied with the old scale and defeated the proposal. Finally in March the assembly passed the act by which Pennsylvania provided for its citizens who were public creditors of the United States.[44]

One of Morris' aims was to settle the accounts of the five national departments which had incurred debts during the war. The assembly accepted the congressional suggestions on this subject and empowered Morris to appoint a commissioner to settle the claims of individuals against the central government. In the application of the act Benjamin Stelle, the commissioner, disagreed with Morris over a point of interpretation. To keep the claims at a minimum Morris insisted that each claim should be carefully scrutinized and disallowed if there was a suggestion of fraud. Stelle on the other hand championed a loose, liberal interpretation which favored questionable claims. It is easy to understand why the assembly upheld the commissioner even though this action constituted a mild rebuke to Morris.[45]

At last Congress adopted the new financial scheme consisting of an impost and supplementary funds, fathered by Morris and championed by Hamilton, Wilson, and FitzSimons. The State assembly quickly approved the proposal with the understanding that it would not be effective until the other states made similar provisions.[46]

In the realm of State finance the Republicans took some steps to bring order into the system of taxation. Morris complained that the tax collection laws were insufficient which was undoubtedly true, for large sums were outstanding. With John Nicholson in high command as comptroller general, Council pressed the counties to collect the deficient taxes. Although the county collectors were fertile with excuses, some improvement was made in this direction. The assembly scrupulously avoided additional general taxes except for the demands of Congress. When extra funds were needed, levies were made on billiard tables, carriages, stage coaches, and imported beverages.[47]

Foreign and domestic trade were of vital interest to the conservative merchant class. As soon as hostilities were declared at an end, the Philadelphia merchants urged immediate opening of the port to British merchant vessels. As this was bound to bring repercussions from the Radicals, Council threw the burden of the decision on Congress where a committee composed of Hamilton, Ellsworth and Wilson refused to commit the national legislature to any formal decision. A week later, however, the city newspapers announced that unofficially they understood that the port was open to vessels of any foreign flag. The objections of delegates of the southern states had prevented the federalist group represented by FitzSimons and Wilson from securing an express declaration from Congress. The North Carolina delegates pointed bitterly to the excuses and technicalities utilized by the Philadelphia merchants to import British goods.[48]

Another incident indicated that the conservative assembly was heartily in agreement with the idea of stronger federal government. Washington had granted a flag of truce to a train of clothing supplies for British prisoners at Lancaster. As the cargo passed through Chester County the supplies were seized by local officials under provision of a State law prohibiting intercourse with the enemy. The incident brought the State into direct conflict with Congress and for several weeks a deadlock ensued. The assembly forthwith repealed its former law because it was in conflict with the ninth article of the Confederation.[49]

Although they were eager to resume trade relations with England, the merchants complained when they learned that the preliminary articles of peace provided that British creditors would encounter no lawful impediments in recovering their debts in full value sterling money. President Dickinson represented to Congress that this provision would prove difficult to Americans who had suffered from the calamities of war and requested that the peace commissioners should secure an extension of time. Congress instructed the commissioners to obtain a definition of that article of the treaty. They did not appreciate the delicate game of diplomacy that was going on in Paris and did not realize that the article was the result of compromise.[50]

Dominated by the mercantile interests, the Republicans neglected the complaints of hard times by the working class. In the summer of 1783 the mechanics and artisans of Philadelphia called for a high tariff to protect their domestic manufactures. Since this would have cut off the British trade which the importing merchant group had been so eager to resume, the pleas of the mechanics fell on deaf ears; the assembly took no action on their petition.[51]

Taking advantage of their growing ascendancy in State politics, the merchant group urged the assembly to consider internal improvements for the advancement of trade and commerce between the hinterland and Philadelphia. The house appointed a committee to investigate the possibility of constructing roads between the Susquehanna and Schuylkill Rivers so as to draw the commerce of the Susquehanna River valley away from Baltimore and divert it to Philadelphia. The assembly also set on foot an inquiry as to whether the State had a frontage on Lake Erie.[52]

Revolt of the Pennsylvania Soldiers

The most spectacular event in John Dickinson's administration came in June, 1783, when several hundred soldiers demonstrated before the State House in Philadelphia. The President and Executive Council of the State were faced with one of the most serious problems that occurred during the period following the Revolutionary War. The immediate result of Council's decision was the hasty removal of Congress from Philadelphia; a remote result was the fact that Congress never returned to the State during the period of the Confederation.

With news of the signing of the preliminary articles of peace with Great Britain, plans were made to disband the continental army. But these soldiers were being sent home without their pay. National leaders were not unaware of the restlessness among the troops. It was rumored that the soldiers had secretly determined not to lay down their arms until they could be assured of their pay. There were also suggestions that politicians were spreading this idea.[53] The episode at Newburgh, New York, where General Washington appealed to the officers not to resort to violence, had been created by the famous "Newburgh Letters," written by John Armstrong, Jr., who within a few weeks became Secretary of Council in Pennsylvania.

In the barracks at Philadelphia were quartered several hundred soldiers of the State line. They composed two groups; most of them had been enlisted for only five months and thus saw no more active warfare than guarding British prisoners; the rest were old soldiers who had taken part in the revolt of 1781. On June 12 their number was augmented by about two hundred men of the Maryland line who stopped in the city on their way home. On the following day the sergeants sent a remonstrance to Congress demanding satisfaction in the matter of their pay. Congress ignored the warning while General St. Clair and Secretary of War Lincoln temporarily quieted the soldiers.[54]

At the same time other trouble was brewing at Lancaster. Two captains of the discontented men in Philadelphia had sent anonymous letters to the soldiers quartered in the barracks at Lancaster. This stirred them to a mutinous disposition concerning their pay. Disregarding Colonel Butler's explanation that arrangements had been made to pay the men, they set off for Philadelphia fully armed under the leadership of Nagle, one of their sergeants. With the incident of the 13th fresh in mind, Congress appointed Hamilton, Ellsworth and Peters to request Council to take some precautionary measures. They suggested that the militia should be called out to stop the progress of the Lancaster mutineers, but Council asserted that the militia could not be relied on to act until violence took place. On Friday morning, June 20, the soldiers from Lancaster marched into Philadelphia, were welcomed by the citizens, and joined the rest of the troops at the barracks.[55]

The combustibles were piled for a conflagration. The mutinous soldiers needed only leaders, and two captains, Henry Carberry and John Sullivan, had already been priming themselves for that niche. They were the men who had sent the anonymous letters to Lancaster. On Friday night they went to the barracks and sought out Sergeant Nagle to complete plans for a demonstration.[56]

Saturday, June 21, proved to be the red-letter day. Shortly after noon when the officers were at dinner, the barracks resounded with the long roll. Two hundred fifty or three hundred men fell in line and made their way to the State House, surrounded it and placed guards at the entrances. A message from the soldiers was handed into Council demanding the right to appoint officers with full authority to bring about a settlement. "You have only twenty minutes to deliberate on this important matter," was the ultimatum. Council rejected the insolent address.[57] Then began a series of meetings between Council and the congressional committee on how to solve the delicate problem. Although the soldiers were served with liquor from nearby taverns and some of them occasionally pointed their muskets at the windows of the State House, the whole group was orderly—if such can be called orderly. At three o'clock, the regular time for adjournment, the members of Congress filed out of the State House and passed through the group of soldiers without insult or injury. At a hurried meeting that night Congress sent a demand to the Council. If President Dickinson could not assure them of protection, they would adjourn to Trenton or Princeton. At the same time they called on Washington to send troops to the city to suppress the disturbance. Since the aim of the rebels was money for their pay, Robert Morris prudently took refuge at the house of a friend.[58]

Congress gave the Council two and a half days to fulfill the demand for protection. On Sunday morning at nine o'clock at Dickinson's house the Council and the congressional committee met. Council insisted it was necessary to consult the militia officers concerning the disposition of the men before attempting to call out that body. On the following day Council declared it was unnecessary and inexpedient to call out the militia and advised conciliation. To avoid the appearance of haste, the congressional committee forebore another twenty-four hours to see whether the State authorities might change their attitude. At Dickinson's house on Monday night the Council took one step by ordering the lieutenant of Philadelphia City and County, the field officers of the militia, and the captain of the Light Horse to confer with them the next morning. The officers agreed with Council that it would be imprudent to call the militia.[59] Receiving no aid, President Boudinot at once issued a proclamation in which he cited the lack of "satisfactory assurances for expecting adequate and prompt exertion of this State for supporting the dignity of the Federal government," and ordered Congress to adjourn to Princeton.[60]

Thereupon the mutiny came to an end. Seeing Boudinot's broadsides posted in the streets and hearing that troops were marching on the city to quell the disturbance, Carberry and Sullivan fled. The soldiers sent their grievances to Council but that body replied that they would not consider them until the soldiers first submitted to their officers. Fearing trouble Dickinson called out at first a hundred militia and then increased it to five hundred. The soldiers acquiesced and gathered before the house of Dickinson who lectured them on their behavior. Soon the Lancaster group also surrendered and began their march back to that town. The mutiny was conquered; Congress had fled from Philadelphia not to return for seven years; and opinion was divided as to the wisdom of Council's actions.[61]

The newspapers were loath to mention the mutiny until at least a week after the fateful Saturday of June 21. When they began to discuss the episode, comment appeared quickly and indicated a marked division along party lines. Bailey's *Freeman's Journal,* the outstanding Radical organ, upheld the actions of Congress, blamed the soldiers for their conduct, and berated Council for its supineness. If there was anything regrettable about the whole event, it was the "blest mild administration of Pennsylvania," according to one writer. He addressed the militia leaders, "If you are guilty" of declaring that no dependence could be placed on the men under you, "be honest and say so; if not, be men and clear yourselves." [62] The strongest suggestion was offered by "Vox Populi" who broadly hinted that questionable actions on the part of Robert Morris and General Benjamin Lincoln were at the bottom of the mutiny.[63]

The conservative press defended the administration of Dickinson and condemned the hasty actions of Congress. One of the earliest references to the mutiny was an editorial comment in the *Gazette* where the writer took the opportunity to read a lesson to the enemies of Morris' financial measures. The failure of the five-per-cent impost was to be regretted for the people "begin to experience the baleful effects of a pernicious opposition. Had it been laid, agreeable to the Financier's plans, the duties . . . would have produced a handsome fund for a speedy diminuation of army debts; and the soldier's distress might have been greatly alleviated by a generous payment, besides the liquidation of his account, on receiving a dismission from the service." [64] Another writer minimized the action of the soldiers with the comment that "our American tumults (if they may be called tumults) are the most orderly, quiet, harmless and peaceable of any in the world." The actions of Congress exhibited neither dignity, fortitude, nor perseverance in the eyes of Republican journalists.[65] Although the *Packet* and the *Gazette* modified their attitude early in July and treated Congress with more respect, the rabid *Independent Gazetteer* continued to laugh at the sacredness and dignity of the national legislature.[66]

The whole affair of the removal of Congress as well as the cause of the mutiny remained shrouded in darkness. The records occasionally point to workings behind the scenes. Soon after Congress had left, Madison observed that many who justified the action of Congress "seem to have their eye remotely on the disgrace of the Executive Councils of the State." [67] It is clear that the Radicals were glad to see Congress depart for more reasons than Madison disclosed. The part played by prominent citizens in causing the mutiny is even more obscure. There were suggestions that the soldiers were encouraged by some civil characters. In ordering a court-martial of the ringleaders among the soldiery, Congress requested the aid of the State in case non-military men were found to be implicated. The court-martial brought no such persons to light and the documents of Carberry and Sullivan give no suggestion that they were the tools of higher-ups.[68] John Armstrong, Jr., Secretary of Council, was particularly sarcastic in his denunciation of Congress, terming it "the grand Sanhedrin of the Nation" whose "wisdom has been long question'd, their virtue suspected and their dignity a jest." [69] Benjamin Rush took a similar attitude.[70]

To smooth over the ill effects of the late transactions, the Republicans took action in two directions. On President Dickinson's suggestion an elaborate dinner was given at the State House to the army officers then in the city. With Dickinson presiding, thirteen patriotic toasts were drunk, accompanied by the firing of cannon and the playing of military marches. The first toast was to Congress and the last to the State of Pennsylvania.[71] The second action of the Republicans took the form of a petition from the citizens asking Congress to return to Philadelphia. After learning that the national body would not return in a few days or a week, the merchants and the Robert Morris group hit upon the plan of petitioning as a sop to satisfy the wounded dignity of Congress. The Republicans had had few kind words to say for Congress until the middle of July when they tempered their bitterness by signing the petition asking the national legislature to return to the city. Written by Paine, the memorial detailed the patriotic endeavors of Pennsylvania during the war, avoided a discussion of the mutiny, and assured Congress that the city would support the national honor if Philadelphia once again became the capital of the nation.[72]

The Radicals in Congress and in Philadelphia were overjoyed when Congress left the city, for they hoped this would diminish the power of Morris and the influence of the conservative moneyed class which was in the ascendant. After the removal the Radicals in Congress led the Pennsylvania delegates to believe that an address from the citizens of Philadelphia would be sufficient to induce a return. But after the address arrived, they insisted on an invitation from Council, and if that was not forthcoming, then they would wait until the assembly convened. "This will do for procrastination," sighed Richard Peters. In Congress the address was committed to Williamson, Duane, Higginson, Arthur Lee, and Izard. Peters predicted that their report "may be very sweet but I will watch lest the Bee be drowned in the Honey." [73] So it was, for the committee simply acknowledged the address but said not a word about accepting the invitation to return.[74]

As the Radicals in Congress demanded more penance from the conservatives of Pennsylvania, the Republicans ate the humble pie set before them. The first demand had been for an address from the people of Philadelphia; it was submitted in July. The second demand was an invitation to return to be extended from Council. This was met in the early part of August. The third demand was that the assembly should extend an invitation. At the end of August the whole question was discussed in the house behind closed doors because Joseph Montgomery feared that the outspoken debate might give further offense to the touchy Radicals in Congress. On the first of September the State delegates laid before Congress the peace offering of the assembly. The national legislature was not only offered the accommodations it had already enjoyed in Philadelphia, but the assembly pledged unanimously to afford speedy and adequate support to maintain the honor and dignity of the federal government. In the meantime the assembly had been very careful to pass all requisitions of Congress. The Republicans would go no further even though some members of Congress thought that the assembly should repudiate the actions of Dickinson and Council or impeach the members of the executive branch.[75] Foiled by the activity of the Radicals in preventing the return of Congress, Republicans like Rush who at first had begged for the national body to return now assumed an indifferent attitude and even declared that "Congress is abused, laughed at & cursed in every Company." [76]

The possible remote effects of the removal of Congress from Philadelphia did not escape the vision of some thoughtful men who feared that it would have an ill influence on American political and financial standing in Europe. In this they were not wrong.[77]

Toryphobia and the Election of 1783

The Radicals constantly asserted that the Republicans were scheming to bring back the tories and restore them to their confiscated estates. Two cases came up in the assembly which illustrated this feeling. Stephen Anderson had moved to Virginia during the war but later returned to Pennsylvania. Although he had been proscribed by Council as a traitor, Republicans argued that Anderson had no relations with the enemy during his absence and that he should be allowed trial by jury. The Radicals construed his actions as suspicious and revealed their fear that this was an opening wedge for the restitution of confiscated property. Appealing to old prejudices, the Radicals were able to defeat the proposed measure. In the case of John Gosling where the facts were not open to double interpretation, the Republicans won their point by reversing his attainder although eight unbending Radicals refused to agree. Fear of the restoration of the proprietaries also gave the Constitutionalists ground for apprehension, especially since the Republicans only occasionally denied such intentions. The Radicals probably learned from John Adams that England was urging that the Penns should be cared for in the treaty of peace. But they would have been shocked to know that Franklin was suggesting to President Dickinson that after the warmth of the times had cooled the divesting act might wisely be reconsidered.[78]

As peace was about to be proclaimed between the United States and England, the Radical militia of Philadelphia resorted to several methods to guard against an influx of exiled tories. They petitioned the assembly to exclude the disaffected from militia elections and asked that the militia should not be disarmed. Ignored by the Republican representatives, they held numerous meetings to focus public opinion on the undesirables. At the meeting of May 29 they resolved that no tories should be allowed to return and that persons harboring despised traitors should feel the displeasure of society. Two weeks later at a mass meeting held at the State House they broadened the scope of the restrictions and appointed a committee to carry out their policies. As an extra-legal body this committee held hearings, passed sentences and ordered persons to leave the city on very short notice. This was 1779 all over again. The Radicals were determined to drive out the "apostate sons of America." [79]

Outlying regions adopted similar measures. In Philadelphia County the Radicals determined to investigate the character of all strangers; if found to be undesirable, they would ask them "peacefully to leave the State." At Newtown they declared against any repeal of the test laws. In Bucks County the townships sent representatives to a county meeting which turned out to be a political rally. They called on the assembly to bar the return of the tories who "supported by a powerful, unbroke, political combination" would triumph over the true sons of the Revolution. "Watch over that great bulwark of equal liberty, the Constitution under which we live . . .," was their cry.[80] Militia battalions in Chester County denounced tories, and similar action was on foot in Cumberland and Berks.[81]

As the month of September wore on, conditions became more complicated. Carleton justified his continued occupation of New York City by pointing out the slowness with which Congress made recommendations for the protection of loyalists, and cited the open hostility of the committees of the city and counties of Pennsylvania toward the tories. Despite this situation several writers in the newspapers continued to urge laws barring the return of tories. It was pointed out that every day tories and strangers were buying up the estates of whigs who had spent their fortunes in the war, and that suits were being commenced to collect British debts from some of the most active whigs.[82]

This clamor was the harbinger of the election of October, 1783. The Radicals fully realized that the Republicans would take the first opportunity to repeal the test acts and restore the College. If the disaffected were allowed to vote what might the returns show? The danger of counter-revolution was imminent, for in October the people voted for Censors to pass judgment on the operation of the Constitution of 1776. The Republicans realized that the cry against tories was electioneering on a grand scale. When John Penn, Jr., visited the State in September, Rush planned to ask him for a tract of land for his darling project, Dickinson College. Living in the Radical stronghold of Cumberland County, John Montgomery realized the political suicide of such an action when he wrote: "I am of opinion we should not aplay [sic] to the Mr Penns. before the Election [in October] and when we do it ought to be as private as Possiable [sic] if it was Known that I waited on them it woud Certainly Confirm the report that young penn was invited by us." [83] But the story got abroad and the Cumberland County Radicals did not fail to point out that the conservatives proposed to change the Constitution in order to restore the Penn family to its rights over the soil and to collect the arrears of quit rents. The charge was published in the Philadelphia newspapers.

What its effect was in other counties is not known, but Montgomery acknowledged that it accounted for the Radical victory in Cumberland County.[84]

Another phase of the campaign was the use of personal abuse. Henry Osborne was an easy target for the Republicans. Emigrating from Ireland only a few years before, he had been one of Reed's favorites, had married a girl of property, and had risen to the post of Escheator General of the State. When his first wife arrived from Ireland in June, his game was over and his career blasted. Although he quickly disappeared into oblivion, the Republicans made capital use of the story. A more important target was George Bryan who the conservatives feared might be elected to the Council of Censors. His past was exhumed and spread before the public in an uncomplimentary manner. All charges from having been a smuggler in the Irish trade during his early years in Philadelphia to his use of inquisitorial methods during the Revolution were cast up to him. The Republicans feared "this grave old lady," as they preferred to dub Bryan, because of his hold on the Radical element. John Bayard, Thomas McKean and Joseph Reed were handled less roughly by the opposition press only because they were not candidates for office.[85]

A new note in the campaign was an attempt of the Republicans to induce the mechanics not to unite with the Constitutionalists. Suffering from an influx of British imports and general hard times, the mechanics had memorialized the assembly to levy a protective tariff so as to increase the wages of laborers, but the assembly ignored the plea. Thereupon the Radicals promised to care for the mechanics if they would vote them into power. The Republicans warned the disappointed working class to beware of a union with the Radicals.[86]

Election returns in October gave ample evidence of success for the Republicans. Although the turnover in membership in the house was about fifty per cent, sufficient conservatives were elected to give the Republicans claim to at least forty seats. It is true there were small islands of Radicals such as the delegation from the Constitutionalist stronghold of Chester County, a number from Lancaster County, most of the Cumberland members, and a scattering from the back-country region; but the Republicans were safe in the house.

More important than the assembly was the Council of Censors. In this body each county, irrespective of population or taxables, was entitled to two members. The returns showed a Republican majority, but not a two-thirds majority which was necessary to call a convention. The conservatives bided their time and hoped to make the most of opportunities. To the Council of Censors had been elected some of the best men of both factions. FitzSimons, Muhlenberg, St. Clair, Wayne, and Irvine were the undoubted leaders of respectability. John Whitehill, James McClene, John Smiley, and William Findley were unequalled proponents of Radical thought at its best.

The outlook in October, 1783, was unusually bright for the Republicans. In some cases they became too optimistic. Scarcely a week after election, and before all the returns had been reported, Benjamin Rush put on rose-colored glasses and wrote exultingly to his friend John Montgomery, "This Victory we hope will restore order & happiness to Pennsylvania & render us once more the envy & admiration of our sister states." He intimated that friend John had won a seat in the Censors from Cumberland County for "At *Carlisle* we were near 400 a head of the palefaced party. *You* had our ticket." [87] Four days later complete returns forced Rush to face reality and to tell Montgomery the bad news: "You were thrown out by *only* 50 Votes." More truthful was Rush's reason for the Republicans' loss of one of the Censor's seats in Cumberland County, when he wrote, "The letter from McClene & Co. [Constitutional faction] with the old story of the restoration of the prop[rietar]y estate lost us the election in your County." [88] Though Montgomery might complain of his defeat, there was always Rush offering consolation and encouragement. "Dont say you will never serve" the people again, counselled the Philadelphia physician. "Their madness will soon be over . . ." "All will end well." [89]

Another Republican not so sanguine as Rush was William Bingham sojourning in England. He did not hide his anxiety over the election but confided his fears to his friend Cadwalader Morris. "Our party," he explained, "do not possess half the activity & address which prevail amongst the factious leaders of the Opposition. These qualities are held but in little Respect amongst *Us,* & we both can remember the time when the Election was attended with the most pointed neglect, by those they were calculated to serve." [90] The aristocratic but practical Bingham realized that such methods must be discarded. When the good news of the election arrived he "was exceedingly rejoiced," and visualized the blessings of a good Constitution for Pennsylvania.[91]

When the house assembled, the Republicans had undisputed control although there was a significant opposition. The conservative George Gray became Speaker. Dickinson and Ewing were re-elected President and Vice-President of Council.[92]

In the wake of the election trailed ugly rumors of contested returns in Philadelphia City and County, Chester County, and Northumberland County. The exposure of irregular voting in these regions brought no credit to the Republicans.

Of the contested returns that in Philadelphia was the most outstanding. Headed by Jonathan D. Sergeant, Francis Bailey, and Lewis Farmer, the

Radicals presented their charges of irregularity, the most important of which was the presence of numerous soldiers of the State line at the election poll. It would appear that General Wayne corralled the soldiers who were in the city, some actually in service, others recently furloughed, and sent them to the State House to vote. Doubting the legality of the soldiers' vote, the judges and inspectors of election counselled with each other and came to no decision; then they sent for Chief Justice McKean for a ruling but the Chief Justice was out of town. Next they summoned Attorney General Bradford but the Attorney General was loath to give an answer on the spur of the moment. Thus for several hours actual balloting was delayed and the soldiers waiting to cast their votes became restive and crowded into the polling room. The delay was interpreted by some that they might not be allowed to vote. At this the army officers used threatening language; in positive terms Wayne declared that his men would vote. As the judges and inspectors did not like the appearance of the soldiers and their officious officers, they did not wait any longer and threw open the window to receive ballots. Prepared tickets had been placed in the soldiers' hands. At the window an army officer stationed himself "to keep order among the soldiers" and also to inspect the tickets which his men handed in. Citizens who came to vote were ordered to stand back until the army men had cast their ballots.[93]

The Radicals marshalled other charges, some of which are not well sustained by the evidence presented. It was claimed that many of the soldiers did not take the oath or fulfill the legal requirements for voting; that soldiers from Maryland, New Jersey, and New England had cast ballots; that the sergeants prevented their men from altering the tickets placed in their hands; that many citizens were over-awed by the military and withdrew without voting. Both sides admitted, however, that of the 1,630 votes cast at the State House, there were 230 more votes than recorded taxables. The Radicals asserted that the ballot box had been stuffed; the Republicans explained that the votes were delivered faster than the clerk could record the names of the voters, that freeholders' sons just reaching the age of twenty-one and not yet on the list of taxables were allowed to vote and that some of the voters might have come from other districts or counties, a practice which was not forbidden at this time.[94]

The contested Philadelphia election was examined by committees in both the assembly and in the Council of Censors. Although the reports of the committees were known to favor the Republicans, they did not rest easily. While the hearing of witnesses was in progress Irvine pleaded with Wayne to attend the Censors, of which he was a member, if only for "the benefit of your advise which we have much occasion for." "The Election business is under examination," he continued. "There is no danger of finishing it too soon." [95] In the early part of 1784 both committees reported that the charges were groundless. The Republicans had won, but at a price to their reputation.[96]

In Northumberland County where the disputed election was closely allied with the vexed Wyoming question, the trouble centered about thirty-five voters, eleven of whom were so-called Indian land men or Yankee squatters, and twenty-four who were Wyoming settlers. Some or all of these voters had not taken the oath of allegiance to the State. The Republicans were bound to oppose these votes as a rebuke to the Yankees in Wyoming. In the Council of Censors this was not serious, for Samuel Hunter and William Montgomery, even after this deduction, won their seats. In the assembly, however, the deduction cut out Frederick Antes. On a strict party vote William McClay, William Cooke, and James Mc-Clenaghen were declared the representatives from Northumberland County. Against this action the Constitutionalists objected vainly, not so much at the exclusion of Frederick Antes as with the principle of excluding Yankee votes. They claimed that even though these men had not taken the oath, they had already been considered by the government as citizens of the State since the Trenton decree.[97]

In Chester County the Radicals asserted that non-jurors had been allowed to vote. The committee, composed entirely of Republicans, tried to stave off further inquiry by insisting that the petitioners submit more specific charges. This ruse was unsuccessful, for Samuel Cunningham, John Culbertson, and John Boyd appeared in the house to amplify the charges. Exactly what took place between these three gentlemen and the committee is not known, but sharp words passed for two weeks; later Cunningham and Culbertson remonstrated to the house against the way they were handled by the committee. Mercilessly the Republicans drove on to a final insult. By a strictly party vote the house decided that these insinuations against the committee were unjust and ill-founded. The main question of whether non-jurors voted in the Chester County election was still unsettled. The Radicals took a new tack. They attempted to make all witnesses concerning the election declare whether they had taken the oath of allegiance to the State. This was speedily killed. Later in February the committee report, adopted by the house, dismissed the whole question.[98]

An echo of the election of 1783 was a contention in some quarters that Hubley and Parr had been elected from Lancaster by unfair means and for ulterior reasons. William Parr, an Englishman by birth, was suspected of being a tory. Adam Hubley had been a county lieutenant whose financial accounts did not seem to balance correctly, or, at least, they were suspected of not balancing. It was charged that he and the force of his powerful family in Lancaster were bent on repealing the State law for settling accounts so as to prevent him from being embarrassed. Opponents of Hubley and Parr asserted that the inspectors and judges at the election were the tools of these two men and aided in stuffing the ballot boxes with two hundred votes to insure the election in their favor. When Hubley and Parr entered the assembly they gave their wholehearted support to the Republicans; so much so, that a correspondent in a newspaper asked whether the house would pass over the questionable accounts of Hubley without scrutiny. Five months later the house investigated with the result that it ordered a credit of fifty-seven pounds to be assigned to Hubley as the balance due him for money spent in the recruiting service. Thus the Republican record was kept clean and the Radicals were silenced.[99]

The post of delegate to Congress did not carry with it the esteem which is usually associated with such an appointment. After the mutiny of 1783 the situation of the Pennsylvania delegates was uncomfortable, to say the least. The Radical element in the national body had carried Congress away from Philadelphia under circumstances which made its return highly improbable. Furthermore, the work completed by Congress was so trivial due to diminished representation and the assent of seven states necessary to pass the least important measures, that many people had little regard for it. During this period the journals grew monotonous with the repetition of "so the motion was lost," which almost inevitably followed every vote.

Of the delegates from Pennsylvania who under normal circumstances would have been re-elected in the fall of 1783, Richard Peters was determined he would not continue. Although he claimed private reasons, other circumstances undoubtedly brought him to the point of refusal. In June he was in the storm center of negotiations between the State Council and Congress over the question of mutiny; the experience was not pleasant and he saw Congress dragged away from the city by his political enemies. Nor did he entertain a very high opinion of Congress, "the Political Comet whose aberrations are beyond calculation," as he described it.[100]

While three of the delegates were finding excuses to get out of Congress, Rush was engineering John Montgomery into an appointment. Montgomery had failed of re-election to the assembly in the fall of 1783 and he keenly felt the defeat. Rush consoled him with his usual "All will end well." [101] For once Rush was correct in his predictions. On November 12 the assembly re-elected Mifflin and Peters, and added John Montgomery, Cadwalader Morris, and Edward Hand, all good Republicans. In the meantime Thomas Mifflin was elected President of Congress, although absent at the time of his election; he consulted Robert Morris before accepting the honor. Peters carried out his original determination and resigned. There was some doubt of Hand's accepting the appointment, but he retained the post. Whether the same doubt existed about Montgomery is not known but Rush cautioned him not to resign because Peters' action had offended the assembly. To supply the place left vacant by Peters, James Wilson was prevailed upon to serve on account of his interest in the Wyoming affair which was again coming to the fore.[102] Until this time the State delegation contained "Not a Limb of the Law." [103]

Domestic Issues

One of the most important social questions which came before the assembly in this session of Republican supremacy was whether theatrical entertainments should be legalized in Philadelphia. Eager to play in the city, Dennis Ryan petitioned the house to repeal the restrictions on the theatre and suggested a tax on entertainments. The Quaker interests opposed the idea and the house made short shrift of his plea.

Interest in the question increased and when Lewis Hallam repeated Ryan's petition there was a slight majority in favor of lifting the restriction. The Presbyterians, Baptists, and Quakers, odd bedfellows indeed, united in opposing relaxation of the law. The assemblymen harkened to their constituents, changed their minds, and defeated the licensing bill by a two-to-one vote. "The Saints and saint-like folk have too much influence," was Cadwalader Morris' opinion.[104] In this vote party lines were obliterated although a sectional division was noticeable; the rural sections generally disapproved the theatre while the supporters were found in the city. The theatre question was settled, but only temporarily, for it came forth again in the near future with increased vigor.[105]

Symbolic of the heights of power which the Republicans had attained was the manner in which they stripped Council of the power to appoint auctioneers. There were three auctioneers for the city of Philadelphia and by a law of 1778 Council was given the power to appoint men to these offices. The income from these posts was very lucrative and became the choice political plums at the disposal of the party in control of Council. If the assembly could control the appointments, the Republicans could share in the spoils.

Resorting to legalistic interpretation, the assembly took from Council the power to appoint auctioneers. At once a group of prominent Republicans applied for the jobs. The old incumbents whom the Republicans removed were William Brown and John Bayard, well-known Radical who several years before had resigned from Council in order to retain the auctioneer's post. They were replaced by Arthur St. Clair and John

Mease. Alexander Boyd apparently had made his peace with the conservatives, for he was reappointed.

The Council entered a formal protest against this increase in the power of the assembly. An assembly committee passed over it lightly and went ahead with its objective. After the new auctioneers were appointed by the assembly, Council accepted them without further protest.[106]

An interesting episode of the period was the Longchamps case. At this time the Chevalier de la Luzerne filled the post of French minister to the United States and Barbé Marbois was consul general. Although only Marbois was actively involved in this serio-comic incident, the affair gave rise to a serious problem between the State of Pennsylvania and the government of France. Members of Congress realized the gravity of the situation but possessed no power to interfere.

The facts of the case are simple. Charles Julian de Longchamps, a Frenchman, had arrived in Philadelphia in September, 1783. He brought with him a genius for getting into trouble and proceeded to apply his talents. Being the nephew of La Luzerne's steward's wife and now residing in the land of the free and equal, Longchamps decided to impress the people with a European title. To certify his claim to this honor it was necessary to have the approval of the French embassy. On the refusal of Marbois to countenance the claim, Longchamps threatened him in vague language. The following day Longchamps took the oath of allegiance to the State of Pennsylvania. On the next day he met Marbois on the street and engaged him in a fight. At once La Luzerne complained to the State Council and demanded that Longchamps should be arrested and handed over to him to be sent back to France for punishment. The arrest of Longchamps started a train of further troubles. When habeas corpus proceedings were instituted to free him, La Luzerne and Van Berkel, the Dutch minister, threatened to leave the State if the prisoner were released. To the disgust of the French embassy and to the embarrassment of the Council, Longchamps eluded his guards and escaped. He was recaptured, brought to a speedy trial, and convicted on all counts.[107]

The Radicals were not too sympathetic with France. Two days after Council asked the Supreme Court whether the French demand for Longchamps could be legally carried out, a broadside appeared to arouse the people against such action. Suggesting that overbearing methods had been used to obtain a verdict against the Frenchman, the writer claimed that the laws of the State were sufficient in the case and that sending Longchamps to France would introduce "an arbitary and very alarming measure." His cause "must be supported in spite of all the Tyrants and Despots in the state . . ." [108] It is fortunate that this issue never came to a head. Before passing sentence, the judges of the Supreme Court had decided that Council could not legally surrender the prisoner to France. The sentence comprised a fine of one hundred French crowns and imprisonment for two years.[109] As far as Pennsylvania was concerned the case was settled. The French government, however, applied to Congress in its demand for Longchamps. Following the policy of judicious delay, Congress let the matter rest. Marbois finally decided to withdraw the demand, and bent over backwards when he interposed his good offices to have Longchamps pardoned.[110]

During the session of 1783-1784 the western Radicals attempted to move the seat of the State capital from Philadelphia. Lancaster was designated for the proposed honor but lost by a margin of eight votes. Taking advantage of the absence of five opponents of removal, the Radicals several days later tried again to move the capital from Philadelphia; they did not count on a shifting of votes which took place in the intervening days, and again they lost. The City, Philadelphia and Northampton Counties opposed removal while Cumberland, Bedford and Westmoreland championed it. The counties lying between these two groups divided and shifted their votes on the measure, probably from jealousy of Lancaster which alone would have benefited from the change. Sectional as well as political considerations dominated the proceedings.[111] According to Radical philosophy large cities were not places for the seat of democratic government. From London Joseph Reed supported the idea of removal because, "The Assembly is not the Assembly of Pennsylvania, but of Philadelphia, and that the most corrupt part of it . . ."[112]

After Congress had left Philadelphia in June, 1783, the Republicans were torn between contempt for that body and adherence to the principles of the Articles of Confederation. This was illustrated in the extinguishment of Indian claims in the western part of the State. Large tracts had been set aside for the reward of soldiers and for redemption of depreciation certificates, but before the land could be surveyed it was necessary to remove the Indian title by purchase according to the traditional policy of the State.

Although a treaty with the aborigines was necessary, Congress was loath to cooperate with Pennsylvania. Despite the provision in the ninth article of Confederation which vested the control of Indian affairs in Congress, the Republican assembly believed that it had a just right to negotiate a treaty without regard to the national legislature. But respect for the union prompted the assembly to seek approval. Since the New England delegates opposed separate action of Pennsylvania, the assembly forged ahead with its plans and Council appointed commissioners to meet with the Indians. This action brought Congress to reason and it also appointed agents to hold a general treaty. After opposition from Massachusetts and Rhode Island was again overcome, Congress enjoined its agents to cooperate with the State commissioners. Waiting for almost a year, the assembly became impatient as numerous delays thwarted the holding of the treaty; finally it ordered the State agents to proceed with the purchase whether the national representatives were present or not. At the last minute the congressional agents cooperated. At the ensuing conferences with the Indians at Fort Stanwix and Fort McIntosh, the Pennsylvania agents scrupulously gave precedence and deference to the continental commissioners. By these treaties all the land within the bounds of the State were freed from Indian claims.[113]

Among certain groups there was increasing envy of the successful operation of the Bank of North America. In 1782 a dividend of almost nine per cent was paid on the stock and in 1783 a dividend of over fourteen per cent. The institution was a closed corporation, the amount of stock was limited, and only those who had invested in 1781 enjoyed the attractive profits.[114] The discontent was voiced by Ebenezer Hazard when he wrote to a friend:

> The present bank has been both useful and pernicious: useful to the stockholders, who got a prodigious interest for their money; and useful to the man of trade, because, by paying a moderate discount he could turn his notes of hand into cash. But it has been prejudical to the middling and poorer clases of people who wanted money on interest; for, as the bank yielded 9, 12 and even 16 per cent, none could be had at the legal rate, which is 6, and many were much distressed for want of money who could give good security, but could not afford to pay so great an interest. The brokers took the advantage of people's necessities, and have lett money out by the month, at 4½, 5, and even 6 per cent per month, which is 54, 60 and 72 per cent per annum. Such folks can always find means to evade the law. A new bank, I think, will tend to prevent such practices, because it will bring more money into market, and consequently make it more plenty.[115]

There was also the fact that Robert Morris by his power in the Bank, his control over federal finances, and his enormous credit facilities could exert a monopolistic force in the financial realm and ruin any businessman at will.

The discontented moneyed men led by Constitutionalists like John Bayard and Jonathan D. Sergeant set plans on foot for a new bank. One of their first acts was to apply to the assembly for a charter. At once the proposal was placed in the hands of a grand committee about equally divided between Republicans and Radicals. The old Bank then petitioned for a hearing and this was handed to another grand committee in which the Republicans predominated. In committee the arguments pro and con were presented by Gouverneur Morris and James Wilson on behalf of the old institution and by J. D. Sergeant, Jared Ingersoll, William Bradford, and Miers Fisher for the new institution. The Bank of North America pleaded its patriotic services and asserted that the assembly had no right to establish two banks in the State. The representatives of the new bank resorted to the cry of monopoly and the dominance of Robert Morris.[116]

The old Bank faced the alternative of taking to its bosom the members of the new organization or seeing a rival institution destroy its exclusive nature. It chose the former by enlarging its issue of stock. Thereupon the new bank withdrew its petition from the house and was satisfied.[117] The bank issue crosscut party lines. William Bradford described it thus: "you might have seen the violent whig, the bitter tory & the moderate man laying their heads together with the earnestness & freedom of friendship: the Constitutionalist and Republican were arm in arm: & the Quaker and Presbyterian forgot their religious antipathies in this coalition of interests." [118] By subscribing for twenty shares Dickinson attracted the resentment of his old friends. Joseph Reed was suspicious of the coalition; "I fear some of our friends will be the dupes at last . . . The Whig Representation seems to be too weak in this new Bank . . ." [119] The ultra-Radicals, however, never swallowed the idea of the bank in any form. A harbinger of future events appeared when the Council of Censors declared that Congress had no right to erect corporations like the Bank.

In 1784 the Bank faced the threat of a new emission of paper money. This condition arose from the strained economic conditions late in 1783 and early in 1784 when a scarcity of circulating cash adversely affected the farmers. Since the Bank did not extend its facilities to the rural regions, the farmers demanded a loan office. Under this pressure a bill was brought forth providing for an issue of one hundred thousand pounds to be loaned out on mortgages on land and property. Hard money Republicans disliked the bill because the money would be made legal tender. To thwart the paper emission Thomas Willing and the Bank offered to lend the State three hundred thousand dollars at five per cent interest. This was refused. The bill did not come to the point of passage during this session but against the protests of the Republicans it was referred to the next house. The eastern mercantile group was meeting increasing pressure from the rural regions. By the time the next house met the whole political picture changed completely.[120]

Another cause of hard times was the action of English merchants who flooded America with their wares. Philadelphia did not escape the resulting depression. Edward Bancroft summarized the situation when he wrote:

> The importation of European goods has been so considerable, within the last six months that the exportable produce of the states probably will not equal it in less than three years; the British are the only manufactures which have afforded any profit; the foreign have sold under prime cost, and there is hardly anything here

to pay for them, except a very little Spanish silver, which is daily carried away, and will soon be all gone.[121]

In this depressed economic situation the United States sought a trade treaty with England, with the object of opening the British West Indies to American bottoms. England was not eager to come to economic terms with the recently revolted colonies, and Sheffield's *Observations* confirmed many Britishers in this position. Two Pennsylvanians, both representative of the Republican mercantile interests, came forth to answer Sheffield. Thomas Paine under his well known pen-name of "Common Sense" gave one rebuttal. More important was the effort of William Bingham who while on a visit to England turned his pen to answer Sheffield in a work which soon ran into the third edition. He looked forward to the hope of being appointed an economic adviser to American commissioners who might be sent to Great Britain to negotiate a trade treaty. The policy of the Republican merchants was to have the States relinquish to Congress all their powers over external trade. This was one of the important instructions which the assembly ordered its delegates to urge on Congress. At the same time the Philadelphia Merchants' Committee sent a feeler to the merchants of Massachusetts concerning the possibility of united action in regard to British trade.[122]

The back-country groups saw an opportunity to shift the tax burden from land to commerce when a bill was presented imposing an additional duty on all British goods and vessels. To this measure the city merchants protested on the basis that however wise it might be, it was at that time premature. The Republicans kept the bill from passage. At the same time the back-country members in coalition with other Radicals passed an act imposing a duty of one and a half per cent on all goods imported into the State. Although the merchants protested, they were able to appoint Sharp Delaney collector of the port of Philadelphia.[123]

The Republican Assault

The conservative revival reached its high-water mark in 1784 when the Republicans attempted to carry out several of their important preliminary objectives, the incorporation of the city of Philadelphia, the restoration of the College of Philadelphia, and the repeal of the test acts. Events proved that the Republicans were moving too fast for the people and that they had underestimated the force and determination of the opposition.

The movement for the incorporation of Philadelphia constantly gained momentum during the years of conservative revival from 1780 to 1784. In 1781 fifty-four persons petitioned for a city charter. The assembly ordered a bill reported but no action was taken. In 1783 a number of petitions for and against incorporation were presented to the house. The Constitutionalists opposed every attempt to grant a charter. On one occasion the Radicals invaded the assembly "with a flaming petition not less than 7 Yards long." This aroused the conservative Delany who proceeded to tell the Radicals and the assembly what he thought of such spectacular methods. This time the bill reached the third reading, was debated and received a favorable committee report but it was referred to the next house for action. Although the bill slumbered through most of the 1783-1784 session, in August several remonstrances were received against it. It is difficult to understand why the Republicans did not press the bill to a final vote; doubtless they were not certain of sufficient support.[124]

The Radicals were fully alive to the dangers of the incorporation bill. They never liked corporations or charters of any type, for combinations of men and of property were repugnant to their ideal of democratic government. The real complaint was that the voting franchise in the city would be restricted to free holders; and they believed that the charter provided loopholes for the evasion of the test laws in the city. They condemned the whole charter movement with one word—"aristocratical." [125]

The assembly was reluctant to go into the problem of the University of Pennsylvania which had been created by the act of 1779 when the Radicals dispossessed the trustees of the old College of Philadelphia and took over control of the whole institution. Every year since that time Dr. William Smith, the ousted provost, memorialized the assembly to investigate his claim for reinstatement. Until September, 1784, the assembly never brought Smith's memorials up for discussion.[126] Undoubtedly the Republicans looked to the Council of Censors to condemn the act of 1779 as unconstitutional.

In 1784 the Republicans launched their first drive to restore the old College. Early in the year they scrutinized very carefully a list of all confiscated estates which Council had set aside as an endowment for the institution. The assembly confirmed about two-thirds of these reservations, disapproved five, and postponed consideration on eight. The city members were then instructed to prepare a bill to confirm to the University such estates as were reserved by Council and confirmed by the assembly. Thus the Republicans in the house asserted the right to review Council's actions.[127]

The real effort to restore the College came later. In March the house decided to postpone action on Smith's memorials until the Censors might take action on similar memorials before that body. In July the members of the corporation of the old College,[128] all conservatives, laid their claims before the Censors, stating that without misdemeanor or breach of trust proved against them, their charter as a corporate body was taken from them by the act of 1779. The house then took up Smith's case and debated it for several days in a committee of the whole. Counsel, headed by James Wilson, was heard on the claims of the old College, and the case of the University was presented by Jonathan D. Sergeant. The committee of the whole recommended that a bill should be reported to repeal the act of 1779 so as to reinstate the old trustees of the College, provided that the trustees of the University may apply the remaining estates toward carrying out the business of the University until the assembly should take further order. On strictly party lines this report was adopted by a vote of twenty-eight to twenty-five and three Republicans were ordered to prepare the bill.[129]

Before action could be taken on the bill, the Radicals were fighting a desperate battle over a more important measure, the repeal of the test laws. By drastic action they prevented the passage of both bills. The Republicans had failed in their attempt to restore the old College.[130]

The repeal of the test laws was the boldest stroke the Republicans had attempted since the Revolution. As in the case of the College charter they did not wish to agitate the question of the test laws until the Censors had taken favorable action or until a convention had been called to revise the State constitution.[131]

By September, 1784, the Republicans had lost all hope of effecting the least change in the Constitution by way of the Council of Censors. As a last resort they decided to use their majority in the assembly to secure the abolition of the test laws in the expectation that it would make available enough new votes among the populace to continue their control of the assembly until further action could be taken on the Constitution. On September 1, Wayne and FitzSimons in the Council of Censors had made a final, unsuccessful attempt to have that body condemn the test laws. On the next day in the house a motion was introduced to appoint a committee to revise the test laws. By the middle of September the house received petitions from Philadelphia praying for alteration of the test laws. The report of a grand committee suggested a bill to allow all white male inhabitants to take the oath of 1777 and to admit these men to full citizenship. There was also a provision that no one should hold office until he had taken the oath and that no one who joined the British army or aided the enemy cause should be capable of voting or holding office. By a report to twenty-nine to twenty-two this report was adopted by the house. The next day the bill passed through the first and second readings and on the following day, September 28, when a motion was made to take up the bill for a third reading, the house divided twenty-five to twenty-five. Speaker Gray cast the deciding vote in favor of the motion.[132]

Blocked in their efforts to stem the action of the Republicans, nineteen of the Radicals left the assembly room. The conservatives were dumbfounded. They had brought the bill to the point of passage and now they were completely baffled by lack of a quorum. In vain did the rump house order the sergeant-at-arms to collect and bring in the absentees. Unable to continue legislative work, the Republicans stood idly by with the fruits of victory snatched from their hands. The Radicals were confident that their constituents would support them in this high-handed procedure. Election was only two weeks away. Jubilant over the defeat of the Republicans in the Council of Censors, the Radicals added another feather to their cap by blocking passage of the Republican laws. Already they had flooded the counties with reports of their victory in the censorial body. The Constitutionalists were correct in believing that the pendulum was swinging again in their favor.[133]

In a cry of indignation and resentment the Republicans appealed to the public through printed handbills in which they justified their whole program and condemned the irregular secession of the Constitutionalist assemblymen. The dignity of the government had been insulted and public business grievously obstructed. The test law excluded nearly one-half of the inhabitants of the State from citizenship, yet these non-jurors had paid their public taxes and many of them were inoffensive and peaceable men. Granted the franchise, these men would support the government of the Constitution of 1776. The Republicans justified the bill to restore the College to the original trustees and vehemently denied that there had been the least intention of returning the proprietary estates.[134] "Friends and Fellow-Citizens, be not deceived. You have been too long the dupes of a few designing men. Think for yourselves." [135] This had the true ring of an election broadside and in effect that is what it was. The conservatives had lost in their struggle over the test laws. The vital blow to the counter-revolution, however, had already been administered by the Council of Censors.

VI

Counter-Revolution Halted (1783-1786)

DURING the period from 1780 to 1784 the Republicans had risen to power in the assembly. Just as they were about to crown their four years of success with the overthrow of the test laws and the restoration of the College, they met disastrous defeat. The Radicals had scotched their plans by preventing a quorum in the assembly. At the same time a more serious disaster had overtaken the conservatives in the Council of Censors which met in the winter of 1783-1784 and again in the late summer of 1784. For seven years the Republicans had waited for the opportunity of overthrowing the Constitution through the legal channel of the Council of Censors. Not only did they lose this battle, but the public turned against them and they forfeited many of the gains they had made earlier in the assembly. Once again the pendulum swung in favor of Radicalism and the counter-revolutionary movement went into eclipse. This story of defeat begins in October, 1783, when the public chose members to the censorial body.

Council of Censors: Radical Triumph

Despite the fact that each county had equal representation in the Council of Censors, the Republicans contemplated the election of the members with enthusiastic optimism. When the return came in, they had good reason to believe that their hope of an alteration in the Constitution might be realized. Like many of their apparent victories, the Republicans again fell just short of success. They had a majority of the Censors but not two-thirds of the entire body. Thirteen Republicans and twelve Constitutionalists had been elected. Republicans tried to muster all of their strength and friends of Wayne urged him to attend because his help was needed.[1]

The Censors began their work with the Republicans in the dominant position. Thomas FitzSimons was elected president and John Rose (Baron Rosenthal) became secretary. Realizing that they did not command two-thirds of the members necessary to call a convention which was the ultimate aim of the conservatives, they planned a new strategy.

They would advance carefully prepared alterations for the Constitution, publish them to the people at large, and then call on the public to bring pressure on the recalcitrant members to vote for a convention.[2]

The important work of the Censors centered in several questions, each of which was submitted to a committee to prepare a report. The first task was to inquire whether the Constitution had been preserved inviolate; the second, whether the public taxes had been justly laid and collected in all parts of the State; the third, whether the articles of the Constitution were defective and in need of amendment. All the committees were predominately Republican.[3]

The question of defective articles and amendment of the Constitution was the initial step looking to a convention. And so the Republicans brought forth the committee report on that subject first. It outlined the most comprehensive view of the Republicans' plans for revamping the frame of government. They called for a bicameral legislature, the lower house to remain essentially as it was; the upper house, to be called the Legislative Council, was to comprise a membership half the size of the lower house and to be elected by the people. All bills could originate in either house except money bills which could be initiated only by the lower house. Each house would pass on the legislation of the other, and the executive would have the power to veto any bill. A vetoed bill, however, could be repassed by the vote of two-thirds of each house.

The executive planned by the Republicans would consist of one man under the title of governor to be elected annually by the people. He would be required to be a resident of the State seven years prior to his election. His powers were mainly those of the executive council then in operation.

Less important innovations in the scheme of government but indicative of conservative plans included the following: The number of years which an official could serve the public in the same post would be unrestricted except in the case of delegates to Congress who could serve only three years out of every six. The residence requirement for voting would be increased from one to two years. Foreigners coming to the State could purchase land on taking the oath; after two years they would be considered free denizens of the State except that a residence of five years would be necessary before they could qualify for election to public office. The residence requirement for members elected to the legislature would be lowered from two years to one. The Republicans proposed to omit the provision then in practice whereby assemblymen who dissented from a measure were allowed to spread their reasons on the minutes. The provision to print bills for public consideration was also deleted. To avoid controversial election returns no one was to be allowed to vote except in the city or county of which he was an inhabitant. The judges of Supreme Court and common pleas would be guaranteed fixed salaries. Their tenure of office, however, would continue only during good behavior instead of for seven years; and they would not be allowed to hold any other office. The conservatives also planned to abolish the whole system of the Council of Censors.[4]

It could not be expected that the Radicals would permit these constitutional innovations to go unchallenged. They voiced their usual charges that the whole proposal was unconstitutional and undemocratic. Forgetting their own actions in 1776, they urged that no constitution should be changed lightly, and charged that the new system would prove expensive, burdensome, and complicated; that it would "tend to introduce among the citizens new and aristocratic ranks, with a Chief Magistrate at their head, vested with powers exceeding those which fall to the ordinary lot of Kings." They referred to the governor's chair as a "throne of royalty," and declared that the voice of "God and nature" proclaimed against such a system.[5]

Blocked in their attempt to call a convention, the Republican majority recessed the Council of Censors until June. Their plan was to arouse the people to bring pressure on the rabid Radicals. Before adjourning, the conservatives issued a strongly worded address to all voters. Very frankly they stated that the problem was to secure a convention. The minority in the Censors held almost half of the seats but represented only one-third of the people. "We have not the most distant prospect," explained the Republicans, "that the gentlemen of the minority will concur in calling a Convention to amend the Constitution, which we have thought, we hope not improperly, the most important part of our business: And it is that you might have an opportunity to instruct them on this subject, that we have at present suspended our deliberations." [6]

The Republicans made use of various methods to influence the people in favor of calling a convention. Benjamin Rush in Philadelphia carried on a correspondence with former friends who were now in the camp of the moderate Constitutionalists in an effort to effect a compromise between the warring groups. He was willing to consider any plan so long as it included the calling of a convention. While the Censors were in their first session, Rush utilized his old friendship with the aged John Armstrong in order to sound him out on the idea. Armstrong replied that deeper than the question of a convention or no convention, was the "unhappy temper too apparent in the people at large;" jealousies had been awakened; mutual confidence and candor had been lost. He continued:

. . . I have earnestly laboured with both partys, that some degree of coalition should be attempted, as prerequisites to the present critical period—but never received a better answer from either town or country, than that I did not well enough know human nature—was too charitable, owing to a better heart than head.

His formula provided that the Censors should agree on the particular things to be altered or amended, and that these points and no others should come before a convention. As he saw it, this was plainly the intent of the wording in the Constitution. If Rush insisted that the convention should reconsider the whole Constitution, then compromise was out of the question. To effect a conciliation Armstrong bluntly explained that Rush demanded too much, such as when he expected the Radical Presbyterians in office to amalgamate with the dominant party, or to relinquish the Constitution and "Generously throw it into the hands of a Convention." This was expecting the impossible. James McLene was not an unreasonable man, Armstrong explained, for in conversation with McClene he learned that the latter was not averse to some alteration in the Constitution.[7]

The chief trouble was that the Republicans in their brief moment of triumph in the Censors went too far. Their appeal to the people was couched in the bitterest terms of party warfare. The changes they proposed in the system of government were too extreme, the scope too vast, and the manner too domineering. Even Rush, ardent Republican that he was, admitted that "Our friends have not conducted matters with the prudence or consideration that was expected from them." [8] In line with this belief, Rush hastened to scale down his demands in order to gain the support of as many moderate Constitutionalists as possible. He would now be satisfied with amendments which two-thirds of the Censors might approve. This position found Armstrong in a more receptive mood, for he agreed that a minimum of two points would be satisfactory, that is, "that the burthens of the people may be lightened from the dead weight of supernumeraries, under which we now grone and cannot much longer labour—And a Compound legislature, at the same time [I] should be extreamely glad . . . that this last could be so quallified, as to get over that bitter pill, & prevailing popular Objection, *that either branch* should possess the power of *an absolute negative*." Armstrong then promised his aid in attempting compromise: "I shall god willing use my utmost endeavours, as prudently as I can to convince & persuade a few of the most tenacious of my acquaintance of each side, supposing it to be the best way, first if possable to gain the leaders . . ." [9] Again he reiterated the absolute necessity of yielding on the part of both factions. He hoped that a program could be worked out so as to be adopted by the Censors at this next session. He strongly decried the use of any forceful or extra-constitutional methods to gain the objectives.

Meanwhile the public received a barrage of literature from both political factions. Arthur St. Clair wrote an article signed "One of the Majority" which was widely circulated. Rush claimed that it had a great effect in opening the eyes of the people, but Rush's opinions in matters concerning the strength of the conservatives was always over-optimistic. In Lancaster County Stephen Chambers found St. Clair's article and another publication signed "One of the Germans," "particularly usefull." In fact Chambers wrote an urgent request to John Rose for as many copies as he could spare of the proposed amendments to the Constitution in the German language because "the Germans want much to read them and judge for themselves as some as ye thinking part of them begin to apprehend they have been imposed on, & I have no doubt that in a little time that a great majority of them will be for the Amendments . . ." [10] Rush reported that in the same county many who had signed the petition against a convention were now signing a counter-petition in which they declared that they had been imposed upon by the Radicals. Although petitions for a convention were circulating in the western part of Cumberland County, the lack of active conservatives nullified their success.[11] In evangelizing the frontier region for political reform, Rush took the opportunity to urge social improvement among the Scotch-Irish Presbyterians. In a letter to the Reverend Linn he stated that the farmers should be taught to be more neat, to clean their fields of dead trees, to build larger and better fences, to convert distilleries into milk houses, to replace whiskey toddy and grog with beer and cider, and lastly, to spend "less time in attending constitutional meetings at taverns, & more time in improving their farms" like the thrifty, industrious Germans.[12] After some delay the clergyman replied that there were two things on which the Scotch-Irish insisted:

> The people here have been drinking with all their might, whiskey & bad rum all harvest. Though the Physician says it will destroy their bodies & the Clergyman, It will ruin their souls. They drink on. They *will* have the *Constitution* & the *bottle* at any hazard whatever.[13]

The policy of conciliation and compromise which Rush and some of his friends were trying to accomplish ran into difficulties. An example from a hot-bed of Radical frontier settlers well illustrates the problem. The Reverend Mr. Knight was a convert to the policy of allaying the ardent Radical spirit of his congregation. His parishioners met in the Spring to remonstrate against the proceedings of the Republicans in the Council of Censors. They were about to sign one of the printed remonstrances when Knight opposed it and counselled moderation. Then they asked him to write a remonstrance. In his draft he avoided the vital question of whether a convention should be called and mentioned as few complaints as he thought would satisfy the people. The dutiful congregation accepted the draft but later made additions to suit their own extreme views.[14]

Muhlenberg made a special effort to appeal to the German population to support the demand of the conservatives for a convention. But Muhlenberg was unfortunate in not possessing an easy style and popular presentation. It can be doubted whether his journalistic endeavors made any impression on his fellow Germans.[15]

The Republicans overshot their mark. By the time the Censors reassembled early in June, the conservatives learned that their appeal to the people had not only been unsuccessful, but that they had completely lost their hold on the censorial body.

Due to an unusual combination of events, the Constitutionalists were now a majority in that body and the hands of the conservatives were completely tied. Samuel Miles, a Republican Censor from the city, suddenly resigned. The cause of this action is not known but it is undoubtedly connected with an earlier event. As was his custom, Comptroller General John Nicholson had reported to the assembly various mistakes or irregularities which he discovered in settling the accounts of public officers handling State monies. Such a report he made concerning Miles. An assembly committee absolved Miles from any irregularity and the Republicans proceeded to pass a resolution acquitting their fellow member of any intention of fraud or perjury in his former financial accounts. Some of Miles' friends then sought Nicholson's scalp and talked about trying to remove him from his post, but the matter was dropped. Soon after the Censors reassembled, Miles sent in his resignation. A new election was ordered and George Bryan, high priest of the Radicals, was the successful candidate.[16]

Other changes took place in the personnel of the Censors. James McLene, a Constitutionalist leader from Cumberland County who did not appear at the first session, now took his seat. William Irvine, Republican from the same county, ceased to attend during the new session. Samuel Davidson, Republican from Bedford County, did not attend. The Constitutionalists gained James Potter from Northumberland County, who was elected to the seat never occupied by Samuel Hunter during the first session. The new composition of the Censors consisted of ten Republicans and fourteen Constitutionalists. John Rose resigned as secretary and his place was filled by Samuel Bryan, one of George Bryan's sons. Henceforth, the committees were dominated by the Radicals.[17]

In the second session of the Censors the Republicans were in the minority. They had given up all hope of a convention or any alteration in the Constitution.[18] Although the more important conservative members like FitzSimons and Muhlenberg fought the Radicals every inch of the way, it was a hopeless battle. The odds were against them; the only thing they could do was to register their dissent in the journals. The Constitutionalists were in an odd position. Their task was to point out the defects in their own frame of government. Undeterred, they went about their work. The report of the committee on the question whether the Constitution had been preserved inviolate detailed charge after charge against the assembly; these charges, however, were against actions of the house when it was controlled by the Republicans. Even the dry journals occasionally sparkled with humor. When the Radicals charged that allowing assemblymen to add a reservation to the prescribed oath of office was a violation of the Constitution, St. Clair jumped to his feet to add that the assemblies so constituted had therefore been unlawful bodies and that all of their acts were in direct violation of the Constitution. The Radicals went so far as to interpret the power of the Censors to cover the actions of the current session of the assembly; accordingly, they passed numerous censures on the Republican house.[19]

Another important committee to report was that on the question whether the taxes had been justly laid and collected in every part of the State. There was relatively little debate on this report and the report itself is the least acrimonious, most probably because of two important factors. A great majority of the taxes had been collected from Republican strongholds while the frontier counties had been very deficient; and it was the conservative Morris who had stabilized the state's financial system as well as the national treasury.[20]

In the last days of the session, the Radicals took special occasion to condemn the Republicans' treatment of the Wyoming settlers and the use of the State military organization at a cost of over four thousand pounds to enforce the claims of the Pennsylvania grantees. It should be understood, however, that the Radicals did not advocate the Connecticut claim. In their eyes the Trenton decree was "a happy event," but the Republicans had not followed it up with wisdom or foresight, nor had the State government acted as guardians of the rights of the Yankees committed to their care. Such action could merit only censure in Radical eyes. It was at this time that the assembly refused to submit certain documents relating to Wyoming and would not allow the request of the Censors to lie on the table. This was interpreted as a grave insult and indignity.[21]

Another question was what laws were to be recommended to the assembly as proper to be repealed because they were contrary to the Constitution. The result was a formidable list of the most important acts passed during the Republican regime.[22]

Finally, the vital question was reached. Should a convention be called? In answer the majority left no doubt when they agreed "That there does not appear to this Council an absolute necessity to call a Convention, to alter, explain, or amend the Constitution." [23] After spending several months in detailing violations of the Constitution and filling page after page of their journals with innumerable examples, how could the Radicals then vote that there was no necessity to alter or amend that document? This predicament they foresaw and justified their conduct by two arguments. In the first place, the Constitution had operated during seven years of war; if the people would follow it as their guide through seven years of peace, they would find no fault with it. In the second place, the faults attributed to the frame of government were not due to the structure of the document, for it was sound in that respect, but they were due to the men in public office who administered the government. If the State were administered by "honest and able men employed to serve the public," if the good of everyone were promoted instead of "hunting down and destroying some of the most faithful friends of the *American* cause," the Constitution would prove to be superior to any other form of government.[24]

In effect the Radicals were preparing an election appeal to the people, calling for justification of their actions and for an endorsement of their political philosophy. Bryan realized the power of propaganda. He had the Censors print five thousand copies of the Constitution in English and the report of the committee on the violations of that instrument, and twenty-five hundred copies in German, so that they might circulate freely over the State.[25] In addition the Radical majority issued an address to the voters. However imperfect the bill of rights and the Constitution might be, the Radicals declared that they were

> firmly persuaded that the constitution of Pennsylvania needs only to be faithfully administered by men, who are honestly disposed to support it according to its true spirit and intention, to be the best system of government in the world.

Unfortunately, they continued, the question of calling a convention "has lain at the bottom of all our disputes." [26] Since no group of men could agree on what changes should be made, they asked that the Constitution should be given a trial for another seven years. The last act of the Censors was to order two copies of their minutes to be sent to Benjamin Franklin.[27] It would be interesting to know that gentleman's observations as he pondered the results of a movement he had fostered and encouraged.

Return of the Constitutionalists

Defeated in the assembly and in the Council of Censors, the Republicans took the offensive in the election campaign of 1784. They detested and feared George Bryan and the ability he displayed in organizing and holding the votes of the Constitutionalists. As a result of this situation their press propaganda consisted of personal attacks on Bryan. He was accused of being the only man who blocked the reprieve for Carlisle and Roberts back in 1778 when seven thousand persons had petitioned the Council for clemency. Prominent Radical assemblymen and Councillors were pictured as "Bryan's tool." That he was characterized as "the old midwife" is one example of the depths to which the political press descended.[28]

A more solid ground of argument was that used by the Radicals when they pointed out that over eighteen thousand persons had signed petitions against calling a convention whereas only two hundred and forty persons had requested a convention. Constitutionalists resorted to the usual tactics of reviewing the actions of the assembly of the past year in the most unfavorable light so as to embarrass the Republicans. The ablest election attack made by the conservatives detailed the extreme partiality with which the Radicals reported on the Constitution in the Council of Censors and the way in which they neglected to censure acts committed by members of their own party. In this respect the Republicans were blacked by the same stick but they did not admit that at election time. Radicals were pictured only as enemies of commerce and industry, and skulkers during the war. "Their patriotism has scarcely extended beyond bawling in a Coffee-house or tavern . . ."[29]

The mechanics were uneasy at this time because the house failed to better their living conditions by neglecting to levy an additional duty on imported manufactures. Torn by the enticements of both major political factions, this laboring class was urged to organize a party of its own and to vote for men who would champion their interest regardless of whether they were Radicals or Republicans.[30]

The election of October, 1784, dealt the Republicans the hardest blow they had received since their emergence in 1780. The counter-revolution went into temporary hibernation. When the people went to the polls on October 12, they turned almost completely against the conservatives. The Radicals captured Philadelphia City and County and all other counties except Chester and York. The extent of the overthrow is demonstrated by the fact that over sixty per cent of the members were new men. The Republicans could count no more than fifteen to seventeen seats in the house. They were almost completely repudiated.[31]

Only in Lancaster County were the election returns seriously contested. The Radicals charged that the Republicans had the ballot box in the borough of Lancaster stuffed with the votes of non-jurors. The new assembly proceeded to disregard the votes cast in that district and seated the men who had the highest votes in the five other districts. Since these were rural regions where the Constitutionalists were strong, the delegation from Lancaster County was all Radical.[32]

The temper of the Radicals was reflected by action taken in Bucks County. Twenty-one leading Radicals from the various townships assembled at Newtown on November 1, elected Richard Backhouse to the chair, and adopted a letter of instructions to their representative in the assembly. Every attempt to encroach on the Constitution must be firmly opposed; the rural regions especially should have a better opportunity to read the bills before they were enacted. They approved the failure to revise the test law; such a change would have had pernicious consequence, but "the spirit of 1776 has not yet lost all its influence among the yeomanry of this state." [33] No less than two-fifths of the inhabitants were non-jurors, and they should not be given the vote. Then the Newtown letter turned to other subjects. It was agreed that the Articles of Confederation had been violated by the State's keeping an armed force in Wyoming without the consent of Congress; and that the early settlers there had been badly treated. They revealed the inspiration of these instructions by referring their representatives to the report of the Council of Censors.

When the assembly convened, its policy for the coming year was indicated in the election of John Bayard as Speaker and Samuel Bryan, son of George Bryan, as Clerk.[34] The policy of the house was to carry out the suggestions of the majority report of the Censors and to undo, as far as possible, all the legislation passed by the Republicans. With triumph and without opposition they set about their task. Republicans like Anthony Wayne and Richard Willing could only sit by and see the work of their counter-revolution speedily reversed.

The house experienced difficulty in selecting delegates to represent the State in Congress. The position of delegate carried with it little prestige. Early in November the house elected Joseph Reed, Cadwalader Morris, William Montgomery, Joseph Gardner, and William Henry. All but Morris were good Constitutionalists. Reed's election was due to a sense of vindication more than anything else. Reed, however, opposed the use of his name and determined not to take his seat unless Congress returned to Philadelphia. Morris resigned. The election of men to fill the vacated seats was delayed time and time again. This was probably due to the progress of a bill to regulate the appointment of delegates which was before the house but which never materialized. In the meantime Joseph Reed died. In February the house elected Matthew Clarkson and David Jackson. A month later Clarkson declined the honor. Finally in April James Wilson and Charles Pettit were chosen, and they accepted. How the Radical house could bring itself to a point of selecting James Wilson is difficult to understand. Several explanations can be suggested. This appointment would take Wilson away from Philadelphia and in one sense deprive the conservatives of their active leader. Moreover, the Wyoming controversy was still pending in Congress and Wilson was conceded to have a legal mastery of that subject.[35]

With power once again in their hands the Constitutionalists determined to rectify certain mistakes of which they found the earlier Republican assemblies guilty. The censure of the assembly in 1783 on Timothy Matlack, stating that he was unworthy of public trust and confidence, was declared unconstitutional and the public proceedings instituted against him were annulled. On the same ground of unwarrantable assumption of power the house rescinded the action of their predecessors in the case of Samuel Miles who had been exonerated by the Republicans from charges of fraud. In this case Pettit tried to strike out the rescinding clause while allowing the censure of the former house to stand, but he was unsuccessful. Another pinprick which annoyed the Constitutionalists was the case of Isaac Austin, brother of an attainted traitor, whom the Republicans had allowed to buy his brother's confiscated property after Baker, a faithful patriot, had purchased it. The Republicans had turned out Baker and handed the house over to Austin. The Radicals now repealed that act, ejected Austin and handed the house back to Baker.[36]

Aside from personalities, the new house took occasion to change certain principles established by the Republicans in former years. Jury trial was provided for persons accused of harboring deserters from French vessels. The act to prevent setting up new states within the confines of Pennsylvania was altered so as to allow trial of offenders in the county in which the act was committed. Former assemblies had exercised the power to vacate roads; now the courts of quarter sessions were granted that power. The excise and tax laws were amended so as to prevent collectors from breaking into houses before oath was made.[37]

The Constitutionalists made a special effort to take care of the judges of the supreme court. The chief justice was granted a thousand pounds a year and the other justices six hundred pound a year; and they were commissioned for seven years. These provisions were made because "fixed and permanent salaries have not been established by act of assembly upon the said judges as ought to have been done." [38] But when the judges asked the assembly for that part of their back pay which they had not received, the request was ignored.

On one of these changes of policy the Republicans put up a stiff fight. This was the bill which would place all the appointive offices with a few exceptions at the disposal of council. Under the list of exceptions the conservatives tried to reserve as many offices as possible to assembly. In two small cases they succeeded. The bill, including the repeal of the appointment of Sharp Delaney as collector of the port, was passed over the protests of the small number of Republicans. The Radicals also determined that all money paid out of the treasury was to be obtained only on warrants from the President and Council. This was a rebuff to the Republicans who in former assemblies had authorized various public officers to draw warrants on the treasurer.[39]

A piece of petty legislation passed by the Radical house in order to embarrass Robert Morris was enacted during this session. Morris had been pressed by Holker to settle the accounts which existed between the two men resulting from Morris' earlier activities in procuring supplies for the French nation. Holker got Congress to recommend to the states to pass laws giving certain privileges to the French agents in State courts in settling their accounts. The Radicals proceeded to pass such a bill against the protest of Morris and despite the arguments of the sixteen dissentients that it gave undue advantages to the French which Americans had not received in French courts. By this strange action against Morris the Radicals favored Holker who on several occasions had roused Reed's ire and had formerly engaged in political activity on the side of the Republicans. The Radicals demanded vengeance on Morris, and took it in this petty form.[40]

To plague Morris further, Comptroller-General Nicholson urged him to settle his accounts with the State respecting the specific supplies which Morris had undertaken to buy for the State back in 1781. Nicholson asserted that the financier owed the State forty-eight hundred dollars, but Morris claimed that that amount had been expended for the general uses of the Federal government. Council authorized Nicholson to take the matter into the courts. The result was that although Morris was cleared and an arrangement was made by the congressional board of treasury to commute the money into supplies, he found the whole affair troublesome and vexatious.[41]

On the matter of the test laws the Republicans gave their opponents no rest. They managed to introduce the subject into the assembly debates whenever possible. In December some conservatives in the house proposed a resolution in connection with a tax measure to the effect that since no man's property could be taken away from him without his consent, and as "it appears that a great proportion of the inhabitants of this State" are disfranchised by the test oaths, a committee should report a bill revising the test laws. The resolution, of course, was killed.[42]

Late in 1784 Benjamin Rush published a pamphlet stating the case of the non-jurors. How widely it circulated, we do not know, but his correspondence indicates that it spurred men from various parts of the State to write to him about the subject. J. Oakely, of Bethlehem, explained that in his community the general temper of the people would admit of no change at that time; but some "Mid-Line," he thought, might break the ground. He suggested an act which would direct non-jurors, who wished to be restored to go before the court of quarter sessions for examination and approbation. This plan, he thought, might be accepted by the people at large. J. W. Hartley of York County indicated that petitions would probably issue from that county in favor of the non-jurors. At the same time he asked Rush for more copies of his pamphlet. An old friend, George Lux, then in Baltimore, suggested to Rush an idea which was probably already well considered by the Republicans, when he wrote: "It is your policy, continually to agitate the question [of the test laws] in Assembly for the relief of the Nonjurors, because though it may miscarry, yet you fix their Children to your Interest, who are continually growing up & entitled to vote, & that body will soon be numerous . . ." [43]

Not satisfied with simply defeating attempts by the conservatives to urge the repeal of the test laws in the house, the Constitutionalists took up the challenge. In March Wayne moved that, since the principal objection made in the last session to revision of the test laws was based on the assertion that it had not been requested by those people, this objection was now removed by petitions lately received by the house from non-jurors. Thereupon he suggested that a committee should report on the petitions. The majority took him at his word. A grand committee of sixteen was appointed, all of whom were strong Radicals except three. In its condescending report, the committee reviewed the actions of the non-jurors during the war and then asked whether such men could expect to enjoy all the privileges arising from the Revolution. These non-jurors were not citizens but only subjects protected benevolently by the government. They did not ask for forgiveness, they did not offer to take the test now. "In fine the most favorable construction we can make for these men is, that they are blind, and have put themselves under the guidance of blind leaders." [44] The committee declared that the government had an unquestionable right to extract tests of allegiance at any time and in any manner, and that it would be dangerous to admit non-jurors to the vote so soon after the war. By a representative vote of forty-two to fifteen, the house adopted the report. No more positive refusal could have been offered. Not only did the Radicals decidedly reject the petitions of the non-jurors, but they justified the action of the minority in the former house. On the minutes they spread their own version of the running away of the nineteen members in September, 1784, because the repeal of the test laws was imminent; they approved and justified the actions of the runaways.[45]

Despite the formal action by the assembly, there is evidence that some of the Radical leaders were beginning to question the wisdom of continuing the test acts. If they would change about face, how could they convert their loyal followers? In the summer of 1785 David Jackson, Constitutionalist delegate to Congress, confided to George Bryan:

> . . . I perfectly coincide with you in opinion that the test laws may now rather be of a mischievous tendency & that there is not so much danger to be apprehended from their repeal as is generally supposed; but the great difficulty is to persuade the real Whigs of this truth—it will require some delicacy & perhaps a little management to make this matter agreeable to their feelings, & indeed considering their sufferings & services in this revolution they ought not to be wantonly offended.[46]

The question was not agitated during the remainder of the session. The matter was allowed to rest until after the fall elections.

While the Constitutionalists were in control of the assembly, Thomas McKean, George Bryan, and Dr. James Hutchinson took the opportunity to have the confiscated estates formerly assigned to the University by Council fully confirmed. The Republicans opposed but, as usual, in vain. Their final effort was to postpone the bill to the next assembly, but the Constitutionalists would take no chances. The last act of the house confirmed the estates to the University.[47]

The persistent and ever optimistic Lewis Hallam again petitioned the Radical assembly for the right to open a theatre in Philadelphia. A committee on the subject reported favorably but the house killed the report by a vote of twenty-eight to thirty-two. The political complexion of the assembly made no difference for the members did not divide on party lines of this social question. Nor can the vote be generalized on sectional divisions. Some Radicals from the back-county voted for and some voted against it. The city, Philadelphia and Bucks counties, which were controlled by Radicals, voted ten to three in favor of the measure. York County, represented mainly by Republicans, split four to four, while the Radicals from Berks voted in favor of the theatre. The causes obviously were due to the religious and moral antecedents of each member.[48]

Launching the Radical Program

Of the numerous objectives entertained by the Constitutionalists four were outstanding. They wanted to fund the Federal certificates held by State citizens; they were obligated to do something to relieve the distress of the artisan class suffering from hard times; they were determined to destroy the Bank; and they thought they could do a better job than the conservatives had done with the perennial Wyoming problem.

The Constitutionalists had very definite ideas in regard to the vast debt owed by the United States to citizens of the State in the form of loan office certificates, quarter master and commissary general certificates. Republicans and Constitutionalists agreed that the certificates issued by the loan office and the various army departments during the war should be funded and the interest paid. But the Radicals believed that this action should be taken by the State, since the national government had failed to secure the approval of all states to the financial plan of 1783 to produce an independent revenue. A committee of public creditors from the Philadelphia area, composed of members of both parties made urgent appeals to the assembly for immediate payment of interest on these obligations. The first action looking to a speedy funding of these certificates was an act of assembly, empowering the President to appoint two additional commissioners to settle the certificates; that is, to reduce them to specie value and to determine how much the interest would amount to in each case. Since the act disregarded the right of Congress and proceeded to have United States certificates settled by commissioners appointed by the State, Dickinson was loath to appoint the commissioners. He made a strong appeal to Congress to provide additional commissioners in the State so that he would not be forced to do it himself. Just before the law went into effect, Congress consented and appointed one extra agent for the State.[49]

More important than the settlement of certificates was the plan which the Radicals adopted to pay the interest on these certificates. The assembly planned to assume all debts due to State citizens from either Congress or the State and to pay the interest by a combination of revenue from the sale of public lands, a general tax, and an issue of paper money. President Dickinson took exception to the plan. He asserted there should be a discrimination between original holders of certificates and dealers in certificates. Collection of the arrearages of back taxes, he thought, would provide sufficient specie to pay off the interest to original holders who were the most deserving group; the back lands could be sold at a fixed price per acre in payment of which the holders of alienated certificates might redeem their investments. Stripped of all verbiage which flowed between Council and assembly over the problem, the crucial struggle was between speculators in depreciated public certificates and property owners who would be called on for additional taxes to fund these certificates.[50]

It seems strange, indeed, that the Radicals should have fathered this funding bill which proved a veritable gold mine for speculators. There were substantial reasons for this. The man at the head of the plan was the moderate Radical Charles Pettit who was known to be a large holder in certificates; it was rumored that he would receive six thousand pounds annually in interest on these securities. He took such a personal interest in seeing the act passed that privately he referred to it as "My funding Plan." [51] Some Radical leaders from the western counties were also speculating in these certificates. Aside from Pettit, other prominent Philadelphia Radicals like Jonathan D. Sergeant were large holders. Although the Republicans as a group opposed the measure, there were several outstanding members of that political persuasion like Benjamin Rush, John Nixon, and Peter Wikoff, who had accumulated a significant amount of the certificates. On the other hand, Dickinson and most of the Council members were not financially interested. Another angle of the story is interesting. Many western members of the assembly looked longingly at the lands beyond the last Indian purchase which were said to be of excellent quality. They wished to secure a right of preemption to this fertile soil. The city speculators proposed a compromise: if the westerners would vote to fund the certificates, the easterners would vote to establish a title to the western lands.[52]

The battle for and against the plan was waged in the newspapers. The committee of public creditors made concerted efforts to counteract Dickinson's opposition to the bill. The bill became law by a vote of forty-seven to eighteen, the latter composing the Republican minority in the house. Their protest was aimed mainly at the fact that the State thus assumed the burden of paying interest on over one-third of the total amount of loan office certificates issued by the United States government whereas actually Pennsylvania had always been rated as only one-eighth of the Confederation.[53]

An important part of the Radical plan was to issue a hundred fifty thousand pounds in bills of credit, of which fifty thousand pounds were appropriated to set up a loan office and the remainder to be used to pay the interest on public obligations. In vain did the Republican merchants oppose this effort to introduce paper money; their argument that it was prejudicial to the commercial interests of the State fell on deaf ears. The memory of the days of 1778-1781 was still green. Furthermore, the Republican policy following Robert Morris' lead was definitely opposed to all paper money schemes. They pointed out that the non-jurors would not accept the new money. The Radicals realized that they were encountering great obstacles. Dickinson and Council had vigorously condemned the measure. Judge Bryan wrote to a friend: ". . . but the paper money! There's the rub! It has too been damned by the Council before its appearance. Indeed there is reason to doubt; there is ground for apprehension." [54] The conservative Bank, of course, opposed the new money.

While the bill was in process of passage, the Radicals insisted that the new emission should not be made legal tender so as to avoid serious depreciation. Some playful Republican then moved that the various officers of government, including assemblymen, should receive their pay in the new paper. The embarrassed Radicals were not content to kill this motion but spread on the record four paragraphs of indignation over such an "unseasonable motion" which had "a manifest tendency to cast an undeserved odium upon the majority of this House."[55] Scarcely did the Constitutionalists realize that the Minister of the Netherlands had already warned his home country of the new emission. It "must have a great influence on the trade of that state," he explained; "for should they compel foreigners to receive this paper money in payment for their goods, it is easy to foresee that the commercial connections between that state and Europe will not only diminish, but will virtually be severed."[56]

The year 1785 saw a decrease in trade at the port of Philadelphia, and general dull times. It was assumed that one of the factors in the tightening financial situation was the excess of imports over exports with a resulting flow of coin out of the State. As the year progressed, evidences of commercial decay appeared. American ships no longer went from England to the continent for goods but returned with only ballast and crew. Bankruptcy became fashionable as public and private credit went to ruin. There were the usual rantings against the purchase of luxuries, trifles, and gewgaws from abroad. Naive observers pointed out that this was the cause of the declining economic situation. An extract from a letter of Robert Henderson, a Philadelphia merchant, gives his view of the situation as well as the political forecast:

> . . . times here still continue as bad as ever[;] hard money is going out of sight very fast and produce still continues high & Business very dull at present but as it is expected we are to have a change in publick Affairs this Fall it is generally believed Business will revive by that time . . .[57]

The importation of British goods and the prohibition of American ships from the British West Indies and other British possessions stirred the people into action. Late in 1784 the house agreed to Congress's request that that national body should be vested with power to prohibit import and export of goods in any vessels belonging to nations which had not made commercial treaties with the United States. It was soon realized that this measure was ineffective. Sentiment was finally consolidated in favor of drastic actions against the British commercial menace. An increasing number of articles appeared in the newspapers calling attention to the tariffs passed by Maryland and Massachusetts.[58]

In the meantime the mechanics and manufacturers of Philadelphia pressed the assembly for a protective tariff. At this time manufacturing was engaged in on a small scale; the moneyed men had not yet found this field a promising one for large investments; they continued to look to importing and shipping. Thus it was the artisan class which had a definite interest in protective tariffs. They had suffered from the post-war depression. After the Republican assemblies had done nothing for them, the Constitutionalists attracted their votes by the promise, vague as it might have been, of taking care of them. There is the suggestion that after they came into power the Radicals found obstacles, if not an actual disinclination, to pass a protective tariff. Not until March did the assembly committee report a bill for this purpose; it hung fire over the summer and was not passed until a few weeks before the election of 1785. As the house did not take decisive action at once, various interested groups resorted to other methods. In March the master cordwainers planned to discourage the importation of boots and shoes by agreeing not to buy, sell, or mend imported shoes. Other groups asked for protection of certain industries such as iron, leather, hemp, and pins.[59]

If there was to be a tariff laid by the State, the Republicans advocated only the principle of revenue. They were more interested, however, in nationalizing the problem by vesting Congress with full power to regulate commerce. The Constitutionalists agreed to this general proposition but at a mass meeting they stressed the encouragement of home manufactures by absolute prohibition or substantial duties on all foreign manufactures. The Republicans tried to ignore this action of their enemy but the Radicals gained in popularity. President Dickinson, on the other hand, stated the Republican view when he declared that Congress should not only have the right to regulate and protect commerce, but it should impose import duties for revenue purposes and should appoint the collectors of this money. Agreeing that the national legislature should regulate commerce, the Radicals feared that too much power might be vested in Congress. Samuel Bryan revealed this jealousy of State rights when he wrote: "the difficulty is how to regulate such powers with the individual importance of the several states to prevent Congress in that event absorbing all power and influence within their vortex." [60] He wanted the duties collected by officers independent of Congress, appointed and removable by the states in which they acted; and the revenue to be paid into each state treasury for its own uses. Finally in September, about two weeks before election, the Constitutionalist assembly passed the protective tariff designed to encourage a host of enumerated manufactures. The duties were largely specific in nature.[61] At last the Radicals had taken care of the artisan class.

It was inevitable that the Constitutionalists would use their unopposed power in the assembly to strike at the Bank of North America. This institution represented to them the citadel of the Republican wealth, the power in the financial affairs of the State, and, above all, a closed corporation controlled by their political enemies. The Radicals wished only for an excuse to attack the financial ogre. The Bank played into their hands by refusing to give credit to the new emission of paper money. So the Radicals adopted the rallying cry that the Bank was destructive to the public interest and set out to demolish the institution. The attack had begun late in 1784 with newspaper articles detailing the vices of the institution. This was followed by numerous petitions to the assembly complaining of the monopolistic features of the Bank.[62]

In March, 1785, Whitehill and Smiley used several of these petitions as a springboard for action. They had the petitions referred to a committee to inquire whether the Bank was "compatible with the public safety and that equality which ought ever to prevail between individuals of a republic." The resulting report reflected what might be called the "official" Radical case against the institution. From every point of view the Bank was incompatible with public safety. The stockholders had cornered the money-market; this monopoly had increased bank profits while money daily grew scarcer. These profits tempted foreigners to invest in the Bank and thus they drew out of the State large sums in interest. This line of reasoning was pursued further when the report suggested that the foreigners might eventually obtain such an influence in the Bank as to make "this enormous engine of power" "subject to foreign influence." But even in the hands of Americans the institution was wholly destructive of republican equality, according to the Radicals. "Already we have felt its influence indirectly interfering in the measures of the legislature."[63] The Bank had threatened not to give credit to the new paper money. Soon the Bank would dictate to the assembly. Before this report was adopted by the house Pettit attempted a compromise by suggesting that the charter should be altered and not repealed. But the Radicals would have no half-way measures; they demanded the end of the institution. One day after the report was adopted, a committee introduced a bill to repeal the incorporating act.[64]

The friends of the Bank made only belated efforts in defense. A few weak articles appeared in the public prints. Late in March the Bank memorialized the assembly for the privilege of being heard, but the house ignored the plea. It is probable that the Bank planned to use the coming summer, when the assembly would be in recess, to influence the people and to prepare its defensive tactics. One method was to refuse discounts; this would have a devastating effect on trade and might convince the people at large of the need of the Bank. James Wilson was the man on whom the Bank interests relied to present their case. By the time the assembly had reconvened late in August, Wilson had prepared a printed pamphlet written with the purpose of influencing Congress and the assembly; pieces in a more popular vein were planned for general consumption among the public. Thomas Willing, president of the institution, made a fervent plea to Wilson, then a delegate in Congress, to take whatever steps he considered necessary for the interest of the Bank. Apparently Willing believed that Congress would object to the proposed repeal of the charter which would constitute "a stab—a mortal stab" to the honor of the national legislature and to the credit of the nation.[65] Meanwhile the Radicals learned that Robert Morris was exepecting the worst and had already planned a new bank under his own name. Furthermore, rumor had it that Morris would attempt to win a seat in the assembly in the fall so as to be in a better position to defend the Bank; if this were the case, warned David Jackson, "it behooves the friends of the constitution to be vigilant & active." [66]

With the reconvening of the house late in August, the Bank launched its formal defense. Again it memorialized the house for the right to be heard. In a most condescending manner the assembly granted this plea. For two days the case was laid before the house, James Wilson speaking for the Bank and Jonathan Dickinson Sergeant for the repeal of the charter. The belief that few set speeches have ever changed votes in the legislative hall was true in this case. In vain did Wilson explain all the benefits which the Bank had conferred on the state and the nation; in vain did the merchants and traders of the city petition for a compromise measure whereby only the charter would be limited and the capital decreased. But the Radicals would not waver. *Cartago est delenda.* One week after Wilson and Sergeant had spoken, the bill to repeal the incorporating act passed. When the Bank affair had first come before that house, the Republicans had mustered eighteen votes; now their strength had declined to twelve. As was customary they left their statement of the case on the *Minutes.* No actual proof, they asserted, had been given that the Bank was injurious to the State. The repeal was a dangerous precedent and an arbitrary exercise of power; in other words, property was at stake. Growing more bold, they claimed that the institution could not be destroyed even by the powers that created it. Finally, the Bank had been established on the recommendation of Congress; common decency required that Congress should be notified of the reasons of the assembly's repeal. This last point had already been answered by Sergeant with characteristic Radical reasoning: "We are not bound by any terms made by Congress—Congress are our creatures!" [67]

Another objective of the Constitutionalists was to deal with the Wyoming problem in their own way. Despite the Trenton decree, the use of the militia, and the strong-arm methods of Patterson and John Armstrong, the Yankee settlers would not be crushed. The outlook was not auspicious, for Connecticut was again taking an active interest in the fate of her orphaned sons of the upper Susquehanna. At New Haven the State assembly extended an encouraging hand to their former citizens, and directed its delegates to press Congress for a trial to the right of soil. When the question came up in Congress, the Pennsylvania delegates were absent. At a later time the agents for the Connecticut settlers did not appear. Thus the matter dropped temporarily in Congress.[68]

Having criticized the Republicans for their management of the Wyoming affair, the Radical house now put its hand to the task. Disposed to use lenient measures, the assembly decided to make a fresh start by sending a committee to the region to inquire what would be necessary for the peace and good order of the inhabitants and the regular administration of justice. During the summer the Pennsylvania delegates thought it best not to move in the business in Congress before the assembly had a chance to act on the report of the committee.

If the Radicals expected the Wyoming problem to be settled easily, they were soon disillusioned. Bayard, Frazer, and Smith reported that the chief complaint concerned the choice and appointment of magistrates, branded the measures pursued by the settlers as subversive, and doubted their declarations of willingness to submit to the government of Pennsylvania. They pointed out that the Wyoming settlers felt free to use violent methods to drive out any Pennsylvania claimants. The committee believed it necessary that Congress should provide for a trial to the right of soil. With this question decided, the State could then determine what steps to take to reduce the disorderly inhabitants to submission. The assembly thereupon instructed the delegates to ask Congress for an immediate decision on the private right of soil. After some parliamentary fencing, the Pennsylvania delegates gained their end, for Congress threw out the petition of the Wyoming claimants on a technicality.[69]

Political Pendulum at Dead Center

The political pendulum in Pennsylvania rarely ceased to move. The Republicans in 1784-1785 had been hopelessly submerged in the assembly. In the October elections the pendulum began to swing back towards conservatism. On their return to power the Radicals became too violent in trying to turn back the clock. They had re-introduced paper money which depreciated; they had funded the certificates with obvious benefit to speculators; and they had destroyed the Bank with gleeful vengeance. These excesses were too much. The voters began to turn to the leaders of respectability.

In the City of Philadelphia there was an unusual situation where both parties agreed unanimously on one man, Benjamin Franklin. Returning from France but a month before election, all hailed him with enthusiasm. The *Packet* voiced the sentiments of the public when it declared eulogistically that Providence had restored Franklin to Pennsylvania, the only man who could command the respect of both warring political factions.[70]

Seeking to profit by Franklin's presence, the Constitutionalists immediately championed him as their leader. The assembly in the hands of the Radicals managed to propagate their political philosophy even while formally addressing him: ". . . we have the happiness of welcoming into the State a person who was so greatly instrumental in forming its free and excellent constitution . . ." The tactful Franklin did not disappoint them. "I hope," he replied, ". . . that the free constitution we now enjoy, may long contribute to promote our common felicity . . ."[71] The Constitutionalist Society asked him to be their candidate for Councillor and he accepted. It was generally agreed that he would be elected to Council and thence to the presidential chair. Earlier plans of the two parties gave way to this man. Morris was no longer considered for the office; Pettit was to be the leading candidate of the Radicals until they learned of Franklin's acceptance.[72]

The Radicals were not so fortunate in their contest for the Philadelphia City and County seats in the assembly. The Constitutional Party and Mechanical Society put up the men who had sat in the last assembly. The conservatives flirted with the laboring group in an effort to detach them from the Radicals; in Philadelphia the Republicans assumed the party name of "Friends of Equal Liberty." At the polls the Constitutionalists received a severe shock. Although the Republicans succeeded in capturing all the seats in Philadelphia City and County, the contest was a close one. All votes were cast for Franklin for Councillor and for William Will for the assembly. But only by a margin of about a hundred votes were Robert Morris, Thomas FitzSimons, James Irvine and George Clymer successful.[73]

In other parts of the State the Republicans made significant, though not decisive, gains. Lancaster replaced its Radicals with conservatives. Chester and York continued to support the Republicans. In Montgomery and Northampton Counties the Radicals won by a hair's breadth.[74] Of the seventy-five members in the house, only thirty-three of the former assembly remained. Of course, a number of the new members were Radicals from the back-country.

One serious contested election gave rise to party quibbling. The trouble arose over two sets of returns from Northampton County. In one of the districts there were ten more ballots than recorded electors. After some petty parliamentary fencing between Whitehill and Hannum, which showed that neither party would trust the other and that the Republicans were holding off for time, the conservatives won their point in declaring Maclay legally elected although Montgomery had three more votes. In Philadelphia the increasing population made it impossible for all the electors to vote in Mulberry ward. These people later petitioned for a division of the ward on the ground that in the October elections nearly half of them were deprived of voting because of the want of time to take their ballots.[75]

When the assembly met, the two factions were almost equally divided. The first few days of any house were always important because of the election of the Speaker and other officers and because the arrival of tardy members might at any time overthrow the calculations of either faction. Such was the case in October, 1785.

During the first few days the Constitutionalists delayed as much as possible in the hope that more of their faith would arrive from the back-country. For the same reason the Republicans counseled haste. On the first day a quorum was prevented by the lack of two members. The four Cumberland Radicals who appeared that day did not have their official return. They had left it in the hands of the county sheriff who explained that it was not quite ready but that he would forward it with Councillor Woods. Radical members of the house thought this augured design. The following day a quorum was prevented by a death in the family of one of the assemblymen. In the meantime, Smiley, outstanding Radical leader from the west, came to town and the house proceeded to business. But the return of the four Cumberland members did not appear, and the Radicals were "now in a critical situation," as the Clerk of the house explained it. They resorted to maneuver; two members absented themselves and thus prevented a quorum. That night and the next morning seven back-country Radicals arrived in town, and Councillor Woods turned up with the return for the four Cumberland members. The Constitutionalists were now ready to begin business.[76]

The early organization of the house indicated the close division between the two factions. Not wishing to lose one of their best men from active service on the floor, the Radicals ran General Mifflin for Speaker. Unwilling to risk defeat, Mifflin had declined to run the day before, but with the advent of the western members, he realized that the Radicals could carry him into the office. The Republicans advanced George Clymer, likewise not wishing to lose Morris or FitzSimons from active service on the floor. The vote stood thirty-three for Mifflin and twenty-nine for Clymer. The vote for Clerk was similar, thirty-three for Samuel Bryan and thirty for Lloyd. These two successive blows dashed the hope which the Republicans had entertained. Apparently they had been confident of success, for in the early days of the house, before the votes had been taken for Speaker and Clerk almost two hundred conservative partisans had filled the gallery; "and till Thursday," explained Samuel Bryan, "not one of our friends." [77]

To capture the office of Vice-President was the aim of both parties. It was understood by general agreement that Franklin would be elected President but that due to his age, he would not be very active in the office. Therefore, the contest for the second office became significant. The Republicans looked to Henry Hill as their best candidate, and had every hope of success; the lack of four votes in the assembly would be compensated for, they thought, by their strength in the Council where they had a majority of two or three. It was to their interest to hurry on the election before more western members arrived. In this they succeeded. The election of President and Vice-President took place about two weeks earlier than in previous years. Very hastily and secretively, according to the Radicals, the Council at five o'clock in the afternoon of October 28 arranged for the election the next morning at eleven. It was believed that the conservatives had adopted this precipitate action because they believed they could muster a majority, and because the Constitutionalists might not have agreed on their candidate. If these were their plans, they were disappointed by an unforeseen event. The night before the election two Radicals from the West arrived in town, and it was rumored that a third had appeared. On learning this news, the conservatives of the Council hurriedly conferred and decided to avoid a third defeat by acquiescing in the election of Charles Biddle, a mild Constitutionalist. On the following day by an almost unanimous vote, Franklin became President and Biddle Vice-President. Franklin's situation in his new office was not easy. At heart a Constitutionalist, he was not in sympathy with some of the important tenets of that faction. Although it was generally understood that his task was to placate the two political factions, the Republicans openly assumed that he would champion their principles.[78]

The election of delegates to Congress brought on another contest between the two factions. John Bayard and Charles Pettit received thirty-nine votes each, St. Clair thirty-six, and William Henry thirty-five. When the ballots were counted, it was discovered that sixty-eight had been cast although there were only sixty-seven members present. On the motion to elect a fifth delegate, James Wilson received thirty-four ballots over his rival Jackson who netted thirty-three. Four months later the Radicals moved to appoint two additional delegates to Congress but this was scotched by Morris and Clymer.[79]

The year 1786 marked a distinct victory for the Republicans on the vexed subject of test laws. Scarcely had the house assembled when petitions were presented for a revision of these acts. A group from Philadelphia who had memoralized the assembly in the last session repeated their request to be removed from a "state of vassalage." Several religious societies in Montgomery County explained the good relief work they had done among the soldiers during the war and then asked for a repeal of the hated laws. A week later an interesting memorial came from the freeholders of Byberry township, in Philadelphia County, reciting that there were not enough voters in the township to fill the elective offices and that it was necessary to bring in men to administer these duties.[80]

Franklin fully approved the abolition of the test laws. This was one of the first aims of his administration, for only two weeks after the house met and soon after the petitions for repeal had been received, he declared in a formal message to the assembly that however proper and necessary those laws might have been at an earlier period, they were at present the cause of much uneasiness within the State; ". . . it is now expedient to revise them."[81] It should be noted that he did not specify how far they should be revised.

At once the Republicans set to work. Morris and FitzSimons proposed that Franklin's message should be referred to a committee. Smiley, leading the Constitutionalists, countered with a proposal to refer it to a grand committee. Wayne suggested a committee of the whole. The Radicals believed that in a grand committee, that is, a committee composed of one member from each county, they could muster sufficient votes from the back-country to defeat the plan. The Republicans wanted to keep the subject before the whole house where they were confident of a sufficient number of votes, or to commit it to a group which they could control. The message was referred to a committee of one member from each county with Morris as chairman. In this group there were eight for and eight against repeal. A deadlock ensued and the committee was dissolved. By a special vote a new committee of five was appointed; all the members were favorable to repeal. Within two days it made a report advocating citizenship for all men except those under attainder or those who voluntarily aided the British during the war. The house adopted this report and within three weeks the bill was transcribed and printed, despite the demand of the Radicals for a vote on important parts of it.[82]

When the assembly re-convened in the early part of 1786 the die-hard Radicals vainly persisted in their opposition. Using strong words and even intimating that they might resort to arms, the Constitutionalists of Dauphin County petitioned the house against the bill. The petition was not even allowed to lie on the table because of its unusual language. Several other petitions were received from the same county. Victorious so far, Morris attempted to broaden the bill. He tried to strike out the provision that non-jurors must take an oath of abjuration and also the clause declaring them to swear that they had never voluntarily aided the British. Both resolutions were negatived. On March 4, 1786, the act passed by a vote of forty-five to twenty-three. The vote discloses a sectional division. The eastern counties, except Bucks, voted solidly for the bill. The western counties, except Westmoreland, voted against it. Cumberland and Bedford Counties divided.[83]

The act revising the test laws contains some interesting features. The preamble condoned the passage of the original restrictions as a war necessity. The non-jurors were now given "another opportunity of testifying their allegiance and fidelity" to the State. They could regain citizenship by taking an oath of allegiance and abjuration before any justice of the peace. The oath included a declaration that the juror had since July, 1776, never voluntarily joined or aided the English forces. Those who had been attainted of treason or who had joined or abetted the savages in their attack against the states were excepted from the scope of the act.[84] The passing of this act was an important milestone in the counter-revolution. As the passions of war were cooling, the Radicals were losing ground. The cry of "tory, tory" became an empty sound. With few exceptions all men in the State could now exercise the franchise.

The domestic issues discussed in the assembly during this session covered a variety of topics. They were for the most part old questions. The nice balance between the two political parties made it difficult to foretell the outcome on any issue. Each faction gained some of its points and lost some points so that the result could best be characterized as a tie. The controversial domestic issues were tariff alterations, the re-charter of the Bank, altering the charter of the Scots' Presbyterian Church, licensing of the theatre and penal reform.

Several manufacturing interests in the State which had not been favored by the general tariff act of 1784-1785 brought their complaints before the house. Exporters trading with Portugal succeeded in having the duties on wines and fruits of that nation repealed. Sugar refiners complained of English competition but did not receive any favorable legislation. Merchants and traders of the city complained that trade and revenue of Pennsylvania were diverted to neighboring states due to the additional tonnage laid on foreign vessels and the additional duty on rum imported in foreign bottoms. Accordingly, the duty on rum was repealed and the tonnage duty on foreign shipping lowered. The shipbuilding trades were to be protected by a proviso which abolished the tonnage duty altogether if the ships, although owned by foreign powers, had been built or would be built in Pennsylvania in the future.[85]

The manufacturers of bar iron were vitally interested in the tariff rates on that product. They asked the house for a higher protective duty. In the past year three hundred tons of nails had been imported; this reduced the price of the domestic product so as to put some forge owners out of business. Accordingly, an additional duty of one penny per pound was laid on all imported nails and spikes. In this connection the house took another action. In order to encourage Whitehead Humphreys, a Republican, to utilize a process he had discovered to manufacture bar iron into steel, the assembly advanced him a small loan. This passed by a close vote of thirty-one to twenty-nine, the Republicans voting for it and the Constitutionalists opposing it. The conflict between the iron manufacturers who were demanding protection and the rest of the people who wanted inexpensive products was coming to the fore, as Jasper Yeates explained when he wrote:

> . . . It strikes me forcibly that the Legislature will not lay a Duty on the foreign Iron imported, unless some practicable System can be devised, ascertaining to them that the Manufacturers here shall not demand exorbitant Rates upon the Sales of what is made amongst us. How to effect this is a Matter of Difficulty, & the Country at large are too much interested in the Prices of Iron, to expect Success without some satisfactory encouragement to this Purpose. It certainly is a Matter of considerable national Magnitude.[86]

Despite the significant number of Radicals in the house, the Bank did not give up its fight against the repeal of the charter. The Republicans called into service the ability of Thomas Paine, pamphleteer extraordinary. Hopkinson planned to join his wit with Paine's forceful arguments in a common literary production in order to make the opponents of the Bank stand out in the most absurd light. The Republicans launched their campaign for the Bank through the usual preliminary step of petitions to the assembly. The president and directors of the institution presented their complaints, stating that the repealing act was injurious to the Bank, inconsistent with the security of a free government because the bill to protect bank notes from the counterfeiters' art had likewise been abolished, and—the strongest argument advanced by the Bank interests—that no facts were proved to justify the removal of the charter. They prayed for the repeal of the repealing act. No immediate action was taken on this petition. When the house re-convened in the spring of 1786 a long petition with six hundred twenty-four signatures was presented in which the methods used last year in repealing the charter were severely attacked. A committee was then appointed to consider the petitions concerning the Bank. Three of the committeemen were for the Bank, two opposed. Concurrent with the renewal of agitation in the assembly, the press broke forth with articles in favor of the Bank. This publicity took the form of attacks on the Radicals and their program rather than constructive argument in favor of the Bank. One writer lamented that since Delaware had chartered the Bank and made Wilmington and New Castle free ports, this would shift the seat of the import and export trade from Philadelphia. Paine asserted that agitation against the Bank was continued in order to divert attention from the Radical speculators who were making twenty to thirty per cent on the paper money issued as a result of their funding bill.[87]

The question came to a head in the assembly in April when the committee made its report. All the arguments against the repeal of the charter were summed up with the words "Precipitancy, prejudice, and partiality." [88] The committee suggested that the repealing act should be rescinded. The western Radicals were joined by a sufficient number of other members in order to negative the measure by a vote of twenty-seven to forty-one. Persisting against these odds, Morris offered what he termed an alternative proposal, that a bill should be reported to suspend the repealing act for a certain number of years. This met a similar defeat. The Bank question was not broached during the rest of the session.[89]

A squabble within the congregation and elders of the Scots' Presbyterian Church in Philadelphia intruded itself on the assembly. The prerevolutionary charter of the Church stipulated that it was subject to the jurisdiction of the mother church in Edinburgh. The Radical part of the congregation did not relish this situation and appealed to the assembly for redress. Then the minister and several other members sent in a petition to counteract the effect of the first address. During the summer of 1786 the controversy raged. Late in August when the assembly discussed the incorporating of certain churches—and numerous churches were incorporated about this time—the whole question of the sanctity of charters was debated. Were charters of non-political institutions nullified by the Revolution? Clymer and FitzSimons denied that they were; Smiley stoutly insisted that the Revolution had wiped out charters and he quoted section forty-five of the Constitution to uphold his contention. Clymer flatly contradicted him with the exception that charters bearing on government such as the charter of the city had expired with the Revolution; he pointed out that under Smiley's thesis private property held under similar charters would be affected. A bill to remove the objectionable clause from the charter of the Scots' Presbyterian church was successful on a test vote by forty-two to eighteen. All but four of the minority were staunch Republicans. They appealed to this act as a precedent dangerous to religious liberties; at bottom, however, it was the threat to the sanctity of charters which annoyed them. Although the group which had lost petitioned for a repeal of the act, nothing was done.[90]

Just as the question over legalizing the theater and stage plays became a burning issue in the assembly of 1784-1785, so did it arouse passion in the assembly of this year. When a new bill came forward in the house, all the Calvinsim of the Scotch-Irish Presbyterians of the frontier region was represented in Whitehill who moved for a fine on every attempt to open a theater. This was lost by eight votes. On the whole question over legalizing the theater, although party lines tended to be erased, in general the back-country Radicals, especially the Scotch-Irish group, voted against the theater, while the conservatives from Philadelphia and those representatives with German names from the middle tier of counties, voted for the theater. At the end of the session in September, 1786, the bill came to a final debate and vote. During the intervening months it had been before the people for consideration. Something happened to change at least eight votes in the house. The bill passed with a provision for a fine of two hundred pounds on any one convicted of staging a play. The blue stocking Radicals continued to impress their moral ideas on the sophisticated Philadelphians.[91]

At this time public attention was turned to the penal laws. In the Constitution it had been suggested that they should be made less sanguinary. In the fall of 1785 a petition signed by Justices McKean and Bryan and other prominent citizens asked for changes in the law and suggested the method of punishment at hard labor "publicly and disgracefully imposed," as an innovation.[92] Although both political factions united on revision of the penal code, they disagreed over some details of the proposed bill which came before the house. The main point at issue was whether discretionary power should be vested in the judges. The Republicans generally wanted to set a definite term of years for the punishment of given offenses which the judges would be required to impose when sentencing offenders. If there were good reasons why the full sentence should not be served, then the offender could resort to the Executive Council which had the pardoning power. The Constitutionalists, on the other hand, insisted that there should be a discretionary power vested in the court whereby light punishment might be meted out at once if the case seemed to merit it. One point was clear in the minds of the assemblymen; the Republicans were unwilling to lodge a discretionary power in the hands of the supreme court which was dominated by their rivals, the Constitutionalists. Council was in the hands of the Republicans and their opponents were just as loath to confer powers, which in turn became favors, on that body. The Republicans, however, could not muster sufficient votes to carry their point. The motions to lower the time of imprisonment for offenses were initiated and carried by the Radicals.[93]

The question of incorporating the city of Philadelphia had been brought up numerous times in past assemblies. Acting on petitions, the house appointed the city members to report such a bill. At this stage a test vote showed only a dozen Constitutionalists opposed to it. In April the bill went through the second reading but was then shelved. Several days before the end of the session in September Smiley brought up the subject either in order to have the bill killed or more likely to make an election appeal to the Radicals of the city. In a speech bristling with quotations from Montesquieu and cases in English History, Smiley opposed all incorporations and more specifically the incoporation of Philadelphia because the Council would be elected only by freeholders who, he asserted, did not number one-quarter of the inhabitants. The Republicans answered that none of them expected the bill to be passed as it was printed for public consideration, but that there would be many changes. They based the plea for incorporation on the need of better regulation of the city, especially in regard to adequate police protection. The enacting clause was lost by a vote of twenty-four to thirty-five. The Republicans let the measure rest though a conservative newspaper indicated that the new house would take favorable action; and it pointed to a recent epidemic of robberies as evidence that a charter was necessary to insure greater protection to the inhabitants.[94]

Problems of the Confederation

Although the members of the assembly had their hands full with domestic issues, there were questions of national import which commanded their attention. At this time three problems assumed importance; they were the payment of interest on United States certificates, the cession of Connecticut's claims to western lands, and the proposed Spanish treaty which threatened to close the Mississippi River to American navigation.

Early in 1786 the assembly took a bold step when it decided to assume on loan all United States certificates held by Pennsylvania citizens, and to pay the interest on them semi-annually. A test vote showed forty-one assemblymen for the measure and twenty-two opposed. The minority consisted entirely of Republicans including Robert Morris, Thomas FitzSimons, George Clymer, and less important lights from Chester, Lancaster, and York counties. The back-counties were solidly for the measure. This act simply continued the system adopted the previous year when the Radicals had granted one year's interest on the certificates. The act of 1786 made the interest a permanent feature.[95]

At the same time the financial situation of Congress became acute. That body saw hope only if it could obtain the five-per-cent impost which it had asked several years before. But to make the impost palatable it had been accompanied by a requisition for supplementary funds. Most of the states had adopted the joint proposals but under different conditions, and several, like Pennsylvania, provided that their grant should not go into effect until it was adopted by all states. New Jersey, for example, flatly refused to comply until New York and Pennsylvania would apply the impost to Federal measures. With the knot tightened by such actions, Congress attempted to have all states agree at least to the impost so that it could go into operation in the near future. Pennsylvania was asked to separate the impost from the supplementary funds and to make it effective without the consent of all states. The assembly, thereupon, passed an act granting to Congress the supplementary funds amounting to over $200,000, which was the State's quota, and the five-per-cent impost. But it stipulated that out of the impost was to be paid annually the interest on all continental debts held by citizens of the State on conditions which the State should prescribe. Nor was the grant to Congress effective until all the states should adopt the impost.[96]

Congress did all in its power to induce Pennsylvania to separate the two grants and to lift the demand that all states must agree to the impost before it could go into operation. On July 27 it ordered the drafting of an ordinance assuming control of the impost as soon as Pennsylvania, New York, and Delaware modified their acts. Then it decided to send a commission with a special plea to the assembly. Rufus King and James Monroe were chosen for this task. After insisting that they were sent to address the whole assembly, and not a committee of that body, King and Monroe discoursed before the house. The chamber was crowded for the event. King had carefully prepared his address but after uttering a few words he lost mental control. Monroe presented the arguments and then King went through his speech without incident. The argument used was that if Pennsylvania persisted in appropriating its continental requisition to its own citizens, there would soon be no contributions made to Congress. Henry Hill was of the opinion that if the members would have been individually questioned on the spot, a majority would have agreed that the impost should be granted without reserve. It was to be otherwise. Some Congressmen believed that if Pennsylvania could be won over, New York would no longer dare to oppose the impost. The commission only wasted its breath. Monroe realized this when he wrote to Madison the day before he addressed the assembly: "Both parties are united in opposition to it." [97] Two days after the congressional delegates had made their plea, the important party leaders, Morris, FitzSimons, and Clymer for the Republicans and Whitehill, Findley, and Smiley for the Radicals, were constituted a committee to frame the reply. The committee agreed that speedy measure should be taken to enable the Federal government to carry out its financial engagements, but the immediate compliance of the State "would involve a breach of the faith of this State, pledged to the public creditors, citizens thereof," unless some other funds were provided to pay the interest. Since the assembly was about to dissolve, it recommended the whole affair to the next house.[98]

The Wyoming controversy and the Connecticut cession of western claims were tied together in a unique transaction of 1786. At this time Connecticut urged Congress to accept the cession of her western claims. Unlike the cessions tendered by the other states Connecticut insisted on retaining a strip one hundred twenty miles wide beyond the western boundary of Pennsylvania. At first the other states opposed this. But it seems that Pennsylvania and Connecticut came to a gentleman's agreement whereby Pennsylvania would acquiesce in the western reservation if Connecticut would in the future withdraw all support from the malcontents in the Wyoming region. The tacit belief at the time was that Connecticut would use the western reservation as a compensation for the claim of the Susquehanna and Delaware land companies. When this became known among the members of Congress, enough of them agreed to the proposition to vote acceptance of the cession offered by Connecticut. Such was the general understanding among the people of Pennsylvania. Of the four delegates from this State in Congress, Wilson and St. Clair were Republicans and Bayard and Pettit were Constitutionalists. There is no evidence that they looked with disfavor on the proposition or that they disagreed among themselves as to the expediency of it. Pennsylvania was interested in this agreement as a means to negative the new extensive claims made by the Susquehanna Company rather than to remove the original Yankee settlers from the Wyoming region. The new State movement was an attempt to include land west of the Wyoming region.[99]

In the fall of 1786 the first real actions were taken by the State assembly to settle the Wyoming controversy on a just basis. John Franklin and John Jenkins, two leaders of the more moderate Yankee group, explained the sufferings of the people in the upper Susquehanna valley and requested a hearing. This was referred to a committee of seven which included the leaders of both political factions. While the Wyoming matters were under discussion, a bill was brought forward to exonerate non-resident landholders from paying taxes on lands in Wyoming until they could be put in possession of their property. Although defended by the Eastern Republicans, this measure was opposed by the Radicals from the frontier counties. On this vote there was an unusual number of absentees in the Republican ranks. The bill was defeated by a vote of twenty to thirty-three. Another measure which indicated how the wind was blowing in respect to Wyoming was the passage of the bill to create Luzerne County so that the Connecticut settlers would enjoy some form of local government. On this measure the Radicals and many of the Republicans agreed. In fact it was Morris and Clymer who had initiated the measure as early as April. The fourteen who opposed the bill in September were mainly Republicans. During this time John Jenkins and John Franklin had visited Philadelphia under safe conduct in order to lay their side of the story before the assembly. Noah Webster urged them to disregard the claim of the Susquehanna Company to the western part of the State but to insist on confirmation of the soil for five miles on both sides of the river.[100]

The crux of the matter now was to agree on some method of confirming the land-titles of the actual settlers in the disputed region. The liberal-minded Republicans and all of the Radicals agreed that this was necessary. In March, 1787, an assembly committee reported that in the earlier session of the house Jenkins and Franklin were told that only claims of individual landholders would be received. The committee also pointed out that news from Connecticut showed that the Susquehanna Company had revived its title to a large area of northern Pennsylvania, directed a method of distributing land, and intimated a plan to erect that territory into a separate state. On the basis of this report a bill was ordered prepared which would provide for confirming the Connecticut claimants who were actual possessors of soil in Luzerne County before the Trenton decree, and that compensation in lands should be made to Pennsylvania proprietors. While this debate was under discussion an interesting side-issue cropped up. It was proposed that three commissioners should go to Luzerne County to carry out the work of confirming the grants. The original bill provided that these officials should be appointed by Council, but George and Daniel Clymer moved to amend so that the appointments would be made by the assembly; this was carried by a two-to-one vote, the Radicals forming the minority. The confirming act finally passed.[101]

The Mississippi River did not come to the serious attention of statemen and politicians until 1785 when the Spanish government sent Gardoqui to negotiate a treaty with the United States.[102] In the summer of 1786 the problem became acute. Jay was required by his instructions to insist on the free navigation of the Mississippi. He and Gardoqui came to a deadlock. In May, Jay asked to be relieved from this part of the instructions and intimated to individual members of Congress that he was working on the basis of a treaty, whereby the United States would relinquish the use of the Mississippi for twenty-five years in return for commercial concessions from Spain. Predisposed by their economic interests, the northern states favored this plan. Looking to the development of the lands at their back door and to the creation of new states with similar interests, the southern states opposed it. The Pennsylvania delegates in Congress at this time were Pettit and Bayard, Radicals, and St. Clair, Republican. Under the dominance of commercial influences in the eastern part of the State, these men cast their votes with New England. Monroe and Madison discussed the possibility of converting the Pennsylvania delegates. Pettit and Bayard being "under the influence of eastern politicks" were not approached by the Virginians.[103] While in Philadelphia, Madison did not see St. Clair, and if he had, he thought that his acquaintance was too slender to warrant broaching the subject; but Madison did speak with Wilson but could not divine his ultimate opinion on the subject. In Congress a few days later there was no doubt of the attitude of St. Clair who gave a detailed defense of the proposed treaty, in which he outlined the beneficial effects to the commercial states and reasoned that a check to Western settlement would be advantageous to the whole union. Pettit's actions also proved to the Virginia delegates that he likewise was lost to southern and western interests. Jay's letter asking to be relieved from his instructions was committed to King of Massachusetts, Pettit of Pennsylvania, and Monroe of Virginia. King and Pettit reported that the committee should be discharged. Monroe was helpless. On August 29, 1786, the important question of repealing Jay's instructions came to a vote, and the repeal was carried by seven northern states, including Pennsylvania, as against five states to the South.[104]

The breach between the North and the South became so great over the issue that for a time it was feared that the states might split up into several confederacies on these sectional lines. Virginia delegates, as the dominant leaders of the southern interests, foresaw that in the event of a division it would be highly desirable to include Pennsylvania, and perhaps New Jersey, with the South so as to prevent too much strength in the eastern section. So the contest centered on Pennsylvania, and Monroe realized that every effort should be made to convert her. "A knowledge that she was on our side," he explained, "wo[ul]d blow this whole intrigue in the air. To bring this ab[ou]t therefore is an important object to the Southern interest." [105]

At this time the people in the western part of the State began to express themselves. One of the planks in Brackenridge's platform for election to the assembly from Westmoreland County was a protest against the proposed treaty; he wanted the assembly to instruct the State delegates to oppose the closure of the Mississippi. Local opinion was voiced in the *Pittsburgh Gazette,* located in the heart of Pennsylvania territory, which would be affected. Should the river be closed, wrote the correspondent, "you are in a ruined and undone situation . . . the only channel is to be shut up thro' which you can never expect to have any regular trade to bring your produce to market." [106] Brackenridge was successful in being elected to the assembly. Already Pettit had written to the aged Franklin, fresh from diplomacy and intrigue at Passy, to ask his opinion on the Spanish treaty. Explaining that he was not familiar with the details of the proposed agreement, Franklin advised delay as the best general solution. Make new propositions or vary old ones, he suggested, so that Gardoqui would be required to write home for instructions. A new Spanish king, with different ideas, or ministers with different views, might bring a solution. In the meantime the United States would be growing stronger and better able to back up its claim.[107]

Brackenridge and the western settlers had been exerting their influence to bring the question before the assembly. The house was about equally balanced between the two political parties, but the eastern Radicals showed little sympathy with their western brethren. The committee report on the petition from the West was made early in March. The Republicans had hoped to suppress the subject. But when it was known that the topic would come up, St. Clair sent an abstract of some of the proceedings in Congress to FitzSimons in preparation for the debate. St. Clair was annoyed that the members of the assembly should air their views on national questions. In the assembly, Brackenridge at first had difficulty in obtaining leave to present the side of the westerners because the Republicans said "that we [Western Radicals] come down like Huns, Goths, and Vandals upon them, and join with those who tear up charters and the most sacred engagements of government."[108] He obtained this privilege and it was one of the few favors extended to him for his support of the re-charter of the Bank. His speech, of course, had no effect, except perhaps that the committee report was postponed rather than killed. In the meantime, the question in Congress gradually subsided as interest was diverted to the Federal constitutional convention; the proposed Jay treaty never materialized.

The three years from 1783 to 1786 marked the revival and the relapse of Radicalism. Although the Radicals had defeated the revision of the Constitution in the Council of Censors and had returned to power in the assembly because of the excesses of the Republicans, they failed to gain wisdom from the mistakes of their political enemies. Controlling the assembly in 1784-1785, they outdid the conservatives in overturning the work of previous years. In their swan song of triumph they failed to realize that they could no longer count on war hysteria and anti-British sentiment. The day of those psychological forces had passed. As level-headed men turned with disgust from the excesses of the Radical assembly of 1784-1785, they realized the seriousness of national problems which could no longer be delayed. The Radical particularistic State rights philosophy of government was not adequate to a satisfactory solution of these problems. For many years the Republicans had waited for the occasion when the public would turn to them for leadership.

VII

TRIUMPH OF THE COUNTER-REVOLUTION (1786-1790)

RECOVERING from their defeat in the assembly in 1784-1785, the conservatives had learned the lesson of proceeding slowly when the tide was running in their favor. They had made considerable gains in the succeeding session and by the fall of 1786 they were well established on the road to victory. The four years from 1786 to 1790 marked the complete triumph of the Republican party. It should be noted that they did not attempt to put their policies into effect in one session but introduced point after point when they believed that the public was ready to support them. They had also learned the value of compromise as in the case of the re-charter of the Bank. The most significant event which played directly into the hands of the Republicans was the adoption of the Federal Constitution which incorporated many of the theories of government advocated by the conservatives.

CONSERVATIVES GAIN STRENGTH

The election of 1786 showed that the Republicans were gradually accumulating more strength. In Philadelphia the struggle took the form of a fight between the two major parties to capture the vote of the immigrant element. Hence the Republicans adopted the party label of Friends to Equal Liberty which had been first used in the previous election. For their ticket they re-nominated the members then in the assembly, except James Irvine, who would not adhere to a strict Republican platform and who was dropped in favor of Jacob Hiltzheimer. Although William Will had been a Constitutionalist, he now cast most of his votes in the assembly for the conservatives. Judging from the election returns, he was a very popular man and was acceptable to both parties. The Constitutionalists, weakened by the momentum in favor of respectability and conservatism, likewise adopted a temporary label when they nominated their men under the title of the University ticket. It contained the more moderate group from the Radical camp. Pettit was interested in finance and speculation.

Frederick Kuhl could draw usually the votes of the populace, but in 1786 he was unable to stem the tide against Radicalism. James Irvine, despite his middle-of-the-road position in the assembly in 1785-1786, was again run by the Radicals, undoubtedly because of his vote-getting ability. William Will was a sure bet for either party. The Radical ticket was really the result of a joint agreement among the Constitutional Society, the Mechanics and Manufacturers, and the Adopted Sons.[1]

In Philadelphia County a coalition ticket was proposed, consisting of Thomas Mifflin who kept on good terms with both parties, Isaac Gray who was a Republican, Elias Boyce and Emmanuel Eyre who were Radicals, and John Nice who had no record. The Republicans however renominated the men then in the house.[2]

The fight in Philadelphia centered over the votes of the immigrant class known as the Lately Adopted Sons. It was asserted that about a week before the election James Hutchinson, J. B. Smith, and Major McCulloch had been sent by the Constitutional Society to solicit the support of the Lately Adopted Sons. At once the conservative press echoed with allusions to "mud," "dirt," "runners of party" and "vile party faction." The Republicans were uneasy, for they were not quite sure what the Lately Adopted Sons would do on the crucial day. They assumed that the Bryanites had captured them, but at the same time they tried to believe that the new society contained only a handful of members.[3]

The issues of the election were based largely on the past record of both parties. In appealing to the mechanics, a conservative pointed to last year's election law by which the polls were ordered closed at eight o'clock; this prevented many of the artisans from voting, for few were free from work by that time. Another charge was that the Constitutionalists had excluded the mechanics from the list of taxables on the plea that it would relieve them from the funding tax, but actually it disqualified them from voting. The conservatives showed that indirectly the Bank was the friend of the workingman; an employer in financial trouble could go to the Bank, secure a loan, and pay his workers; otherwise they would lose their wages. This had been the case since the annihilation of the Bank charter. When taxes came into the picture, the conservatives always pointed out how the Radicals had loaded the State with far more than its just proportion of continental debts and speculated on the last issue of paper money. Of the back-counties in this election little is known except that in Cumberland the various sections of the county were not unanimous in choosing candidates. Although several sets of candidates were proposed, each had Robert Whitehill at the head, testifying to his leadership among the Radicals of that region. Whatever the ticket might be, it could be assumed that the county would support the Constitutionalist faction.[4]

The outcome of the election was another victory for the conservatives. The outstanding overturn was in Bucks County which had sent a complete Radical delegation to the assembly since the beginning of the Revolution. By a two-to-one vote Bucks County returned representatives who voted with the city conservatives. Figures which are available show that Robert Whitehill retained his lead above all other Radicals in Cumberland County. The report of votes from a Republican newspaper claimed that the Republicans in Lancaster County received well over eight hundred votes, while the Radicals, a number of whom had been in the assembly in 1784-1785, received a maximum of eleven votes. The crucial district, however, was the City of Philadelphia where William Will had the votes of both factions; the remaining four conservatives won by a three-to-two lead over their opponents. In Philadelphia County a similar situation existed where both parties apparently joined in supporting Thomas Mifflin and Isaac Gray. The truly Republican members on the ticket received an outstanding majority. In all, seven eastern counties went Republican while the rest of the State went Radical. The dominant party could count thirty-six seats, the minority twenty-nine, while the remaining five seats were divided among absentees or members who did not vote consistently on party lines. The outlook promised a Republican program; this, however, would move slowly due to the close division in the house. Conservatives believed that eventually they could convert the hinterland to their views.[5]

The only aftermath of the election was a disputed return from Bedford County as to whether Abraham Cable or Joseph Powell was justly entitled to fill the third seat of that county in the assembly. The conflict also involved the seat in the Council which was contested between George Woods, Republican, and James Martin, Constitutionalist. The upshot was that the Republican candidate was seated in Council. The contest over the disputed seat in the assembly was more protracted. On November 2 just as Speaker Mifflin was about to qualify Piper and Cannon, Robert Morris objected and said that the whole thing should be sent to committee. On the following day the committee reported that Cannon and Piper were duly elected, and they were admitted to their seats. Then began the conflict between Cable and Powell for the third seat for Bedford County. Powell was a Radical, and Whitehill and Smith wanted the Speaker to send for witnesses but this was defeated. After a committee reported in a way that gave Powell a very good claim to the seat, no matter how much the Republicans opposed, they were forced to capitulate and admitted Powell to his seat late in February, 1787.[6]

The election of President and Vice-President was not very vital to either party. Franklin had the full support of both factions and was unanimously re-elected. For the second office, however, there was divided opinion. Charles Biddle, a moderate Constitutionalist, had been elected Vice-President in 1785. The Constitutionalists supported him again as well as some of the more liberal Republicans. But other Republicans, feeling the need of complete triumph for their party, put up Peter Muhlenberg as an opposition candidate. It was the opinion of Biddle who had much influence with the Germans that Muhlenberg had been advanced to draw these votes away from him. In the election Biddle won by a close margin. The Republican organ, the *Independent Gazetteer,* gave its support and approval to Biddle. It appears that the extreme wings of both factions wished to displace Biddle because of his middle-of-the-road attitude. Some Republicans opposed him because he was instrumental in appointing Tench Coxe a commissioner to the Annapolis Convention, after Coxe had offended the directors of the Bank.[7]

When the legislature assembled a quorum late in October, there were evidences of conservative assertiveness. Morris, Clymer, and FitzSimons wanted to dispense with the custom introduced by the Radicals of asking each member whether he had taken the oath of allegiance and whether he held any office contrary to the Constitution. The Republicans declared this was not required by the Constitution and that it was improper. The clerkship of the house was a plum in the gift of the dominant party. Since the overturn in 1784 Peter Z. Lloyd had been resting from the duties of that office which were exercised by Samuel Bryan. In 1785 Lloyd lost by only three votes. This year the Republicans were determined to reinstate him, which they did by a vote of thirty-two to fourteen. Thomas Mifflin was re-elected Speaker.[8]

The election of delegates to Congress also mirrored the increasing conservative power. St. Clair and Pettit were re-elected. The new members were William Irvine of Carlisle, Samuel Meredith, and William Bingham, of Philadelphia. The delegation was representative of Republican ideals. Pettit, Bingham, and Meredith had commercial and financial interests at heart, while Irvine and St. Clair reflected the respectability of army officers. The instructions to the delegates were prepared by a committee headed by Robert Morris. "Perusal of foederal measures and foederal interest will be the principal object of your attention." If the interests of Pennsylvania should come into competition with the national interests, then Pennsylvania should recede only so far and in proportion as the other states submitted.[9]

Glorying in their increased strength and realizing that the trend of popular opinion was favoring them, Republican papers directed merciless shafts at their political opponents. Soon after John Smiley arrived in the city to take his seat in the Council, he was ironically hailed as the

Demosthenes of the Mountains who was already "blowing the trumpet in Zion" against the inevitable incorporation of Philadelphia and the restoration of the Bank.[10] He was reported as openly threatening that the minority would resort to the bayonet if either of these policies were attempted. Early in 1787 the Radicals resorted to a new type of propaganda admirably suited to the uneducated class in which they found their chief support. A cartoon with the caption "Zion Besieg'd & Attack'd" depicted the Radical forces entrenched on a rock-ribbed fortification representing the Constitution. The Bankers, led by Robert Morris and Gouverneur Morris, assaulted the fortress by direct attack and by undermining. But the Constitutional fortress withstood all the efforts of the enemy.[11]

In February, 1787, a new president of Congress was to be elected. Both the Northern and Southern delegates wanted to place a favorite local son in the chair. The resulting compromise was the election of St. Clair from Pennsylvania. In March when Pettit's term as delegate expired, the house elected John Armstrong, Jr., to succeed him. Thus the State delegation to Congress was completely conservative in its personnel.[12]

The tariff was one of the several problems which the assembly had to deal with in this session. Manufacturers of bar iron called for a protective duty on that product imported into the State. When a duty of forty shillings per ton was proposed, it was defeated by a decided vote of eighteen to thirty-nine. The opposition came almost solidly from the back-country, doubtless because the people in general believed that protective duty on bar iron would send the domestic price sky high. To meet this opposition the iron interests proposed a provision that the current price of bar iron of domestic manufacture would not exceed twenty-eight pounds per ton. But the opposition was adamant and the proposal went down in defeat by an overwhelming vote. In the tariff measures various interests clashed. The shipwrights complained that the duty on all cordage imported into the State discouraged the building of vessels, and prayed a reduction. The ropemakers of the city then remonstrated against such an idea. In the end the shipwrights won the issue for the duty on cordage was reduced one-half.[13]

With a conservative majority in the assembly, the Republicans launched a new effort to re-charter the Bank of North America. This was an object dear to their hearts, and they promoted a continual newspaper campaign to keep the issue before the public. Although the assemblymen from the western region generally opposed the Bank, when they arrived in Philadelphia, sometimes the blandishments of Robert Morris and his colleagues had their effect, as was the case of Brackenridge who supported the Bank.[14]

At this time the question was not so much whether the Bank would be re-chartered, for the Radicals realized that that was inevitable, but whether the new charter would modify the broad powers granted in the first charter. Although Radical leaders like Findley and Whitehill tried to postpone action on the subject, friends and stockholders of the Bank petitioned for a modification of certain powers, doubtless believing that such a compromise would bring them victory. Assured by James Wilson that a limitation of time or amount of capital in the proposed charter would not affect the charter granted by Congress, the directors of the Bank felt constrained to accept such a compromise. Robert Morris was opposed to these limitations. Those who urged the restrictions, he asserted, were the Constitutionalists who always opposed the Bank and tried to influence the country members. They were joined by another group, those who had applied to a former assembly to incorporate a second bank; most of these men, Morris explained, were not Constitutionalists, but opposed the Bank on grounds of its financial policies. Whether with an ulterior purpose or not, Morris maneuvered the question on the floor so that the house would vote first on the question of repealing the repealer act, and secondly on the question of imposing limitations. FitzSimons explained that some members feared that if they voted for the first proposal, they might be deserted on the second. So he pledged to vote for restrictions in order to gain full support for the more important question of reviving the Bank's charter. The restrictions were proposed to obviate the monopolistic features of the institution. There was the fear of the undue influence of foreign stockholders and the fear of the manipulation of holdings of stock in order to influence election of Bank directors. Constitutionalists like Whitehill called for rotation of men holding the offices of directors and insisted that each stockholder should have only one vote.[15]

It was the Bank issue which eventually ruined Brackenridge politically. In the middle of December a group of western assemblymen gathered at McKean's residence and discussed politics. Brackenridge had already become a devoted follower of Morris on the Bank question. When some of the Radical Westerners suggested that Morris and his friends were striving for personal emolument rather than for serving the public, Brackenridge snapped back that the people were fools and Morris was a great leader. This story eventually got into the press; Brackenridge could not match his antagonist Findley; and in fact Brackenridge lost re-election to the assembly in the following year.[16]

Finding themselves in the minority in the assembly, the Constitutionalists resorted to the old strategy of attempting to beat down opposition by flooding the house with petitions against the revival of the Bank charter. At the same time the Radical press constantly attacked the Bank. But in

March the Republicans were successful in re-chartering the institution by a vote of thirty-five to twenty-eight. They were forced, however, to accept some restrictions. The charter was limited to fourteen years. Its capital was set at two million dollars. There was a provision to prohibit the bank from monopolizing or engrossing merchandise. Copies of the by-laws and regulations made by the directors were to be filed with Council. On the Bank question the votes in the assembly followed a close sectional division, the eastern part supporting the Republicans and the western opposing them.[17]

One of the most interesting maneuvers made by the Radicals during this session of the assembly was the almost successful attempt to move the seat of the State government from Philadelphia to Harrisburg. Taking the conservative Easterners by surprise, Findley called for a vote on the subject; by a purely sectional division he carried his motion by a majority of four votes. The city, Philadelphia, Bucks, Chester, Lancaster, Montgomery, and Northampton counties opposed the idea, but the frontier counties were solidly for it. Just exactly what was at the bottom of this action is not entirely clear. But Arthur St. Clair offered some suggestions which are enlightening. He thought it best not to give the removal idea serious opposition "or it will end in transferring it [the capital] to Lancaster, and perhaps detaching the Members from that County from the [Republican] Party."[18] St. Clair thought that the real objective was Lancaster. Scarcely had Findley won his tentative victory when the conservative press attacked his motion. Since Philadelphia was the commercial hub of the State, it should be the political center; since two-thirds of the population was located east of the Susquehanna River, the only logical seat of government was the Quaker City. This was the gist of the Republican arguments. The truth is that the conservatives had been caught off their guard, and their defense reflected haste and lacked the tone of sincere conviction. It is interesting to note that Brackenridge continued to adhere to the eastern group, for the "Western Chatham" spoke at length in the house in favor of Philadelphia. Several weeks later the Republicans marshalled their forces, called for a reconsideration of the motion and effectively killed it.[19]

It was not until March, 1787, that the Republicans succeeded in completing the abolition of the hated test laws. In 1786 they had gained their greatest victory in this respect, but there still remained the abjuration of the King of Great Britain which some persons felt that they could not take. So the house modified the test laws by requiring only a simple declaration of allegiance to the State as the only qualification for voting and holding office. The fact that no vote was spread on the record is mute evidence that the question was no longer a burning issue. Early in

1789 a movement was started to abolish the last vestige of the test laws, the oath of allegiance, which was still a thorn in the side of Quakers and Mennonites who, it was claimed, were migrating to Virginia and Canada to avoid this restriction. In March, 1789, the house removed this final reminder of the stormy days of a decade gone by.[20]

At this period Pennsylvania was not only concerned with domestic issues. As people recognized with increasing alarm that the Articles of Confederation would not guarantee a strong republic, they turned their attention to the possibility of amending those articles. Republicans were particularly alert to the unsatisfactory state of affairs.

Although the Annapolis Convention was a failure in itself, there were larger issues involved. The future course of the government of the United States was at stake, and according to the views of some contemporaries the possibility of a new revolution depended on one state, Pennsylvania. Virginians believed that the New England members were trying to break up the states into two or possibly three separate confederacies. The success of the plan, they asserted, depended on whether New England could convince Pennsylvania to join the northern group. It is true that none of the Pennsylvania delegates to the convention attended except Tench Coxe because they were waiting in Philadelphia for the arrival of the New England delegates. These northern delegates were late and the commissioners at Annapolis adjourned. Although leading Pennsylvanians looked toward a form of federal government republican in nature and possessed of sufficient energy, some men were contemplating another mode of departure. William Bingham advocated the grouping of the states into several confederacies along lines of mutual interest. This idea was just appearing in the newspapers by the early part of 1787. Four months earlier Benjamin Rush informed Richard Price of speculation among "some of our enlightened men" for three confederacies bound together by an offensive and defensive alliance. Rush's only comment on this was: "Perhaps necessity, or rather divine providence, may drive us to it."[21]

The question of the seat of Congress was always subject to discussion. Pennsylvania had a direct interest in this topic because there was the possibility that the national body might return to the Keystone State. By February, 1787, the Southern states had agreed to remove to Philadelphia and had marshalled their forces to effect the plan. At one time only the lack of sufficient representation from Delaware prevented removal to the Quaker City. But before the Delaware delegates showed up, the representation from South Carolina lapsed. Believing that since Philadelphia carried the stigma of June 19, 1783, perhaps another place in the State would be more attractive, John Montgomery asked Irvine to try to interest Congress in Carlisle. On two other occasions Pennsylvania lost the fight for Congress by the defection of one member. In the first case Peleg Arnold of Rhode Island "was overcome by the exertions made to convert him," and the proposal failed.[22] The Southern members were opposed to New York because they suspected that the East would not concur in a permanent residence so long as the national body had its temporary residence in New York. The Southern members pressed removal from New York with increasing fervor. Arthur Lee, of course, was opposed to the Quaker City from first to last. He believed that the commercial superiority of Philadelphia, increased by the residence of Congress, would give the Pennsylvania merchants a decided control over commerce, if not a monopoly. The second attempt to remove to Pennsylvania was defeated by the lack of Schurman of New Jersey who found it more important to keep an appointment with a ferry boat to take him home than to vote on the seat of Congress.[23]

As the year 1786 neared its close, the State assembly entered on the task of appointing delegates to the Federal Convention to revise the Articles of Confederation. This action was taken before Congress had made the recommendation to the states. The type of men who were in the minds of some people became evident in one of the Philadelphia newspapers several days before the passing of the act. Asserting that the State should appoint its best men to the delegation, a correspondent reported that Benjamin Franklin, Thomas Mifflin, Robert Morris, James Wilson, George Clymer, Thomas FitzSimons and John Armstrong, Jr., were under consideration. The law by which the delegates were appointed included all of these men except Franklin and Armstrong. Gouverneur Morris and Jared Ingersoll were added to the official list. Three months later by a special act Franklin was included. During the struggle in the early part of 1787 over the seat of Congress William Irvine privately suggested an additional reason why the national body should be located in Philadelphia. If Congress and the Convention could sit at the same place, he thought, it might facilitate the business of the latter body by an interchange of ideas between the two groups.[24]

The newspapers reflected some of the ideas on national government which were passing current at this time. Voting by states was condemned as unjust; representation proportioned to population and the economic importance of each state appeared to be a fairer method. Federal power to raise revenue and to regulate commerce were accepted as powers necessary for any effective national government. Federal assumption of State debts was broached as early as October, 1786. A more daring writer suggested that Congress should be made the supreme executive head of the nation. Each state should have an assembly and a legislative council.

Congress should appoint the governor of each state and the governor's signature would be necessary for the enactment of state laws. Another writer stressed the division of the powers of government and took the opportunity to advocate two houses of the national legislature. This, of course, was what the Republicans had been calling for in the state government. Rush informed an English friend "that there is little doubt of our adopting a vigorous and compounded federal legislature." [25]

Many people looked to the Federal Convention as the only hope for a strong American government. In June, the Republican editor, Eleazer Oswald, privately expressed the opinion that the people considered the members of the Convention "as their political saviours," and expected some "mighty changes" in government.[26] George Fox believed that much of the future happiness of the nation depended on the deliberations of the Convention; he likewise entertained great expectations.[27]

If the conservatives placed all their hopes in the Federal Convention, the Radicals were very dubious of the proceedings going on behind closed doors at the State House in the summer of 1787. The conservative character of the Pennsylvania delegation made them uneasy because it contained no members from the rural region, and the rest of the delegates, except Franklin, represented urban finance and commerce. The inclusion of Gouverneur Morris, who was looked upon as a citizen of New York and not of Pennsylvania, was an additional grievance which created suspicion in Radical minds. Early in August the Radical press began to criticize the members and the work of the Convention although there were only the vaguest rumors afloat as to what turn the actual proceedings were taking. The opposition press replied with counter-accusations and with the charge that Bryan and J. B. Smith were circulating pamphlets through the State in order to create public disapproval of the new frame of government whatever form it might take. By the end of August the people were divided into three groups, as David Redick, a western assemblyman in Philadelphia, viewed the situation. The "infernal" spirits were determined to oppose whatever the Convention did, right or wrong; the "earthly" spirits, to acquiesce in its work; and the "celestial" spirits, to risk everything to support the new government if it were "wholesome" or to oppose it vigorously if it were undemocratic.[28]

Realizing that they had a safe majority, the Republicans in the assembly were determined to call a convention to discuss the ratification of the Federal Constitution. A struggle in Congress delayed the action of that body in formally submitting the document to the states. Not until September 27 did Congress agree to such action. In the meantime the State assembly had determined to adjourn on September 29. On the 28th Clymer proposed that a convention should be called. At once the Radical minority fought for delay. They argued that the matter should be referred to the next assembly, that Congress had not submitted the Constitution to the states, and that the Republicans were guilty of undue haste. These Radical speeches were unavailing, for the Republicans carried their motion for a convention by a vote of forty-three to nineteen.[29]

Balked in their attempt to stave off a convention, the Radicals decided to use the last weapon at their command. In the afternoon session of the 28th it was necessary to set the date and state the conditions under which the delegates should be elected to the convention. But the afternoon session could not be held because the nineteen Radicals refused to attend and thus prevented a quorum. This desperate remedy was not new to the Constitutionalists, for they had used it with startling success in the September days of 1784 when it proved a crushing blow to Republican zeal. Also remembering that earlier experience, the Republicans were determined not to be defeated a second time by the same ruse. The Speaker sent the sergeant-at-arms for the nineteen delinquent members but none of them appeared. So the house was forced to adjourn until the next morning, September 29, the last day of the session.[30]

Over night the Republicans gained a strong point in their favor. In New York Bingham had sent a courier with the news that Congress had officially submitted the new frame of government to the states. When the assembly convened on Saturday morning, the Radicals continued to absent themselves. Thereupon the resolution of Congress was read and the sergeant-at-arms and the assistant clerk were dispatched with it to the absentees to prove that one of the strongest objections had been removed. But this did not alter the determination of the seceding members who resolutely refused to attend. Then the mob intervened; conditions had changed since 1779, for this time the mob championed the Republicans. The populace dragged James McCalmont and Jacob Miley to the State House and thrust them into the assembly. Although the situation was unusual, the quorum was technically completed, and the house proceeded to business over the protests of the victimized Radicals. Finally resigned to his fate, McCalmont attempted to change the meeting place of the convention from Philadelphia to Carlisle; when no one seconded the motion, he proposed Lancaster. Although the members from that county fell in with the idea, it was defeated by a vote of two to one. At last the Republicans carried out their plans when it was agreed that the election should be held on the first Tuesday in November, that the number of delegates should be the same as the number of assemblymen, and that the convention should sit in Philadelphia. The Radicals would not admit defeat, for on this same day they were at work on an address justifying their position. Before the campaign over ratification swung into full blast in the press, the annual election of assemblymen afforded a brief interval.[31]

Test of Strength over the Federal Constitution

The election in October, 1787, created little stir. It was but one spoke in the whole wheel of politics of the time; the hub of this political wheel was the heated debate over the Federal Constitution. The Republicans identified themselves with the new frame of government. In Philadelphia, for example, they assembled under the name of "Friends to the Federal Constitution" to make up their ticket for assemblymen. Another interesting feature of this meeting occurred after the name of each candidate was approved. A resolution was passed by which everyone present was considered "honor bound" to support the ticket on election day. In Cumberland County John Montgomery, standard bearer of the conservatives in that region, correctly predicted that the Radicals would carry the county, and added that he did not expect one Republican from the whole territory west of the Susquehanna River, except in York County, to obtain a seat in the house.[32]

Although not without a significant Radical representation, the election guaranteed a Republican assembly. Five eastern counties, representing twenty-six seats, sent an all conservative delegation which constituted the main strength of the party. The back-counties sent men of the democratic stamp mixed with a few who did not hold strictly to party lines. A factor in favor of the Republicans was the number of absences among western members; this naturally decreased the Radical voting strength. The house this year revealed a close connection between sectionalism and politics. In general, the older, more populous counties were conservative; while the newer, sparsely settled regions were inclined to be Radical.

Despite the strong feeling which welled to the surface over the Federal Constitution, the election for assemblymen produced only two minor cases of irregularities. A petition from Dauphin County declared that the election had not been held according to Hoyle and therefore John Carson, Republican, should be debarred from his seat. With little ceremony the house dismissed the petition on the basis of lack of evidence. A more serious case occurred in Bedford County where Saylor and Cable tied for election but only because one vote had not been counted. On the questionable ballot had been written the name for Councillor and another name for assemblyman, but the voter had neglected to clip the ballot apart before he handed it in. Carrying out the letter of the law, the officials of election did not count it. Declaring that no fraud was intended, the assembly counted the ballot and declared Saylor elected.[33]

The Republicans again won control of the house. There was a smaller turnover in the membership of the house than at any time since the Revolution. A number of counties returned all of their former members; many other counties changed only one member. Forty-nine members, or seventy per cent, of the old house retained their seats; twenty-one new members appeared. The house continued its former organization. Mifflin was unanimously re-elected Speaker, and Peter Lloyd retained the Clerkship. At the end of October Franklin was unanimously re-elected President. The only contest centered around the Vice-Presidency. Peter Muhlenberg was elected with forty-two votes while Daniel Redick lost with thirty-one.[34]

Although the old Congress still flickered like a guttering candle, the assembly continued to elect delegates to that body. Preparatory to the election, the grand committee met at Hasall's Tavern and determined on five men to fill the posts. William Irvine and Samuel Meredith received almost unanimous votes. The other successful candidates were John Armstrong, Jr., and William Bingham, both well-known conservatives, and James R. Reid from the back-country.[35]

As soon as the assembly passed the resolution calling a convention to debate the ratification of the Federal Constitution, the battle royal was on between the opposing forces. Speeches before public assemblies and articles in the press provided the media for influencing voters to elect delegates for or against the proposed frame of government. The struggle was the bitterest of all during the period since the adoption of the State Constitution of 1776. Both parties realized that the fight in Pennsylvania was part of the larger struggle throughout the nation.

The first shot in the newspaper campaign was fired by the dissenting Radical members of assembly when they justified their conduct to their constituents and asked them to elect delegates to the convention who would oppose the new frame. The arguments they offered provided the core of most of the later newspaper barrage. In the first place these Radicals contended that these delegates from Pennsylvania to the Constitutional Convention had been chosen entirely from the city, did not represent the landed interests, and were for the most part members of the Republican party. Furthermore, these delegates had been sent to revise and alter the Articles of Confederation and not to concoct a whole new framework of government. That the assembly had been too hasty in calling a ratifying convention, attempting to act even before the official recommendation had been received from Congress, proved another strong argument advanced by the Radicals. The violent seizure of the two members in order to secure a quorum was deprecated in the strongest terms. Finally, the Radicals laid down the minimum changes which they were willing to accept. These changes provided for granting power to Congress to regulate commerce, to equalize and collect the impost, and to possess full jurisdiction over maritime affairs; the exercise of internal taxation, on the other hand, was to be left with each individual state.[36]

The Republicans displayed as much activity as their opponents in utilizing the newspapers to good effect. Six conservative assemblymen promptly answered the dissenting Radicals point by point. They explained how the Constitutionalists had acquiesced in the election of delegates entirely from Philadelphia, and made repeated use of the maxim that in a democracy the minority must give in to the majority. Among numerous other statements issued by the Federalists, the one by Pelatiah Webster was outstanding for its clear logic and undoubted force. A flood of less important or repetitive contributions on both sides of the question flooded the press in the seven weeks between September 28 and November 6.[37]

Leading conservatives made a definite effort to secure good writers for their newspaper campaign. As early as September 15 Thomas FitzSimons had asked Noah Webster to write a defense of the new Federal system. Urged by Wilson and Rush, Tench Coxe wrote four articles on the same subject with the intention of circulating them not only in Pennsylvania but also in New York and Virginia. By this activity Rush and Wilson aimed to neutralize the Radical propaganda of the back-country. One of Coxe's articles they proposed to circulate on handbills through the western counties.[38]

The Radicals found their strongest pamphleteer in the author of a long series of articles signed "Centinel," now generally believed to have been written by Samuel Bryan, son of the Radical George Bryan. Three of these had appeared before the election of delegates to the Convention and undoubtedly had their effect in giving backbone to the splitting Radical faction. Writings by an "Old Whig," "The Democratic Federalist," and a pamphlet by John Nicholson, comptroller general, had their influence in holding Radicals to the true democratic principles. The Constitutionalists identified Robert Morris and the Bank group as the leaders of the Federalist forces and attacked them accordingly.[39]

Popular meetings provided another method of propaganda utilized principally by the Federalists. On October 6 a large group attended at the State House. After settling a list of candidates for assembly, James Wilson gave a long speech on the principles of the new Constitution in which he answered arguments of the opposition. Then Rush painted a golden picture of the advantages which would flow from the adoption of the new frame, and concluded that if this were his last moment on earth he would exhort his fellow citizens to support the Constitution. A few days before election of delegates, both parties held meetings and proposed their slate of candidates. Taking no chances, the Federalists made certain that their candidates would support the Constitution before they nominated them.[40]

In some of the back-counties a desperate struggle was taking place. Late in September Tench Coxe had prophesied that the adoption of the Federal Constitution would rend the Radical party to pieces. This became evident as the struggle in Cumberland County progressed. On October 3 the Federalists held a large meeting at the court house in Carlisle with Major-General John Armstrong presiding. They condemned the defection of the nineteen Radicals from the assembly and approved the new Constitution. A Republican reported enthusiastically to a friend that the first impression of the majority of people was favorable to the new frame. Of one of the die-hard Radicals, he observed: "Brown is bellowing against it, but his Audience is very small." Then he continued: "The Constitutionalists are splitting here about a Convention—Whitehill against Watts—The People of the Hills ag[ain]st those in the Valley—The Republicans are not able to do more than help them on & foment their Divisions . . ."[41] Another observer found all ranks of people engaged in the dispute, fighting "almost man against man."[42] In Northampton County the Federalists met at Bethlehem on October 22, chose a slate of delegates for the Convention, warmly approved the Constitution and required each candidate to declare publicly to the meeting that he would vote for ratification. The German element in the hinterland gave the Republicans some uneasiness, though they noted with pride that only one of the nineteen runaway assemblymen was of that nationality while twelve Germans, representing both political factions, had voted for a convention.[43]

Stripping aside the propaganda and bluster, it is evident that the opposing forces in the State were almost equally balanced. William Bradford, Jr., looked forward to "very serious disputes" over the issue and considered the situation grave.[44] Writing from New York, Grayson understood that the pros and cons were nearly equal in Pennsylvania. In the same city Carrington was informed that the Federalists of the Keystone State were damaging their cause by over-zealous activity; he expected, however, a coalescing of the two parties in favor of the Constitution. With more direct knowledge Gouverneur Morris admitted that he did not know whether the Federalists would be strong enough to secure ratification. Philadelphia and the neighborhood he found enthusiastic for it, "but I dread the cold and sower temper of the back Counties."[45] A sidelight on the campaign is revealed by Samuel Powell who heard that R. H. Lee made a short stay at Chester where he prepared and distributed printed papers against the Constitution, but "escaped the resentment of the People."[46]

The election campaign passed off without disorder until late on election night, when a disorderly crowd gathered before the house of Alexander Boyd, a well-known Radical. At his residence lived seven noted Constitutionalists: Smiley, Baird, and Smith who were members of Council; and McLene, Piper, Findley, and McCalmont, members of the assembly. The crowd made a noisy demonstration, threw stones at the door and windows, called the inmates damned rascals, and suggested that they should be hanged. Without further ado, the crowd dispersed.

When this matter came before the assembly, the triumphant Republicans balked at giving their opponents immediate satisfaction. McLean and Findley complained of the incident as an indignity to the honor of the assembly and submitted depositions by Boyd and Baird to support the facts. Richard Peters, William Lewis, and Thomas FitzSimons bedeviled the offended Constitutionalists by suggesting that the case should be committed before taking further action. The Radicals were outraged, called for a vote, and lost. The documents were committed. Later the same day, however, a report was made, and the house formally condemned the riot and asked Council to issued a proclamation to apprehend the offenders. Council complied and offered a reward of three hundred dollars. Herewith the incident died; no offenders were discovered; and the Radicals were forced to swallow the insults unavenged. The Republicans were riding the road to triumph.[47]

The result of the election was an overwhelming majority for the Federalists. Exactly what influence the campaign had on the result is not too clear. The data in the accompanying table indicates that there was a reaction against the Federalists when the people elected assemblymen in October, but these conservative losses were made up by the time the people elected delegates to the ratifying convention. If this was the case, the Federalist gains during those four weeks must be ascribed to their propaganda and organization.[48]

The only votes of the election which have been found are those for the City of Philadelphia. They show the enormous strength of the conservative party at that time. On the Federalist ticket Latimer polled the highest place with 1215 votes and Thomas McKean lowest with 1157. Hoping that his name would draw votes away from the dominant party, the Constitutionalists placed Franklin on their ticket. He received 235 votes; the other Radical candidates were only mild Constitutionalists but they could attract no more than 150 votes.[49]

The strength of the Federalists came from numerous groups. Public creditors supported the movement because it promised a stronger government which had the power to make good its obligations and to pay interest on its bonds. This group was located in the eastern part of the State in

	Election of Assemblymen, Sept., 1786		Vote to call Ratifying Convention, Sept. 27, 1787		Election of Assemblymen, Oct., 1787		Vote in Convention to ratify Constitution	
	Republicans	*Radicals*	*For*	*Against*	*Republicans*	*Radicals*	*For*	*Against*
City	5		4		5		5	
Philadelphia .	5		4		5		5	
Bucks	4		4		4		4	
Chester	6		6		6		6	
Lancaster ...	6		6		6		5	1
York	6		4		3	2	6	
Cumberland .		4		3		4		4
Berks	1	4	5			5		5
Northampton.		4	2	1	1	3	4	
Bedford	1	2	1	2		1		2
Northumberland		2	1	1	1	1	2	
Washington .		4		4		4	2	2
Franklin		2		2		2	1	1
Montgomery .	4		4		1	3	4	
Dauphin	1	2	1	2		2		3
Westmoreland	1	2	1	2		2		3
Fayette		2		2		2		2
Luzerne.....	Absent				1		1	
Huntingdon .					1		1	
	40	28	43	19	34	31	46	23

NOTE: In the assembly of 1787-1788 the party affiliation of four members is not obtainable; they were from the counties of York, Bedford, Dauphin and Westmoreland.

the urban areas. Dr. Beard has shown that at least nineteen Federalist members of the convention were interested in public securities about this time; all of them came from the eastern counties.[50] Another group was composed of former officers of the continental army who had always favored the ideals of the Republicans. Eight members of the convention were members of the Cincinnati, all of whom were Federalist. Other groups included stockholders of the Bank, most of the lawyers and preachers, those who had suffered from the evils of paper money, mechanics who depended on commerce and navigation, and in general, those connected in any way with trade.[51]

The ratifying Convention which assembled in November contained a varied group of delegates. There were the old leaders of the Republicans like James Wilson, Benjamin Rush, Frederick Muhlenberg; and now Thomas McKean was in the same camp. Supporters of the party included other men who had also been active in the counter-revolution, men like Gray, Wayne, Chambers, Slagle, Hartley, and Scott. The Radicals also sent their outstanding leaders. The two Whitehill brothers, William Findley, and John Smiley defended democratic ideals with the support of their ardent but less prominent followers like Hoge, Lincoln, Lutz, Brown,

Todd, and Harris. The Radicals relied more on men who had experience in public life than the Federalists. Three quarters of the Radical delegates had served in the assembly, Executive Council or the Council of Censors whereas only half of the Republicans had such experience under the Constitution of 1776.[52]

The Convention lasted from November 21 till December 15. It was in effect a debating society, for it was a foregone conclusion that ratification would be the result. The first week was consumed over questions of procedure while the remainder of the session was devoted to the merits and defects of the new frame of government. Essentially, the Anti-Federal opposition rested on the fear that the individual states were asked to surrender too much of their sovereign power to the Federal government. This was nothing new, for the Radicals had always acted on a political philosophy which made the State more important than the national government. Findley and Smiley elaborated their position with unalterable firmness, while their followers sat silently by and voted when the occasion arose. Although the Federalists were more active in the debate, the floor was usually yielded to Wilson who was not only well-grounded in theory of government but had the advantage of attending the Constitutional Convention. His long, labored arguments became the pride of the Republicans and filled columns of the newspapers, largely because the Anti-Federalist press remained inactive.[53]

Seeing defeat inevitable, the Radicals shifted ground and suggested compromise. Findley asserted that they did not hold that the proposed Constitution should be rejected, but that if certain safeguards were adopted they would be willing to approve it. He advanced a series of fifteen amendments, similar to the first ten amendments later adopted. But he asked something more. His object was to adjourn the convention to give the people at large an opportunity to discuss the Constitution and the proposed amendments, to learn what the other states were doing on the same subject, and to offer the amendments to Congress before the Constitution should finally be adopted. Realizing that the Radicals were making a desperate play for time, the Republicans made short work of the proposals and immediately called for a vote on ratification. By a division of forty-six to twenty-three, the Constitution was adopted. On the following day the members of the Convention marched in colorful procession with officers of the State, city, and University to the court house where the ratification was formally announced to the people.[54] The counter-revolution was in full swing.

To crown their victory the Federalists of Philadelphia and the neighboring region determined to make a bid for the capital of the United States. In the midst of the closing debates of the Convention memorials were presented, asking that a ten-mile area in Philadelphia and surrounding counties might be offered to Congress with exclusive jurisdiction for the seat of government. For reasons which might easily be assumed, it is only necessary to note that the petitioners were landholders of the region in question. The Radicals disapproved on the ground that the convention did not have the right to act on such a proposal and that, if adopted, it would violate the State Constitution. They refused to vote for or against the motion. On the closing day the convention adopted the proposal and included an invitation to Congress to use the public buildings of Philadelphia until a permanent residence had been fixed.[55]

Defeated but undaunted on the issue of the Federal Constitution, the minority appealed to the public. On the day when the vote for ratification was carried, the Radicals prepared a lengthy address to their constituents in which they stated their case against the new frame of government. They attacked the secrecy of the Constitutional Convention, the fact that it framed a new form of government instead of amending the Articles of Confederation, the haste and intimidation employed by the assembly in calling the ratifying convention, and the precipitance in electing delegates to the Convention. They pointed out that less than nineteen per cent of the voters of the State had elected the delegates to the convention, and that forty-six members who voted for ratification had been chosen by only 6,800 voters, or about ten per cent of the taxables in the State. In a bitter tone they outlined the amendments which they had proposed and again asserted their willingness to approve the new government if these provisions were included. This was followed by a lengthy attack on detailed parts of the Constitution. Through the address they insisted that the State Constitution was undermined by the act of ratification and that there was danger that the democratic palladium of liberty would crumble to pieces.[56]

The conservatives went on their way merrily celebrating their success. In Philadelphia a boat was wheeled through the streets with sailors taking mock soundings. "Three and twenty fathoms," they called out, referring to the number of the minority, "*foul* bottom." "Six and forty fathoms—sound bottom—safe anchorage." At Easton the enthusiasm was more restrained. After the four deputies of Northumberland County had made an enthusiastic report of the reasons why they voted for ratification, a public meeting presided over by Alexander Patterson of earlier Wyoming notoriety, declared approval and gave hearty thanks to the deputies. At York the Federalists rang bells and discharged cannon to announce the happy event. In Chambersburg the sound of cannon was accompanied with a happy flow of wine. Commenting on some Franklin County Radicals, a joyful Republican reported: "James Johnston drank his wine but would not huzza. James McLean was in town but kept out of the way . . .," while the conduct of Baird who voted against ratification was "much reprobated." [57]

Serious repercussions followed the attempt of a small band of Federalists determined on staging a public celebration at Carlisle located in the heart of the Radical Cumberland Valley. The day after Christmas a few conservatives dragged a cannon to the public square and stacked barrels for a bonfire. At once the opposition appeared from all directions. In short order a riot was under way from which the Federalists were forced to retreat with bloody noses and broken heads. The Radicals took possession of the square, threw a copy of the Constitution into the flames with shouts of "Damnation to the 46 members, and long live the virtuous 23." On the following day the Federalists issued forth once more, this time with the benefit of firearms, and proceeded to hold their belated celebration. As soon as this was completed, the Radicals paraded through the streets with effigies of Chief Justice McKean and James Wilson which were consigned to the flames. At night the Federalists assembled at Postlethwaite's Tavern to enjoy a supper and patriotic toasts.[58]

Unmindful of the increasing Radical resentment, the Federalists in Cumberland County determined to press their advantage. They prepared depositions which singled out leaders of the mob, and forwarded the documents to the Supreme Court for action. Since McKean had been vilified, he asked his associates to issue warrants for the arrest of twenty persons. Bryan counseled delay, pointing out the danger to the court's prestige if the arrests could not be carried out. During the delay Federalists and Anti-Federalists in Cumberland and Franklin counties formed associations to forward their respective political aims. Tension increased. John Montgomery, a leader among the conservative minority, explained that "they are Violent on Both Sides . . . we [Federalists] are in a very Disagreeable unhapey Situation in this place nothing Ever happned So bad amongst us neaghbours pass Each other without Speaking . . ." [59] Viewing the situation from a distance, moderates feared that the Federalists might carry the affair too far. Some wanted to cast it into oblivion; others believed that punishment of the offenders was necessary to demonstrate the ability of the existing government. The Anti-Federalists of Cumberland continued to issue sympathetic addresses to the minority members of the Convention.[60]

At last the affair in Carlisle came to a head. After failing for some time to have the warrants served, Squire Agnew managed to round up seven of the rioters whom he jailed until he could receive further instructions from the Supreme Court. This action aroused the country. Before the militia assembled on March 1, five Radicals met with some Federalists to seek a compromise. They agreed to release the prisoners and to send a joint petition to Council to quash the proceedings. With great demonstration the militia numbering from a thousand to fifteen hundred men marched to the jail and hailed the freeing of their martyrs. Eight weeks later John Montgomery reported that all was quiet in the frontier town. When the Radicals had intimated that McKean was afraid to show himself in Carlisle, the Chief Justice determined to visit the place. On learning this news, the Anti-Federalists turned about face and planned to pay him the compliment of waiting on him as he entered the village. Good sense and compromise prevailed but the spirit of opposition to the Federal Constitution still burned in the breasts of the irreconcilables.[60a]

Last Stand of the Radical Forces

The press continued to pour forth a prolific stream of defense and attack. On the Radical side "Centinel" and "Philadelphiaensis" kept up a running fire after the State had voted for ratification. At first "Centinel" devoted his energies to a statement of the Radical case but after the State adopted the Constitution, he made increasingly vigorous attacks on leading Republicans, especially James Wilson and Robert Morris. The other writer, under the name of "Philadelphiaensis," generally conceded to have been Benjamin Workman, a recent immigrant from Ireland and at this time a tutor at the University of Pennsylvania, engaged in similar newspaper attacks.[61]

The Federalists used a different type of journalistic approach. The wit of the day, Francis Hopkinson, wrote a clever skit in which he compared the Federal Constitution to a new roof. Having furnished the conservatives with this convenient catch-phrase of which they made liberal use, Hopkinson was severely attacked in the press by the opposition. Other Federalists, especially Tench Coxe, circulated their writings in states where the contest over ratification was still undetermined. Rush asked Irvine to have all New York newspapers publish extracts from his speech in the Convention. Tench Coxe continued to write answers to the opposition. Under various signatures he replied to R. H. Lee's attack on the commercial powers of Congress, and assailed the benefits of State sovereignty which in his opinion did "all the mischief in Pennsylvania." Although his articles appeared in the newspapers of the State, he planned to have them republished in New England, New York, and in the South. On several occasions he sent his articles to Rufus King when the contest was waxing hot in Massachusetts.[62]

Although the Federalists rejoiced at the gradual accession of a half dozen states to the new government by the beginning of February, Radical opposition crystallized in Pennsylvania. The lack of an official answer to the address of the minority embarrassed individual Federalists scattered through the Scotch-Irish back-country. Already losing his hold on his whiskey-guzzling congregation because he preached abstinence, John Black, of Marsh Creek, found that the lack of Federalist vindication distressed the faithful conservatives in York County. "In the meantime," he complained, "the anti-foederalists are triumphing as if the publications on their side were unanswerable . . ." [63] The Radicals of neighboring Franklin County petitioned the assembly to take a bold course. It should bring to account the delegates to the Constitutional Convention for exceeding their powers; it should completely reject the Constitution which had been adopted by the ratifying convention; and it should protect the State Constitution from subversion. This was indicative of the new tactics employed by the Anti-Federalists, but the conservatives were not surprised for they had informed each other of the intended avalanche of petitions. The rumor was well-founded. During the month of March the hinterland sent petitions, bearing over five thousand names, to the assembly with the plea that the Constitution should be rejected by the legislature and that the State delegates should be ordered to vote against it in Congress. Some Federalists, like Rush, now admitted privately that their hasty action in rushing through ratification was responsible for this hornets' nest of opposition.[64]

In the western part of the State the Radicals were not inactive. The situation was explained from a partisan slant by Thomas Scott in a letter to Rush in the early days of March, when he wrote:

> Altho many who think not for themselves, think not well of the federal Constitution becaus Tom had long ago told them, that dick had told him, that Henry had told him, that Messr. Finley, Smiley &c had told him it was a bad one, yet the voice of oposition is Scarcely heard, except in a small Circle in Fayette county, where Mr. Smiely rides Triumphant on the wings of Fame, and where after rideing the Cirquet of his Small domean, he Collected to the tune of 30 or 40 holy Grunters, and after mounting the Rostrum and retailing to them Centaniel, Old Whiganical and other Newspapar nonsense for the space of three hours Concluded, that before the hell-born plan should be the Constitution of the united states, he would spend the last blood in his vanes and farthing in his Treasury . . . In a word he laboured to stir the people up to arms but could not well direct them to the Emediate object against which their arms should be used, and therefore happily thought of petitioning the Genl. Assembly . . .[65]

William Findley continued inveterate against the new plan. Aside from deprecating "the methods of Violence and deception" used by his enemies, he believed that fewer changes should have been made; after Congress gradually learned to exercise its additional powers, further amendments would then be in order. He agreed to the requirement that only nine states should be necessary to ratify changes. "I do not object to the construction of the new system," he explained to a friend, "but to the powers as they extend to internal objects, and eventually leaves us no means of relief or protection in the State governments . . ." [66] In addition to speaking in public he contributed articles to the press to forward his views. In Federalist Pittsburgh where Brackenridge upheld the Constitution, it was rumored that Findley and Smiley alarmed the people to the point of inciting them to arms.[67]

David Redick represented the type of Radical who was willing to accept the new order. He advised cheerful submission to the majority. He was attacked on the basis of a rumor that he had written to the followers of Shays in Massachusetts telling them to oppose the Constitution. But he disclaimed any desire to create civil war and asserted he was attempting to reconcile the Radicals to the inevitable.[68]

When news of the ratification by Virginia reached western Pennsylvania, Federalists in the Pittsburgh area assembled on Grant's Hill, listened to an address by Brackenridge, cheered and threw their hats in the air. Bonfires blazed, youths danced, and from a distance Indians watched the proceedings in silence. Nine states had ratified; the Radicals were defeated.[69]

In the eastern part of the State the two factions called each other odious names and complained of mutual artifice and deception. Charges of fraud in settling the public accounts years before were revived against Mifflin and Morris who found it necessary to make formal denials. Two personal letters, written by George Bryan, were intercepted and gleefully spread before the public by the Federalists. As the various states signed acts of ratification, the hopes of the Federalists rose. Men like Rush tended to ignore the opposition or to consider it as a mere handful of malcontents. On July 4 the grand Federal procession gave Philadelphians a treat of pageantry more brilliant than they had ever witnessed, and provided the Republicans with a triumph they had not experienced since the Revolution. The parade was the visible sign of the ascendancy of the conservative, moneyed, merchant group. It was the counter-revolution coming into its own.[70]

Defeated in their struggle against the adoption of the Constitution, the Radicals were not crushed. They made one last desperate effort to obtain their revised objectives. This was the convention at Harrisburg, in September, 1788, which was the swan song of Radical democracy in Pennsylvania. The movement for the Harrisburg convention did not spring up over night. As early as February George Bryan explained privately that plans were on foot to hold a meeting, but that the outcome would depend on the actions of those states to "which we look to hold up the Standard of Liberty." [71] In March one of Bryan's henchmen proposed a method of sending circulars throughout Pennsylvania, New York, and Virginia with suggestions for a modified Constitution. The new movement, however, originated in Cumberland County. A meeting, held in East Pennsborough, resulted in an invitation to the other counties to send delegates to Harrisburg in September for the two-fold purpose of consolidating the friends of amendments and of nominating delegates for election to the new national House of Representatives. There was some response to this appeal, for early next month a meeting was held at Greensburg, where a committee of correspondence was established to stir up sentiment in favor of amendments. At Uniontown two deputies were chosen to attend the proposed convention. About the same time, forty Radicals from the townships of Bucks County met to choose delegates. This organization and selection of delegates in various counties was carried out with such care and secrecy that the Republicans were completely unaware of it.[72]

A varied group met at Harrisburg on September 3, 1788. Representatives from fourteen counties appeared; the remaining five counties of York, Northampton, Westmoreland, Montgomery, and Luzerne failed to send delegates. Of the thirty-three members present, eight had formed part of the minority in the ratifying convention, fourteen had had experience in the State assembly, the Council or in the Censors, and two had been members of Congress. Fifteen, however, had no political experience beyond holding local offices. The leader of the group was George Bryan, aided by such men as Pettit and McClenaghan of Philadelphia, Whitehill and Hoge of Cumberland, and John Smiley of Fayette. Among the unknown members was young Albert Gallatin who prepared a set of resolutions for the meeting; although they were not adopted, the gist of them was contained in the resolutions which were adopted. In a mild, concilatory tone the convention called on the people of the State to acquiesce in the organization of the new government, declared the necessity of speedy revision by a general convention, and drew up a petition to the assembly requesting that body to obtain amendments by a general convention of all the states. Then the Radicals listed twelve changes which they deemed essential to protect the people and the states from the potential tyranny of strong federal government.[73]

The Federalists had little cause to worry about the action taken at Harrisburg. Bingham had joyously exulted that it had defeated the purpose of the Anti-Federalists because he understood few counties sent delegates. The Philadelphia Republicans were irritated, however, because the Radical meeting had been arranged and held without their knowledge. Until the proceedings were published in the city newspapers, the conservatives were consumed with curiosity. Moderates pointed out the conciliatory tone of the meeting and suggested that the Federalists should act in a similar spirit and agree to amendments.[74]

Twice during the following year the Radicals re-echoed the sentiments of the Harrisburg Convention in the assembly. In October they attempted to refer to the next session the amendments submitted by Massachusetts, New York, and Virginia. By a vote of twenty-four to thirty-eight they lost. Four months later Virginia proposed a convention of the states to consider amendments. Again the Radical minority vainly attempted to have the house endorse this plan. But by a two-to-one vote the Republicans politely rebuked Virginia for its presumption. Having won their victory in the adoption of the Federal Constitution, the conservatives would not consider the idea of entrusting it to any revising body. The demand for the essential rights of the people, however, was too strong to be resisted, and in March, 1790, the assembly adopted the first ten amendments without opposition. Essentially, this was a Radical victory, for these amendments constituted some of their demands; the action was indicative of the compromise spirit which was infusing state political circles.[75]

Steps Toward the Goal

Just as the election of assemblymen in 1787 was overshadowed by the larger issue of ratification of the Federal Constitution, so the election of 1788 was of minor consequence because of the approaching election of delegates for the new Congress. There were no major issues. In Philadelphia the Republicans attempted to confound their opponents by hurling charges based on the Harrisburg convention. It was asserted that at the meeting the Radicals had made amendments and civil war alternatives, that the whole incident was the result of dark, secret conniving, and that in some districts the people were told that the convenion had been called by order of Congress. After the official proceedings of the convention had been published, the Federalists asserted that the real object of the Radicals at Harrisburg was to marshall their forces for the approaching election. In Montgomery County Federalists pleaded with the faithful not to split their tickets for assemblymen.[76]

The election left the house much the same as it had been. Forty-eight of the sixty-nine members were re-elected, and the Republicans retained control by a two-to-one majority. By unanimous vote Richard Peters was escorted to the Speaker's chair. In the election of executive officers of the State, the Republicans brushed away one more vestige of Radical supremacy. The first and second offices were filled by first-line Republicans. Franklin who had served his three years was ineligible. Although he had favored the Republicans on most issues, he had been originally proposed by the Constitutionalists. Thomas Mifflin became President by a unanimous vote. A few days before the election Charles Biddle, a mild Radical, had resigned as Vice-President to accept another office. In his place was elected David Redick, a Radical willing to accept the Federal Constitution, but desiring amendments. Feeling that failure of re-election would constitute a great personal mortification, Redick undoubtedly suffered the anticipated humiliation, for by twenty votes he lost and George Ross, an unflinching conservative, became Vice-President. The executive and the legislative branches were in control of the conservative forces.[77]

The important political activity of the fall of 1788 centered in the choice of senators and representatives for the new Congress. Taking no chances on the composition of the next assembly, the expiring session in September chose the two senators. Long before this session convened on September 2, George Clymer and William Maclay had been talked of for the posts, but political winds shifted quickly. A number of citizens waited on Robert Morris and received his consent to serve; thereupon he and John Armstrong, Jr., were considered the logical candidates. The Anti-Federalist forces considered their old standard bearer, Franklin, whom they planned to team with the moderate William Irvine; but there were drawbacks to this plan. Some even thought of taking up Maclay who was feeling bitter at being dropped by the Republicans. When it was pointed out that Irvine had been appointed by Congress to settle accounts in the Treasury Department, James McLene considered it "as A Scheme hatched" to put Irvine out of the running. In the ensuing two and a half weeks developments occurred so that the day before election the Republicans discovered that Armstrong could muster only seven out of thirty-three votes. Armstrong's youth and inexperience in public life were handicaps and the Republicans turned to their original choice of William Maclay. On the morning of the election Armstrong and Muhlenberg were withdrawn by their respective parties, and the ballots showed sixty-six votes for Maclay, thirty-seven for Morris, and thirty-one for the luckless Irvine. Irvine's friends reported that the Maclay clique arranged at the last moment to freeze him out. Thus Morris and Maclay became the first senators to Congress from Pennsylvania.[78]

More unique was the popular election of members of the national house of representatives. When the question of the date of the election came up in the assembly, thirteen Republicans wanted to set it for the first Wednesday in January. This was overwhelmingly opposed. The eastern Federalists might have believed that mid-winter weather would decrease the Radical vote. The date was set for the last Wednesday in November. Eight representatives and ten presidential electors were to be chosen by the people. The Republicans realized that they could be sure of success only if the election was held on the statewide basis and not by districts. It was the only election of this type held under the Constitution of 1776.[79]

The Radical ticket for representatives was designed to appeal to various groups. Pettit and McClenaghan represented the merchant and public creditor classes in Philadelphia. Daniel Heister and Peter Muhlenberg were Republicans placed on the ticket to attract the German vote. William Irvine was a Republican from Cumberland County, and William Montgomery a Westmoreland Constitutionalist. The Radical appeal was based on the plea that although they wished to see the new national government launched, amendments to the Constitution were absolutely necessary. Their appeal ended with a typical warning: "The liberties of our country are at stake." [80]

The Republicans chose their candidates at a convention at Lancaster. Each county held meetings where delegates were chosen to attend the nominating convention. In Northampton County the delegates were instructed to choose men who possessed integrity, industry, and extensive economic background. They were ordered to compose a slate containing two merchants, a man versed in manufactures, an eminent lawyer, and four "substantial yoemen." [81] In Philadelphia the committee of wards agreed on a ticket to be submitted at the State convention. At Lancaster, twenty-eight delegates represented all counties but Luzerne; the number and prominence of the eastern delegates dominated the conference with James Wilson at the helm. The ticket agreed on included Clymer and FitzSimons from Philadelphia. The remaining six had been members of the ratifying convention: Muhlenberg from Montgomery, Wynkoop from Bucks, Chambers from Lancaster, Allison from Franklin, Hartley from York, and Scott from Washington.[82]

The issue of the election was largely on party lines. Republicans declared that the Radical ticket was composed of men who had introduced the test laws and tender acts, had enforced the burdensome militia law on the farmers, had squandered the confiscated property, loaded the State with more than its share of the public debt, and had driven specie out of circulation by the last paper money emission. The Federalists pointed to their own candidates as men interested in opening new avenues of commerce which would benefit sailors and mechanics; in fact, some of their candidates had already established manufactures which were supporting hundreds of inhabitants.[83]

After the two tickets had been submitted to the public, the Germans kicked up the dust and declared their political independence Although one-third of the population of the State was of that nationality, they asserted the Federalists had placed only one German on their ticket and the Anti-Federalists only two. So the Germans proposed to alter the

Federalist ticket by dropping Allison and Chambers and inserting Peter Muhlenberg and Daniel Heister, two Germans, on the opposition slate.[84]

Although only six of their eight candidates were successful, the Republicans won a complete victory. Chambers and Allison lost to Peter Muhlenberg and Daniel Heister. It was the hybrid German ticket which decided the election; in other respects the vote was on strictly party lines. This is the first time that returns are available which show that the Germans threw off the party leadership and voted on lines of nationality. There were, however, some surprising exceptions, for the German insurgency took place not in York and Lancaster counties where that nationality was very prominent, but in Northumberland, Montgomery, and to a lesser extent in Philadelphia City and County, and in Bedford County. Another aspect of the election was the relative strength of the two parties. Although the Radicals had been gradually losing power in the Council and assembly over a period of several years, this statewide popular election showed that they could still muster a force which undoubtedly made the Republicans feel very uncomfortable. The change of one thousand or fifteen hundred votes could have spelled disaster to the conservative forces.[85]

Little interest was shown in the choice of presidential electors. The conservative slate, known variously as the "Lancaster Ticket" and "Federalist Ticket," was headed by James Wilson and seven lesser lights. The "Harrisburg Ticket," representing the Radicals' choice was less outstanding. The result was a complete victory for the conservatives. Although it was assumed that Washington would be President, Alexander Hamilton became nervous over the thought that if a few votes were withheld from Washington, John Adams might win first place. Late in January he proposed to James Wilson that two or three votes in Pennsylvania should be diverted from Adams. This plan was carried out, for Adams received eight votes and Hancock two.[86]

In the meantime the rigid Radicals in Council displayed their attitude toward the new Federal frame of government. A proposed message to the assembly expressing the universal joy over the adoption of the Constitution by the states came to a vote in Council where three members opposed it. A statement in the message that the ill feeling over the document "had been gradually lulled" provoked five Radical Councillors to ask for a re-wording of the idea, for they were not willing to agree that the opposition had capitulated. With the majority of the Council Republican, these protests went unheeded.[87]

To keep up a semblance of national government until the new Congress would meet, the assembly elected three delegates to the expiring legislature. They were John Armstrong, Jr., James R. Reid, and Tench Coxe.[88]

The struggle over the Federal Constitution and the election of State senators and representatives did not divert the Republicans from their plans of carrying out reforms at home. In this session the four important issues which received attention were the licensing of the theatre, the revision of the penal code, the restoration of the College, and the incorporation of Philadelphia.

An old question which was settled during the year was that of licensing the theatre to stage performances. The actors, Hallam and Henry, had been petitioning the house perennially. In November, 1787, these two men in the name of the American Company asked for the repeal of the law prohibiting dramatic entertainments. But the motion was killed. It was not until the fall of 1788 that favorable action was taken. A committee reported in favor of the theatre with the explanation that far from being the "corruptor of mankind," the stage constituted "the great Mart of Genius, and as such, a natural and necessary concomitant of our independence." [89] At once the Quakers protested and the house thought it convenient to ask Hallam to withdraw his request. After the fall elections were over and the house reconvened early in 1788, the agitation was revived. The Philadelphia members worked on a bill for repeal of the prohibition, while petitions carrying several thousand names were presented both for and against the measure. Opposition to the theatre came mainly from the Radical back-country members who, as the newspapers pointed out, would be least affected by the action. When the Radicals saw defeat ahead, they tried to insert in the bill a provision that the actors of each performance should pay a stipulated fee to the State treasury. This was defeated. The bill passed by a majority of eight votes.[90] In overthrowing the political aspects of Radical democracy, the counter-revolutionary forces thus invaded the social sphere and cast off the Presbyterian and Quaker control of public morals. Truly a change was taking place.

The new penal code passed by the assembly early in 1786 had removed the death penalty for a number of offenses, substituted imprisonment, and lightened other punishments. Also a complete change had been effected in the mode of punishment. The new system provided for taking the prisoners out of jail and putting them to work on public improvements, such as cleaning streets and digging ditches. The prisoners wore a distinctive costume; those accused of serious offenses wore ball and chain, the less serious offenders drove wheelbarrows. And hence the prisoners under this new system were nicknamed the "wheelbarrow" men. Scarcely had the new law gone into operation when an important Republican newspaper began to condemn the liberal features of the new rules of punishment, and implied that it was the work of the Radicals who could justify their act only on the ground that it was an experiment. An increase in burglaries was noted and ascribed to the new system. For almost two years the system was in operation. But there was increasing opposition. In the fall of 1788 the *Packet* issued a vehement cry against convicts working in public and voiced popular clamor for a return to the practice of solitary confinement. It was not until 1790, however, that the wheelbarrow system was abolished.[91]

The assembly continued on its work of sweeping away the vestiges of Radical supremacy in the State. To the conservatives one of the most galling symbols of Radicalism was the University. The petitions of William Smith, former Provost of the College, at last found a favorable reception. In March, 1788, his petition was committed to a grand committee elected by ballot. Although Findley and McLene were included in the committee, it was overwhelmingly conservative. This action was met by a counter-petition from the faculty of the University which was intended to neutralize Smith's plea. For once Rush's predictions were correct when he remarked of Bryan and his colleagues in the University: "I view them as oxen decorated with ribbons, parading the streets of a great city previous to their being lead to the place of their destruction."[92] By the fall of 1788 the attack was already under way when a Radical writer used the same argument to defend the University as had been used by the Republicans in 1779. The assembly, he counseled, should not act on the presumption that the faculty or trustees were Anti-Federal, or that they were usurpers, and added apologetically that perhaps Federal ideas might have rendered the late commencement more entertaining. In February the house declared that the rescinding of the charter in 1779 had been founded on no just cause of forfeiture but was a direct violation of the Constitution. Although the restoration was inevitable, the crucial question involved the disposition of the estates which provided the endowment of the University. A spirit of compromise prevailed. The University was forced to hand over the buildings and equipment to the College, but was allowed to retain the estates set aside for it since 1779.[93]

After insisting on the incorporation of the City of Philadelphia over a number of years, the Republicans finally gained their victory in 1789. In November of the previous year the city members of the assembly were authorized to report a bill providing for incorporation. Opposition to the bill was negligible. The arguments offered in favor of the change centered mainly on the need of better municipal administration in regard to health and police regulation. Along with other important questions brought up in the fall session, nothing was done until the election had been held. In February the city members and Speaker Peters met at Hassler's Tavern to discuss and perfect the measure. When it came to a test vote in the house only six members opposed, all inveterate Radicals from the back-country. On March 11 the bill became law. Framed on popular principles, it gave little uneasiness to those who formerly had been averse to the proposal. It took control of the City from the hands of the Executive Council and the assembly and put it in charge of a board of aldermen and a common council, headed by a mayor. The Republicans were not slow to put their favorite measure into practice, for the elections for councilmen and aldermen were held in April. The aldermen elected were all old-line conservatives like Samuel Miles, Hilary Baker, Francis Hopkinson, John M. Nesbitt. For mayor they chose Samuel Powell who had been the last mayor of Philadelphia before the war. Certainly the Revolution was over when a man like Powell was reinstated at the head of the City. The members of the council also represented the old Quakers and conservative merchant element. As Powell emerged in this election, so among the councilmen was Benjamin Chew who made his first public appearance since the Revolution. Times had changed. Men of wealth, social prestige, and respectability were coming to the front.[94]

Final Victory: The Constitution of 1790

As the remaining vestiges of Radical democracy crumbled, the Republicans began an attack on the last fortress, the Constitution of 1776. In 1777, 1778, and 1783-1784 they had attempted to overthrow the Radical frame but each time they had failed. The fourth attempt was crowned with success.

One of the earliest suggestions for a convention to alter the frame of government appeared in June, 1788, when a correspondent in the *Gazette* said that the State ratification of the Federal Constitution automatically abrogated parts of the State court. He declared that a session of the Council of Censors was too expensive, but he admitted the real fear by remarking that the Censors would be controlled by the Radicals. The attack began in earnest as soon as the Federal Constitution had been ratified by the State. The Republicans pointed out inconsistencies between State and Federal forms of government and demanded that the former must give way. Aside from these objections to the Radical Constitution, the old stock arguments were brought forth and repeated. The Executive Council was growing cumbersome and expensive, since the number of counties had increased from twelve in 1776 to nineteen in 1788. A single executive and bicameral legislature would be more effective in checking hasty and ill advised lawmaking.[95]

In the second session of the assembly which met in the spring of 1789, the conservatives decided to act. On the night of March 19 about thirty members congregated at the City Tavern and worked out plans for appealing to the public. On the following day Wynkoop moved the house to address the people at large, requesting them to indicate whether they wished for a convention to alter the Constitution. The resulting address pointed out that the people had that right. The reasons for a change were then listed. The Federal Constitution must be predominant; expenses of the State had been too great, and the single legislature needed a check; and the bicameral system of Congress was suggested as a model. There was also the complaint that the Council was not elected on the basis of population. The conservatives realized that the Radicals would advance the argument that the Council of Censors would meet within a year and a half; to this they answered that it would take two years or more until a convention could be called by the Censors, if the Censors would be so disposed. Four days later the assembly adopted these resolutions by a vote of forty-one to seventeen, the minority consisting of the unremitting Constitutionalists from the back-country. The Radicals offered their reasons against a convention. The Constitution provided a regular machinery for amendments in the Council of Censors, and this body would meet next year. It was not true, they continued, that the government under the prevailing frame had laid heavy financial burdens on the State. Another denial was given to the charge that the State and Federal Constitutions clashed. Furthermore, it was possible that the Federal Constitution might soon be changed by considerable amendments. On general principles they maintained that frequent changes in government would create a disrespect for constituted authority. Forging ahead, the Republicans ordered the resolutions of March 24 printed on handbills for distribution throughout the State.[96]

It is difficult to learn what maneuvering initiated the movement for a new constitution except that Benjamin Rush claimed he was active in it. A few weeks before the matter came on the floor of the house, Gerardus Wynkoop, William Maclay, Thomas FitzSimons, and James Wilson had met at Rush's residence and discussed plans. Oddly enough, Robert Morris did not have a hand in the work, and although he was absent at the time, he was not even consulted in the business. But he gave his full support to the movement and looked for a frame of government which would be "capable of protecting Life & property and of establishing a due execution of justice."[97]

The assembly called on the Executive Council to join in forwarding the plan for a convention. The members of Council split on the question and by a party vote of six to seven declined to comply. Making the most of this rebuff, the Radical minority in the assembly issued a long appeal to the people against the resolutions of March 24, in which they repeated their former arguments. Their appeal to class feeling emerged when they declared that the Republicans planned an upper house where *"the better born may be separated from the common countrymen."* [98] Newspaper articles appeared for and against the movement but added little to the official arguments already given on both sides of the question. Republicans stressed the fact that Georgia had recently adopted a new constitution in which it discarded the unicameral idea.[99]

The Radicals made attempts to organize their strength in some of the back-counties. In Franklin they called a meeting in which they formally disapproved of the measure taken by the conservative majority, asserted the assembly did not have power to initiate steps toward altering the prevailing form of government, and arranged to draw up remonstrances. The Republicans reported that in Cumberland County vigorous measures were taken to oppose the call for a convention, even to the extent of threatening to burn the houses of those who signed petitions for that purpose.[100]

As time went on some Republicans doubted whether they could carry through their favorite project. Robert Morris assured Richard Peters that in Philadelphia everyone was "Ripe for a Change." "There is nothing to fear;" he continued, "you must therefore push on boldly for it will not do to look back," and assured him of his willingness to cooperate in the cause.[101] George Clymer decided not to meet the assembly, because the violent feeling against Congress for refusing to come to Philadelphia "would rather injure than aid the cause of the convention." [102] Although Republicans in Philadelphia urged rural conservatives to be diligent in having petitions signed, and had expected a great flood of such memorials, the response was not so favorable as they had anticipated.[103] This was one of the important reasons for the Republicans' pessimism.

When the September session of the assembly opened, the conservatives followed Morris' dictum that it would "not do to look back," and pushed ahead with their program. Wrangling over the matter for several days, the grand committee finally reported that the majority of the people wanted a convention in preference to the Council of Censors, and indicated that only "a slender opposition" had been encountered. This report suggested that the convention should be called at Philadelphia at the end of November. The house did not accept the committee report at once. On the following day, the Radical minority made two attempts to inject their own ideas into an otherwise inevitable situation. First they asked the assembly to formulate a plan by which the opinions of the citizens of the State could be canvassed on whether a convention was desired. This suggestion was defeated by a two-to-one vote. They then tried to have the meeting place changed from Philadelphia to Lancaster. This proposal met a similar fate but by a closer vote. At last the house agreed to the original report to call the convention; the vote stood thirty-nine to seventeen. With an expiring gesture the Radicals protested in vain and spread upon the journals the reasons for their opposition.[104]

To justify their actions the Republicans resorted to a method formerly employed by their opponents. Since early spring they had conducted a vigorous campaign to secure signers to petitions for a convention. By September they reaped a harvest of over ten thousand signatures; less than six hundred persons had remonstrated against a convention. Under similar circumstances the Radicals had rescinded the call for a convention in 1779. Now they were forced to taste their own medicine. In the press "Centinel" asserted that the number of petitioners for a convention composed but a small fraction of the taxables of the state, in fact only about one-seventh. To this he added the accusation that James Wilson had attempted to change the election laws to favor the Republicans but had failed. Forgetting his own party's action eleven years before, the writer termed the assembly's action "high treason."[105] There is only one reason to explain why the Republicans did not take a vote of the people on the subject; the returns on the statewide election for congressmen and presidential electors demonstrated that while the Republicans had a majority of the votes, it was a majority so slight that the shifting of several hundred ballots could change victory to defeat. This would never support their contention that everyone except "a slender opposition" clamored for a convention.[106]

As soon as the issue had been settled and the assembly had called a convention, the house anticipated adjournment. This was especially true of the Western members who wanted to get home to mend fences and inject backbone into the opposition movement. Early in October young Albert Gallatin tried to persuade the Western voters to denounce the actions of the assembly and to refuse to elect delegates to the convention. But all of this came too late. The western counties elected full delegations to the convention, and ironically Gallatin was one of those so chosen.[107]

The election of assemblymen in the fall of 1789 took place almost unnoticed. One reason was that the Radicals were so far discredited as to be submerged by the increasing wave of conservatism. Another cause was the election of members to the Constitutional Convention. The best leaders on both sides were placed on the ticket for this purpose, hence only men second in abilities or in popular favor were available to run for the assembly. One observer thought the new legislative body was completely destitute of men of talent.[108]

The Republicans maintained their control in the new house. Richard Peters continued as Speaker, while Mifflin and Ross were unanimously re-elected President and Vice-President of Council. At once the house arranged to regard the new Federal Constitution as uppermost by adding provisoes to the oaths required of assembly members to the effect they were binding only in so far as they were not altered by the new national frame of government.[109] The action of this house during the ensuing year was unimpressive and drab. Most of the important aims of the conservatives had been accomplished except the crowning work of rewriting the State Constitution, and that work was then in progress.

Meeting in Philadelphia late in November, the State Constitutional Convention assembled a varied group of deputies. The conservatives had undisputed control. They sent a strong representation of legal talent from Philadelphia when they elected James Wilson, William Lewis, and Thomas McKean. These men were supported by an impressive group of followers such as Mifflin, Gray, Tyson, and Irvine. Though only a handful, the old Radicals sent their steady and reliable leaders, Robert Whitehill, William Findley, John Smiley, and James McLene. Three-fifths of the members had previous experience in public life. Thomas Miffln became presiding officer. Half a century later Albert Gallatin wrote that the convention "was one of the ablest bodies of which I was a member and with which I was acquainted." [110]

The important work was done in the committee of the whole which provided greater freedom of debate and less formality in parliamentary procedure. By unanimous vote McKean became chairman of this important committee, and was granted the unusual privilege of a member on the floor. When a piece of business was completed by the committee, it was reported to the convention; if adopted it was then referred to a committee of nine where it was properly phrased for inclusion in the final document. William Findley was chosen chairman of this committee of nine by a unanimous vote. The rest of the members were Republicans.[111]

These unanimous votes may seem odd until it is explained that a spirit of conciliation, unknown in Pennsylvania since the Revolution, descended upon the convention. In the early days of the session Findley and Wilson had a confidential talk in which the Radical leader explained that if Wilson and other conservatives would refrain from violent attacks on the Constitution which was held dear by the unbending Radicals, they would make greater headway and preserve harmony in attaining the desired alterations. Wilson took the advice; and he and Findley cooperated in launching a sane discussion of amendments. Wilson no longer attacked the Radicals and Findley skillfully pointed out the weaknesses of the document of his followers. As a further gesture, the old Constitution was taken as the basis on which to propose amendments. With the ground prepared, Findley and other members asked Wilson to initiate resolutions for amendments because it was known that he had come with a proposed draft in his pocket.[112]

The essential features of the new Constitution were a bicameral legislature, a single executive with a check on the law-making activities of the assembly, tenure of judges during good behaviour, and fixed salaries for the judiciary. Most of the debate occurred in working out the details, and it was on these details that the members split into opposing camps, not along the old party lines, but on the basis of aristocratic versus democratic theories of government. The aristocratic group, composing but a core of the ultra-conservatives, usually lost to the great majority of members formed by a coalition of Radicals and moderate conservatives. For example, Ross proposed that the upper house of assembly should be elected by the lower house, whereas Gallatin and Wilson argued for popular election of senators. Gallatin also strove for a larger representation in the lower house and for an extension of the franchise. Findley wished to retain some of the forms of the old Constitution when he proposed an advisory council to check the governor. The only vestige of his suggestion was the creation of the office of Secretary of the Commonwealth. Several of the provisions for popular education are also credited to Findley.[113]

The Convention found it necessary to agree on a method of transition from the old to the new government. There was the fear that confusion in public business would result if all the office-holders were discharged at one time, which undoubtedly would have been the case. A committee of four, headed by Findley, prepared a *modus operandi.* Laws not inconsistent with the new Constitution would continue in force; the President and Executive Council would exercise their authority until the third Tuesday in December, but no vacancies in Council would be filled; all officers appointed by Council would continue in power until the first of September, 1791; judges of the Supreme Court would serve out the term of their commissions. The first Senate would consist of eighteen members, who along with the President, would be elected in the same manner as assemblymen.[114]

After ordering the proposed Constitution to be printed for public distribution, the Convention adjourned on February 26, with plans to reassemble on August 9. During the first session of the Convention and the months following its adjournment, the general satisfaction of the people with its work was remarkable. The newspapers contained very little comment on the subject. From Carlisle, located in the heart of the Radical country, John Montgomery wrote in August that no petitions would be offered against it, and that very little was said about it. The second session of the Convention lasted from August 9 to September 2. A few details were altered but no important changes were made in the

Constitution. On the last day the document was adopted. There was no provision for submitting it to a vote of the people, nor did that seem necessary, for apparently everyone accepted it. The day following the promulgation of the Constitution, fifty-six members of the assembly considered their power suspended by the new act; the Speaker did not take the chair, and the members ceased to meet. Thus the assembly, under the old frame of government, committed constitutional suicide so suddenly that the Clerk could not learn how to complete the records.[115]

The Counter-Revolution was accomplished. It took fourteen years to complete the curve from the days in 1776 when the conservatives lost their control until 1790 when they returned to complete leadership in the State. This does not imply that they restored conditions exactly as they had been in 1776. Times had changed; the past could not be recalled. The Republicans, for example, made no serious attempt to limit the suffrage by property qualifications. But in the Constitution of 1790 they secured a form of government under which they could feel safe from the excesses which characterized the State under the Radical regime. To make their triumph more complete they had inaugurated a national government which exemplified their political ideals.

NOTES

Abbreviations

Due to frequent citation, the following abbreviations have been used in the notes.

AHA:	American Historical Association.
Burnett:	Burnett, E. C., comp., *Letters of Members of the Continental Congress.*
Eve. Post:	*Pennsylvania Evening Post.*
Freeman's Journ:	*Freeman's Journal, or the North American Intelligencer.*
Gazette:	*Pennsylvania Gazette.*
Gemein. Phil. Corr:	*Gemeinnutzige Philadelphische Correspondenz.*
HSP:	Historical Society of Pennsylvania.
Indep. Gaz.:	*Independent Gazetteer, or the Chronicle of Freedom.*
JCC:	*Journals of the Continental Congress* (Library of Congress edition).
Journal:	*Pennsylvania Journal and Weekly Advertiser.*
Journ. Censors:	*Journal of the Council of Censors.*
JPA:	*Journal of the Pennsylvania Assembly.*
LC:	Library of Congress.
MHS *Colls.:*	*Collections* of the Massachusetts Historical Society.
NYHS *Colls.:*	*Collections* of the New York Historical Society.
NYPL *Bull.:*	New York Public Library *Bulletin.*
Pa. Arch.:	*Pennsylvania Archives.* All references are to the first series unless otherwise noted.
Packet:	*Pennsylvania Packet, or the General Advertiser.*
PCR:	Minutes of Supreme Executive Council in *Pennsylvania Colonial Records.*
PMHB:	*Pennsylvania Magazine of History and Biography.*

P.R.P.: Post-Revolutionary Papers, Archives Division, Harrisburg, Penna.

PSL: *The Statutes at Large of Pennsylvania.*

R. P.: Revolutionary Papers, Archives Division.

Susq. Trans.: Transcripts of the Papers of the Susquehanna Company in the possession of Julian P. Boyd.

Notes to Preface

1. Lincoln, *Revolutionary Movement in Pennsylvania, 1760-1776.*

2. Selsam, *The Pennsylvania Constitution of 1776: A Study in Revolutionary Democracy.*

3. E. Bruce Thomas, *Political Tendencies in Pennsylvania, 1783-1794,* was published after the present work was completed. He confined his investigation to the formal legislative records, some newspapers, and contemporary pamphlet literature.

Notes to Chapter I

1. The tendency of recent research on colonial population has been to decrease the estimates given by contemporaries. Stella Sutherland, *Pop. Distr. in Col. Amer.,* pp. 120-168, did much spade work in tabulating and analyzing the returns of taxables in *Pa. Arch.,* 3rd ser., XII-XXII, which apply mainly to the year 1779. These records however are incomplete, and Miss Sutherland did not use as a check on her results the list of taxables for 1779 and 1786 on which representation in the assembly was based. For number of taxables, see *JPA,* Sept. 6, 1786, p. 295; *Packet,* Sept. 11, 1786; neither of these lists is complete, but *cf.* Warville, *Travels,* p. 180. The estimate of 380,000 persons given by Boudinot, *Journal,* p. 97, is obviously too high. Rossiter, *Century of Population Growth,* p. 47, gives the data for 1790. Various contemporary estimates of population for the period 1775-1790 have been compiled by Greene and Harrington, *American Population before Federal Census of 1790,* pp. 7-8, 116-120. On immigration: *Gazette,* Sept. 22, 1784; *Packet,* June 3, 1785; "Philadelphua" in *Herald,* Aug. 10, 1785; Bingham to Price, Dec. 1, 1786, MHS *Proceed.,* 2 ser., XVII, pp. 360-362. On emigration: Bancroft to Frazer, Nov. 8, 1783, Bancroft, *Formation,* I, p. 333; Coxe to Livingston, Feb. 15, 1789, Burnett, VIII, p. 821n.; "Lucullus" in *Gazette,* Nov. 5, 1788; "A Citizen of Philadelphia" and unsigned articles in issues of Feb. 4, 25, Mar. 4, 1789.

2. Rossiter, *op. cit.,* pp. 11, 13, 142. *Packet,* Aug. 22, 1786, under New York date-line, suggests that Philadelphia contained about 32,200, excluding strangers. *Cf.* Sumner, *Financier and Finances,* II, p. 144; *Packet,* Sept. 20, 1783. T. Coxe, *View,* pp. 311-314. York in 1788 boasted 2,884; MS. "Extracts" from Committee Minutes, Nov. 11-21, 1788, York Co. Hist. Soc.

3. "Report of Committee on Linguistic and National Stocks," AHA *Report for 1931,* I, pp. 124-125. *Cf.* older study by Rossiter, *op. cit.,* p. 272, whose results gave a larger percentage of English stock and a smaller proportion of other stocks. On the Germans, see Barker's discussion, AHA *Report for 1931,* I, pp. 291-294.

4. W. F. Dunaway's article on the English element in *PMHB,* LII, pp. 317-341; and the same author's *Hist. of Penna.,* pp. 73-95.

5. Warville, *New Travels,* pp. 186-187. Rush, *Manners of the Germans.* They used little slave labor.

6. On Muhlenberg, see Seidensticker's article in *PMHB,* XIII. Fred. Muhlenberg to Henry Muhlenberg, June 28, 1784, Muhlenberg MSS, contains the uncomplimentary reference which Seidensticker omitted from his translation. For a sample of Muhlenberg's attempt at political writing, see his "Freymüthige Gedanken" broadside, Gilpin Coll.; and the articles signed "Ein Deutscher" in *Gemein. Phil. Corr.,* Feb. 13, 20, Mar. 13, 1782. Lincoln, *Rev. Mov. in Penna.,* pp. 25-37. J. Bayley to Wharton, June 27,; R. McAllister to Wharton, Aug. 28, 1777; *Pa. Arch.,* V, pp. 405-406, 558-560. A. McLean to Bryan, Sept. 3, R. P., XV, p. 6. Burd to Yeates, July 2, Yeates, MSS. "De Witt" in *Packet,* Mar. 18, 1777; "Philerene" in *Eve. Post,* Mar. 18, 1777; letter in *Gazette,* Dec. 4, 1782. *Indep. Gaz.,* Oct. 25, 1787. There was a German Society in Philadelphia but there is no evidence that it had any political significance.

7. Helfenstein to Wharton, Jan. 11, 1778, *Pa. Arch.,* 2 ser., III, p. 162.

8. *E. g.* "Anzug eines Briefs" in *Gemein. Phil. Corr.,* Mar. 24, 1784; "Ein Deutscher Burger" in *ibid.,* May 17, 1785. MS. Council Minutes, Jan. 29, 1778, I, pp. 201-202. *JPA,* Aug. 6, 1784, p. 263.

9. The correspondence of Benjamin Rush contains numerous interesting references to the Scotch-Irish Presbyterians. But since Rush always guided his pen by his prejudices, the letters must be used with great care. Rush to Armstrong, Mar. 19, July 30, 1783; Linn to Rush, July 25, 1784; in vol. 41, pp. 33-34, 81. Rush to Linn, May 4; to Nesbitt, Aug. 27, 1784; in MS. "Letters and Thoughts," I. Rush to John Bayard, June 25, 1784, vol. 39, p. 33. "Candid" in *Indep. Gaz.,* Feb. 5, 1785.

10. Cabeen, "Society of Sons of Saint Tammany," *PMHB,* XXVI. Hugh Campbell, *Friendly Sons of Saint Patrick.* Hazard to Belknap, June 14, 1784, *Belknap Papers,* pt. 1, pp. 355-356, comments on origin of the name Tammany. In 1790 the Hibernian Society was formed which did not have the exclusive character of the Saint Patrick organization; *Gazette,* Apr. 7, 1790; and also Campbell, *op. cit.*

11. W. F. Dunaway's article on the French, *PMHB,* LIII, pp. 332-342. On the Jews, see *Freeman's Journ.,* Jan. 21, 1784; *Journ. Censors,* Dec. 27, 1783. The French minister in 1785 reported only 7,700 Catholics in the combined population of Pennsylvania and Delaware; Marbois to Vergennes, Mar. 27, 1785, Bancroft, *Formation,* I, p. 421.

12. Levers to Matlack, Nov. 15, 1777, R. P., XVII, p. 1. Hubley to Matlack, July, 1777, *ibid.,* XIII, p. 66. J. Maxwell to Irvine, n. d., Irvine MSS, X, p. 76. Irvine to Wayne, Mar. 20, 1781, Wayne MSS, XII, p. 76. Thos. Scott to J. Nicholson, June 1, 1783, Hand Papers, p. 44

13. Okeley to Rush, Dec. 25, 1784, Rush MSS, vol. 43, p. 107.

14. *Indep. Gaz.,* Sept. 10, 1785, quoting *Carlisle Gazette.* Jos. Hall to Rush, Aug. 28, 1786, Rush MSS, vol. 33, pt. 1, p. 115, complained that Pittsburgh lacked a postal service. "N" in *Indep. Gaz.,* Mar. 8, 1787.

15. *Indep. Gaz.,* Aug. 8, 1787. Scott to Rush, Mar. 3, 1788, Rush MSS, vol. 43, p. 121. A. Campbell to Bryan, Mar. 9, 1788; Hart to Campbell, Mar. 7, 1787, Bryan MSS.

16. "A Federal Centinel" in *Gazette,* Sept. 10, 1788. Rossiter, *Century of Population Growth,* p. 35.

17. Spotswood to J. Belknap, June 19, 1788, MHS *Colls.,* 6 ser., IV, p. 410.

18. *PSL,* June 14, 1777, ch. 757, sect. 7, IX, p. 121. For typical notices of election, see *Indep. Gaz.,* Sept. 27, 1783, and *Packet,* Sept. 26, 1788.

19. *PSL,* Mar. 23, 1778, ch. 790, IX, pp. 223-225.

20. *PSL,* Sept. 13, 1785; Sept. 19, 1786; Sept. 13, 1787; chs. 1176, 1242, 1307, XII, pp. 25-52, 290-296, 502.

21. *JPA,* June 17, 1777; Nov. 28, 1778; pp. 146, 246-247.

22. Thos. Whitesides *et al.* to Council, Oct. 20, 1778; Hartley to Reed, Mar. 17, 1779; Memorial, Oct. 9, 1781; *Pa. Arch.,* VII, pp. 19-20, 2 ser., III, pp. 220-223, 279-281. MS. Council Minutes, Feb. 13, 16, 1779, I, pp. 481-482, 484. *JPA,* Nov. 23, 1781, pp. 520-522. *Journ. Censors,* Dec. 30, 31, 1783; Jan. 3, 1784.

23. MS. *JPA,* Oct. 31, Nov. 3, 17, 1783, pp. 8-10, 20-21, 71. *JPA,* Nov. 3, 5, 1783; Nov. 12, 1784; Nov. 14, 1787; pp. 13, 31; p. 17, p. 56. Petition, Oct. 30, 1788, Nead Papers. *Freeman's Journ.,* Oct. 20, 27, 1784. *Packet,* Nov. 2, 1786.

24. "Demophilus" in *Packet,* Sept. 17, 1776. Marshall, *Diary,* Oct. 31, 1776, p. 100.

25. "A True Friend to Liberty" in *Journal,* Sept. 3, 1777. He suggested a more complicated method. The freeholders in each ward and township should meet four to six weeks before election and settle on a ticket. Then two men from each township should assemble and form two

or three tickets from the names submitted from each township. These composite tickets would then be offered to the voter on election day.

26. "An Inhabitant of Cumberland County" in *Journal,* Oct. 1, 1783. *Carlisle Gazette,* Sept. 27, 1786. *Gazette,* Nov. 12, 1788. For a case of political double-crossing, see *Indep. Gaz.,* Oct. 11, 14, Nov. 1, 15, 22. Dec. 20, 27, 1783.

27. *Packet,* Apr. 8, 1777. *Gazette,* Apr. 28, 1779. "Constitutionalists and Mechanics" in *Freeman's Journ.,* Oct. 5, 1785. "A Friend to Equal Liberty" in *Indep. Gaz.,* Oct. 10, 1786. A. Boyd to Jas. Young, Dec. 29, 1778, *Pa. Arch.,* 2 ser., III, p. 340.

28. The following summary is based on Selsam, *Pennsylvania Constitution of 1776;* Harding, "Party Struggles over the First Pennsylvania Constitution," AHA *Annual Report for 1894;* Lincoln, *Revolutionary Movement in Pennsylvania;* and Bolles, *Pennsylvania, Province and State.*

29. Proceedings of the conference are in *JPA,* pp. 34-44.

30. Proceedings in *ibid.,* pp. 50-96; the first volume of the original manuscript is in Arch. Div., Harrisburg.

31. Burnett, I, pp. 522n.-524n., 534-536. T. Willing, "Autobiography," Balch, *Willing Letters,* p. 126. Morris to J. Reed, July 21, Burnett, II, p. 19.

32. Allison to Robert ——————, Aug. 20, 1776, *PMHB,* XXVIII, p. 379.

33. There has been much speculation as to who wrote the Constitution. James Cannon and Benjamin Franklin were generally considered to have had an important share in the work. Since Cannon was a tutor at the College of Philadelphia and was accused of injecting unsound theoretical principles not grounded in practical experience, the Radicals preferred to point to Franklin as the author of the new frame; *e. g.* "Audax" in *Freeman's Journ.,* Sept. 29, 1784.

34. Constitution, sect. 19.

35. Wilson to Yeates and Montgomery, Aug. 10, Roberts Coll., was dubious of the value of the Council of Censors from the first. Rush to Wayne, Sept. 2, Stille, *Wayne,* p. 40, at this early date looked hopefully to the Censors.

36. "Consideration" in *Gazette,* Oct. 30.

37. *JPA,* pp. 88-89.

Notes to Chapter II

1. *Journal,* Oct. 16, 1776; "Scaevola" in the same issue. "Lucius" in *Packet,* Oct. 15. Broadside, Oct. 17, Gilpin Coll. *Packet,* Oct. 22. Marshall, *Diary,* Oct. 17, p. 97, described the meeting as composed of "a large number of respectable citizens.

2. Marshall, *Diary,* Oct. 17, 21, pp. 97, 98. *Packet,* Oct. 22.

3. Geo. Stevenson to Col. Wilson, Nov. 4, R. P., VI, p. 25. *Journal,* Oct. 30. *Packet,* Nov. 5.

4. "Demophilus" in *Packet,* Oct. 22.

5. "Consideration" in *Gazette,* Oct. 30. See also "W" in *Packet,* Oct. 22.

6. *Packet,* Nov. 5. Broadside, Nov. 2, Gilpin Coll.

7. Marshall, *Diary,* Nov. 2, pp. 101-102.

8. *Packet,* Nov. 12. For votes, see *Pa. Arch.,* 6 ser., XI, pp. 315, 382. Marshall, *Diary,* Nov. 5, 6, p. 102.

9. Collinson Read to John Dickinson *et al.,* Nov. 18, Bradford MSS, II, p. 194. He enclosed a remonstrance to the assembly (not in Bradford MSS.) and reported that the people were generally dissatisfied with the election. The assemblymen elected were all Radicals but the vote was small, the highest successful candidate receiving 109 votes and the lowest 60 votes. The Bedford delegates claimed that only 113 persons voted in Berks County while five times that number protested against the election; *Journal,* Mar. 19, 1777.

10. Stevenson to Wilson, Nov. 4, R.P., VI, p. 35.

11. *Journal,* Nov. 22, 1776; Feb. 19, 1777, for Brown's defense.

12. "Union" in *Packet,* Nov. 19. "Andrew Marvel" in *ibid.,* Nov. 26. "Phocion" in *Journal,* Mar. 12, 1777, asserted not over 2,500 voted. "Addison" in *Journal,* May 14. Cumberland County Declaration, March, 1777, Lamberton Coll., II, p. 19. Complete election returns for 1776 have not been found. Benjamin Rush, *Observations,* p. 19n., claimed that not over 1500 of the 2500 who voted for assemblymen took the oath required by the September ordinance.

13. *E. g.* Cumberland Co. Declaration, March, 1777, Lamberton Coll., II, 19, HSP. Remonstrance from Bedford County, *Journal,* March 19.

14. John Dickinson in *Indep. Gaz.,* Jan. 18, 1783, fn., explained that he proposed the terms of the agreement. The address of the Bedford County members, *Journal,* March 19, is less definite. It stated that the agreement was adopted by a vote but that on the following morning the Radicals denied what they had done. "Phocion" in *Journal,* March 12. "DeWitt" in *Packet,* March 18.

15. *JPA,* Nov. 28, 1776. Address of Bedford members, in *Journal,* Mar. 19, 1777. "Phocion," in *ibid.,* Mar. 12. Rush, *Observations,* p. 3. John Montgomery to James Wilson, Apr. 21, 1777, Society Coll., explains how many of the Cumberland County committee had no authentic information of the various methods of taking the oath until five months after the event.

16. John Dickinson's statement, *Indep. Gaz.,* Jan. 18, 1783, fn. Address of Bedford members in *Journal,* Mar. 19, 1777.

17. *JPA,* Feb. 8, 25, Mar. 4, pp. 110, 114, 123. *PCR,* Mar. 5, 6, XI, pp. 173-174. "An Inquirer" in *Journal,* Feb. 19; "Phocion" in issue of Mar. 12, asserted that in the election of February a total of only seventy votes was cast.

18. *E. g. JCC,* Nov. 11, 14, 22, VI, pp. 940, 951, 975, 976n. Bd. of War to Council of Safety, Nov. 21, Burnett, II, pp. 160-161.

19. Francis Johnston to A. Wayne, Nov. 17, Stille, *Wayne,* p. 45.

20. *JCC,* Nov. 25, 30, VI, pp. 979, 995. Saml. Chase to Md. Council of Safety, Nov. 26, *Arch. of Md.,* XIII, p. 482. Pres. Hancock to Washington, Nov. 26, Force, *Amer. Arch.,* 5 ser., III, p. 852.

21. Burnett, II, p. 165n.

22. *JCC,* Dec. 2, 9, VI, pp. 999, 1015. Council of Safety to Lancaster Comm., Nov. 14, Force, *Amer. Arch.,* 5 ser., III, pp. 672-673. Report of meeting of "Real Whigs," R. P., VII, pp. 1, 5. *JPA,* Dec. 11, p. 101. J. Moore *et al.* to Pres. Wharton, Dec. 3, Gratz, Coll. John Patton to James Read, Dec. 4, Col. & Rev. MSS, p. 43, declared he could not get one man in the battalion to march. Wm. Leas of York Co. Committee informed Council of Safety, Dec. 27, R. P., VII, p. 96, that all authority of the Council was denied in York. The battalions would not march and he suggested using the Westmoreland militia then on its way to Philadelphia to force the York militia to turn out. This action he thought would help to establish the authority of the Council.

23. *JPA,* Dec. 10, 14, 1776; Jan. 13, 1777, pp. 101, 102.

24. Saml. Adams to Mrs. Adams, Dec. 19; W. Whipple to J. Langdon, Dec. 24; M. Thornton to Pres. of N. H., Dec. 25; Saml. Adams to J. Warren, Dec. 25, 1776; F. L. Lee to L. Carter, Jan. 14, 1777; Burnett, II, pp. 179-180, 187, 188, 189, 217. Scharf and Westcott, *Phila.,* I, p. 333. *JCC,* Dec. 12, 1776, VI, p. 1027.

25. Address of meeting of Sufferings of the Quakers, Dec. 20, 1776, signed by John Pemberton, clerk; Force, *Amer. Arch.,* 5 ser., III, p. 1309. Broadside, Dec. 20, Gilpin Coll.

26. Scharf and Westcott, *Phila.,* I, pp. 334, 335.

27. R. Morris to James Wilson, Jan. 31, 1777, Society Coll., HSP. Wm. Hooper to R. Morris, Feb. 1, facsimile in Henkels, *Catalogue* 1183, pp. 24-25, declared that the exclusion of Wilson "would work an essential political Evil" in Congress. Hooper considered George Ross, one of the other Pennsylvania delegates, whimsical and eccentric.

28. Benj. Rush to R. Morris, Feb. 11, Burnett, II, p. 246. *JPA,* Feb. 5, 6, pp. 108, 109.

29. Wilson to St. Clair, Feb. 19, Konkle, "Wilson," II, p. 109.

30. Wilson to Morris, Feb. 28, Henkels, *Catalogue* 1183, pp. 53-54. *JPA,* Feb. 22, p. 114. W. H. Smith, *St. Clair Papers,* I, p. 392n, states that Wilson's return was due to the entreaties of Washington but does not cite the source of his statement.

31. Wilson to St. Clair, Feb. 8, Henkels, *Catalogue* 1183, item 82.

32. Benj. Harrison to Morris, Jan. 8, Burnett, II, p. 208.

33. Rush to Morris, Feb. 8, Henkels, *Catalogue* 1183, item 82. Thos. Burke, "Abstract of debates," Feb. 26, *State Recs. of N. C.,* XI, p. 385. Those who opposed Burke were Samuel Adams, Witherspoon, Wilson and Sherman. *JCC,* Feb. 17, 25, 27, VII, pp. 127, 157, 164. Congress reassembled in Philadelphia on March 12.

34. Rush to Morris, Feb. 11, Henkels, *Catalogue* 1183, item 426. *Ibid.,* item 92. Rush to Morris, Feb. 8, Burnett, II, p. 240.

35. Rush to Morris, Feb. 22, Henkels, *Catalogue* 1183, item 93.

36. Burke, abstracts of debates, Feb. 8; Rush, "Diary," Feb. 10; Burnett, II, pp. 240-241, 244-245.

37. E. Rutledge to R. R. Livingston, Oct. 2, 1776, Burnett, II, p. 113. Force, *Amer. Arch.,* 5 ser., III, p. 1214. Regulations of Council of Safety, Dec. 31, 1776, R. P., VII, p. 112. *PSL,* Jan. 29, June 13, 1777, chs. 738, 755, IX, pp. 34-40, 109-110.

38. James Lang to Jacob Howell, June 22, 1777, R. P., XIII, 27. Bolles, *Penna.,* p. 159, citing letter of Baron de Bonstellin.

39. Rush, "Diary," Feb. 4; Burke, abstract of debates, Feb. 1, 15, Pres. of Congress to Md. assembly, Feb. 20; R. Sherman to Gov. of Mass., Apr. 23; Burnett, II, pp. 234-235, 249-253, 266, 340. *JCC,* Feb. 15, Apr. 15, VII, pp. 124, 267.

40. "To the six men . . .," Jan. 22, in *Eve. Post,* Mar. 15. The address of the Bedford County members, Jan. 3, and the remonstrance appeared in *Journal,* Mar. 19.

41. "Hampden" and "To Hampden" in *Eve. Post,* Mar. 13, 15. Woods, Smith and Rhoads in *Journal,* Mar. 19, 26. *JPA,* Mar. 20, p. 131.

42. Declaration of people of Cumberland County, March, 1777, Lamberton Coll., II, p. 19. Wilson to Atlee and Yeates, Mar. 13, Roberts Coll. The declaration is doubtless the enclosure referred to in Wilson's letter.

43. "Phocion" in *Journal,* Mar. 12. In his article in *Packet,* Mar. 25, he suggested that the people should agree to vest the next assembly with power to propose amendments to the Constitution, and then provide sufficient time for consideration.

44. "Hampden" in *Eve. Post,* Mar. 13.

45. "De Witt" in *Packet,* Mar. 18; "Philerene" in *Eve. Post,* Mar. 18. "Demophilus" in *Gazette,* Mar. 19.

46. "Common Sense" in *Packet,* Mar. 18. Other articles were by "Philadelphia" in *Gazette,* Mar. 26, and by "G" in *Journal,* Mar. 26.

47. *Eve. Post,* Mar. 20. The meeting was held March 18 with Charles Willson Peale in the chair and Thomas Young as secretary. Sellers, *Peale,* p. 158, believes the address displays earmarks of Peale's composition.

48. *Packet,* Apr. 8. *Eve. Post,* Mar. 20.

49. Slough to Yeates, Mar. 28, Prov. Del., I, p. 57. Yeates to Col. Burd, Mar. 29, Balch, *Letters and Papers,* pp. 258-259, expressed his feelings thus:

> . . . we probably shall have much confusion and disorder before the new constitution is fairly fixed. Many are determined to oppose it at all events, and many to support it at all hazards. . . . *The Clamors of the Red-Hot Patriots Have Subsided into Easy Places and Offices of Profit! The posts of mere Trust* go a begging! No one can be found to accept *them.* Whenever I reflect on the times, I am seized with the blue devils . . .

50. Sharp Delaney to A. Wayne, Mar. 28, Stille, *Wayne,* pp. 50-51.

51. Report of meetings of Oct. 17, Nov. 2, 1776, in *Packet,* Oct. 22, Nov. 5. *Ibid.,* Nov. 12. "A Friend to Liberty" in *Journal,* Nov. 13. Broadside, Nov. 8, Gilpin Coll.

52. *E. g.* remonstrances from Bedford County to assembly, March 19, 1777; from Cumberland County, March, Lamberton Coll., II, p. 19.

53. *JCC,* April 14, 1777, VII, p. 264. Wm. Duer, statement, March 9, 1779, Burnett, IV, pp. 98-100. *JCC.* Apr. 9, 11, 30, 1777, VII, pp. 246-247, 254, 264, 314.

54. *JCC,* Apr. 15, 16, VII, pp. 268-269, 271. Wm. Duer to President of N. Y. Convention, April 17, 1777; N. Y. delegates to the same, April 21, 29; Burnett, II, pp. 331, 337, 344. On April 24, Congress asked President Wharton and the State Board of War to call out and equip three thousand militia. Neither assembly nor council is referred to in this requisition; *JCC,* VII, p. 296.

55. Memorial in *Packet,* May 20.

56. Wm. Duer, statement, March 9, 1779, Burnett, IV, pp. 98-100. In this statement Duer disclaimed any attempt to embarrass the Radicals by his proposal.

57. "A Friend to Union," *Journal,* April 23, 1777. Remonstrance, May 6, 1777, Gratz Coll., Penna. Convention. *Packet,* May 20.

58. Circular letter in *Eve. Post,* May 24. Memorials in *Packet,* May 20. Broadside in Henry MSS, I, 17, HSP; endorsed June 3, 1777. This memorial address to the assembly pointed out that the Constitution had not been ratified by the people at large, and that the subscribers had supported the assembly only because of the danger from British attack.

59. Rush's work originally appeared under the signature of "Ludlow" in *Journal,* May 21, 28, June 4. The four letters were later issued as a pamphlet. Replies to "Ludlow" were made by "Whitlock" in *Eve. Post,* May 24, 27, and in *Packet,* June 10; by "Common Sense" in *Journal,* June 4. Other articles in *Journal* were by "Addison," May 14; "An Associator," May 27; "A Native of Pennsylvania," June 11. In the *Eve. Post* were "A Citizen," May 24; unsigned article, May 27. "Addison" in *Packet,* May 27. *Eve. Post,* June 7, gives an account of the York meeting.

60. Rush to Wayne, May 19, June 5; Peters to Wayne, May 27; in Stille, *Wayne,* pp. 68-70.

61. "A Native of Pennsylvania" in *Journal,* June 11.

62. *Packet,* April 8. Members of the Constitutionalist committee were Charles W. Peale, James Cannon, David Rittenhouse, Thomas Young, and Thomas Paine. Two addresses to assembly from Whig Society, *Packet,* May 20, 27. Sellers, *Peale,* p. 158, is of the opinion that the addresses bear strong earmarks of Peale's authorship. *JPA,* May 22, 24, 28, 29, June 11, pp. 133-136, 142.

63. *JPA,* June 17, p. 146.

64. Council to assembly, June 11, MS. Council Minutes, I, pp. 55-56. War Board to Assembly, in *Eve. Post,* June 14. *JPA,* June 12, 17, pp. 142, 145-6.

65. *Eve. Post.,* June 17. Report of Mifflin's meeting with the people at the State House of June 11, in *Gazette,* June 18. Reed to Washington, June 18, Sparks, *Corr. of Am. Rev.,* I, pp. 389-390.

66. Hubley to Pres. Wharton, July, R. P., XIII, p. 66.

67. Marshall, *Diary,* July 30, Aug. 21, pp. 120-121, 123.

68. Arch. McClean to Vice-Pres. Bryan, Aug. 13, Sept. 3, R. P., XIV, p. 45; XV, p. 6. Same to same, Aug. 31, *Pa. Arch.* V, pp. 536-538. These letters give a good picture of opposition to the Radical government in York County at this period.

69. "Hampden" in *Eve. Post,* Mar. 13, 1777.

70. Sharp Delaney to Anthony Wayne, Mar. 28, in Stille, *Wayne,* p. 51.

71. *Packet,* May 14. Cadwalader to Washington, Mar. 12, 1778, Sparks, *Corr. of Amer. Rev.,* II, p. 84.

72. Eph. Blaine to Pres. Wharton, Apr. 7, 1777; John Piper to James Marten, July 20; *Pa. Arch.,* X, pp. 299, 438. Hugh Davison to Council, May 15, 1778, R. P., XXXI, p. 30. MS. Council Minutes, April 10, Sept. 12, Oct. 31, 1777; Apr. 2, 1778, I, pp. 38, 139, 244; appx., p. 14.

73. Geo. Campbell to Pres. Wharton, Mar. 30, 1777, R. P., X, p. 57.

74. Col. Kirkbride to Pres. Wharton, Aug. 24, R. P., XVI, p. 66. MS. Council Minutes, June 9, 10, 20, Aug. 6, I, pp. 52, 54, 65, 95.

75. Robert Lollar *et al.* to Pres. Wharton, Nov. 18, 1777, R. P., XVII, p. 6. Arch. McClean to Geo. Bryan, Aug. 31, 1777; McAllister to ————, Aug. 28; Ed. Shippen to Geo. Bryan, Aug. 7, 1778; *Pa. Arch.,* V, pp. 536-538, 558; VI, p. 682. MS. Council Minutes, July 23, 1778, I, p. 323.

76. *PCR,* Mar. 20, 1777, XI, p. 186. MS. Council Minutes, Apr. 9, I, p. 37. Matlack to Reed, June 20, *Pa. Arch.,* V, p. 379. Reed to Council, July 22, Reed, *Reed,* I, pp. 301-303.

77. Thos. McKean to John Dickinson, Aug. 15, 1777 (Copy), McKean Papers, I, p. 9.

78. John Montgomery to James Wilson, Apr. 21, 1777, Gratz Coll., Members of Old Congress, HSP.

79. Wm. Lyon to Pres. Wharton, July 7, *Pa. Arch.,* V, pp. 416-417. Deposition of Loughead, July 26, 1777; commission of July 26, 28, R. P., XIV, pp. 3, 4, 6, Pres. Wharton to Washington, June 25, 1777, *Pa. Arch.,* 2 ser., III, p. 108. MS. Council Minutes, June 11, July 26, 1777; Feb. 28, 1778; I, pp. 80, 88, 222.

80. Demand and deposition of Galbraith, Sept. 29, 1777; Robt. Levers to Pres. Wharton, Oct. 8; R. Galbraith to same, Oct. 31, 1777; Feb. 6, 1778; R. P. , XV, pp. 60, 72; XVI, p. 39; XIX, p. 57. Warrant for arrest, Nov. 17, 1777, *Pa. Arch.,* VI, p. 12. MS. Council Minutes, July 28, Sept. 15, 1777, I, p. 89, 143.

81. Slough to Yeates, Mar. 28, 1777, Prov. Del., I, p. 57.

82. Burd to Yeates, Dec. 24, 1777, Walker, *Burd Papers,* p. 100.

83. Yeates to Burd, Feb. 15, 1778, Shippen Family Papers, III, p. 27. Wm. Lyon to Geo. Bryan, Feb. 2; J. D. Sergeant to Pres. Wharton, May 13; *Pa. Arch.,* VI, pp. 228, 496. James Read to Matlack, Feb. 7, R. P., XIX, p. 61. "A Friend to Union" in *Journal,* Apr. 23, 1777.

84. Council to John Morris, Aug. 2, 1777, *Pa. Arch.,* 2 ser., III, p. 114.

85. John Montgomery to James Wilson, Apr. 21, Gratz Coll., Members of Old Congress, HSP.

86. Marshall, *Diary,* Aug. 5, 8, p. 122. John Hubley to Council, Aug. 8, 1777; Arch. McClean to Geo. Bryan, Oct. 11; McClean to Wharton, Oct. 25; R. Galbraith to Pres. Wharton, Oct. 31, 1777; Feb. 6, May 16, 1778; R. P., XIV, p. 37; XVI, pp. 1, 28, 39; XIX, pp. 57, 86; XXXI, p. 34. J. D. Sergeant to Pres. Wharton, May 13, 1778, *Pa. Arch.,* VI, p. 496. David Harris to Pres. Wharton, Nov. 24, 1777; James Read to Matlack, Feb. 7, 1778; R. P., XVII, p. 19; XIX, p. 61. Burd to Yeates, Sept. 30, 1778, Yeates MSS. *JCC,* June 27, XI, p. 662.

87. Minutes of Council of Safety, Dec. 2, R. P., VII, p. 1; account of the meeting, *ibid.,* p. 5.

88. *PSL,* Mar. 17, 1777, ch. 750, IX, pp. 75-94. The act of June 19, *PSL,* ch. 760, IX, pp. 131-132, removed the requirement that a field officer

must be a freeholder. *JPA,* Mar. 3, 4, pp. 122-124. By the act of Dec. 30, 1777, however, the assembly exempted its members from the militia act; *PSL,* ch. 781, IX, p. 189.

89. Col. Kirkbride to Pres. Wharton, Aug. 24; Rich. McAllister to Pres. Wharton, Oct. 23; R. P., XIV, p. 66, XVI, p. 19. MS. Council Minutes, Oct. 25, Dec. 6, I, p. 178, appx., pp. 10-13. Pres. of Congress to Washington, Apr. 25, Burnett, II, p. 341. John Armstrong to Pres. Wharton, Apr. 28; Arch. McClean to Geo. Bryan, Aug. 31; *Pa. Arch.,* V, pp. 324-325, 536-538.

90. Wharton to Elias Boudinot, Dec. 13, 1777, R. P., XVII, p. 48.

91. Wayne to Pres. Wharton, Feb. 10, John Armstrong to Pres. Wharton, Jan. 22, 1778; *Pa. Arch.,* VI, pp. 251, 413. Maxwell's memorial is in *ibid.,* 2 ser., III, pp. 184-185. R. McAllister to Pres. Wharton, Jan. 22, R. P., XIX, p. 34. *JCC,* Dec. 4, 1777, IX, p. 1002.

92. Reed to Pres. Wharton, Feb. 1, *Pa. Arch.,* VI, pp. 218-220.

93. Excerpt of address to Friends, Dec. 20, 1776, Force, *Amer. Arch.,* 5 ser., III, p. 1309. MS. Council Minutes, Mar. 15, 1777, I, pp. 14-15.

94. Wm. Lyon to Pres. Wharton, July 7, *Pa. Arch.,* V, pp. 416-417.

95. Hubley to Matlack, July, 1777, R. P., XIII, p. 66.

96. Marshall, *Diary,* July 30, pp. 120-121.

97. Arch. McClean to Geo. Bryan, Oct. 11, R. P., XVI, p. 1. *PSL,* June 13, 1777, ch. 756, IX, pp. 110-114. *JPA,* May 23, 28, 30, June 6, 7, 13, pp. 133, 135, 136, 140, 143. "Ignotus" in *Packet,* June 10; "Pro Bono Publico" in *ibid.,* June 24. *Eve. Post,* July 3.

98. Council to John Harris and Robert Elder, Nov. 8, 1777, R. P., XVI, p. 63.

99. Pres. Wharton to Wm. Henry, July 31, 1777; Bryan to John Weitzel, May 22, 1778; R. P., XIV, p. 14, XXI, p. 47. MS. Council Minutes, Aug. 15, I, pp. 103-104. For this problem on the frontier, see Saml. Hunter to Pres. Wharton, Oct. 27, *Pa. Arch.,* V, pp. 717-718. The non-jurors were called on for blankets for the army in the ensuing winter; MS. Council Minutes, Nov. 8, 1777, I, Appx., pp. 18-21. George Kreibil's son was fined for not exercising with the militia. When the elder Kreibil was asked to prove that the boy was only seventeen years old, he was told that his evidence could not be admitted until he took the test oath. This he refused to do, because the clause requiring abjuration of the king bothered him. Kreibil's declaration, July 18, 1777, *Pa. Arch.,* V, pp. 432-433.

100. Geo. Bryan to Mrs. Bryan, July 4, *PMHB,* XLI, p. 383.

101. Council to James Young, July 4, R. P., XIII, p. 43.

102. *JCC,* July 31, Aug. 12-14, 29, VIII, pp. 591-592, 633-642, 695. In the vote in Congress the Pennsylvania delegates split on party lines:

Roberdeau and J. B. Smith voted with the Radicals; Morris, Wilson, and Clymer, with the conservatives. *PCR,* Aug. 12, XI, p. 264. Laurens asserted that private conversation between an unnamed member of Congress and Secretary Matlack of the State Council was received for good evidence by Congress although contradicted by other members who conversed with Councilmen; Laurens to Pres. Rutledge, Aug. 12, 15, Burnett, II, pp. 439, 440.

103. *JCC,* Aug. 28, VIII, pp. 694-695. MS. Council Minutes, Aug. 31, Sept. 1, I, pp. 118-120, 125.

104. MS. Council Minutes, Sept. 3, I, pp. 123-125. Memorial, Dec. 19, 1777; Observations, Jan. 31, 1778; R. P., XVIII, p. 6, XIX, p. 47. Burd to Yeates, Sept. 6, 16, 1777, Yeates MSS. *JCC,* Sept. 3, 4, 6, VIII, pp. 707, 713-714, 718-719, 722-723. Bryan to Pres. Laurens, Sept. 2; Wharton to Pres. Laurens, Sept. 5; Council to Congress, Sept. 6; Quaker remonstrances of Sept. 9, 1777, Apr. 26, 1778; *Pa. Arch.,* V, pp. 509-511, 574, 586, 593. Other protests are in broadsides, Sept. 3, 5, Gilpin Coll., II, ff. 226-228; V, f. 670. See also protest of Sept. 12 and letters of Henry Drinker, Dec. 13, *PMHB,* XV, pp. 122-123, 235-237. *Packet,* Sept. 10. Laurens to Gervais, Sept. 5, 9, Burnett, II, p. 481. Other members of Congress privately voiced their disgust with the Quakers: *e. g.* James Lovell, R. H. Lee, and John Adams; *ibid.,* II, pp. 484-487.

105. Eliz. Drinker, *Journal,* Sept. 15, p. 49n. *JPA,* Sept. 14-16, pp. 151-152. *PSL,* Sept. 16, ch. 762., IX, pp. 138-140. McKean to S. Adams, Sept. 19, McKean Papers, I, p. 11. *JCC,* Dec. 9, IX, pp. 1012-1013. Council to Congress, Jan. 5, 1778, R. P., XIX, p. 6. Marshall, *Diary,* Dec. 11, 1777, p. 149. Resolutions of Bd. of War, Dec. 8; Jones to Duane, Dec. 17; Jones to Matlack, Dec. 18; memorial of Dec. 19; *Pa. Arch.,* VI, pp. 74-75, 102-103, 106, 111-115. The important documents are in *An Address to the Inhabitants of Pennsylvania . . .,* a statement by the Quakers. The best secondary account, written from a sympathetic view, is Sharpless, *A Quaker Experiment in Government,* II, ch. 7, which contains numerous extracts from original sources.

106. *JCC,* Jan. 29, Mar. 2, 1778, X, pp. 98, 211. *PCR,* Apr. 21, 1778, XI, p. 468. Council's letter of Jan. 5, in *Pa. Arch.,* VI, p. 158. Ed. Pennington to Thos. Wharton, Mar. 25, *PMHB,* VI, pp. 364, 366. J. B. Smith to Matlack, Jan. 19, R. P., XIX, p. 25.

107. *JCC,* Mar. 10, 16, May 14, 15, X, pp. 238, 260, XI, pp. 497, 503. J. B. Smith to Pres. Wharton, Mar. 16, Burnett, III, pp. 130-131. Clark, Henry and Smith to Pres. Wharton, Mar. 18; Council to A. Clarke *et al.,* Mar. 27; Council to Pres. of Congress, May 1; *Pa. Arch.,* VI, pp. 367-368, 389-90, 523. *PSL,* June 1, ch. 794, IX, p. 243. Extracts of Chew to Morris, Mar. 31, is in Henkels, *Catalogue* 1183, item 375. See *ibid.,* Morris' reply, Apr. 6, item 44. Council was irritated because the arrests had been made by civil authorities of the State, yet Congress directed the disposition of the prisoners.

108. G. Morris to R. Morris (May 11, 1778), Burnett, III, p. 230. *JCC,* Sept. 15, 1777, VIII, p. 746. *JPA,* Sept. 13, 14, pp. 151, 152.

109. *JPA,* Sept. 16, pp. 152, 154, 157.

110. J. Adams, Diary, Sept. 18, Burnett, II, 497. On the 14th Adams wrote to his wife, *ibid.,* 494, "It is the determination not to leave this State." Dyer to Jos. Trumbull, Sept. 28, *ibid.,* 502-3, explained, "we thought it not best at this time to remove out of this State least in this Critical Situation of affairs there should be a total defection of this State."

111. *JCC,* Sept. 27, 30, 1777; June 27, 1778; VIII, p. 753; XI, p. 662. J. Lovell to Saml. Adams, Feb. 6, 1778, Burnett, III, p. 73.

112. D. Roberdeau to Pres. Wharton, Oct. 10, *Pa. Arch.,* V, 658-659. Roberdeau did not name the "real Friends of our State" in Congress who originated the idea. It appears that the whole plan was hit upon on the spur of the moment when Roberdeau found that no election for assemblymen was held in York and assumed that the people were so confused that the day of election had irrevocably lapsed. Roberdeau later discovered that the official date of election was the second Tuesday in October and not the first as he had previously assumed. This tenuous excuse has a hollow ring; Roberdeau was attempting to explain away a plan which stirred up the Radical officials of the State. His letter is the only one which has been found bearing on this suggested plan.

113. Matlack to sub-lieutenants of Phila. County, Oct. 10, R. P., XV, p. 77. Marshall, *Diary,* Oct. 14, p. 135. Roberdeau to Pres. Wharton, Oct. 14; Arch. McClean *et al.* to G. Bryan, Oct. 17; *Pa. Arch.,* V, pp. 672, 682-683. The only evidence of a disputed election was in Northumberland County, but the assembly did not go into it; *Pa. Arch.,* 6 ser., XI, pp. 277-279. The returns from only five counties have been found. If these are representative of the whole State, the number of voters was very small.

114. *JPA,* Nov. 20, 1777, Feb. 20, 1778, pp. 160, 184.

115. *Pa. Arch.,* 6 ser., XI, pp. 345-346. Konkle, *Bryan,* p. 153.

116. MS. Council Minutes, Oct. 17, 1777, appx., p. 3. *PSL,* Oct. 13, ch. 766, IX, pp. 149-151.

117. MS. Council Minutes, Oct. 21, Dec. 4, I, appx., pp. 8-9, 35-36. Burd to Yeates, Dec. 5, Walker, *Burd Papers,* pp. 99-100, railed at the granting of legislative authority to the Council of Safety.

118. Roberdeau to Pres. Wharton, Jan. 26, 30; deposition of James Christy, Feb. 3, 1778; R. P., XIX, pp. 41, 46, 52. Deposition of Geo. Stewart, Jan. 31, *Pa. Arch.,* VI, p. 217. Gouvr. Morris to Jos. Reed, Apr. 9, 1778, Burnett, IV, pp. 150-151.

119. *PSL,* Sept. 10, ch. 814, IX, pp. 287-288. MS. Council Minutes, Oct. 1, I, pp. 370-371.

120. Robt. Levers to Matlack, Dec. 8, 1777, R. P., XVII, p. 37.

121. Mifflin to R. H. Lee, Nov. 5, Lee MSS., II, no. 13. In October an assembly committee was ordered to frame a memorial to Congress

about several disaffected persons in the quartermaster and commissary department who oppressed the true friends of the common cause; *JPA,* Oct. 9, p. 154.

122. Council to Pa. delegates, Feb. 7, 1778, R. P., XIX, p. 59.

123. *JCC,* Apr. 15, 1779, pp. 453n.-454n. When the delegates demanded to see the letter Morris refused on the ground that it was private; G. Morris to Jos. Reed, Apr. 9, 1779, Burnett, IV, p. 151.

124. Pres. Wharton to Thos. McKean, Feb. 15, R. P., XIX, p. 69.

125. Nath. Greene to McKean, June 3; McKean to Greene, June 9, McKean Papers, I, pp. 17, 19. Hooper to Geo. Bryan, Aug. 31, *Pa. Arch.,* 2 ser., III, pp. 236-237. Memorial, Mar. 6, *Pa. Arch.,* VI, p. 335.

126. Arch. McClean to Geo. Bryan, Oct. 11, 1777, R. P., XVI, p. 1.

127. Arch. McClean *et al.* to Bryan, Oct. 17, *Pa. Arch.,* V, pp. 682-683.

128. Robt. Galbraith to Pres. Wharton, Feb. 6; John Weitzel to Pres. Wharton, May 25, 1778; R. P., XIX, p. 57; XXI, p. 55. Marshall, *Diary,* Mar. 26, 28, 29, May 22, 23, June 2, 12, Aug. 6, 1778, pp. 174, 175, 182-184, 187, 195. With his Quaker background Marshall could understand the religious scruples of the Mennonists and made efforts to release them from jail.

129. Alex. McDowell to Geo. Bryan, June 1, *Pa. Arch.,* VI, p. 572. "Candidus" in *Packet,* June 17, saw no reason why these religious groups could object to the test. Another writer in the same issue took alarm at the rumor that the Quakers had determined to disown all members who should take the oath. *PSL,* Sept. 10, 1778, ch. 813, IX, pp. 284-286.

130. *E. g.* Wm. Ellery to Gov. Cooke, Mar. 1, Burnett, III, p. 103.

131. Armstrong to Geo. Bryan, July 29, Lamberton Scotch-Irish Coll., II, p. 35.

132. "A Pennsylvanian," "Belisarius" and "Philadelphensis" in *Packet,* Feb. 25, Aug. 15, 20; also issue of July 25. "Casca" and "Astrea de Coelis" in *Eve. Post,* July 16, 18. *Pa. Arch.,* 2 ser., III, pp. 199-200. Sellers, *Peale,* p. 187. S. Adams to P. Thacher, Aug. 11, Burnett, III, p. 368. Durand, *New Materials,* p. 181.

133. Council to Reed, Aug. 21, Sept. 8, R. P., XXIII, pp. 35, 64. Scharf and Westcott, *Phila.,* pp. 386-387.

134. MS. Council Minutes, Nov. 7, 1777, I, appx., pp. 16-17; June 20, 1778, p. 312. *PSL,* Jan. 2, Apr. 1, May 25, chs. 779, 795, 799, IX, pp. 177-180, 236-238, 249-250. *JCC,* Apr. 8, June 4, X, pp. 322-323, XI, p. 569. *JPA,* Dec. 26, 1777; Mar. 21, Apr. 1, May 25, 1778; pp. 177, 197, 203, 211.

135. *PSL,* Mar. 20, 1777, Mar. 23, 1778, chs. 752, 791, IX, pp. 93-103, 225-277.

136. Council to Assembly, Aug. 18, R. P., XXIII, p. 31. MS. Council Minutes, Aug. 3, I, p. 332. *JCC,* June 8, XI, p. 579. *PSL,* Sept. 7, ch. 809, IX, pp. 272-274. Laurens to Pres. Lowndes, Aug. 5, Burnett, III, p. 360.

Notes to Chapter III

1. "Hampden" in *Packet,* Sept. 28, 1778. For answers, see "A Plain Dealer," and "Z," in *ibid.,* Oct. 3.

2. J. Yeates to Col. Burd, Oct. 10, Balch, *Letters and Papers,* p. 267.

3. "T" in *Packet,* Oct. 10.

4. "An Elector of Philadelphia" in *ibid.,* Oct. 13.

5. Thos. Mifflin *et al.* to A. Wayne, Nov., 1778, Stille, *Wayne,* p. 165. Benjamin Harrison to R. Morris, Nov. 5, Henkels, *Catalogue* 1337, p. 9, expressed joy over the Republican resurgence.

6. Reed to Gen. Greene, Nov., 1778, quoted in Bolles, *Penna.,* II, p. 44. "A Dialogue" in *Packet,* Oct. 31, asserted that not one-quarter of the potential electors took the oath before June 1.

7. Jacob Morgan, Jr., to Geo. Bryan, Oct. 14, Prov. Del., IV, p. 68. Judges of Lancaster County to Council, Oct. 20, *Pa. Arch.,* VII, pp. 19-20. *Ibid.,* 6 ser., XI, p. 281. *JPA,* Nov. 7, p. 234.

8. MS. Council minutes, Oct. 17, 21, Nov. 13, 1778; Jan. 2, 9, 25; Feb. 11, 13, 16; Apr. 10; I, pp. 376, 379, 401, 436, 442, 457, 479, 481-482, 484, 532. *JPA,* Nov. 23, 24, 1778; Feb. 12, 16, 1779; pp. 241-243, 310, 315. Robt. Smith to And. Boyd, and And. Boyd to Council, Nov. 26, 1778; Council to James Claypoole, Feb. 16; Wm. Scott and Robt. Stevenson to Council, Feb. 25; Thos. Hartley to Pres. Reed, Mar. 17, 1779; *Pa. Arch.,* VII, pp. 97, 193, 206-207; 2 ser., III, pp. 279, 281; see also *ibid.,* 6 ser., XI, pp. 423-424. Half a dozen conservatives appealed to Anthony Wayne to leave the army for a short time in order to forward party affairs in Chester County; Thos. Mifflin *et al.,* to Wayne, Nov., 1778, Stille, *Wayne,* pp. 165-166. The case of the York County Councillor involved the unusual angle of interference in local politics by a Continental officer. Eichelberger was a deputy commissary of purchases for Congress; naturally the Radical Council had no love for him and accepted at face value the unfavorable reports of his unruly behavior at the election. The conservative Hartley minimized this part of Eichelberger's activities.

9. *JPA,* Nov. 5, 6, pp. 231-232. Eight members were not on record as to the oath. The reservation read:

> The subscriber hereby expressly reserving to himself full liberty to adopt and pursue such measures as he may judge necessary for collecting the sentiments of the people, on the subject of calling a new convention, to revise, alter, amend, or confirm the said Constitution—and reserving also, full liberty of cooperating, as well with his fellow citizens, in calling the said convention, as with the said convention, if called.

10. Col. Stewart to A. Wayne, late 1776, Stille, *Wayne,* p. 161. *JPA,* Nov. 20, 21, p. 240. Biddle asked to resign due to health and private affairs. James Smith had asked not to be reappointed due to ill health.

11. The Radical list with votes was: Roberdeau 28, Clingan 27, Armstrong 27, Shippen 27, Biddle 28, Atlee 27 and Searle 27. The Republican candidates received the following: Gray 20, Wilson 24, Cadwalader 23, Miles 24, Saml. Morris, Jr., 23, Samuel Howell 23, and John Nixon 23. *Packet,* Nov. 24. The low number of votes for the Radicals is explained by the absence of the Chester County representatives and a number of Radical members from the back-country.

12. *JPA,* Nov. 30, 1778; Mar. 2, 1779; pp. 248, 328.

13. MS. Council Minutes, Dec. 1, I, p. 412. *JPA,* Nov. 25, p. 244. "A Republican" in *Journal,* Feb. 24, Mar. 3, 1779. No positive evidence has been found about such an understanding. But Reed's resignation from the assembly on November 25, the resolution to ask the people to vote on a convention passed on the 27th and 28th, and the almost unanimous vote for Reed as President on December 1, give grounds for the assumption that the three events were inter-related.

14. Extract from Gerard's report translated in Durand, *New Materials,* 177-178. *Packet,* Dec. 5.

15. Wayne to Reed, Jan. 24, 1779, Stille, *Wayne,* pp. 177-178. T. Cushing to Reed, Mar. 15, *Pa. Arch.,* VII, pp. 250-251. "Sully" in *Packet,* Feb. 2. "A Republican" and "Brutus" in *Journal,* Feb. 17, Mar. 17.

16. *Packet,* Jan. 7, and "Candid" in issue of Jan. 21. MS. Council Minutes, Jan. 12, I, p. 444. The Republican candidate is not known; he was described as a gentleman of character, fortune and influence.

17. Rush to David Ramsay, Nov. 5, 6; Rush MSS., "Letters and Thoughts," vol. 4, p. 35.

18. *JPA,* Nov. 27, 28, pp. 245, 246, 247. Broadside, Nov. 28, Du Simitiere Coll., f. 126. Less important questions to be discussed by the convention were: should the executive powers have the right to appoint justices of the peace and field officers of the militia; should the President and Vice-President of the State hold office more than three years; should delegates in Congress be eligible three years in succession; and how could the several oaths in the Constitution be adapted to cover any alterations made in the frame. All officers of the State were allowed to stand for election to the convention. The resolves were well circulated. Five thousand copies in English and the same number in German were published as broadsides; also they appeared in the newspapers for one month. The Executive Council was invited to approve the resolutions which it conveniently ignored.

19. "A Serious Address" in *Packet,* Dec. 1, 5, 10, 12; two unsigned articles in issue of Dec. 17, 29; "A Faithful Patriot" and "A Constitutionalist" in *ibid.,* Feb. 4, 16. "A Multitude" in *Gazette,* Feb. 3. An unsigned article in *Packet,* Dec. 17, suggested that the talk about the incorporation of the City of Philadelphia which would give the voters power to elect their own magistrates and to establish courts was designed to influence the citizens to vote for a Convention.

20. Andrew Boyd to Jas. Young, Dec. 29, *Pa. Arch.,* 2 ser., III, p. 340.

21. Marshall, *Diary,* Jan. 23, pp. 210-211. Whitehill criticized the twenty-three hundred pounds spent on the inaugural dinner, but he blamed Morris, Mifflin, and Potts, the committee in charge of the affair.

22. General form of remonstrance, 1779, and the numerous remonstrances printed in *Pa. Arch.,* 2 ser., III, pp. 243-79. Memorial which circulated in the city, in *Packet,* Feb. 9. As early as January Robt. Whitehill told Marshall that in York and Cumberland Counties a memorial to be signed by "some one thousand" was in preparation; Marshall, *Diary,* Jan. 23, pp. 210-216.

23. "Sully" in *Packet,* Feb. 2. Other articles are: "Agricola," "Dialogue," and "Phocion" in *Packet,* Feb. 13, 20, 27. "Agricola" and "A Republican" in *Journal,* Feb. 24.

24. *JPA,* Feb. 18, 23, pp. 316, 319. *Pa. Arch.,* 2 ser., III, pp. 344-379. *Packet,* Mar. 2. *Gazette,* Mar. 3. Timothy Matlack under signature of "T. G." in *Packet,* Mar. 2. Andrew Boyd to James Young, Dec. 29, *Pa. Arch.,* 2 ser., III, p. 340.

25. Address to the Citizens of Pennsylvania by the Republican Society, signed by Richard Bache, chairman; *Gazette,* Mar. 24. See also "DeWitt" in *Packet,* Mar. 11.

26. *JPA,* Feb. 27, pp. 324-326. Address to Citizens, *Gazette,* Mar. 24. The Republicans pointed out that 14,000 or 16,000 signatures represented far from a majority of the voters of the State.

27. To Caesar Rodney, Mar. 8, Ryden, *Rodney,* p. 297. The article on Reed was by "A Republican" in *Journal,* Mar. 3; see also "An Impartial Inquirer" in *Packet,* Mar. 30.

28. The pertinent articles which appeared in the *Packet* and *Evening Post* have been collected and reprinted, usually in full in NYHS *Colls.,* XXI, XXII. W. Conyngham and Joseph Wharton also took part in the newspaper campaign on the side of the conservatives; Reed to R. H. Lee, Apr. 15, 1780, Lee Papers, II, no. 142. The best biography of Deane is by G. L. Clarke, *Silas Deane* (N. Y., 1913), but it has little to say about the Pennsylvania side of the conflict.

29. To R. Morris, Jan. 26, NYHS *Colls.,* XI, p. 441. "Common Sense" in *Packet,* Dec. 31, 1778, Jan. 2, 5, 7, 9, 1779. In Congress Gouverneur Morris attacked Paine in sarcastic tones; Sparks, *G. Morris,* I, pp. 203-204.

30. Open Letter to Reed by Deane, Feb. 6, 1779, NYHS *Colls.,* XXIII, p. 380. Reed to Deane, Feb. 24, *ibid.,* XXI, pp. 382-383. G. Morris to Reed, Apr. 9, Burnett, IV, p. 153.

31. Matlack's address in *Packet,* May 18. NYHS *Colls.,* XXI, pp. 100-101, 103-123, 137-140. Sparks, *G. Morris,* pp. 203-204. If "Americanus" was Gouverneur Morris, as his biographer, Sparks, suggests, then it is probable he was the same "Americanus" who in 1779 was in the pay of the French minister; see Conway, *Paine,* I, pp. 135-136.

32. R. H. Lee to A. Lee, May 23, Burnett, IV, p. 228.

33. *JCC,* May 3, June 8, 10, XIV, pp. 542-543, 704, 713. N. Scudder to R. H. Lee, June 15, Burnett, IV, p. 271. "T" in *Packet,* May 8. Reed supported Lee despite the dictionary of 1776 in which Arthur Lee cast doubts on Reed's fidelity to the American cause; J. Lowell to A. Lee, Sept. 17, 1779, Burnett, IV, p. 424.

34. To W. A. Atlee, Nov. 13, 1779, Pa. Misc. box 10, LC.

35. Sellers, *Peale,* p. 200.

36. Gerard to Vergennes, Jan. 10, 17, May 29; extracts quoted in Conway, *Paine,* I, pp. 133-135. Peale to Henry Laurens, Mar. 6, in Sellers, *Peale,* p. 213. Paine to R. Morris, Nov. 2, 1781, NYHS *Colls.,* XXII, p. 525. *Gazette,* June 30, July 14, 21, 1779. "Cato" and "Common Sense" in *Freeman's Journ.,* Jan. 2, 9, Mar. 13, 1781.

37. Wm. Floyd to Gov. Clinton, Dec. 21, 1779, Burnett, IV, p. 544. *JCC,* Mar. 22, 27, 1780, XVI, pp. 277-278, 291-292. Lewis Weiss to John Ettwein, n. d., and reply, *PMHB,* II, pp. 153-156.

38. Sam. Adams to James Warren, Oct. 20, 1778, Burnett, III, pp. 458-459. *JCC,* Oct. 2, XII, p. 974. Reed to War Board, Mar. 8, 1779; Bd. of War to Reed, Mar. 9; Bd. of War to Pulaski, Mar. 9; *Pa. Arch.,* VII, pp. 230-234.

39. McKean to Congress, Nov. 19, 1778; Thompson's examination before Congress; Col. and Revol. MSS., pp. 22-24, 34-37. MS. Council Minutes, Dec. 31, 1778; Jan. 6, 1779; I, pp. 433, 439. Thompson to Reed, Jan. 7, *Pa. Arch.,* 2 ser., III, pp. 262-263. G. Morris to Reed, Apr. 9, Burnett, IV, p. 152.

40. Reed to B. Galbraith, June 30, *Pa. Arch.,* VII, pp. 522-523.

41. Reed to McKean, Aug. 10, *ibid.,* VII, pp. 637-638.

42. *JPA,* Feb. 24, pp. 320-321. "Simplex" and "Sidney" in *Packet,* Feb. 22, Apr. 24. "Latimar" in *Freeman's Journ.,* Aug. 8, 1781, revealed that when the vote on McKean was taken, Potts and several other Republicans left their seats in the assembly. An examination of the *Journals* discloses the absence of Potts, Edie, Rhoads, and Davison for at least one month.

43. Quoted in W. Irving, *Life of Washington,* IV (N. Y., 1860), IV, p. 13.

44. The evidence and documents concerning these charges are in *Trial of . . . Arnold* (1865 ed.), pp. 13-33 and *passim.*

45. Burke and Reed, Jan. 26, 1779, Burnett, IV, p. 43. Same to same, Feb. 28; Reed to Burke, Jan. 28; *Pa. Arch.,* VII, pp. 170-171. "The Case of the Sloop *Active,*" pamphlet, Aug., 1779; copy in Henry MSS. *JCC,* Jan. 19, 21, Mar. 6, 16, Apr. 6, 9, 19, 24, 28, Sept. 29, Oct. 13, 21, 1779; Mar. 21, 1780; XIII, pp. 86-92, 97, 134-137, 281-286, 320, 424-

425, 435, 472, 507-508, 527-529; XV, pp. 1122, 1166, 1194-1196; XVI, pp. 273-274. *Packet,* Nov. 12, 17, 19, 1778. *Gazette,* Oct. 4, 1780. "An American" in *Packet,* Apr. 22, 1779. The best secondary account of the affair is H. L. Carson, "The Case of the Sloop 'Active'," *PMHB,* XVI; and J. F. Jameson, ed., *Essays on the Constitutional History of the United States,* pp. 17-23.

46. *JCC,* Sept., 1779, XV, p. 1028. Wilson to Wm. Lewis and J. Jay, Sept. 6, 1779, Konkle, "Wilson," II, p. 132.

47. MS. Council Minutes, Jan. 30, Feb. 25, 1779, I, pp. 460-463, 493. *Trial of . . . Arnold, passim.* Matlack to J. Jordan, Feb. 18, *Pa. Arch.,* VII, p. 194. *JCC,* Mar. 1, XIII, p. 263. B. Fell, "Diary," Mar. 1, Burnett, IV, p. 85. Pettit to Greene, May 23, Greene Papers, V, no. 61.

48. Reed to Pa. delegates, Jan. 30, 1779, *Pa. Arch.,* VII, p. 174.

49. F. A. Muhlenberg to Henry Muhlenberg, Oct. 11, 1780, Muhlenberg MSS.

50. *JCC,* Mar. 26, 1779, XIII, pp. 374-378. On the correspondence between Council and Congress, see Paca to Bryan, Mar. 4; F. Lewis to Clinton, Mar. 8; Paca to Council, Mar. 9; Burnett, IV, pp. 88-89, 92-95.

51. Laurens, notes of debates, Mar. 26, Burnett, IV, pp. 119-120.

52. *Ibid.,* Mar. 29, p. 123. Gouverneur Morris understood that Reed complained to the Assembly of his attempts to delay settlement of the Arnold affair in Congress; G. Morris to Reed, Apr. 9, 1779, *ibid.,* p. 152.

53. MS. Council Minutes, Mar. 25, April 5, 15, I, pp. 513, 524-525, 453-455. Fell, "Diary," Mar. 26, 27, Apr. 3, 15, 28, Burnett, IV, pp. 120-121, 133-134, 157, 181-182. *JCC,* Mar. 26, 27, 29, 30, Apr. 3, 15, XIII, pp. 374-377, 379-380, 389-390, 393, 412-417, 454n.-455n. *JPA* Apr. 5, p. 359. Reed to St. Clair, Apr. 26, Smith, *St. Clair Papers,* I, p. 468.

54. *Trial of . . . Arnold,* notes, pp. 167-168. *JCC,* Feb. 2, 10, 12, XVI, pp. 120, 153, 161-162.

55. *JCC,* Jan. 23, Feb. 1, 10, 18, 23, 24, Mar. 23, 24, XIII, pp. 105, 131-132, 160-161, 206, 247-250, 360-363. Fell, "Diary," Feb. 1, 24, Mar. 23, 24, Burnett, IV, pp. 54, 63, 81, 114, 117. MS. Council Minutes, Jan. 25, 26, I, pp. 457-458. At this time Clarkson was defending Arnold in the newspapers; *Packet,* Feb. 9, 13. Clarkson to McKean, Jan. 26, 1781, McKean MSS. I, p. 40.

56. *E. g.* William Gibbons to John Gardner, Mar. 9, 1779, Gardner Papers, p. 14.

57. "A Fair Dealer" and "Mobility" in *Packet,* Dec. 3, 10, 1778. *PCR,* Dec. 8, 10, XI, pp. 639-640.

58. MS. Council Minutes, Jan. 12, 1779, I, p. 444. *Packet,* Jan. 16.

59. MS. Council Minutes, May 5, I, p. 562. Matt. Smith to Gouvr. Morris, June 7, *Pa. Arch.*, VII, p. 472. Wm. Bradford to Pres. Reed, May 25, *ibid.*, 2 ser., III, pp. 299-300. Matlack to Hollingsworth, June 16, R. P., XXVIII, p. 21.

60. Memorial, May 12, *Pa. Arch.*, VII, pp. 392-395.

61. St. Thos. Jenifer to Gov. Johnson, May 24, Burnett, IV, p. 232. See also Wm. Blodgett to Nath. Greene, May 24, Greene MSS, V, no. 64.

62. Marshall, *Diary*, May 25, p. 217. See also Elizabeth Drinker, *Journal*, May 22, p. 116.

63. *Packet*, May 27. *Gazette*, May 26, June 2. Broadside, May 25, Du Simitiere Coll. f. 130. The men appointed to investigate Morris were: Timothy Matlack, Thomas Paine, David Rittenhouse, Charles W. Peale, Captain Blewer, and Jonathan B. Smith. The committee on prices, headed by Wm. Henry, contained prominent Radicals like Dr. James Hutchinson, George Schlosser and Colonel Bradford.

64. *Packet*, May 29. Draft of petition, May 16, R. P., XXVII, p. 66. Pettit to Greene, May 29, Greene MSS, V, no. 84.

65. Marshall, *Diary*, May 27, p. 218.

66. "To the Committee of the City" in *Packet*, July 1, 1779. See also *ibid.*, June 5.

67. Reed, *Remarks on a Late Publication*, p. 41. M. Smith to Thos. Jefferson, July 30, Burnett, IV, p. 348. "Address of the Committee" in *Gazette*, July 7. Reed to Brodhead, July 21, *Pa. Arch.*, VII, p. 572. Silas Deane to Simeon Deane, July 27, NYHS *Colls.*, XXII, pp. 22-24.

68. Morris to committee of complaints, June 18, 1779; committee to Morris, July 21; *1776, Americana* (Rosenbach Catalogue), pp. 67-68. Morris to committee, June 28; Gerard to Morris, July 7; committee to Morris, July 21; Henkels, *Catalogue* 1183, pp. 34-35, 187, 194-195. *Gazette*, July 7, broadside, July 21; *Packet*, July 24, 31. "Junius" in *Packet*, July 7, Broadside, Gilpin Coll., II, p. 242. John Fell, "Diary," July 28, Burnett, IV, p. 347. John Jay to Pres. Reed, Aug. 22, *Pa. Arch.*, VII, p. 662. *JCC*, July 28, 30, Aug. 2, XIV, pp. 894, 898, 912-915. About the same time Morris was under fire from unsympathetic congressmen for having retained the records of national finance too long; Laurens to Morris, July 8, Burnett, IV, pp. 303-306.

69. James Read to Geo. Read, Aug. 7, Read, *G. Read*, pp. 350-351.

70. J. Jay to Gov. Clinton, Aug. 27, Burnett, IV, p. 390. See also Wm. Fleming to Jefferson, July 13, *ibid.*, pp. 315-316.

71. *Gazette*, July 21, 28. *Packet*, July 15, 24, 27, 31. Broadside, July 11, signed by James Roneys, Du Simitiere Coll., f. 143.

72. Broadside addressed to "Fellow Citizens," Aug. 2, 1779, Du Simitiere Coll., f. 143. Also in *Packet,* Aug. 5. For the election of the committee, see *Gazette,* Aug. 4. The votes were 2115 to 281. Marshall, *Diary,* Aug. 6, p. 228.

73. "Address of the General Committee" in *Gazette,* Aug. 13. "C. S." in *Packet,* Aug. 14.

74. Marshall, *Diary,* June 14, 16, 18, 28, July 6, 15, 21, pp. 220-222, 224, 226, 227. Matt. Smith to Pres. Reed, July 31, *Pa. Arch.,* VII, p. 606. *Gazette,* June 16, 23. *Packet,* July 3, 20, 22, Sept. 14.

75. Langworthy to Pres. of Congress, July 25, Burnett, IV, pp. 344n.-345n. Peale, extract from autobiography, Sellers, *Peale,* pp. 198-199, assumed credit for having kept the mob under control. Silas Deane to Simeon Deane, July 27, NYHS *Colls.,* XXII, pp. 22-24. *JCC,* July 26, Sept. 18, XIV, pp. 888-889; XV, p. 1086. *Packet,* July 31.

76. "Address of the Committee" in *Gazette,* July 14, Aug. 25.

77. *Packet,* July 27. *Gazette,* Sept. 15. *JCC,* Sept. 14, XV, p. 1049. Dan. Roberdeau *et al.* to Pres. Reed, Aug. 4, 12; *Pa. Arch.,* VII, pp. 621-622, 643.

78. *Packet,* Sept. 10.

79. Peale, extracts from autobiography, Sellers, *Peale,* pp. 203, 205.

80. *Ibid.,* pp. 205-208. S. Patterson to C. Rodney, Oct. 9, Ryden, *Rodney,* pp. 323-324. Eliz. Drinker, *Journal,* Oct. 4, 5, pp. 121-122. *PMHB,* II, 392; V, pp. 475-476. Fell, *Diary,* Oct. 4; Laurens to J. Adams, Oct. 4; Burnett, IV, pp. 468, 470. Reed, *Reed,* II, appx. "S.—C.—" in *Packet,* Oct. 16.

81. Morris to Wilson, Oct. 5, 6, 7, 8; Wilson to Morris, Oct. 6; Konkle, "Wilson," II, pp. 141-150. Wilson to Morris, Oct. 7, Henkels, *Catalogue* 1137, p. 11. Wm. Atlee to Mrs. Atlee, Oct. 12, Atlee MSS. Matlack to McKean, Oct. 4; McKean to Reed, Oct. 7; Bryan to McKean, Oct. 10; *Pa. Arch.,* VII, pp. 732, 835, 744.

82. Reed to assembly, Nov. 13, *PCR,* XII, p. 168. "S.—C—" in *Packet,* Oct. 16. *Gazette,* Oct. 20. *JPA,* Oct. 5, 10, pp. 384, 388.

83. *JCC,* Oct. 6, XV, p. 1147. Saml. Holten, Diary, Oct. 6; Arnold's two letters to the Pres. of Congress; Burnett, IV, p. 477 and note. Edw. Burd to Col. Burd, Oct. 9, Balch, *Letters,* p. 280. Gouverneur Morris made the motion to refer Arnold to the state.

84. *JPA,* Nov. 2, p. 391. *Packet,* Nov. 13. *Journal,* May 31, 1780.

85. Matlack to Sam. Adams, Oct. 22, in *Pa. Arch.,* VII, p. 763. *PSL,* Sept. 24, ch. 847, IX, pp. 394-395. No official list of taxables for 1779 has been found; the following table is from *Packet,* Dec. 29, 1785.

Counties	*No. of representatives from 1776-1779*	*No. of representatives by 1779 law*	*No. of taxables in 1779*
City of Philadelphia ..	6	5	3,681
Philadelphia County ..	6	9	7,066
Bucks	6	5	4,067
Chester	6	8	6,378
Lancaster	6	11	8,433
York	6	8	6,281
Cumberland	6	7	5,092
Berks	6	6	4,662
Northampton	6	5	3,600
Bedford	6	2	1,201
Northumberland	6	3	2,111
Westmoreland	6	3	2,111
	72	72	54,683

The number of taxables for some of the frontier counties was approximated. By the new apportionment Lancaster County assumed added importance in the eyes of politicians as it almost doubled its number of seats in the house.

86. *JPA,* Nov. 10, 16, 1779; June 1, 1780; pp. 395, 396, 501. McKean to Wm. Atlee, Nov. 13, 1779, Pa. Misc., box 10.

87. For over a year in 1777 and 1778 the trustees did not meet. Late in 1778 Robert Morris and Francis Hopkinson were elected trustees, an action which indicated no attempt to compromise with the Radicals. MS. Trustees' Minutes, II, pp. 96, 107, 109.

88. *PSL,* Jan. 2, Apr. 1, 1778, chs. 775, 796, IX, pp. 170-171, 238-245.

89. MS. Trustees' Minutes, II, pp. 120-138, 143-148. Wm. Smith to Pres. Reed, and "T. G." in *Gazette,* Mar. 17, 31. "A Pennsylvanian" in *Packet,* July 5.

90. MS. Trustees' Minutes, II, p. 151, which gives the committee report not printed in *JPA,* Sept. 10, p. 366.

91. *JPA,* Sept. 29, Oct. 2, 3, pp. 378-382. MS. Trustees' Minutes, II, p. 153. Wilson and Lewis were appointed by the trustees only the day before the assembly heard the arguments. "N. G." in *Gazette,* Sept. 29. "A Universalist" in *Packet,* Nov. 25.

92. Ramsay to Rush, July 3, 1779, Rush MSS., 7257, pp. 7-9. MS. Trustees' Minutes, III, pp. 22, 31, 45, 47. Marshall, *Diary,* Dec. 24, 29, p. 233.

93. "Numa" in *Packet,* Mar. 9. B. Daugherty to Col. McPherson, Mar. 19, Prov. Del., V, p. 31.

94. Ed. Burd to Yeates, Mar. 23, Walker, *Burd Papers,* pp. 107-108. Daugherty to McPherson, Mar. 19, *loc. cit. Packet,* May 15. Council

attended the assembly to hear the arguments. This was an unusual procedure; MS. Council Minutes, Mar. 18, I, p. 508.

95. *JPA,* Sept. 10, 23, Nov. 24, pp. 366, 373, 402-403. A copy of the bill as printed for consideration is in Bryan MSS.

96. *PSL,* Nov. 27, ch. 874, X, pp. 33-39.

97. *JPA,* Nov. 18, 1779, p. 399. *Packet,* Nov. 23. The eight opposers were Radicals.

98. Letter to "Reverend and Dear Sir" in *Packet,* Dec. 25, 1779. Konkle, *Bryan,* p. 190, thinks this was written by George Bryan.

99. Although slave registry lists were kept in each county as a result of the act, only a few of them have been located. If all were available, a clearer picture of the opposition might be possible. The list for Bucks County is in Davis, *Hist. of Bucks Co.,* p. 797, covering the period 1780-1782. He found that slaves were held in twenty townships and one borough; three townships had no slaves. As a rule slaves were most numerous in townships settled by Hollanders. Townhips in which Quakers were most numerous contained about one-third of the slaves of the county; but few were held in townships settled by Baptists and Presbyterians. A contemporary copy of the slave registry for Chester County is in Abolition Society Papers. It lists 462 slaves for life and 25 for a term of years. The registry for Washington County is printed in Crumrine, *Washington County,* pp. 257-259, which was part of Westmoreland County when the original act was passed. Albert, *Westmoreland County,* pp. 447-450, prints the list for that county. It shows 695 slaves, a high number for a frontier county. Many were held by prominent men and rigid Scotch-Irish Presbyterians. Two such clergymen were slaveholders. Ellis and Evans, *Lancaster County,* p. 71, indicates that the Scotch-Irish, Welsh, and Episcopalians were the principal holders in that county.

100. *JPA,* Feb. 15, Mar. 1, pp. 424-425, 435. The minority votes were distributed thus by counties: Philadelphia 3, Chester 2, Lancaster 6, Berks 2, Northampton 3, Northumberland 1, Westmoreland 2. Philadelphia City and Cumberland County were solidly for the measure on every vote.

101. Bryan to Sam. Adams, quoted in Bancroft, *Hist. of U. S.,* V, p. 413, wrote: "Our bill astonished and pleases the Quakers. They looked for no such benevolent issue of our new government, exercised by Presbyterians." "A Whig Freeholder" and "Philelentheuros" in *Gazette,* Jan. 26. *PSL,* Mar. 1, ch. 881, X, pp. 67-73.

102. J. E. Potter, "Pennsylvania and Virginia Boundary," *PMHB* XXVIII, pp. 424-425.

103. *JPA,* Dec. 4, 1778, Mar. 25, 1779, pp. 244-245, 250-251.

104. Reed to militia officers of Northampton County, Aug. 3, 1779, *Pa. Arch.,* VII, p. 616. See also Reed to Benj. Blythe, June 21, 1778; Reed to Sam. Hunter, Aug. 3, 1779; *ibid.,* pp. 496-498, 615.

105. *JPA,* Feb. 24, Mar. 2, 1780, pp. 429-430, 437-440.

106. B. Rush to McHenry, Jan. 19, 1780, *PMHB,* XXIX, p. 63.

107. Armstrong to Searle, Dec. 15, 1779; Armstrong to Washington, Jan. 12; Armstrong to Reed, Jan. 24; O. Ellsworth to S. Lyman, Jan. 25; Armstrong to Gates, Feb. 16, 1780; Burnett, IV, p. 537; V, pp. 7-8, 13-14, 16, 37-38. Ed. Burd to Yeates, Dec. 31, Society Coll. *JCC,* Nov. 19, XV, pp. 1290, 1292. *JPA,* Nov. 18, 22, 1779; Jan. 10, 29, Feb. 14, 1780; pp. 398, 401, 412, 413, 422. The house elected John Bayard, George Bryan, John Jacobs, John Bull, and William Henry delegates to the convention; only Bull and Henry attended.

108. R. Morris to Silas Deane, Mar. 31, NYHS *Colls.,* XXII, pp. 117-118. *JCC,* Feb. 29, Mar. 29, XXV, pp. 219, 269. *JPA,* Mar. 21, 23, May 27, 29, 30, 31, pp. 450-453, 498-501. *PSL,* May 31, ch. 911, X, pp. 204-205. "A Countryman" in *Journal,* Feb. 23. "A. B." in *Gazette,* Mar. 8. B. Rush to John Adams, Apr. 20, MS. "Letters, Facts," Rush MSS., 4406. Marshall, *Diary,* May 3, 4, 20, pp. 240-241, 243.

109. R. R. Livingston to R. Schuyler, June 9, Burnett, V, p. 202. Charles Pettit to ————, July 13, quoted in Greene, *Greene,* II, p. 313. Sam'l. Postelthwaite to Wm. Irvine, June 9, Irvine MSS, III, p. 44. Pres. Reed to Wm. Henry, late August, Jordan, *Wm. Henry,* p. 127. A convenient summary of paper money emissions is given in Harlow, "Aspects of Revolutionary Finance," *American Historical Review.* XXXV, pp. 46-48.

110. MS. Council Minutes, Apr. 30, May 14, 20, 1780, I, pp. 556-557, 582-583. "F," "A Citizen of Pennsylvania" and "Embargo" in *Packet,* Aug. 7, Sept. 16, 25, 1779. *PSL,* Oct. 8, 1779; Feb. 28, Mar. 22, 1780; chs. 859, 876, 904; IX, pp. 421-432; X, pp. 43-45, 175-176. *JPA,* Sept. 16, 1779; May 19, 1780; pp. 369, 495. *JCC,* Aug. 19, 21, 25, Sept. 8, 1779; June 20, 21, 22, 26, 27, 28, 1780; XIV, pp. 979-980, 986-987, 994-995; XV, pp. 1036-1037; XVII, pp. 538, 542, 544-548, 563, 565-569.

111. Reed to Washington, Sept. 7, 1779; Reed to Congress, May 6, 1780; *Pa. Arch.,* VII, pp. 684-686; VIII, p. 229. *PSL,* Sept. 22, 1780, ch. 917, X, pp. 227-228. *JCC,* May 22, XVII, p. 446.

112. See *JCC,* Jan. 4, Nov. 22, 1777; Jan. 5, May 21, Oct. 7, 1779; Nov. 4, 1780; also XV, pp. 1371-1372; XVI, pp. 196-197; XVIII, pp. 828-829.

113. Morris to assembly, Sept. 28, 1781, Sparks, *Dipl. Corr. of Amer. Rev.,* XI, pp. 478-483. *JCC,* XVII, p. 563. *PSL,* Mar. 27, 1778; Apr. 3, Oct. 10, 1779; chs. 794, 840, 866; IX, pp. 230-235, 360-375, 443-448.

114. June 3, 1780, Burnett, V, p. 190.

115. Comm. at headquarters to Pres. of Congress, June 12, July 13, 18; to Reed, June 12, July 13; Burnett, V, pp. 209, 211-212, 261-263, 273-274, 277. *JCC,* July 19, 26. Reed to Congress, July 30, *Pa. Arch.,* VIII, pp. 467-468.

116. Lewis, *Bank of N. A.*, pp. 17-19, 22. *Gazette,* July 5; "C. S." in issue of June 28. *Journal,* June 21. *JCC,* June 22, XVII, pp. 542, 548-550. Thomas Paine, *Dissertation on Government,* pp. 19-20. R. Morris to S. Deane, July 3, NYHS *Colls.*, XXII, p. 172. See comments in letters by R. R. Livingston, June 16; E. Gerry, June 11; J. Walker, June 17; P. Schuyler, June 18; J. Madison, June 23; E. Carroll, June 27; Pres. of Congress, July 21; Burnett, V. pp. 205, 220, 223, 224, 235, 239, 280.

117. *Journal,* Aug. 9, 23, Oct. 4, 25, Nov. 15. *JCC,* July 13, 14, Aug. 15, XVII, pp. 609, 610-611, 733. Comm. at Headquarters to Comm. of Phila. Citizens, July 10; to Pres. of Congress, July 18; Burnett, V, pp. 255-256, 277. Lewis, *Bank of N. A.*, pp. 22, 23.

Notes to Chapter IV

1. *PCR,* Oct. 2, 3, 6, 11, 12, 13, 17, 27, 1780, pp. 495, 499, 502-505, 509, 520. D. S. Franks to Council, Oct. 20; Wm. Hamilton to Council, Oct. 22; Matlack to David Franks, Nov. 18; David Franks to Reed, Nov. 21, 22; Reed to Franks, Nov. 23; *Pa. Arch.*, VIII, pp. 589-591, 611, 615, 617. *Packet,* Oct. 3, 14. Wilson to Deane, Jan. 1, 1781, NYHS *Colls.*, XXII, p. 270. Walker, "Life of Margaret Shippen," *PMHB, XXIV-XXVI.*

2. "A Plain Dealing Whig" in *Packet,* Oct. 10.

3. *Gazette,* Oct. 18. Regarding the Constitution, Wayne observed to President Reed: "It will be time enough to take that up when we have fully determined whether we shall have any left to contend for;" Wayne to Reed, Nov. 7, Reed, *Reed,* II, p. 314.

4. *JPA,* Sept. 20, p. 708.

5. Clement Biddle to N. Greene, Oct. 12, Henkels, *Catalogue* 1092, pp. 53-54. Thomas McKean to ————, Oct. 26, Atlee MSS. F. Johnston to Irvine, Oct. 16, Irvine MSS., III, p. 108. Johnston to ————, Oct. 16, *PMHB,* XXXI, pp. 249-250. Fred. Muhlenberg to Henry Muhlenberg, Oct. 11, Muhlenberg MSS., observed on the election: "You may judge how much the Constitutionalists have been disappointed that their ticket has been such a failure. At first they even wanted to fall back upon their former men, but that would not do at all."

6. *JPA,* Nov. 3, p. 527. Muhlenberg's political attitude was stated at this time in a personal letter to his brother, Oct. 11, *loc. cit.:* "I have never thought of supporting 'suspect,' moderate men, but the principle of the *yellow whigs* [ultra Radicals], to allow none that is not of their own stripe, to show his head, I take exception to, especially as they are more noisy than inclined to do real service. They care more for the emoluments than for the welfare of the country." An approximate alignment of assemblymen was as follows:

	Old members re-elected	*New members*	*Total*
Anti-Constitutionalists	7	24	31
Radicals	18	14	32
Uncertain or absent	4	5	9
	—	—	—
	29	43	72

7. *JPA,* Nov. 14, p. 532. *Gazette,* Nov. 15. Reed to Wm. Henry, Dec. 2, Reed, *Reed,* II, p. 290.

8. *JPA,* Nov. 22, p. 540. Harmar to Irvine, Nov. 26, Irvine MSS., III, 119, described the election as a "tight pinch." He gives the votes cast: Montgomery received 60; the other four successful candidates 31 each; of those not elected Ingersoll and Sergeant received 30 each, and Hutchinson 26.

9. A. Lee to E. Gerry, Nov. 26, Burnett, V, p. 439n.

10. *JPA,* Nov. 7, Dec. 18, pp. 529, 557. *PSL,* Dec. 23, ch. 926, X, pp. 259-264.

11. *JPA,* Nov. 11, pp. 522-523. *JPA,* Dec. 8, 12-14, 18, pp. 547, 551, 552, 555. *PSL,* Nov. 18, ch. 920, X, pp. 223-8. "A Constitutionalist" in *Packet,* Dec. 5; unsigned articles in *Gazette,* Nov. 29, Dec. 6. Harmar to Wayne, Nov. 26; Johnston to Wayne, Dec. 7; Edwards to Wayne, Dec. 12; Irvine to Wayne, Dec. 15; Wayne to Johnston (Dec. 16?); Wayne to Reed, Dec. 16; Johnston to Wayne, Dec. 18; Wayne MSS., XI. Johnston to Irvine, Oct. 16; Johnston to ————, Oct. 16; Johnston to Wayne, Oct. 31; *PMHB,* XXXI, pp. 249-250; XXIX, pp. 496-497.

12. Wayne to Johnston, Dec. 16, 1780, Wayne MSS., XI, 50.

13. Reed to Potter, Dec. 27, R. P., XLII, 44. MS. Council Minutes, Dec. 27, III, p. 485. La Luzerne to Vergennes, Jan. 7, 1781, French Arch. Transc., XV, no. 113, states that 12,000 to 15,000 louis tournois had been sent to camp by Reed. Documents on the mutiny are in Reed, *Reed,* II, pp. 319-37; *Pa. Arch.,* VIII, pp. 698-700, 701, 704, 709; *PCR,* XII, pp. 593, 596. La Luzerne to Vergennes, Jan. 7, 11, 21, French Arch. Transc., XV, provides a vivid story; although he is in error on occasional minor points, his account cannot be overlooked because he was in a position to learn the significant information which came into Philadelphia. Hazard, *Register* II. *Bland Papers,* II. 32 letters are in Du Simitiere Collection, 53 letters in Wayne MSS., XI, pp. 101-125, XII, pp. 2-44. Burnett, *Letters,* V, pp. 513ff.; Henkels, *Catalogue* no. 698, items 985, no. 1280, pp. 30-34; no. 738, p. 17; no. 694, p. 107. *JCC,* Jan. 24, XIX, p. 79-83. The newspapers gave no hint of the revolt until January 24, *e. g. Gazette.*

14. Irvine to Wayne, Jan. 22, Wayne MSS., XII, p. 35.

15. *PCR,* Jan. 6. Proclamation, Jan. 15, Reed, *Reed,* II, pp. 333-4. S. R. Fisher, "Journal," Jan. 18, *PMHB,* XLI, p. 404. Reed's explanations, n. d., Pa. Broadsides, box 10, f. 146, LC. La Luzerne understood

that Reed informed the soldiers of the merchants' refusal. Reed to assemblymen of Westmoreland and Bedford Counties, Jan. 23; Reed to Committee and assembly, Mar. 16; *Pa. Arch.*, VIII, p. 709, IX, p. 14. *JPA,* June 2, 11, pp. 657-662.

16. *PSL,* Sept. 29, 1781, ch. 951, X, pp. 364-366.

17. Reed to Greene, June 16, Reed, *Reed,* II, p. 355.

18. Irvine to Wayne, July 6, Irvine MSS., IV, p. 71.

19. MS. JPA, Dec. 18, 22, 1780, pp. 109-110, 122-123. *PSL,* June 25, Sept. 29, 1781, chs. 946, 951, X, pp. 346, 364-366. Reed to Assembly, *JPA,* Feb. 13, p. 568. See also Reed to Assembly, June 21, *PCR,* IX, pp. 219-220.

20. The bill was printed for consideration in *Packet,* Dec. 19, 1780. *JPA,* Dec. 23, p. 565. See also *ibid.*, Nov. 17, 21, 28, 1780; Feb. 13, Sept. 19, 1781, for petitions.

21. E. Cornell to N. Green, Nov. 10, 1780, Staples, *Rhode Island,* p. 321. "Brutus" in *Packet,* Nov. 14; "T. G." in issue of Dec. 6. Madison to Jones, Nov. 21, 28, Burnett, V, pp. 453, 461-62.

22. *Gazette,* Nov. 22. S. R. Fisher, "Journal," *PMHB,* XLI, p. 325. Madison to Jones, Nov. 28; John Sullivan to Pres. of N. H., Dec. 3; Burnett, V, pp. 461, 473. *Packet,* Nov. 28, Dec. 12. The assembly continued the suspension of the legal tender of continental money, which had been inaugurated by the Radicals earlier in the year. It officially recognized the exchange between continental paper and the new state money at 75 to one; *PSL,* Dec. 23, chs. 923, 924, X, pp. 247-251.

23. Irvine to Wayne, June 6, Wayne MSS., XIII, p. 31. Lovell to Holten, Feb. 8; Carroll to Gov. Lee, May 5; Madison to Jefferson, May 5; Va. delegates to Jefferson, May 8; J. Johnson to A. Jones, May 8; Johnston to Burke, May 8; Lovell to Holsten, May 8; Burnett, V, p. 565, VI, pp. 32-33, 77-80, 83. Lovell's letter of May 8 refers to the uproar in Philadelphia about money; sailors with clubs paraded the streets instead of working for paper. Beer houses demanded hard money for drink. Horatio Gates to Robert Morris, June 3, NYHS *Colls.*, 1878, p. 459, explained that he had just traveled through the backcountry which resounded with execrations at the downfall of paper money; the blame "was scattered without reserve" on Congress, the Executive Council and others. Madison to Jefferson, Apr. 3, Henkels, *Catalogue* 694, p. 108. *Gazette,* May 2. *Packet,* May 8. *Freeman's Journ.*, May 9. *PSL,* Apr. 3, ch. 935, X, pp. 283-288. *PCR,* XII, p. 716.

24. Reed to Searle (Summer, 1781), Reed, *Reed,* II, p. 295.

25. "Impartial" in *Freeman's Journ.*, May 30. Other articles in the controversy were by "A Citizen of Philadelphia" in *ibid.*, May 9, 23, June 6; "Philadelphia," May 9; "Timoleon," May 16; "Walsingham" in *Journal,* May 16.

26. *PSL,* Dec. 23, 1780; Feb. 20, Apr. 7, 1781; chs. 924, 927, 939, X, pp. 249-251, 256-257, 301-308. MS. JPA, Feb. 14, 19, pp. 157, 169-170. "A Thoughtful Whig," in *Journal,* Mar. 28; "Uniform," "State Money" and "Specie or the Real Exchange," in *ibid.,* Apr. 11. "An Alarm Gun" in *Freeman's Journ.,* May 2. As early as Dec. 13, 1780, Pelatiah Webster ("A Citizen of Philadelphia"), writing in *Gazette,* had given a full statement of the arguments against legal tender.

27. Root to Gov. of Conn., Jan. 29; Livermore to Pres. of N. H., May 13; Burnett, V, p. 547; VI, p. 86. Proclamation, May 11; Reed to Pettit and C. Biddle, May 10; *Pa. Arch.,* IX, pp. 129-132. "At a Town Meeting" in *Freeman's Journ.,* May 16.

28. "A Revolutionist" in *Freeman's Journ.,* June 6.

29. Hiltzheimer, "Diary," June 2, *PMHB,* XVI, p. 102. R. Peters to Wayne, June 3, Wayne MSS., XIII, p. 22. Irvine to Wayne, June 6, *ibid.,* XIII, p. 31, had high praise for Morris' speech before the assembly on finance. Varnum to Gov. Green, June 8, Staples, *Rhode Island,* p. 344. *PSL,* June 21, ch. 945, X, pp. 337-344. *JPA,* June 4, 11, pp. 658, 664. Pres. of Congress to Washington, July 14; Osgood to Lovell, Aug. 28; Burnett, VI, pp. 146, 199. Reed to Morris, July 27, *Pa. Arch.,* IX, p. 312. Morris to Washington, June 15, NYHS *Colls.,* 1878, pp. 461-462.

30. *JPA,* May 29, 1780. *Pa. Arch.,* 4 ser., III, p. 768. *PCR,* July 10, XII, pp. 414-418. Only occasional glimpses of Searle have been found; *e. g.* his relations with the conservative Charles Thomson: Holten, "Diary," Jan. 10, 1780, Burnett, V, p. 10n., wrote, "Yesterday Mr. Searle cained the Sec'y of Congress and the Sec'y returned the same salute." Thomson to Jay, Oct. 12, 1780, *ibid.,* V, p. 420, explained that the purpose of the mission was supposed to be a "profound secret," but "I am mistaken in the Character of the man if his business and mission remain long a secret after his arrival" in Europe.

31. J. Adams to Reed, Sept. 20, 1780, Pa. Misc., box 10, LC. McKean to J. Adams, Dec. 18, McKean MSS., I, p. 38. Reed to Wm. Henry, Dec. 2; Searle to Reed, Feb., 1781; Reed, *Reed,* II, pp. 290, 455. A number of letters dealing with the mission are in *ibid.,* II, pp. 450-465. Reed to comm. of assembly, Apr. 6, 1781; Reed to Morris, July 27, Aug. 27(?), *Pa. Arch.,* IX, pp. 62-64, 311-312, 376. Most of the extant documents on this topic are cited by Mildred Lombard, "James Searle: Radical Business Man," *PMHB,* LIX, pp. 284-294.

32. Reed to Pres. of Congress (Nov. 17, 1780 ?); Reed to Washington, May 17; Reed to Pres. of Congress, May 23, 1781; *Pa. Arch.,* VIII, p. 609; IX, pp. 46, 162. *JCC,* Nov. 16, 18-20, XVIII, pp. 1062-1063, 1068, 1075-1077. Lovell to Gerry, Nov. 20, Burnett, V, p. 453. *PSL,* June 7, ch. 943, X, pp. 325-326. Reed to assembly, MS. JPA, Mar. 1, pp. 199-200. *PSL,* Dec. 22, 1780; June 7, 1781; chs. 922, 943, X, pp. 243-247, 325-326. The Radicals claimed that the powerful merchants contrived to retain the partial embargo so as to give them an unusual commercial advantage; "A. B." in *Freeman's Journ.,* Sept. 19, 1781. This article also

gives some interesting statistics on the decline of flour exports after the partial embargo was laid. Reed, *Remarks on a Late Publication,* p. 43, later said that his enemies ascribed the embargo to his influence "because it concealed a real and most profitable monopoly carried on by a few individuals, under the mask of public character." He also attributed to the same group the modification requiring exporters to give up one-third of their cargo of flour.

33. *PSL,* Apr. 7, 9, chs. 939, 940, X, pp. 301-314.

34. *Ibid.,* Dec. 23, 1780, Apr. 5, 1781; chs. 925, 937, X, pp. 252-258, 296-298. *JCC,* Mar. 22, XIX, pp. 295-296. Wolcott to Gov. Trumbull, Mar. 24; Wolcott to Lyman, Apr. 3; Burnett, VI, pp. 35, 44.

35. La Luzerne to Vergennes, Mar. 14, 1781, French Arch. Transc., XV, no. 127. W. Houston to T. McKean, [March], McKean MSS., I, p. 45. Reed to Greene, Nov. 1, Reed, *Reed,* II, pp. 374-375. *JPA,* June 25, 26, pp. 680-681. Morris, MS. Diary, July 2, I, p. 10. Reed to Morris, July 3, 6; Morris to Reed, July 4; *Pa. Arch.,* IX, pp. 244-246, 250-251. *JCC,* July 6, XX, pp. 723-724. John Armstrong to Cad. Morris, July 6, Roberts Coll., no. 724, was much pleased with the appointment of Morris to the national post; only a few months before this, Armstrong had been advocating the very policy of restrictions which Morris opposed.

36. Reed to Greene, Nov. 1, 1781, Reed, *Reed,* II, p. 376.

37. *Ibid.,* pp. 372-373. "Censor" in *Freeman's Journ.,* Dec. 26, 1781.

38. *Packet,* Dec. 12. Hiltzheimer, "Diary," Jan. 1, *PMHB,* XVI, p. 102. "An Epistle from Titus to Timothy," broadside, Du Simitiere Coll., f. 155. A manuscript notation identifies the characters and explains the incident. Although the broadside is undated, it is the present writer's opinion that it was written before the quarrel and was undoubtedly a cause of the affray.

39. On Duane: the following articles in *Freeman's Journ.:* "Sinon," May 9; "Lucilius," and "Pro Bono Publico," May 16; "Plain Truth," May 23, June 6, 27, Aug. 22, Oct. 10; "Liberty," June 13; "Old Plain Truth," June 27. Duane's reply is in issues of Aug. 1, 8. On Gouverneur Morris: "Many," May 23; Morris' replies in May 30, June 20; "Candor," May 30; "Lucius," June 6, July 4, 25; "A Citizen," June 27. Reed to G. Morris, July 24, *Pa. Arch.,* IX, p. 308. As on other occasions, Christopher Marshall was pulling the strings behind the scenes with the aid of John Bayard. Marshall explains that the articles signed "Plain Truth" were by "Sr. James Jay"; Marshall, *Diary,* June 14, 22, p. 277.

40. S. R. Fisher, "Journal," Apr. 3, 1781, *PMHB,* XLI, p. 422. *JCC,* Dec. 8, 1780; Jan. 9, 1781; XVIII, pp. 1129-1130; XIX, pp. 40-41. Reed to Congress (Dec. 6 ?) *Pa. Arch.,* VIII, p. 639. Ed. Burd to J. Yeates, May 1, 1781, Walker, *Burd Papers,* p. 125. Campbell, *Sons of St. Patrick,* pp. 121-122, 139. Johnston to Wayne, Oct. 31, 1780, *PMHB,* XXIX, pp. 496-497.

41. McKean to Reed, Dec. 12, 1780, Gratz Coll., MOC. Reed to McKean, Dec. 13, R. P., XLII, p. 11. S. R. Fisher, "Journal," Dec. 6, 13, *PMHB*, p. 330. *PCR*, Dec. 11, 13, XII, pp. 564-565, 567.

42. "Tenax," "Legality," "Philadelphia," "Latimer" and "Anti-Quibbler" in *Freeman's Journ.*, July 17, 25, Aug. 1, 8, 15, opposed McKean. "Jurisperitus" (Pen-name used by McKean), "A Citizen of Philadelphia," "A. F.," and "Senator" in issues of July 24, Aug. 1, 8, 15, defended McKean. Issue of Aug. 22 contains McKean's identification of his assailants; Clajon's denial in Aug. 29, Sept. 12. McKean to the printers, Aug. 6, McKean MSS., I, p. 90.

43. Murray's statement, *Journal*, July 11; the oration is in issue of July 18.

44. *JPA*, Mar. 2, 1781, p. 30. *PSL*, Oct. 1, ch. 953, X, pp. 367-368. "Philotheuros" in *Packet*, Dec. 2. Unsigned "Letter on Slavery" in *Journal*, Jan. 31, Feb. 5, 21; and "Freeman" in the issue of Apr. 25. Unsigned article, Frazer's reply, "Cato" and "Freedom" in *Freeman's Journ.*, June 13, 20, Sept. 19, 26.

45. Bryant to Atlee, Mar. 26, 1781, Konkle, *Bryan*, pp. 234-235. *JPA*, Dec. 23, 1780, p. 564. Bill published for consideration in *Packet*, Mar. 10. "A Pennsylvanian" in *ibid.*, Mar. 24, 31. W. A. Atlee to T. McKean, July 18, McKean MSS., I, p. 59.

46. MS. JPA, Feb. 22, 1781, pp. 183-185. *JPA*, Mar. 30, p. 602. *PSL*, Mar. 31, Apr. 2, chs. 932, 933, X, pp. 278-282. See also the case of Isaac Austin, which later became a burning issue: *PCR*, May 8, XII, pp. 720-721; "A Constitutionalist" in *Freeman's Journ.*, July 4.

47. "Juvenis" in *Freeman's Journ.*, Oct. 3. H. W. Archer to Wayne, Sept. 26, Wayne MSS., XIV, p. 72. In election for Councillor Mifflin received 425 votes, Dickinson 278, and John Bayard 604.

48. "A Citizen of Philadelphia," "Uniform," "A Constitutionalist," "Mercator," and "An Observer" in *Freeman's Journ.*, Sept. 12, 19, 26, Oct. 3 postscript, 5, Nov. 7. "An Elector" in *Journal*, Oct. 3.

49. "A. B." in *Freeman's Journ.*, Sept. 19, 26.

50. *JPA*, Nov. 8, 9, p. 502. La Luzerne to Vergennes, Nov. 23, 1781, French Arch. Transc., XIX, f. 106, reported that the vote was 28 for Muhlenberg and 27 for his competitor, and that a sick member was brought in to give the deciding vote. The *JPA* throws no light on this situation, nor does it report just which members attended for the first time on November 9. By comparing various data it appears that four members, Holgate, Lindsey, Kohler, and William Montgomery in all probability entered on the 9th, to make a decisive vote for a Speaker possible.

51. "Candour" in *Freeman's Journ.*, Jan. 16, 1782. *PCR*, XIII, p. 112. La Luzerne informed Vergennes, *loc. cit.*, that Bayard would probably have been chosen President, had his election as Councillor not been contested.

52. MS. Council Minutes, Sept. 11, III, p. 390. Pres. of Congress to Pres. of Penna., Sept. 11; A. Clarke to J. Caldwell, Oct. 2; Burnett, VI, pp. 216, 232. *JCC,* Sept. 10, Oct. 5, XXI, pp. 947, 1037. *PCR,* Sept. 18, XIII, p. 61. Morris, "Diary," quoted in Sparks, *Dipl. Corr. of U. S.,* XI, p. 473n. *JPA,* Sept. 29, Oct. 1, p. 696.

53. *PCR,* IX, pp. 188 ff. "Censor" in *Freeman's Journ.,* Jan. 9, gave the Radical version that the militia denied that they were forced to vote. The votes for Councillor were given as follows in *Journal,* Oct. 13, 1781:

	Mifflin	*J. Bayard*	*John Dickinson*
No. & So. Liberties	274	98	—
Germantown	130	132	258
Wentz	21	374	20
	425	604	278

The only votes available for assemblymen from Philadelphia County are from *Pa. Arch.,* 6 ser., XI, pp. 353-354:

Matthew Holgate	1326
Daniel Hiester	1311
Jos. McLene	1311
George Smith	1310
George Gray	1162
Thomas Rees	830
Henry Hill	691
George Campbell	675
Samuel Penrose	664

54. Moore to Irvine, Dec. 29; Thos. Irwin to Genl. Irvine, Dec. 21; Irvine MSS., V, p. 26. *Pa. Arch.,* 2 ser., III, pp. 220-223. *JPA,* Nov. 10, 16, 20, 23, 26, 27, Dec. 1, 3, 10-12, 14, 15, 20, 1781; Feb. 20, Mar. 11, 27, Apr. 6, 1782; pp. 504-505, 512, 515, 520-526, 531, 536-541, 567, 589, 607, 620-623. "A Friend to Constitutional Government" in *Journal,* Dec. 17. "A Lover of Justice and Fair Enquiry" in *Packet,* Nov. 27. Unsigned article, "Censor" and "A Constitutionalist" in *Freeman's Journ.,* Dec. 5, Jan. 2, 16, 23. "Ein Deutscher" (Frederick A. Muhlenberg) in *Gemein. Phila. Corr.,* Feb. 13. Bryan to Atlee, Dec. 31, 1781, Konkle, *Bryan,* pp. 237-239, brings out fact that Reed was accused of having had his hand in the questionable affair because he called out the militia. Reed felt the charges serious enough to refute them; *JPA,* Nov. 27, pp. 525-526.

55. *PCR,* 1782, XIII.

56. Reed to Wayne, Nov. 1, Reed, *Reed,* II, p. 376. *JPA,* Nov. 16, 17, 21, pp. 512, 513, 516.

57. Hiltzheimer, "Diary," Oct. 24, *PMHB,* XVI, p. 160. *Freeman's Journ.,* Oct. 24, 31. Extracts from Anna Rawle's diary in W. B. Rawle, "Laurel Hill . . .," *PMHB,* XXXV, pp. 385-414. See also Eliz. Drinker, *Journal.*

58. *JCC,* Oct. 30, Nov. 2, *JPA,* Dec. 5, 20, 22, 26, pp. 524, 546, 553, 557. La Luzerne to Vergennes, Dec. 30, Fr. Arch., Corr. Pol., observed that the Eastern commercial merchant class was bending its efforts to throw the tax burden on the landed proprietors, and that Morris did not urge the taxing of commerce.

59. *JPA,* Feb. 25, 26, 28, Mar. 2, 23, Apr. 12, pp. 571-582, 604, 631-633. *PSL,* Mar. 27, Apr. 13, Sept. 20, chs. 961, 970, 988, X, pp. 385-400, 446-457, 507-58. *Freeman's Journ.,* Feb. 6. J. Hanson to J. Hall, Mar. 11, Burnett, VI, p. 311.

60. *PSL,* Apr. 15, ch. 983, X, pp. 492-493. *PCR,* June 15, 17, XIII, p. 304. *JPA,* Aug. 19, p. 659.

61. Nicholson, *Brief View . . .,* p. 222. MS. Council Minutes, Dec. 12, 1781, pp. 111, 518. *JPA,* Nov. 26, 1781; Mar. 19, Apr. 1, 5, Aug. 19, 1782; Feb. 17, 25, Mar. 8, Sept. 19, 26, 1783; pp. 523, 596, 610, 617, 658, 708, 826, 839, 857, 964.

62. *JCC,* Nov. 18, XXI, p. 1091. Morris to governors of the states, Nov. 17, Wharton, *Dipl. Corr.,* VI, p. 840.

63. Philip Marsteller to Geo. Bryan, Mar. 23, 1782, Bryan MSS., Misc.

64. *JPA,* Nov. 22, Dec. 5, 1781; Feb. 23, 1782; pp. 517, 518, 570. "Censor" in *Freeman's Journ.,* Feb. 20, 1782.

65. J. T. Gilman to J. Bartlett, July 9; B. Huntington to A. Huntington, July 13; Burnett, VI, pp. 380-382. *JPA,* Mar. 28, p. 608. *JCC,* July 3, 8, XII, pp. 373n, 376n. The resolves of the meeting of July 5 are printed in *Gazette,* July 10. The committee to frame the petitions was composed of Blair McClenaghan, Charles Pettit, Thomas FitzSimons, John Ewing, and Benjamin Rush. "Leonidas," *Gazette,* July 10. "A True Friend of his Country" and "Vox Populi" in *Freeman's Journ.,* July 17, 24.

66. *JCC,* Aug. 5, 30, XXII, pp. 429-447, 539-540. *JPA,* Aug. 20, 21, 23, 24, 28, pp. 6, 9, 663, 672-673, 675-676. The petitions to Congress and to the assembly appeared in *Indep. Gaz.,* Sept. 7, 14; and in a broadside, Penna. Broadsides, f. 146, LC.

67. Lewis, *Bank,* pp. 33, 120.

68. *JCC,* Dec. 29, 31, XII, pp. 1184, 1190. Lewis, *Bank,* p. 37. See also Hiltzheimer, "Diary," Jan. 23, P*MHB,* XVI, p. 161. Pettit to Nath. Greene, Feb. 14, Henkels, *Catalogue* 1290, pp. 78-79.

69. *JPA,* Mar. 26, pp. 606-607.

70. *JPA,* Feb. 23, 25, Mar. 26, Apr. 1, pp. 569, 572, 606-607, 649-650. *PCR,* Feb. 20.

71. A. Lee to F. Dana, July 6, Burnett, VI, p. 379.

72. Pennsylvania adherents also complained that the price of land was higher than the price paid by Virginia settlers under Virginia law; *JPA,* Nov. 17, 1781, p. 513.

73. Scott to Reed, Oct. 19, *Pa. Arch.*, IX, pp. 439, 440. *PSL,* Apr. 13, ch. 973, X, pp. 462-464. *JPA,* Mar. 13, p. 592.

74. *JPA,* Mar. 4, Apr. 13, 1782, pp. 585, 633-634. Abernethy, *West. Lands,* p. 263.

75. Pres. Moore to Wm. Irvine, Dec. 17, 1781; R. Morris to John Cannon, Apr. 4, 1782; Irvine MSS., V, pp. 21, 69. Irvine to Wayne, July 2, 1782, Wayne MSS., XVII. Irvine to Washington, Mar. 30; Irvine to Pres. Moore, May 9; Craig, *Pittsburgh,* pp. 172-173, 178-182. MS. PCR, Nov. 29, 1781, III, pp. 503-504. Moore to Irvine, May 30; Huffnagle to Moore, Mar. 8; Alex. McClean to Moore, June 27; depositions of John Robinson and of H. H. Breckenridge, June 20 and July 4; *Pa. Arch.*, IX, pp. 511-512, 552, 564-566, 572-573. *PCR,* Aug. 27, 1782, XIII, p. 356. *JPA,* Feb. 27, Mar. 2, pp. 579, 584. N. C. delegates to Gov. of N. C., Sept. 11, Burnett, VI, p. 472. *JCC,* Sept. 5, 13, XXIII, pp. 548, 549, 575. Abernethy, *West. Lands,* pp. 267-268.

76. *JPA,* Nov. 15, 1781; Mar. 2, 4, 25, Apr. 5, Sept. 12, Nov. 27, 1782; Jan. 23, Feb. 7, 15, Aug. 20, 1783; Mar. 18, 1784; pp. 511, 582, 584, 602, 617, 698-699, 757, 789, 815, 825, 892; p. 191. *PSL,* Sept. 26, 1783; Sept. 9, 10, 1784; chs. 1016, 1107, 1108, XI, pp. 196-203, 359-371. Hayes to Moore, Sept. 20, 1782, *Pa. Arch.*, IX, pp. 637-638.

77. James Burd to James Yeates, March 9, 1784, Yeates Papers, HSP. *JPA,* Sept. 2, 17, 1783, pp. 914, 949; Mar. 9, 1784, pp. 176-177.

78. *JPA,* Apr. 8, 1783, p. 619.

79. *Ibid.*, Nov. 22, 23, Dec. 18, 1781, pp. 518, 519, 532-533, 540, 542-543. *PSL,* Dec. 22, ch. 956, X, pp. 373-376.

80. La Luzerne to Vergennes, Dec. 27, 1781, French Arch., Corr. Pol. See also his letter of Oct. 16. *JPA,* Nov. 13, 26, pp. 516, 522-523. Hiltzheimer, *Diary,* Nov. 5, p. 46. *Gazette,* Jan. 9, 1782. The opposition in the house against the merchants' petition doubtless came from the Constitutionalists. Bryan to Atlee, Dec. 31, 1781, Konkle, *Bryan,* p. 238.

81. *JPA,* Mar. 16, 25, Apr. 12. *PSL,* Apr. 10, ch. 967, X, pp. 418-420.

82. Wm. Henry to Geo. Bryan, July 29, Bryan MSS. Henry to Moore, July 2, 30; Wm. Henry to ————, July 15, 22; Henry to Bradford, n. d.; invoice of merchandise seized by Henry; Wm. Henry MSS., I, pp. 77, 141, 142, 145, 149, 235; II, p. 131. Wm. Bradford to Henry, July 8, *PMHB,* XXII, p. 112. Madison to Randolph, June 18, Burnett, VI, p. 373. *PSL,* Sept. 20, ch. 987, X, pp. 497-505. *PCR,* June 27, July 8, XIII, pp. 317, 328-329. *JCC,* July 1, XXII, pp. 362-363. The following articles in *Freeman's Journ:* "A Citizen," June 5; "Laocoon," June 19; "A Plain Farmer" and "An Advocate for Public Good," June 26; "Christopher Clodhopper," July 10; "A Dream," July 17; statements by J. and A. Hubley, July 24, Aug. 21; "A Constant Reader," Aug. 14, 1782; sale of the goods, May 28, 1783. Articles in *Indep. Gaz.:* Wirtz's statement and "Fabritius" in issues of Aug. 24, Sept. 7.

83. *PSL,* Dec. 27, 1781, ch. 957, X, p. 377. *JPA,* Nov. 19, Dec. 17, 19, 26, 27, 1781, pp. 515, 540-541, 543, 544, 557, 558. Bryan to Atlee, Dec. 31, Konkle, *Bryan,* pp. 237-238, explained concerning the debate in the house:

> . . . I am well informed that Mr. —— stood up & acquainted the house that he had a very important matter against one of the judges to disclose; he was sorry for it as he respected him personally, but his duty did not allow him to be silent, &c., &c. He then said, as we are upon their salaries, the 2nd Justice [Atlee] has received pay and rations, ever since the year 1778, as Commisary of Prisoners. Such was the import of Mr. ——'s speech. A full silence ensued as to his information; whether it prevented an amendment of your allowance is uncertain, but it is clear that they left £ 400 standing in the bill; Mr. Evans and mine are at £ 300. It is whispered, I suppose injuriously, that Mr. E—— says he is contented . . .

84. Atlee to his wife, Apr. 16, Atlee MSS.

85. Two unsigned articles and "A Countryman" in *Freeman's Journ.,* Dec. 19, Jan. 16, Mar. 13. *JPA,* Mar. 7, Apr. 11, 16, Sept. 21, pp. 587, 628, 640-646, 710. In the following year the house considered a petition which asserted that three judges were sufficient. This was aimed at ousting George Bryan; *JPA,* Sept. 19, 1783, p. 954.

86. *JPA,* Mar. 24, pp. 202-203. MS. Council Minutes, Feb. 26, VII, p. 73. *Freeman's Journ.,* Apr. 21. Reed to Bradford, May 2, Reed, *Reed,* II, p. 414.

87. "Ein Deutscher" (Frederick Muhlenberg) in *Gemein. Phil. Corr.,* Feb. 20, 1782. "Oeconomy" in *Journal,* Sept. 21, 1781; also see issue of Sept. 19. "Candidus" in *Packet,* Nov. 24. *JPA,* Nov. 10, 20, Dec. 6, 1781; Feb. 20, 28, 1782; pp. 507, 515-516, 534, 566, 580.

88. *JPA,* Apr. 10, 13, Nov. 8, 1782, pp. 626-627, 728. *Freeman's Journ.,* Aug. 28.

89. *JPA,* Nov. 29, Dec. 21, 1781; Feb. 26, Aug. 23, Sept. 4, 7, 1782; Feb. 27, 1783; pp. 528, 573-577, 666-671, 682-683, 686-687, 839. Also Jan. 19, Feb. 10, 1784. Wetherill, *Free Quakers,* p. 124. Sharpless, *Quaker Experiment,* II, pp. 213-218.

90. *Freeman's Journ.,* Aug. 28; "Cato" in issue of Sept. 11. *Packet,* Sept. 5, 18. "Ein Deutscher" in *Gemein. Phil. Corr.,* Feb. 13. *JPA,* Aug. 15, 23, 24, Sept. 5, 6, 21, pp. 657, 666, 672, 683, 685, 691, 711. *PCR,* May 21, XIII, pp. 286-287.

Notes to Chapter V

1. The Radical position described here is based on a broadside addressed "To the Inhabitants of Pennsylvania" by "A Freeholder," Du Simitiere Coll., vol. 962, f. 167. It is the ablest of all Constitutionalist electioneering

articles. "Z" in *Gazette,* Oct. 8, 1783, suggested that George Bryan was the author. Other articles stating the Radical position are by "Cato" in *Freeman's Journ.,* Sept. 11; a correspondent and "A Plain Common Freeman" in issue of Oct. 2.

2. "A Pennsylvanian" in *Gazette,* Sept. 11. "Reflector" in *Journal,* Sept. 25, attacked the idea that a qualification for office should be an independent income.

3. "Brutus" in *Indep. Gaz.,* unsigned article, Sept. 11. "Verus," "Honestus," and "A Plain Common Freeman" in *Freeman's Journ.,* Sept. 18, 25, Oct. 2. "A Pennsylvanian" in *Gazette,* Sept. 11; "Beza," "A. B.," and "Honestus" in *ibid.,* Oct. 2. The personal attacks continued after the election. Freneau was characterized as "Poetaster to the *skunk-scented* association," and "Poor Bailey," editor of the Radical organ, was accused of not being able to write without aid from the same association; *Indep. Gaz.,* Oct. 15.

4. *PCR,* XIII, p. 413.

5. "An Enemy to Aristocracy" in *Gazette,* Jan. 15, 1783. Rush to ——————, Oct. 15, 1782; Rush MSS., vol. 41, p. 5. "W. C." in *Freeman's Journ.,* Oct. 30.

6. Madison to Randolph, Oct. 8, Burnett, VI, p. 499. "Civis" in *Indep. Gaz.,* Oct. 5, which Dr. Burnett, p. 499n, probably correctly surmised was aimed at Lee. Randolph to Madison, Nov. 2, Henkels, *Catalogue* 694, p. 157. Rush to Montgomery, Nov. 5, Rush MSS., vol. 43, pp. 74-5, likewise refers to Lee as being definitely identified with the Constitutionalist faction in the election. Reed to Bryan, Dec. 13, Susq. Trans., thought Lee's actions unfortunate and wished that he had more gracious manners.

7. S. Wharton to G. Read, Nov. 10, Read, *Read,* pp. 369-370, referred to the "keen mortification" of the Radicals in losing the Presidency. Rush to Montgomery, Nov. 5, Rush MSS., vol. 43, pp. 74-75. *JPA,* Oct. 1, p. 717. *Gazette,* Nov. 27, Dec. 11; "A Friend to the Constitution" in *ibid.,* Dec. 11.

8. Muhlenberg to Peters, Nov. 12, Peters Papers, IX, p. 59. Rush to Montgomery, Oct. 15, Nov. 5, Rush MSS., vol. 41, p. 5; vol. 43, pp. 74-75. Ingersoll to Clymer, Nov. 7, Clymer MSS., p. 47. Wilson to Bingham, Nov. 25, Gratz Coll. *JPA,* Nov. 11, 12, pp. 732, 734.

9. The following pointed to Reed as the author of the "Valerius" articles: Rush to Montgomery, Nov. 26, Rush MSS., vol. 43, p. 76; extract of letter from Lancaster, *Indep. Gaz.,* Feb. 8; "Sidney" in *Journal,* Feb. 12. Reed to Bryan, Dec. 25, Reed, *Reed,* II, p. 390, made an interesting comment: "The wild fire lighted up by Valerius will, I hope, be reduced to regular element, which will both warm and animate us. We must, if possible, keep it up." Poem addressed to "Dr. Slop" in *Indep. Gaz.,* Feb. 15, suggests Dr. Hugh Shiell; "An Epigram" in *ibid.,* Mar. 11, might refer to Timothy Matlack. Hazard wrote to Belknap, Apr. 9, *Belknap Papers,* pt. 1, p. 203: " 'Who is Valerius?' is a question which has been asked often, and I believe never truly answered. He conceals himself."

10. "Valerius" in *Freeman's Journ.,* Nov. 6, 13, 20, 27. Dickinson's articles in *Gazette,* Dec. 24, 1782; Jan. 1, 8, 15, 22, 1783. Unsigned article in *Freeman's Journ.,* Nov. 20. Address of 61 Pennsylvania army officers in *Gazette,* Dec. 18. Testimonies to Dickinson, Nov. 14, Ashmead MSS., p. 38. Probably more defenses of Dickinson would have appeared but for the fact that it was known at least a month in advance that he would make his own answer; Rush to Montgomery, Nov. 26, Rush MSS., vol. 43, p. 76.

11. "Valerius" in *Freeman's Journ.,* Jan. 15, 1783. This interesting angle was pursued in the press. "A Member of the Assembly," *ibid.,* Feb. 5, asserted that Wilson was not Advocate General when elected a delegate and that he had not held the former office since June, 1782. "Philo-Valerius" in *ibid.,* Feb. 12, declared this was false and that Congress should investigate the situation.

12. "A Son of Saul" in *Freeman's Journ.,* Nov. 13. Muhlenberg was defended by "Ein Pennsylvanier" in *Gemein. Phil. Corr.,* Nov. 26.

13. "Hamden," "An Enemy to Disguised Tories and Traitors," and "Sidney" in *Gazette,* Dec. 11, 18, 1782; Feb. 26, 1783. "Hamlet's Ghost" and "Sidney" in *Journal,* Feb. 12, 19. Rush to ————, Nov. 5, Rush MSS., vol. 43, pp. 74-75. At this time Reed was not on the most friendly terms with Thomas McKean. When the latter nominated Reed as successor to Livingston, Reed exclaimed to his friend Bryan, Dec. 25, 1782, Reed, *Reed,* II, p. 390, that "Mr. McKean had an opportunity to have obliged me, but as he did not make use of that, I presume this is by way of compensation . . . I very well know how to estimate the value of his friendship . . . I shall put an end to the nomination." Reed knew he had no chance of success while power was wielded by Robert Morris, the "hostile Colossus, who not only bestrides all the other officers of Congress, but even Congress itself." Reed to Greene, Mar. 14, *ibid.,* p. 393, also characterized Morris as "the Dominus Factotum, whose dictates none dare oppose . . ."

14. *E. g.* Rush to Dickinson, n. d., *PMHB,* XXIX, pp. 224-225. Volume of papers on "Reed-Cadwalader Controversy" in Cadwalader MSS.

15. Hazard to Belknap, Jan. 17, 1783, *Belknap Papers,* pt. 1, pp. 182-3, explained the origin of one of these appelations:

> . . . nicknames have been liberally bestowed. That of Skunk Association is intended to designate the heads of one of the parties, [radicals] which has lately held the reins of government. It gets the name of *Skunk* from a person to whom that appelation was given some time ago, who is said to have been a great newspaper author. People generally suppose Mr. Sergeant (a lawyer) to be the person.

16. "Intelligence Extraordinary" and "A Quondam Friend" in *Freeman's Journ.,* Nov. 13, Dec. 18. Hazard to Belknap, Dec. 18, *Belknap Papers,* pt. 1, pp. 168-169, complained of the filthy press.

17. To Hopkinson, Dec. 24, 1782; Franklin, *Writings* (Smyth ed.), VIII, p. 647.

18. Rush to Montgomery, Nov. 5, 1782, Rush MSS., vol. 43, pp. 74-75. "Let us look out in time for Censors. No man who has been in office or power since the Revolution, I think ought to be in that Counsel." He continued with, "What do you think of Col: Richard Butler? . . . I am sure he must think with us."

19. Rush to Montgomery, Apr. 14, 1783, Rush MSS., vol. 41, p. 24. Despite this, Rush found that the accounts from the counties were encouraging; Rush to Cadwalader, Apr. 26, Cadwalader Papers, II, p. 67.

20. *Journal,* Feb. 5, 1783. *Indep. Gaz.,* Feb. 8. The officers of one of the Lancaster County battalions publicly congratulated Dickinson; *Freeman's Journ.,* Apr. 30.

21. The cases of Proctor and Oswald can be followed in *Indep. Gaz.,* Oct. 1, 1782; Jan. 11, 1783; *Freeman's Journ.,* Oct. 2; Hiltzheimer, "Diary," Jan. 1, 3, 4, 6, *PMHB,* XVI, pp. 163-164. Hazard to Belknap, Nov. 27, MHS *Colls.,* Belknap Papers, pt. 1, p. 164, was disturbed by the larger issue of the freedom of the press. For the newspaper warfare, see the following: *Indep. Gaz.,* Jan. 11, 18. "Adrian" (pseudonym of George Bryan) in *Freeman's Journ.,* Jan. 15. "Jurisperitus" (pseudonym of George Bryan) in *ibid.,* Feb. 5. Hopkinson's reply under signature "One of the People" in *Packet,* Jan. 25; his poem in issue of Feb. 1. "Civis" in *Indep. Gaz.,* Feb. 1. "A Bye-Stander" in *ibid.,* Jan. 25. "Cicero" in *ibid.,* Feb. 15, likened McKean to Jeffries. Procter in *Packet,* Feb. 1.

22. *JPA,* Feb. 20, 24, Mar. 18, 21, Sept. 9, 1783, pp. 832, 834-836, 869, 879, 934. MS. JPA, Feb. 12, 1784, pp. 280-282.

23. *JPA,* Sept. 19, Nov. 29, Dec. 4, 1782; Feb. 24, Mar. 5, 22, Sept. 23, 1783; pp. 708, 758, 776-778, 835, 854, 880, 960. Reed to Bryan, Dec. 3, 1782, Susq. Trans. Matlack's memorial to the assembly is in *Indep. Gaz.,* Oct. 10, 1782. On Mar. 25, 1784, he wrote again to the assembly, Prov. Del., V, p. 105. *Gazette,* Dec. 19, 1782. Matlack to Jacob Rush in *Freeman's Journ.,* Jan. 21, 1784.

24. The temporary boundary line was approved by the Assembly Mar. 22, 1783, *JPA,* pp. 880-1. *Pa. Arch.,* X, p. 8.

25. Abernethy, *West. Lands, passim.* S. Wharton to Wm. Trent, Nov. 15, 1782, Ohio, MSS. Madison to Gov. Harrison, Nov. 15, Burnett, VI p. 542. Wharton to Geo. Read, Nov. 17, 1782, Read, *Read,* p. 374, observed that numerous persons "of both sides are of opinion that this State [of Pennsylvania] would be large enough if confined to the Allegheny Mountains, and it would be wisdom to acquiesce in the proposition of an independent State." Hugh Williamson to Gov. of N. Car., Nov. 18, Burnett, VI, p. 545, believed that the people of Vermont and "their abettors in the Minor States" were persuading the people in the West to revolt.

In the assembly of 1781-1782 charges had been brought against Pentecost and Cannon for rebellious activity in Western Pennsylvania. The issue hung fire for several years and it was never definitely settled. *JPA,*

Feb. 12, 19, 22, Mar. 3, 12, 13, 21, Sept. 9, 1783, pp. 821, 828, 834, 850, 862, 865, 878, 933. MS. JPA, Nov. 17, 1783; Feb. 11, 1784; pp. 77, 274.

26. Minutes from private journal of assembly, Nov. 19, 1782, *Pa. Arch.*, IX, pp. 666-667. *JPA,* Nov. 16, 19, pp. 741-744. *PSL,* Dec. 3, ch. 1000, XI, pp. 14-16. *PCR,* Jan. 9, 11, 1783, XIII, pp. 477-478. Madison to Randolph, Dec. 3, Burnett, VI, p. 552.

27. The quotations are from Finley to Dickinson, Apr. 28, 1783, and Finley to ————, Mar. 18, *Pa. Arch.*, X, pp. 40-41, 43. Instructions from Dickinson, Feb. 6, *ibid.*, X, pp. 163, 164, show that Finley followed the line of argument outlined by Council. *PCR,* Jan. 11, 16, XIII, pp. 478, 481.

28. Madison's notes, Jan. 27, *JCC,* XXV, p. 866. Madison to Randolph, Jan. 29, Burnett, VII, p. 25.

29. Wolcott to Edwards, Nov. 29, 1776; Lewis to McKesson, Jan. 31, 1777; Burnett, II, pp. 166-168, 231. J. B. Smith to Pres. Wharton, Mar. 19, 1778, *Pa. Arch.*, VI, p. 371. *JCC,* May 13, 14, 16, 17, June 23, 1778.

30. Sherman to Gov. of Conn., Dec. 20, 1779; Pres. of Congress to Gov. Trumbull, Dec. 24, 1780; Burnett, IV, p. 534; V, p. 497. Wolcott to Laurens, Dec. 27, 1780, NYPL *Bull.*, I. *JCC,* Dec. 12, 1780, XVIII, pp. 1147-1148.

31. *JPA,* Mar. 12, 1781, p. 587. *PCR,* July 20, Oct. 8, 1781, XIII, pp. 8-11, 79. Reed to Pa. delegates, July 23; Pa. delegates to Reed, July 26; Reed to Pa. delegates, Oct. 8; *Pa. Arch.*, IX, pp. 306-307, 434. Jacob Johnson to Z. Butler, June 17; Wm. H. Smith to Butler, Aug. 1, 1781; Susq. Trans., VI. *JCC,* Nov. 3, 1781, XXI, p. 1092. A. McDougall to Gov. Clinton, Mar. 12, 1781, Burnett, VI, p. 26.

32. *JCC,* Nov. 14, 1782; June 27, July 16, Aug. 12, 23, 28, Oct. 18, 1782; Jan. 3, 1783; XXI, pp. 1115-1116; XXII, pp. 354-356, 389-392; XXIII, pp. 461, 528-529, 533-536, 665; XXIV, p. 845. Madison's notes, Jan. 1, 3, 1783, *ibid.*, XXV, p. 845. Conn. delegates to Gov. Trumbull, June 5, July 1, 2, 1782; Burnett, VI, pp. 368, 376-377. *PCR,* Mar. 8, June 21, 24, Oct. 19, 1782; Jan. 6, 1783; XIII, pp. 217, 313, 314, 399, 474-476; Council to assembly, Mar. 7, 1782; 34 official documents on Wyoming, 1782; *Pa. Arch.*, IX, pp. 510-511, 679-724. "Connecticut Claim, Part I," Penna. Broadsides, f. 146, LC. *Freeman's Journ.*, Jan. 22, 29, Feb. 5, 1783. T. Smith to ————, Oct. 18, 1781, Prov. Del., III, p. 108.

33. Wyoming petitions in McAllister Coll. O. Wolcott to Mrs. Wolcott, Feb. 1, 1783, Burnett, VII, p. 28. Patterson to Dickinson, Oct. 28, 1783, Susq. Trans., VI. *JPA,* Jan. 28, Feb. 20, 25, Mar. 8, 11, Aug. 27, Sept. 1, 2, 10, 1783; pp. 798, 830-831, 837, 859, 860, 902, 913, 914, 935. *PCR,* Feb. 1, 18, XIII, pp. 497, 509.

34. MS. JPA, Jan. 30, 1784, pp. 227-30.

35. MS. JPA. Feb. 6, Mar. 10, 11, pp. 255, 402, 403-4; *JPA,* Mar. 25, pp. 204-5. John Franklin to R. Sherman, Mar. 5, Susq. Trans., VI.

36. *JPA,* Dec. 8, 1783, Mar. 31, Sept. 9, 10, 1784, pp. 73, 216-217, 323-326. MS. JPA, Jan. 22, 23, 29, Feb. 3, 4, 10, 23, 1784, pp. 193, 194, 218, 236, 240-241, 243, 270, 325-326, 442-447. The petition of the Penna. landholders, Mar. 19, Susq. Trans., VI, lists 23 names, most of whom were Republicans; the outstanding Radical, Jonathan D. Sergeant, was the prominent exception.

37. *JCC,* Jan. 23, Apr. 24, May 10, June 2, July 27, XXVI, pp. 45-46, 280-282, 363n., XXVII, pp. 526, 603-605. MS. JPA, Jan. 29, Feb. 14, pp. 218-220, 288-292. Letters in Burnett, VII, pp. 453-454, 506-507, 553-554, 561, 575. Dickinson to Pa. delegates, Feb. 16, 24, *Pa. Arch.,* X, pp. 204, 210. Wilson and Bradford to Dickinson, July 3, MS. Letters of Council, I, p. 208. C. Thomson to Jefferson, Oct. 1, NYHS *Colls.,* 1878, p. 192. *Mercury,* Oct. 8. Pa. delegates to Dickinson, Mar. 7, Apr. 2, Gratz Coll., Members of Old Congress, I, 69.

38. MS. JPA, Feb. 9, 10, pp. 268-270. *JPA,* Sept. 15, p. 335.

39. *JCC,* Jan. 24, 1783, XXV, p. 862. Madison's notes, Jan. 24, Mar. 4, 5, *ibid.,* pp. 862, 919. A. Lee to S. Adams, Mar. 5; Lee to Warren, Mar. 12; Hamilton to Washington, Apr. 9; S. H. Gorham to N. Gorham, Aug. 5; Burnett, VII, pp. 68, 77, 131, 251-252. Reed to Greene, Mar. 4, Reed, *Reed,* II, p. 393. In *Freeman's Journ.:* "Belisarius," Jan. 22, Feb. 19; "Lucius," Mar. 12, Apr. 2, 9, 23; "Honestus," Apr. 30. "Civis" in *Indep. Gaz.* asserted that Arthur Lee was author or prompter of the "Lucius" articles.

40. *JPA,* Nov. 1, 2, 11, 21, 26, 29, Dec. 4, 1782; Jan. 25, 29, 1783; pp. 717-720, 733-34, 747, 755-761, 796, 800-801. *JCC,* Nov. 12, 20, Dec. 4, XXIII, pp. 723n., 761, 850. Madison's notes, Dec. 4, 1782; Feb. 26, 1783; *ibid.,* XXIII, pp. 860-862; XXV, p. 915n. Va. delegates to Gov. Harrison, Dec. 10, Burnett, VI, p. 558. *Gazette,* Oct. 16, Nov. 18, 1782; Jan. 1, 1783. Petition in *Indep. Gaz.,* Sept. 14, 1782.

41. Howell to W. Arnold, Aug. 3, Gratz. Coll., Members of Old Congress. Howell to Gov. of R. I., July 30; Madison to Randolph, Dec. 10, 1782; S. Wharton to Del. Council, Jan. 6, 1783; Burnett, VI, pp. 399, 559, 560; VII, p. 2. *JCC,* Dec. 6, 12, 16, 17, 1782; Jan. 24, 28, 30, 1783; XXIII, pp. 770-772, 778-779, 798-809, 811; XXIV, pp. 99-105. Madison's notes, Dec. 6, *ibid.,* XXIII, p. 864. *JPA,* Jan. 22, p. 788. "A Citizen of Rhode Island," in *Freeman's Journ.,* Nov. 6, 13, 20; Staples believed that the author was David Howell. "A Friend to Rhode Island," in *Gazette,* Nov. 27, Dec. 4. *Freeman's Journ.,* Dec. 4, 18, 1782; Jan. 1, Feb. 12, Mar. 26, 1783. "I. L." in *Indep. Gaz.,* Feb. 4. Paine to Morris, Nov. 28, Henkels, *Catalogue* 1183, pp. 197-199; Dec. 7, Rosenbach, *Catalogue,* p. 72. Staples, *R. I.,* p. 428. Conway, *Paine,* p. 193n.

42. Madison's notes, Feb. 18, *JCC,* XXV, p. 901. When the motion to open the doors came to a vote, Pennsylvania alone voted in the affirmative.

43. *Ibid.,* Jan. 27, 28, Feb. 19, 26, Mar. 11, XXV, pp. 866-973 *passim. JCC,* Mar. 18, 20, XXIV, pp. 188-192, 199-201. The new revenue proposal included a specific duty on enumerated articles and a five per cent duty on all other articles; the plan was to continue not longer than twenty-five years; the collectors were to be appointed by each state but could be removed by Congress; by taxes the states were to raise $1,500,000.

44. *JPA,* Mar. 15. *PSL,* Mar. 21, ch. 1021, XI, pp. 81-91. The act was rather complicated. The state quota of federal supplies for 1782 and 1783 amounted to $480,000. The assembly increased this to $600,000, half of which was to be used to pay interest on U. S. certificates held by state citizens. The remaining $300,000 was to be paid to the federal treasury.

45. *PSL,* Mar. 20, ch. 1020, XI, pp. 71-80. *JCC,* Aug. 11, 15, Sept. 10, 23, XXIV, pp. 449, 511-512; XXV, pp. 935, 962. *JPA,* Dec. 3, p. 774.

46. *PSL,* Sept. 23, ch. 1039, XI, pp. 162-166. Like the first impost proposal this act was never put into effect by Pennsylvania.

47. Morris to Dickinson, Jan. 20, *Pa. Arch.,* IX, p. 740. Correspondence on tax collection is in P. R. P., XLII, p. 42; XLIII, pp. 23, 43; and in Nicholson Letter Book, 1783. *PSL,* Mar. 20, ch. 1018, XI, pp. 65-68.

48. FitzSimons to Dickinson, Apr. 12, 1783; Dickinson to Pa. delegates, Apr. 18; *Pa. Arch.,* X, pp. 28, 38. Madison's notes, Apr. 18, *JCC,* XXV, p. 961. *JCC,* Apr. 22, XXIV, p. 267. *Freeman's Journ.* and *Gazette,* Apr. 30. Hawkins and Williamson to Gov. Martin, Sept. 26, 1783, Burnett, VII, p. 310. *Gazette,* May 14.

49. Dickinson to Council, Jan. 4, 1783; Dickinson to Hannum, Frazier, and Taylor, Jan. 4; MS. Letters of Council, II, pp. 13, 14. *JPA,* Jan. 15, pp. 782-3. *PCR,* Jan. 19, 21, 22, 25, 27, Feb. 18, 20, 21, Mar. 6, 22, 24, Apr. 10; XIII, pp. 484-486, 490-491, 509-526, 538-540, 563. *PSL,* Mar. 20, ch. 1019, XI, pp. 68-70.

50. Dickinson to Pa. delegates, Mar. 19, *Pa.* Arch., X, pp. 7-8. *JCC* Mar. 20, May 30, XXIV, p. 204n, 372-376. Madison's notes, Mar. 20, *ibid.,* XXV, p. 936.

51. "A Whig" in *Indep. Gaz.,* Mar. 26; account of mechanics' meeting in issue of July 19. "A Friend to Mechanics" in *Gazette,* June 25. *Reminiscences of Carpenters' Hall,* p. 20. *JPA,* Aug. 28, Sept. 4, pp. 906, 927.

52. *JPA,* Aug. 27, Sept. 15, 20, 1783, pp. 902-903, 944, 956. *Cf.* Jefferson to Madison, Feb. 20, 1784, Bancroft, *Formation,* I, p. 344, on rivalry between Pennsylvania and Virginia for the western trade.

53. Madison's Notes, Feb. 20, *JCC,* XXV, p. 906. Moses Hazen to Wm. Henry, Feb. 23, *PMHB,* XXII, 113. Peters to Steuben, Apr. 23, Burnett, VII, p. 150. Washington to J. Jones, Mar. 12, Henkels, *Catalogue* 694, pp. 20-21, complained that a civilian from Philadelphia came to camp and

industriously circulated reports that the public creditors would support the soldiers in their demand for back pay.

54. John Armstrong, Jr., to H. Gates, June 16; Va. delegates to Gov. Harrison, June 17; E. Boudinot to ministers at Paris, June 15; Burnett, VII, pp. 189n-190n., 189, 221-224.

55. Wm. Henry to Pres. Dickinson, June 17, *Dipl. Corr. of U. S.,* I, p. 14. R. Butler to Wm. Butler, June 17 (copy), Irvine MSS., VIII, p. 23. Madison's notes, June 19, *JCC,* XXV, p. 971. *PCR,* June 19, XIII, p. 603. Collins, *Congress at Princeton,* p. 14. The decision of Dickinson and Council not to call out the militia or to take other steps to prevent the entry of the Lancaster rebels into the city later constituted the chief charge leveled by the Radicals against the administration; "Valerius" in *Freeman's Journ.,* Apr. 7, 1784.

56. Wm. Butler to Irvine, Aug. 6, Irvine MSS., VIII, p. 46, was of the opinion that Carberry and Sullivan should have been in an insane asylum long before this time. Collins, *op. cit.,* pp. 14-16.

57. *PCR,* June 21, XIII, p. 605.

58. J. N. Byers to Irvine, July 1, Irvine MSS., VIII, p. 26. Boudinot to Washington, June 21, 2 letters; Va. delegates to Gov. Harrison, June 24; B. Hawkins to Gov. Martin, June 25; Boudinot to ministers at Paris, July 15; Burnett, VII, pp. 193-199, 221-224. Madison's notes, June 21, *JCC,* XXV, pp. 973, 974. *JCC,* June 21, XXIV, p. 410. "Conyngham's Reminiscences," Wyoming Hist. Soc. *Proceed.,* VIII, p. 211.

59. Boudinot to Elisha Boudinot, June 23, Burnett, VII, p. 195. *PCR,* June 22, 23, XIII, pp. 606, 609. The first hint of coolness between Council and the Congressional committee appeared on June 23 when Hamilton asked Council to carry on the negotiations in writing which was flatly refused.

60. Burnett, VII, pp. 195-6.

61. Dickinson to Col. Huntington, June 26, MS. Letters of Council, II, p. 37. Rush to Montgomery, June 27, Rush MSS., vol. 41, p. 32. Hiltzheimer, "Diary," June 25, *PMHB,* XVI, p. 165. Dickinson to Boudinot, July 27, *Pa. Arch.,* X, p. 62. Boudinot to Washington, June 26; E. McComb to Pres. Van Dyke, June 30; Burnett, VII, pp. 199-200, 206. *PCR,* June 25, XIII, p. 611. The two standard contemporary sources on the mutiny are the report of the congressional committee, *JCC,* July 1, XXIV, pp. 412-421; and Dickinson to Assembly, Aug. 18, *PCR,* XIII, pp. 654-666. The best secondary account is V. L. Collins, *Continental Congress at Princeton.*

62. "A Lover of Facts" in *Freeman's Journ.,* July 16.

63. *Ibid.,* July 23.

64. *Gazette,* June 25.

65. *Packet,* June 28. See also *Indep. Gaz.,* June 28.

66. *E. g. Packet,* July 2, 5, 9; *Indep. Gaz.,* July 5.

67. Madison to Randolph, June 30, Burnett, VII, p. 208.

68. Burd to Yeates, July 10, Yeates MSS. Sullivan to Moylan, June 30, *Dipl. Corr. of U. S.,* I, p. 27. Carberry to his mother, June 26; Boudinot to Dickinson, July 1; Boudinot to ministers at Paris, July 15; Burnett, VII, pp. 208n., 208-209, 221-224. N. C. delegates to Gov. Martin, *N. Car. State Records,* XVI, p. 852. Rush to Montgomery, July 4, Rush MSS., v. 43, p. 89. Madison to Jefferson, Sept. 30, Burnett, VII, p. 303, remarked that "the real plan and object of the mutiny lies in profound darkness."

69. Armstrong to Gates, June 26, Burnett, VII, p. 200n.

70. *E. g.* Rush to Montgomery, June 27, July 2, 7; Rush MSS., vol. 41, pp. 32, 33; vol. 43, p. 88.

71. *Indep. Gaz.,* July 9; *Journal,* July 23; *Gazette,* July 23. Rush to Montgomery, July 12, Rush MSS., vol. 43, p. 93.

72. Petition is printed in *Gazette,* Aug. 6, without signatures. Collins, *op. cit.,* pp. 87-89, prints the signatures. Rush to Montgomery, July 7; Montgomery to Rush, July 8; Rush, MSS., vol. 41, p. 33; vol. 43, p. 90. Paine correctly informed Washington that the address was signed by the principal men of the city. Du Ponceau, quoted by Collins, *op. cit.,* p. 86, noted that "Peale & other persons of his stamp" were assiduous in obtaining signers. Ellsworth to Reed, Aug. 7; L'Hommedieu to Gov. Clinton, Aug. 15; Burnett, VII, pp. 253-254, 266.

73. Peters to FitzSimons, July 26, Gratz Coll., MOC.

74. Boudinot to Willing, July 30; Higginson to Gordon, Aug. 5; Burnett, VII, p. 251. *JCC,* July 23, 28, XXIV, pp. 444n, 452. *Gazette,* Aug. 6.

75. Muhlenberg to Peters, Aug. 30, Peters Papers, IX, p. 64. *JCC,* Aug. 13, Sept. 1, XXIV, pp. 507-508; XXV, pp. 530-531. *JPA,* Aug. 20, 27, 29, pp. 893, 904, 910. Madison to Randolph, Sept. 8, Burnett, VII.

76. Rush to John Montgomery, Oct. 30, Rush MSS., vol. 41, p. 48. Rush to Montgomery, July 29, Sept. 27, *ibid.,* pp. 36, 42.

77. Montgomery to Rush, June 30; Jefferson to Madison, Dec. 11, 1783; Monroe to Gov. of Va., May 14, 1784; Burnett, VII, pp. 205-6, 390, 527. Burd to Yeates, July 10, 1783; Yeates MSS. Adams, Franklin, and Jay to Pres. Boudinot, Sept. 10, 1783, Boudinot, *Boudinot,* I, p. 380. Collins *Congress at Princeton.*

78. Franklin to Dickinson, Mar. 23, Gratz Coll. Benj. Vaughan to Earl of Shelburne, Dec. 10, 1782; Jan. 12, 1783; MHS *Proceed.,* 2 ser., XVII, pp. 428, 432. *JPA,* Nov. 30, 1782; Mar. 13, 1783; pp. 760-769, 863-864. *PSL,* Mar. 13, ch. 1013, XI, pp. 48-49.

79. "Proceedings of the Freemen . . . of Philadelphia," *Packet,* June 17. See also issues of May 31, July 8, 31. *Freeman's Jour.,* Mar. 19. *Indep. Gaz.,* June 21, 28, Aug. 2.

80. *Packet,* Aug. 7.

81. *Gazette,* June 4. *Indep. Gaz.,* June 21. *Packet,* June 17, 25, Aug. 7. *Freeman's Journ.,* June 4.

82. Carleton to Congress, Aug. 17, in *Freeman's Journ.,* Sept. 10. "Recollective" in *Packet,* Sept. 13. "Sic Vos Non Vobis" in *Indep. Gaz.,* Sept. 13.

83. To Rush, Sept. 30, Rush MSS., vol. 41, p. 43.

84. John Black to Rush, Sept. 15; Rush to Montgomery, Sept. 27; Rush MSS., vol. 41, pp. 39, 42. "An Inhabitat of Cumberland County" in *Journal,* Oct. 1. *Ibid.,* June 25, 1783.

85. "Z" in *Gazette,* Oct. 8. "The Ranger," "An Assemblyman," "A Voter," "A Spectator," and an unsigned article in *Indep. Gaz.,* Oct. 8, postscript, Oct. 11, Oct. 14, postcript.

86. "A Brother Mechanick" and "A Friend to All Mechanics" in *Indep. Gaz.,* Oct. 11. An important episode of double-crossing in local politics was aired in the same paper, Oct. 11, 14, Nov. 1, 15, 22, Dec. 20, 27. Few articles appeared on the larger issues that were really at stake over the possible alteration of the Constitution.

87. Rush to Montgomery, Oct. 20, Rush MSS., vol. 41, p. 45.

88. Rush to Montgomery, Oct. 24, Rush MSS., vol. 41, p. 46.

89. Rush to Montgomery, Oct. 26, Rush MSS., vol. 41, p. 47.

90. Bingham to Cad. Morris, Nov. 6, Strettel MSS., I.

91. Bingham to Morris, Dec. 29, Strettel MSS, I.

92. MS. JPA, Oct. 30, p. 4.

93. FitzSimons to ————, n. d., Prov. Del., I, p. 26, was of the opinion that about 150 soldiers were involved.

94. MS. JPA, Nov. 12, 18, 22, 1783; pp. 57, 76, 94-95. *Journ. Censors,* Nov. 19, Dec. 30, 31, 1783. "A Friend to the Army" in *Indep. Gaz.,* Oct. 25.

95. Irvine to Wayne, Dec. 10, Irvine MSS., VIII, p. 83. Wayne to Irvine, Dec. 9, Wayne MSS., XIX, p. 33, was equally anxious about the outcome of the investigation.

96. MS. JPA, Feb. 23, 28, pp. 326, 353. *Freeman's Journ.,* Jan. 21. *Journ. Censors,* Jan. 6.

97. MS. JPA, Oct. 30, 31, Nov. 3, 10, 17, 25, 1783; Feb. 28, 1784; pp. 5, 8-10, 20-21, 52, 71, 161-169, 353-354. *Journ. Censors,* Nov. 26.

98. Delaney to Wayne, Dec. 9, Wayne MSS., XIX, p. 34. MS. JPA, Nov. 3, 5, 13, 28, Dec. 2, 3, 1783; Feb. 16, 1784; pp. 14, 31, 59, 62-63, 116, 132-135, 138-140, 296.

99. Extract of letter from Lancaster, in *Indep. Gaz.,* Oct. 25, 1783. *Freeman's Journ.,* Mar. 31. "The Watchman" in *ibid. JPA,* Mar. 31, Aug. 18, pp. 216, 284.

100. Two other delegates, James Wilson and Thos. FitzSimons, also wished to leave the national body. Their reasons were not disclosed, but undoubtedly the fact that Congress was no longer sitting in Philadelphia made it impossible for them to attend the sessions and to carry on their business at the same time. Peters to Chas. Thomson, Oct. 20, Thomson Papers, I. MS. JPA, Oct. 31, p. 6. FitzSimons to Peters, Prov. Del., I, p. 26.

101. Rush to Montgomery, Oct. 26, Rush MSS., vol. 41, p. 47.

102. MS. JPA, Nov. 12, p. 56. Mifflin and Peters received unanimous votes. Montgomery polled only forty-three ballots because, as Rush explained, he had "done too much mischief" to the Radicals ever to be forgiven by them; Rush to Montgomery, Nov. 15, Rush MSS., vol. 41, p. 49. Wilson was unanimously elected, Feb. 14, 1784; MS. JPA, p. 293. Peters to Gray, Nov. 16, Peters Papers. M. Slough to Hand, Nov. 12, NYPL *Bull.,* I, p. 229. Rush to Montgomery, Dec. 2, Rush MSS., vol. 41, p. 50. It appears that Jasper Yeates was considered as a candidate for Congress at this time; Hartley to Yeates, Dec. 2, Yeates MSS. C. Morris to Thomson, Feb. 12, Thomson Papers. C. Morris to J. Read, Feb. 13, Burnett, VII, p. 439. Morris, MS. Diary, Nov. 12, III. MS. JPA, Nov. 12, 21, 26, pp. 56, 86, 107.

103. C. Morris to Bingham, Jan. 5, Roberts Coll., 722.

104. Morris to Thomson, Feb. 12, 1784, Thomson Papers.

105. *Indep. Gaz.,* Nov. 15, 25, 29. *Journal,* Dec. 24. *Freeman's Journal,* Feb. 11, 18, 25, Mar. 3, 1784. *JPA,* Nov. 10, 13, 1783; Jan. 21, 28, Feb. 3, 6, 9, 12, 16, 1784; pp. 21, 27, 89, 102, 112, 117, 122, 126, 133, 138.

106. MS. JPA, Nov. 10, 22, Dec. 3, 5, 1783; Feb. 4, 19, 1784; pp. 51, 90-94, 137, 145-146, 243, 311. MS. Council Minutes, Feb. 20, 25, pp. 38, 40. *PSL,* Dec. 9, ch. 1063, XI, pp. 225-227. The votes followed party lines.

107. The documents on this case are too numerous to list individually. See *Pa. Arch.,* XI, index, "Longchamps."

108. Broadside, June 28, 1784, signed "An Independent Patriot," Du Simitiere Coll., vol. 962, f. 175. See also *Freeman's Journ.,* June 30, July 14. Du Ponceau in *ibid.,* July 21, bitterly attacked the high-handed attitude of the French.

109. *Pa. Arch.,* XI, pp. 491-494. Under the title "Cause importante," the trial was printed in *Courier de l'Amerique,* July 27, Aug. 3, 10, 17, 24, Sept. 28, Oct. 5, 12, 19. Part of this account was translated and printed in *Freeman's Journ.,* Aug. 4, 11, 18. A. J. Barthold, "French Journalists in the United States, 1780-1800," *Franco-American Review,* Winter, 1937,

pp. 217-219, explains how Pennsylvania suppressed the *Courier de l' Amerique* because it printed the details of the trial. Additional sources of information of the Longchamps affair can be found in Burnett, VII, VIII, index, "Longchamps"; NYHS *Colls.,* 1878, pp. 187, 191-192, 194; McKean Papers, Bryan MSS., and Gratz Coll. in Hist. Soc. of Penna. A brief account of the episode is by Albert Rosenthal, "The Marbois-Longchamps Affair," *PMHB,* LXIII, pp. 282-293, who falls into error on passage of the bill concerning immunities of ambassadors; his account would have been enriched by use of the Philadelphia newspapers.

110. This can be followed in *JCC,* XXVIII, XXIX; Burnett, VIII; *Dipl. Corr. of U. S.,* I; and two letters between Jay and Marbois in Rosengarten Coll.

111. MS. JPA, Feb. 7, 1784, p. 259. JPA, Mar. 27, Apr. 1, pp. 210-211, 248.

112. Reed to Bradford, May 2, 1784, Reed, *Reed,* II, p. 412.

113. Dickinson to Pa. delegates, Apr. 29; Lee and Butler to Dickinson, Sept. 11; Pa. commissioners to Dickinson, Oct. 4; *Pa. Arch.,* X, pp. 45, 332, 346. Hand to Montgomery, Aug. 13, Burnett, VII, p. 583. Pa. delegates to assembly, Sept. 25, Gratz Coll., Members of Old Congress. Montgomery to Cad. Morris, Mar. 5, Strettel MSS, I. *JPA,* Sept. 12, 1783, p. 940. *JCC,* Apr. 21, May 1, Sept. 20, Oct. 22, 30, 1783, XXIV, pp. 264-265, 319-320; XXV, pp. 591-596, 717-719, 762-767. Madison's notes, Apr. 2-5, 1783, *ibid.,* XXV, p. 954. Gerry to Jefferson, Aug. 24, Austin, *Gerry,* I, p. 455. A. Lee in *PMHB,* XLIII, p. 267. *Pa. Arch.,* X, pp. 111, 316-317, 357-358, 360-361, 395-396; XI, p. 510. "Marbois on the Fur Trade," *American Historical Review,* XXIX, p. 730. Chase, *Our Revolutionary Forefathers.* H. H. Brackenridge wrote an article on the Indians in *Freeman's Journ.,* May 28, 1783, in which he advanced a plan of driving the natives to the north and west where the unfavorable climate would exterminate them.

114. Lewis, *Bank,* p. 152. The dividend of 1783 was the highest paid during the 1780's.

115. To Belknap, Jan. 24, 1784, *Belknap Papers,* Pt. 1, pp. 301-2.

116. MS. JPA, Feb. 10, 24, 26, 28, pp. 270, 333, 346, 352. Cad. Morris to Chas. Thomson, Feb. 12, 18, Thomson Papers, II. "To the Public" by Willing, FitzSimons, Wilson and G. Morris, *Packet,* Mar. 2. Burd to Yeates, Mar. 4, Walker, *Burd Papers,* pp. 130-131. Yeates to Burd, Mar. 8, Shippen Papers, XIII, p. 7. Russel, *Salomon,* p. 269. "Liberty" in *Freeman's Journ.,* Mar. 10.

117. Lewis, *Bank,* appx. V, VI, pp. 136, 139, 140-147. MS. JPA, Mar. 16, p. 421-422. Burd to Yeates, Mar. 4, Walker, *Burd Papers,* 130-131, indicated that the committee by a majority of one or two favored the incorporation of the new bank. This probably had much to do with forcing the old bank to extend its subscription.

118. Wm. Bradford to ————, Feb. 13, 1784, Wallace Coll., Bradford Papers, I, p. 125. See also Cad. Morris to Chas. Thomson, Feb. 12, Thomson Papers, I.

119. Reed to Bradford, May 2, Reed, *Reed,* II, p. 413. G. Morris to Hamilton, n. d., Sparks, *G. Morris,* I, pp. 267, 268.

120. MS. JPA, Mar. 18, 1784, p. 433. *JPA,* Dec. 5, 1783; Jan. 31, Mar. 31, Apr. 1, Aug. 24, Sept. 27, 1784; pp. 66, 108, 218, 245-247, 296, 358-359. "Philo-Patria" in *Freeman's Journ.,* Apr. 14. Burd to Yeates, Aug. 25, Walker, *Burd Papers,* p. 132.

121. Bancroft to Wm. Frazer, Nov. 8, 1783, Bancroft, *Formation,* I, p. 333.

122. Phila. Merchant Comm. to Mass. merchants, Jan. 3, 1784, Society Coll., signed by Charles Pettit, Thomas FitzSimons, J. M. Nesbitt, J. Ross, Isaac Hazelhurst, Clement Biddle and John Nixon; all supported the Republicans except Pettit and Biddle who were moderate Constitutionalists. Bingham to Cad. Morris, Dec. 29, 1783; Jan. 1, 1784; Strettel MSS. *Gazette,* Dec. 17, 1783. *JCC,* XXVI, pp. 70-71.

123. MS. JPA, Feb. 16, Mar. 1, 4, 5, pp. 296-297, 355, 375, 380. *PSL,* Mar. 15, ch. 1076, XI, pp. 262-265.

124. Muhlenberg to Peters, Aug. 30, 1783, Peters Papers, IX, p. 64. *JPA,* Aug. 29, Sept. 1, 4, 6, 10, 16, 26, 1783; pp. 910, 912, 928, 929, 935, 966-967. MS. JPA, Nov. 8, p. 43. *JPA,* Aug. 10, 1784, p. 270. "Agricola" in *Gazette,* June 13, 1781.

125. "Democraticus" in *Packet,* Sept. 2, 4, 1784; unsigned article in issue of Sept. 20. Petition in *Journal,* Sept. 10.

126. *JPA,* Nov. 29, 1781; Mar. 18, 1782; Feb. 14, 1783; pp. 528, 596, 824.

127. MS. JPA, Feb. 4, 5, 1784, pp. 244-248, 250-251.

128. Thomas Mifflin, John Cadwalader, Robert Morris, John Redman, Samuel Powell, James Wilson, Thomas Willing, George Clymer, Alexander Wilcocks, William White.

129. Montgomery to Irvine, Sept. 15, Irvine MSS., VIII, p. 112. MS. JPA, Mar. 4, p. 377. *JPA,* Sept. 4, 16-18, 21, pp. 311-312, 337-339, 343-344. *Journ. Censors,* July 16, Aug. 27, pp. 95-96, 129-134. "An Assemblyman" in *Freeman's Journ.,* Sept. 15.

130. Address of the Republican majority, *JPA,* Sept. 29, appx., justified this bill with the statement: "We conceive the safety of all incorporated, even personal, property in Pennsylvania to depend upon the successful issue of that bill."

131. *JPA,* Mar. 3, 5, pp. 164-5, 168-9.

132. *Journ. Censors,* Sept. 1, p. 155. *JPA,* Sept. 2, 9, 10, 16, 26, 28, pp. 324-325, 327, 336-337, 352-358, 360-361.

133. For the exodus of the nineteen members, see report issued by the rump assembly, *JPA,* Sept. 29, suppl., pp. 1-3. They ordered two thousand handbills to be printed, describing "the tumultuous manner in which the

House of Assembly has been broken up." See also *JPA,* Mar. 4, 1785, p. 179, which reprinted the minutes of the last day of the 1784 session, and Apr. 8, 1785, pp. 308-311, on the same topic. The Radicals always justified the running away of the nineteen members, sometimes on the ground that it was a safeguard provided by the Constitution; *e. g.* "One of the Dissenting Assemblymen" in *Packet,* Nov. 14, 1787.

134. In March the assembly had received a memorial from the Penns for a revision of the divesting act; MS. JPA, Mar. 17, p. 425; copy of the memorial in Wilson Papers, X, p. 10. "A Plebeian" in *Freeman's Journ.,* Sept. 1, 8, spread the alarm of the return of the propietaries.

135. "To the Citizens of Pennsylvania," *JPA,* Sept. 29, 1784, appx.

Notes to Chapter VI

1. Muhlenberg to Wayne, Dec. 18; Irvine to Wayne, Dec. 18; Wayne MSS, XIX. Composition of first session of Censors:

	Republicans	*Constitutionalists*
Philadelphia City	Samuel Miles Thomas FitzSimons	
Philadelphia County	F. A. Muhlenberg Arthur St. Clair	
Bucks		Joseph Hart Samuel Smith
Chester	Anthony Wayne James Moore (*vice* John Evans deceased)	
Lancaster	Stephen Chambers	John Whitehill
York	Thomas Hartley Richard McAllister	
Cumberland	William Irvine	James McLene (did not attend 1st session)
Berks		James Read Baltzer Gehr (in early days voted with Republicans)
Northampton	John Arndt	Simon Driesbach
Bedford	David Espy Samuel Davidson	
Northumberland	Samuel Hunter (did not attend 1st session)	William Montgomery
Westmoreland		John Smiley William Findley
Washington		James Edgar John McDowell

2. *Journ. Censors,* Nov. 13, p. 5. Josiah Harmar understood that he was to be appointed secretary of the Censors, but declined; Harmar to Censors, Nov. 13, Irvine MSS., VIII, p. 82. Rush to Montgomery, Nov. 15, Rush, MSS., vol. 41, p. 49.

3. *Journ. Censors,* Nov. 19, Dec. 17. At this time Joseph Reed was on his way to Europe. Realizing that the Republican majority might condemn his administration as President, he asked the Censors to inform him if anything came up concerning him; he would instantly return from Europe and "confront the men who shall question my character, or arraign my conduct as President . . .;" Reed to Censors, Nov. 24, *Journ. Censors,* Dec. 9.

4. *Ibid.,* Jan. 19, 1784.

5. *Ibid.,* dissentients' reasons.

6. *Ibid.,* Jan. 21. This address was ordered to be printed along with the report of the committee on amendments. Broadsides, Jan. 21, Gilpin Coll., II, f. 269.

7. Armstrong to Rush, Jan. 6, Rush MSS., vol. 41, p. 51. See also Rush to John Bayard, June 25, *ibid.,* vol. 39, p. 33. Another Presbyterian Constitutionalist with whom Rush corresponded was John Black in the rural section of Cumberland County. Black was sorry to hear that no convention would be called, and "that the odium must fall upon *our* Denomination . . .;" Black to Rush, Jan. 8, *ibid.,* vol. 41, p. 53.

8. Rush to Montgomery, Feb. 17, *ibid.,* vol. 41, p. 57. William Linn from a Presbyterian stronghold in the back-country realized the same situation when he wrote: "I wish some expressions had been omitted in the address of the Majority;" Linn to Rush, Mar. 6, *ibid.,* vol. 41, p. 59.

9. Armstrong to Rush, Feb. 28, *ibid.,* vol. 41, p. 58.

10. Chambers to Rose, Apr. 5, *PMHB,* XXII, pp. 500-501. St. Clair's article, in *Freeman's Journ.,* Feb. 18, 25, Mar. 3, apparently did not circulate widely in the back-country; John King to Rush, July 17, Rush MSS., vol. 41, p. 80.

11. John King to Rush, July 17, *loc. cit.* Rush to Arndt, Mar. 31, Gratz Coll., Decl. of Indep. McLene was the active radical agent in Cumberland County who circulated petitions against a convention; J. Maxwell to Irvine, n. d., Irvine MSS., X, p. 76.

12. Rush to Linn, May 4, Rush MSS., "Letters and Thoughts," I, pp. 17-19.

13. Linn to Rush, July 25, Rush MSS., vol. 41, p. 81.

14. Black to Rush, July 24, *ibid.,* vol. 41, p. 82.

15. "Freymüthige Gedanken . . ." signed by "Einen freyen Deutschen Burger der Staats," broadside, Gilpin Coll., III, f. 549. F. A. Muhlenberg to Henry Muhlenberg, June 28, Muhlenberg MSS., establishes the author-

ship. He stated that he also wrote some articles in English but they have not been identified.

16. Hiltzheimer, *Diary,* Mar. 1, p. 61. MS. JPA, Mar. 15, 19, pp. 417-419, 440-441, 443. *JPA,* Mar. 27, pp. 207-209. MS. Journ. Censors, Sept. 6, 7, III, pp. 802-803, 806-811. Miles to Ed. Burd, Apr. 6, Prov. Del., V, p. 51, mentions his resignation but gives no reason. On this point Konkle, *Bryan,* p. 260, suggests that Miles resigned due to embarassment but does not state his source. "One of the People" and "Senex" in *Freeman's Journ.,* Apr. 7. *Indep. Gaz.,* June 26, gives votes of the election: Bryan 350, McKean 115, Wm. Lewis 1, W. A. Patterson 8. Apparently the Republicans did not seriously enter any candidate.

17. *Journ. Censors,* June 7, pp. 81, 82.

18. Irvine to Wayne, June 15, Wayne MSS., XIX, p. 43. S. C. Morris to ———, July 6, Henkels, *Catalogue* 698, p. 79. Rush to Montgomery, July 12, Rush MSS, vol. 41, p. 76, fell back on his optimistic philosophy: "There will be no convention. It is all for the best . . . A few years hence we shall be in a better Situation both as to knowledge & numbers to reform the Constitution. Besides, the worse it is the more certainly it will mend itself." Hartley to Yeates, July 9, 14, Yeates MSS, also viewed the Republican cause as hopeless.

19. MS. Journ. Censors, Aug. 16, II, p. 326. *Journ. Censors,* Aug. 24, 27, 30, pp. 112-128, 134-143.

20. For report see MS. Journ. Censors, Aug. 31, III, pp. 740-784.

21. *Ibid.,* Sept. 3, 6, 10, 11, 14, 20, III, pp. 804, 821-822, 835-868, 873-882.

22. *Journ. Censors,* Sept. 20, pp. 173-176.

23. MS. Journ. Censors, Sept. 16, III, pp. 888-889. Vote was 14 to 10.

24. "Address from Council of Censors to the freemen of Pennsylavania," *Journ. Censors,* Sept. 24, pp. 176-178. Broadside, Sept. 24, Gilpin Coll., II, f. 277.

25. MS. Journ. Censors, Sept. 1, III, pp. 787-789.

26. *Ibid.,* Sept. 24, III, pp. 1019-1023, 1041.

27. *Ibid.,* Sept. 25, III, p. 1048.

28. *Freeman's Journ.,* Sept. 1. In the same paper, poem, Sept. 22; "Audax," Sept. 29; "An Alarm," Oct. 6. "A Citizen of Pennsylvania" in *Gazette,* Sept. 22, 29. In the *Indep. Gaz.:* "A Friend to Mercy" and "Jack Retort," Sept. 4; "A Kick for the Journal," Sept. 18; unsigned article, Sept. 24. "An Alarm" was written by one of the minority of the Council of Censors and appeared as a broadside; Gilpin Coll., II, f. 279. Men singled out for attack by the Radicals were Jacob Rush, Benjamin Rush, Sharp Delaney, John Montgomery, James Wilson, Robert Morris, Dr. William Smith, and Dr. William White. "Audax" in *ibid.,* Sept. 29,

took the opportunity to deny that the Constitution had been written by schoolmaster Cannon and proudly boasted that Franklin had a large hand in it.

29. "One of the Minority of the Censors," Oct. 1, Penna. Broadsides, f. 146, LC. *Freeman's Journ.*, Sept. 29. "A Watchman" in *ibid.*, October 6. The official election plea of the Republicans was contained in the address of the majority issued by the assembly when the nineteen Radicals walked out in September; it justified all the actions of the session, argued for the justice of repealing the test laws and for restoring the College, and denied rumors that the Penn Proprietors were to be restored: *JPA,* Sept. 29, appx. Hartley to FitzSimons, Oct. 7, Prov. Del., IV, p. 121.

30. "Arminius" and "An Old Mechanic" in *Indep. Gaz.*, Oct. 9. It is probable that the resulting Radical victory in Philadelphia City and County was caused by promises made by that party to the laborers; "A Mechanic" in *Indep. Gaz.*, Jan. 8, 1785.

31. Where the returns are available, it appears that in individual counties the conservatives were completely outvoted, *e. g.* in Cumberland County the Radicals polled about 638 votes, the conservatives about 166; in Philadelphia City the Radicals polled about 1013 votes, and the conservatives 380. Charles Biddle, Councillor-elect from Berks County explained later how his popularity with the Germans drew votes away from candidates of German origin; Charles Biddle, MS. autobiog., pp. 211-212. Biddle asserted, p. 216, that the Republicans expected him to join their party. It was asserted that two-thirds of the members of the new assembly were Presbyterians.

32. *JPA,* Nov. 1, 12, pp. 4, 16-18; the votes on which the assembly based its action show that the Republicans polled only about four per cent of the votes in these five districts; *ibid.*, Aug. 31, 1785, pp. 350-351. Extract from letter in *Freeman's Journ.*, Oct. 20, 1784; "A Citizen of Pennsylvania" in *ibid.*, Oct. 27. On Northumberland County, see *JPA,* Nov. 1, 2, p. 4.

33. *Freeman's Journ.*, Nov. 10.

34. *JPA,* Nov. 3, p. 6. On Samuel Bryan, Rush to ———, Oct. 30, Rush MSS., vol. 41, p. 94, remarked: "Young Bryan applied to Mr Shallus [Assistant Clerk] in a day or two After the event of the election was made public, to know whether he would act as his deputy as Clerk of the Assembly. The young Cub seems as if he thought the right of being a pensioner upon the State was hereditary in his family." Shallus was a Republican; young Bryan needed his help in the new work.

35. *JPA,* Nov. 16, 17, Dec. 10, 1784; Feb. 11, 15, 16, 19, Mar. 26, Apr. 6, 7; pp. 20-21, 23, 60, 131, 139, 141, 148, 249, 293. Reed to DeBerdt, Oct. 17 (misdated for Nov. 17), Burnett, VII, p. 612n.

36. *JPA,* Dec. 11, 15, 17, 20, 1784; Mar. 22, 1785; pp. 61-62, 66-67, 81, 82, 235-236. *PSL,* Feb. 18, ch. 1134, XI, pp. 441-444. Austin's petition to assembly, Feb. 5, Phila. Co. Papers, vol. X, Arch. Div., Harris-

burg. As late as Sept. 1785 the Republicans attempted to restore Austin; *JPA,* Sept. 20, pp. 388-389.

37. *PSL,* Apr. 5, 31, Sept. 13, chs. 1161, 1168, 1179; XI, pp. 576-581; XII, pp. 5-6, 58-61. For the scope of the Radical program, see *JPA,* Dec. 17, pp. 79-81.

38. *JPA,* Dec. 17, p. 79. Also Mar. 28, p. 253. *PSL,* Mar. 25, ch. 1142, XI, pp. 514-516.

39. *JPA,* Feb. 17, 22; Mar. 17, 18, Apr. 2; pp. 79-81, 88-89, 223-224, 226-228, 280-282. *PSL,* Apr. 4, Sept. 17, chs. 1158, 1184; XI, pp. 556-560, XII, pp. 86-88.

40. Morris to Clymer *et al.,* Oct. 30, 1784, Society Coll. Morris to J. Wilson, Feb. 19, 1785, Konkle, "Wilson," II, p. 304. "A Citizen of Philadelphia" in *Packet,* Oct. 19, 1785. *JPA,* Mar. 25, Apr. 2, pp. 246, 269-272. *PSL,* Apr. 2, ch. 1156, XI, pp. 542-545.

41. G. Bryan to Atlee, June 23, 1785, Konkle, *Bryan,* p. 272. Nicholson to Pres. Dickinson, May 17; Nicholson to R. Morris, May 19, June 21; Nicholson to J. Gardner, July 1; Nicholson to Wm. Bradford, July 11, 1785; to Chas. Pettit, Feb. 13, 15; to Bradford, Apr. 20, 1786, Nicholson, Letter Book I, pp. 312-316, 317, 326, 330, 335-336, 463-464, 466-467, 482-485, 486-489, 535-536. R. Morris to Commrs. of Bd. of Treasury, June 4, 1785; Nicholson MSS., "Letters to & from Federal Officials," Arch. Div. *PCR,* Sept. 15, 1786, XV, pp. 83-84. *JPA,* Sept. 16, 23, 27, Dec. 7, 1786, pp. 307, 308, 322, 333-334.

42. *JPA,* Dec. 17, pp. 75-77. The Republicans asserted that two-fifths of the people of the state were affected by the test laws. They pointed out that the test oaths tended to throw government into the hands of immigrants; this was a direct reference to the Scotch-Irish communities in the backcountry which the Radicals controlled. *Indep. Gaz.,* Jan. 22. "A Friend to Equal Liberty," in same issue, asserted that Republicans and non-jurors composed two-thirds to three-quarters of the population.

43. Lux to Rush, Feb. 18, Rush MSS., vol. 43, p. 10. J. Okely to Rush, Dec. 24; Hartley to Rush, Jan. 8; *ibid.,* vol. 43, p. 107, vol. 41, p. 105. Rush, *Considerations upon the Present Test Laws.*

44. *JPA,* Apr. 8, pp. 302-305. For Wayne's resolution, see Mar. 24, pp. 244-246.

45. *Ibid.,* Apr. 8, p. 308.

46. David Jackson to G. Bryan, July 13, 1785, Bryan MSS., Misc. At this time the Republican press printed a petition allegedly signed by numerous important Radicals including George Bryan. When he denied the signature, the conservatives went to some trouble to prove that he had actually signed the petition. See the petition in *Indep. Gaz.,* May 7, and *Mercury,* May 13; comments by "Plain Truth" in *Indep. Gaz.,* Apr. 9, Sept. 3.

47. *JPA,* Sept. 16, 20, 21, pp. 378-379, 388-389, 390.

48. *Ibid.,* Mar. 15, 26, 30, pp. 219, 250, 264-265. "Leander" in *Herald,* Aug. 10.

49. Dickinson to Assembly, Dec. 14, *JPA,* pp. 65-66. Dickinson to Pa. delegates, Dec. 20, Jan. 18; to Pres. of Congress, Dec. 20, Jan. 18; Wm. Henry and Jos. Gardner to Dickinson, Feb. 7, *Pa. Arch.,* X, pp. 369-371, 405. *PCR,* Feb. 26, XVI, p. 372. *JPA,* Nov. 8, Dec. 4, pp. pp. 11, 46. *JCC,* Dec. 23, Jan. 25, 26, 28, Feb. 11, 16, 23; XXVII, p. 706n.; XXVIII, pp. 18n, 19n., 20-21, 24n., 61-63, 73-74, 92-93. *PSL,* Dec. 1, Mar. 20, chs. 1118, 1161, XI, pp. 389-391, 534. *Gazette,* Dec. 1, 15. *Mercury,* Nov. 12.

50. Council to assembly, Dec. 4, Feb. 1, *PCR,* XIV, pp. 271-275, 328-342. *JPA,* Dec. 5, 24, Feb. 3, pp. 52-54, 97-101, 106-107. "Justus" in *Freeman's Journ.,* Feb. 15.

51. Pettit to Greene, Mar. 23, Henkels, *Catalogue* 1316, p. 22. "A Citizen of Pennsylvania" in *Gazette,* Sept. 22, 1784. "A Mechanic" in *Indep. Gaz.,* Jan. 8, 1785.

52. Rush to Montgomery, Dec. 10, Rush MSS., vol. 41, p. 101. "Civis" in *Indep. Gaz.,* Feb. 2, 9. "A Citizen of Philadelphia" in *Gazette,* Feb. 3, 1790; see also W. Bradford to ————, Feb. 12, 1785, Wallace Papers, Bradford MSS., I, p. 152. MS. funding receipt books, Arch Div., Harrisburg.

53. *Mercury,* Dec. 24. *Packet,* Jan. 13, Feb. 18. "Civis" in *Freeman's Journ.,* Feb. 9. "A. B.," "A Dutchman," "Plain Truth," "A Public Creditor," "To the Printers" in *Packet,* Feb. 11, 19, Mar. 5, 8, 12. *JPA,* Feb. 23, Mar. 7, 8, 16, pp. 153-154, 185-186, 188-190, 192-195, 212-214. *PSL,* Mar. 16, ch. 1137, XI, pp. 454-486. A statement of Nov. 27, 1784, in Nicholson, Letter Books, I, pp. 262-263, showed over $2,500,000 due to Pennsylvanians on loan-office certificates and over $3,000,000 in other forms of debts. The funding bill was not pleasing to Congress where it was considered "rather antifederal"; D. Jackson to Bryan, July 27, Bryan MSS. After Pennsylvania's action Madison was pessimistic over what Congress could do regarding the domestic debt; Madison to Jefferson, June 16, Burnett, VIII, p. 143.

54. Bryan to Atlee, Mar. 29, Konkle, *Bryan,* p. 271. *Packet,* Feb. 18, 24. "A Loan Office Certificate Holder" and "A Looker" in *Indep. Gaz.,* Jan. 1, 8. *JPA,* Feb. 26, p. 160. *Herald,* Jan. 8, Mar. 22, Sept. 3.

55. *JPA,* Apr. 6, pp. 291-293.

56. Van Berkel to States General, Mar. 15, Bancroft, *Formation,* I, p. 417.

57. Robert Henderson to Wm. Gardner, July, 1785, Henderson Letter Book. Conditions at the beginning of the year were apparently good. Without comment the *Packet,* Jan. 3, announced that on Dec. 25, 1784, there had been 209 vessels in the wharves, including coasters and river craft; and that since May 1, 1784, upwards of 900 vessels had entered the custom house. This was certainly an improvement over the year 1781-1782 when the custom house entered only 115 vessels from domestic

and foreign ports; Records of Port of Philadelphia, Arch. Div., Harrisburg. On general conditions, see *Packet,* Jan. 28; "One of the People" in issue of June 4. *Herald,* Feb. 22, June 8, 18. *Packet,* July 9, Aug. 12. The decrease in immigration is noted in *Packet,* May 12, June 2; *Herald,* Apr. 23, June 1, 11, July 2.

58. *PSL,* Dec. 15, ch. 1119, X, pp. 391-392. *Herald,* Mar. 5, May 4. *Packet,* May 14, 19, June 3, 13, and "Boston" in issue of June 18.

59. *JPA,* Nov. 16, 17, 1784, Mar. 18, 19, 22, 1785, pp. 21, 24, 226, 232, 240. *Packet,* Mar. 12. "A Constitutionalist" in *Indep. Gaz.,* Jan. 15.

60. Samuel Bryan to Geo. Bryan, May, 1785, Bryan MSS. Dickinson to assembly, Aug. 25, *PCR,* XIV, pp. 523-524. G. Bryan to Atlee, June 23, Konkle, *Bryan,* p. 272. *Packet,* June 21. "Crito" in *Mercury,* Apr. 1. *Freeman's Journ.,* Apr. 13. *Herald,* July 9. *Mercury,* June 3. *JPA,* Apr. 6, 8, pp. 288-289, 300.

61. *JPA,* Aug. 29, 30, Sept. 3, 12, pp. 335, 341, 355, 360. *PSL,* Sept. 20, ch. 1188, XII, pp. 99-104.

62. "A Citizen" in *Mercury,* Dec. 10; petition in *Herald,* Feb. 26; "Strictures on the Bank and on Paper Money" in *Packet,* March 31; "Colbert" in *ibid.,* Apr. 1. *JPA,* Mar. 12, pp. 233-234. Bryan to Atlee, Mar. 29, Konkle, *Bryan,* pp. 271-272.

63. *JPA,* Mar. 28, pp. 253-4.

64. *Ibid.,* Mar. 28, 29, Apr. 4, pp. 254, 258, 285-286. Chas. Thomson to Mrs. Thomson, Apr. 6, *PMHB,* XXV, pp. 430-431.

65. Willing to Bingham, Aug. 29, Balch, *Willing Letters,* pp. 111-112. Willing to Wilson, May 12, *ibid.,* pp. 107-108. Robert Henderson to Wm. Gardner, May 14, Henderson Letter Book. Chief Justice Smith to Lord Sydney, Apr. 18, Bancroft, *Formation,* I, p. 428. "A Pennsylvanian" in *Packet,* Mar. 29; Thos. Paine to FitzSimons, Apr. 19, in *ibid.,* Dec. 17, 1785. "Crito" in *Mercury,* Apr. 1. *JPA,* Mar. 29, p. 285. For articles against the Bank, see: "A Pennsylvanian" and "Philadelphensis" in *Indep. Gaz.,* Dec. 24, Jan. 19; petition in *Freeman's Journ.,* Feb. 23; *Packet,* Mar. 31; "No Aristocrat" in *Herald,* Aug. 31; Isaac Smith to ———, Henkels, *Catalogue* 698, p. 49.

66. Jackson to G. Bryan, July 27, Bryan MSS. Bryan to Atlee, June 23, Konkle, *Bryan,* p. 272.

67. Quoted in Konkle, *Bryan,* p. 273. *JPA,* Aug. 30, 31, Sept. 5, 6, 10, pp. 340, 353, 355-357, 410-412. *PSL,* Sept. 13, ch. 1179, XII, pp. 57-58. Gouverneur Morris, "Address to the Assembly . . . on the Abolition of the Bank . . .," Sparks, *G. Morris,* III, pp. 437-465, lists ten objections to the Bank which he answers. Assembly debates in *Herald,* Sept. 7, 8, 14. M. Carey, *Debates on the Bank.*

68. See the numerous documents in *Pa. Arch.,* X, pp. 398-400, 405, 449, 453, 672-674, 681-684, 696-698. N. Webster, "Diary," Nov. 30,

1784, Ford, *Webster,* I, p. 87. *JCC,* Jan. 13, XXVIII, pp. 3n-4n. Gardner to Bayard, Feb. 11, Gratz Coll.

69. Pettit to Wadsworth, May 11, 1786, Susq. Trans., VI. D. Jackson to Bryan, July 13, 18, 1785, Bryan MSS. *JPA,* Mar. 10, Apr. 8, Aug. 30, Sept. 8, pp. 202, 301-302, 341-343, 360. *JCC,* Sept. 21, XXIX, pp. 725-731, 777.

70. Sept. 23. *Cf. Memoir of Geo. Logan,* p. 38.

71. *JPA,* Sept. 15, pp. 376, 377. See also *Packet,* Sept. 17, 19.

72. Hopkinson to Jefferson, Sept. 28, Hastings, *Hopkinson,* pp. 390-391. Pettit to Greene, Sept. 21, Henkels, *Catalogue* 1328, p. 55.

73. *Packet,* Oct. 6, 7, 10; *Freeman's Journ.,* Oct. 5. *Indep. Gaz.,* Oct. 8, 15; "A Philadelphia Mechanic" in issue of Oct. 8. *Mercury,* Oct. 14, gives the votes as sent in by "A Correspondent." Illustrative are the following: Franklin for Councillor 2347; for assembly: William Will 2310; the other Republicans polled from 1224 to 1240 votes; the unsuccessful Constitutionalists from 1109 to 1135.

74. *Indep. Gaz.,* Oct. 29.

75. Samuel Bryan to G. Bryan, Nov. 3, *PMHB,* XLII, pp. 286-288. Arthur Bryan to G. Bryan, Nov. 3, Bryan MSS. *JPA,* Nov. 19, 23, 24, Dec. 5, pp. 48, 52, 53, 57-58, 79-80, 158-159. Petition, Phila. Co. Papers, X, Arch. Div., Harrisburg.

76. Samuel Bryan to G. Bryan, Nov. 1, Bryan MSS., Misc.

77. *Ibid. JPA,* Oct. 27, p. 5.

78. Samuel Bryan to G. Bryan, Nov. 3, *PMHB,* LXII, pp. 286-288. Biddle, *Autobiog.,* p. 198. *Herald,* Nov. 2. "A Republican" in *Mercury,* Nov. 4. John Hunter, "Diary," Nov. 16, *PMHB,* XVII, pp. 76-82. *JPA,* Oct. 29, p. 8.

79. *JPA,* Nov. 11, Mar. 25, Apr. 3, pp. 36, 236, 248. A. Bryan to G. Bryan, Nov. 3, Bryan MSS. Hiltzheimer, *Diary,* Nov. 11, p. 76. *Herald,* Nov. 12. The other candidates and their votes on the first election were: David Jackson 34, William Irwin 33, Joseph Gardner 32, James Wilson 32, John Armstrong 31, Samuel Meredith 29. J. Bayard to S. Bayard, Dec. 1, Burnett, VIII, p. 266.

80. *JPA,* Nov. 3, 10, pp. 14-15, 33-34.

81. Franklin to Assembly, *ibid.,* Nov. 11, p. 38.

82. *JPA,* Nov. 11, 23, 25, Dec. 13, pp. 39-40, 54-56, 66-67, 92-93. "Myself" in *Herald,* Nov. 12. "A Freeman" in *Indep. Gaz.,* Dec. 31. Robert Morris to S. Deane, Dec. 5, NYHS *Colls.,* XXIII, pp. 471-472.

83. *JPA,* Mar. 1, 2, 3, 4, pp. 177-8, 181, 183, 188-189, 194.

84. *PSL,* Mar. 4, 1786, ch. 1204, XII, pp. 178-191.

85. *JPA,* Nov. 11, Dec. 7, 19, 1785, Apr. 3, 7, Sept. 19, 1786; pp. 36, 84, 105, 135, 248, 255, 260-261, 264, 311, 328. *PSL,* Dec. 24, 1785, Apr. 8, 1786, chs. 1198, 1227, XII pp. 126-7, 233. Assembly debates in *Packet,* Sept. 13, 1786. "Caution" in *Freeman's Journ.,* Dec. 7, 1785. "Mutuality" in *Mercury,* July 7, 1786. "An Importer" in *Packet,* Aug. 30, 1786.

86. J. Yeates to E. Burd, July 6, 1786, Shippen Family Papers, XIII, p. 73. Petition, Nov. 30, Nead Papers. *JPA,* Nov. 30, Dec. 7, 1785, Apr. 7, 1786; pp. 68, 84, 266-267. Wilson to Little, Dec. 27, Konkle, "Wilson," II, p. 309b.

87. Paine to Claypoole, n. d., NYPL *Bull.,* II, p. 393. Hastings, *Hopkinson,* pp. 392-393. *JPA,* Dec. 23, Mar. 3, 15, 29, pp. 130, 184-188, 210, 242. *Packet,* Mar. 6. "Common Sense" in *ibid.,* Mar. 25, 28, Apr. 4. "Plain Sense" in *ibid.,* Mar. 29. *Mercury,* Mar. 31. Paine's articles in *Packet,* Apr. 7, 20, June 20; "Atticus" in *ibid.,* May 8, 22, June 28.

88. *JPA,* Apr. 11, pp. 245-248. Hiltzheimer, *Diary,* Mar. 31, Apr. 1, pp. 82-83.

89. *JPA,* Apr. 7, pp. 264-266. Paine to Dan. Clymer, Sept. (21), Clymer MSS., p. 50, is an enlightening letter.

90. *JPA,* Mar. 1, 4, Sept. 5, pp. 176, 189-193, 290-291; Nov. 17, 24, pp. 42, 49. Assembly debates, Aug. 24, 25, 28, Sept. 5, in *Packet,* Aug. 26, 28, 30, Sept. 7. *PSL,* Sept. 6, ch. 1235, XII, pp. 258-260. "A Friend to Civil and Religious Liberty" in *Indep. Gaz.,* Oct. 9.

91. *JPA,* Nov. 16, 17, 21, 29, Dec. 12, pp. 42-45, 50-51, 64-65, 90-91. Assembly debates, Sept. 21, *Packet,* Sept. 23. *PSL,* Sept. 25, ch. 1248, XII, pp. 313-322. "The Shade of Roscius" in *Carlisle Gazette,* Mar. 1.

92. *Packet,* Sept. 14. *JPA,* Sept. 7, pp. 357-358.

93. Hopkinson's articles, signed "Jus" and "X," in *Packet,* Sept. 1, 2, 4, 11. *PSL,* Sept. 15, ch. 1241, XII, pp. 280-290.

94. *JPA,* Dec. 19, Mar. 18, Apr. 6, Sept. 22, pp. 105, 224, 261, 321. Assembly debates, Sept. 22, in *Packet,* Sept. 25, 26. *Indep. Gaz.,* Oct. 17, Nov. 22.

95. *PSL,* Mar. 1, ch. 1202, XII, pp. 158-164. *JPA,* Feb. 27, pp. 69-70. New Loan Certificate Interest Ledgers, Arch. Div., Harrisburg. A cursory examination of interest payments made the first six months after the passage of the bill disclosed at least twenty assemblymen who voted for the measure and were certificate holders. The names of four members were found who voted against the measure.

96. St. Clair to Wilson, Mar. 2, *PMHB,* XXXVI, pp. 117-118. *JCC,* Mar. 31, XXX, p. 147. *PSL,* Apr. 8, ch. 1226, XI, pp. 228-233. *JPA,* Apr. 6, pp. 259-262.

97. Sept. 12, Bancroft, *Formation,* II, p. 393. See also Monroe to Madison, Sept. 1, King to Gov. of Mass., Sept. 17; Burnett, VIII, pp. 457, 468.

98. *JPA,* Sept. 15, 20, 21, pp. 306, 313, 315-16. *Packet,* Sept. 20. *JCC,* July 27, Aug. 11, 14, Sept. 25, XXX, pp. 443, 444, XXXI, pp. 511-513, 515, 687-688. Hill to Washington, Oct. 1, Bancroft, *Formation,* II, pp. 397-398. King before Mass. H. of Rep., Oct. 11, Burnett, VIII, p. 480.

99. S. M. Mitchell to W. M. Johnson, Feb. 21; Monroe to R. H. Lee, May 24; Pettit to J. Wadsworth, May 27; Grayson to Madison, May 28; Monroe to Jefferson, June 16; Burnett, VIII, pp. 309, 365-366, 368-369, 373, 391-392. Pettit to Wadsworth, May 11; Wm. Montgomery to L. Myers, June 22; Susq. Trans., VI. Franklin to Pa. delegates, May 10; Pettit to Franklin, May 7; J. Franklin to Doc. Hamilton, June 8; *Pa. Arch.,* X, pp. 759-760, XI, pp. 3, 106. *PCR,* May 10, 11, 29, XV, pp. 19, 20, 28. *JCC,* May 11, 22, 24, 25, XXX, pp. 256n, 296, 299-304, 307. Burd to Yeates, June 8, Walker, *Burd Papers,* p. 138. *Packet,* June 19, July 3. *Mercury,* June 23. Letter of Aug. 17, *Historical Journal,* II, pp. 215-16. Like many such understandings which are made with the wink of an eye and nod of the head, the conditions of the agreement were not too clear. As Pettit remarked (to Franklin, May 7, *loc. cit.,*): "But these Things being understood rather than expressed, may be differently conceived of by different Minds, and therefore I cannot pretend to say what Interpretations may hereafter be given on this Subject."

100. Pa. delegates to B. Franklin, Dec. 31, 1785; W. H. Smith to Montgomery, May 14, 1786; Montgomery to Council, May 20; Pa. delegates to Franklin, June 9; Van Campen to Armstrong, June 27; *Pa. Arch.,* XI, pp. 456, 760, 762, 765-766; XI, 4-5, 26. Chas. Biddle to Assembly, *PCR,* Feb. 23, XIV, p. 644. Pickering to J. Gardner, Mar. 9; Pel. Webster to W. S. Johnson, Mar. 31; Pettit to J. Wadsworth, May 11; John Jenkins, Diary, Sept. 23, Oct. 1; Susq. Trans., VI. *Mercury,* Mar. 24. *Packet,* Feb. 25, June 16, July 3, 19, Aug. 24, Sept. 18. *JPA,* Feb. 24, Mar. 9, Apr. 3, Sept. 11, 14, 23, pp. 164-165, 202-249, 300, 305, 323-325.

101. *PSL,* Mar. 28, 1787, ch. 1285, XII, pp. 436-440. *JPA,* Mar. 7, 27, pp. 162-163, 185-186.

102. For comments on the Mississippi question in 1785, see "Candidus" in *Indep. Gaz.,* Feb. 12, 1785, *Packet,* Feb. 22, Mar. 22, *Mercury,* Feb. 25, Mar. 22. Wilkinson to Hutchinson, June 20, *PMHB,* XII, p. 56. Bryan to Atlee, June 23, Konkle, *Bryan,* p. 273.

103. Monroe to Gov. Henry, Aug. 12, 1786, Burnett, VIII, p. 425.

104. King to Monroe, July 30; Thomson, debates, Aug. 18; Monroe to Jefferson, Aug. 19; W. S. Johnson, speech, Aug. 21; Burnett, VIII, pp. 407, 439-440, 444-445, 448-449. St. Clair to Monroe, Aug. 20, Smith, *St. Clair Papers,* I, pp. 599-600. Madison to Monroe, Aug. 15, 1786, *Doc. Hist. of Const.,* IV, p. 23. *JCC,* Aug. 29, XXI, pp. 595-596. *Packet,* Aug. 28.

105. Monroe to Madison, Sept. 3, Burnett, VIII, p. 461. Otto to Vergennes, Sept. 10, Bancroft, *Formation,* II, p. 390. Monroe to Gov. Henry, Aug. 12, Burnett, VIII, p. 424.

106. Quoted in Newlin, *Brackenridge,* p. 74. *Packet,* Oct. 7.

107. Franklin to Chas. Pettit, Oct. 10, *Works,* Smyth ed., IX, pp. 544-555.

108. Brackenridge in *Pittsburgh Gazette,* Apr. 28, quoted in Newlin, *Brackenridge,* p. 81. *Gazette Publications,* pp. 41-52. *JPA,* Mar. 8, p. 140. St. Clair to FitzSimons, Mar. 10; Madison to Jefferson, Mar. 19; Burnett, VIII, pp. 554, 561. For comment by two other western Pennsylvanians, see Redick to Irvine, Jan. 20; Duncan to Irvine, Jan. 31; Irvine MSS., IX, pp. 58-60.

Notes to Chapter VII

1. *Mercury,* Oct. 7; *Indep. Gaz.,* Oct. 7; *Packet,* Oct. 7.

2. *Mercury,* Oct. 6; *Indep. Gaz.,* Oct. 7.

3. *Indep. Gaz.,* Oct. 7, 9.

4. "A Friend to Equal Liberty" and "Quernus" in *Indep. Gaz.,* Oct. 10. Articles in issues of Oct. 10, 12, mirrored Republican relief on the question of the immigrant element. "A Pennsylvanian" in *Packet,* Oct. 5. "Jos. Langertone" in *Indep. Gaz.,* Oct. 9, described a vision in which he saw thirty-four Radicals condemned by the Lord "to everlasting ———." Later Judge Bryan was censured for having given pre-election stump speeches in Philadelphia; *ibid.,* Oct. 9. The Republicans considered their victory as a mandate to restore the Bank; *ibid.,* Nov. 27.

5. Sam. Vaughan to R. Price, Nov. 4, MHS *Proceed.,* 2 ser., XVII, pp. 355-356. Paine to FitzSimons, Nov. 19, Conway, *Life of Paine,* pp. 219-220. *Indep. Gaz.,* Nov. 1, Dec. 4. *Carlisle Gazette,* Sept. 27, Oct. 4.

6. *Pa. Arch.,* 6 ser., XI, pp. 27-46. *JPA,* Nov. 3, 8, Dec. 9, 1786; Feb. 24, 1787, pp. 15, 23-24, 69-70, 120. D. Espy to Speaker Mifflin, Nov. 18, Prov. Del., III, p. 28. Hiltzheimer, *Diary,* Dec. 9, 1786, p. 108. Assembly debates, Nov. 2, 3, in *Packet,* Nov. 3, 4.

7. *Packet,* Nov. 4, shows Biddle received 36 votes and Muhlenberg 33. Biddle, *Autobiog.,* pp. 211-213. *Indep. Gaz.,* Nov. 1, 4, 6; "A Plebeian" in *ibid.,* Nov. 3.

8. *JPA,* Oct. 26, p. 5; fuller report in *Packet,* Oct. 27.

9. Assembly debates, Oct. 30, 31, Nov. 1, in *Packet,* Oct. 31, Nov. 1, 2. Joseph Montgomery, John Bayard, Joseph Redman, and Matthew Clarkson had also been put in nomination. "A Friend to Pennsylvania" in *Indep. Gaz.,* Oct. 30. *JPA,* Nov. 1, 8, 11, pp. 25, 56. Another innovation was that the house on George Clymer's suggestion determined not to stipulate the time of the appointments. Congress, however, interpreted

this to mean until the following October for all the delegates except Pettit; *JCC,* Feb. 12, 1787, XXXII, p. 31n.

10. *Indep. Gaz.,* Nov. 4, 1786.

11. Cartoon in Library Company of Philadelphia. This is the only political cartoon dealing with state politics which has been found for the period 1776 to 1790. Although it is not a good example of caricature, its story is unmistakable. This was bitter medicine for the Republicans who replied with slanderous newspaper attacks and singled out Peter Markoe, Edward Pole and William Findley as the originators of the drawing. Markoe's love of liquor provided a choice object for filthy attacks on this Poet Laureate of the Adopted Sons; *Indep. Gaz.,* Feb. 14, 20, 26, 28, Mar. 9.

12. Otto to Vergennes, Feb. 16, 1787, Bancroft, *Formation,* II, p. 411, reported that St. Clair was federal and attached to French interests. *JPA,* Mar. 24, p. 178.

13. *JPA,* Dec. 5, 13, 29, 1786; Feb. 26, Mar. 10, 1787; pp. 62, 75-76, 107-108, 121, 142. *PSL,* Mar. 15, ch. 1276, XII, pp. 403-409.

14. *E. g.* Rush to Price, Oct. 27, MHS *Proceed.,* 2 ser., XVII, p. 354. *Packet,* Nov. 7, Dec. 6, 11, 13.

15. Minutes of Directors of the Bank, Nov. 23, Balch, *Willing Letters,* pp. 132-133. Assembly debates, Nov. 22, 29, Dec. 13, in *Packet,* Nov. 25, Dec. 2, 25. *JPA,* Nov. 16, 22, Dec. 13, pp. 38-39, 46, 76-78. Memorial from stockholders of Bank to assembly, *ibid.,* Dec. 18, pp. 84-85. Whitehill's proposals during the debates, *ibid.,* Dec. 28, pp. 101-105. These proposals were defeated by only four to six votes. Tench Coxe, writing under the pseudonym of "Another of their Constituents," suggested nine limitations on the Bank in his pamphlet *Thoughs Concerning the Bank of North America.* Brackenridge and Hiltzheimer assumed that since the assembly could not revoke a charter without trial by jury, the house needed only to put the stockholders in possession of every privilege their original charter had given them; Hiltzheimer, *Diary,* Dec. 13, p. 109.

16. *Indep. Gaz.,* Jan. 5, Mar. 14. Newlin, *Brackenridge,* pp. 77, 78.

17. Jos. Hart to G. Bryan, Jan. 2, Mar. 7, Bryan MSS. *JPA,* first two weeks of March, notes receipt of numerous petitions on this subject. On March 12 petitions were received with a total of almost 1200 signatures. A petition is printed in *Indep. Gaz.,* Feb. 8. *JPA,* Dec. 13, 28, 1786; Mar. 13, 16, 17, 1787; pp. 58-59, 104-105, 132-133, 145-146, 155,160, 163-164. *PSL,* Mar. 17, ch. 1278, XII, p. 412. "Machiavel," "Patriot," "Independent" and poem in *Freeman's Journ.,* Jan. 3, Feb. 7, 28, Apr. 25. "A Fellow Citizen" in *Indep. Gaz.,* Feb. 28.

18. St. Clair to FitzSimons, Mar. 10, Prov. Del., IV, p. 113.

19. "Civis," "N," "A Freeman," "Delaware," and extracts from Brackenridge's address in *Indep. Gaz.,* Mar. 7, 8, 15, 20, Aug. 15. *JPA,* Mar. 3, 21, pp. 132, 171. From the counties which opposed the measure

there were five members absent; Findley seized this opportunity to put his motion to a vote.

20. *JPA,* Mar. 3, 1787, pp. 133-134; Feb. 16, 1789, pp. 73-74. *PSL,* Mar. 29, 1787; Mar. 13, 1789; chs. 1294, 1396. *Gazette,* Feb. 4, 1789, Petition, Feb. 17, 1787, *Pa. Arch.,* 2 ser., III, pp. 98-99.

21. Rush to Price, Oct. 27, 1786, MHS *Proceed.,* 2 serv., XVII, p. 353. Monroe to Madison, Sept. 3, 1786, *Doc. Hist. of Const.,* IV, p. 25. Madison's notes, Feb. 21, 1787, *JCC,* XXXIII, p. 742. In the letters by Bingham which have come to light, he does not mention the ideas others attributed to him; *e. g.* Bingham to Price, Dec. 1, 1786, MHS *Proceed., op. cit.,* p. 350. On Annapolis Convention, see Tench Coxe to Pres. Franklin, Sept. 19; Coxe to Md. Commissioners, Sept. 16; *Pa. Arch.,* XI, pp. 60-63.

22. Madison to Randolph, Apr. 15, Henkels, *Catalogue* 694, p. 128.

23. Montgomery to Irvine, Mar. 27, Irvine MSS., IX, p. 65. N. Mitchell to Pres. of Del., Feb. 10, Gratz Coll., Members of Old Congress. Mitchell to G. Bedford, Feb. 10; Madison to Washington, Apr. 16; Jay to J. Adams, May 12; Lee to Washington, May 13; John Armstrong to Irvine, June 20; Burnett, VIII, pp. 579, 583, 596n., 612. *JCC,* Apr. 10, 21, May 10, XXXII, pp. 167-169, 227, 284; Madison's notes, Apr. 11, 12, *ibid.,* pp. 732, 733.

24. Irvine to Wilson, Mar. 6, Burnett, VIII, p. 551. *PSL,* Dec. 30, 1786; Mar. 28, 1787; chs. 1258, 1280, XII, pp. 351-352, 423-424. *Indep. Gaz.,* Dec. 27, 1786. In the issue of Oct. 15, 1787, the votes of the delegates were given thus: Robert Morris, Clymer, and Mifflin, 63 each; Ingersoll, 61; FitzSimons, 37; Wilson, 35; and G. Morris, 33. The unsuccessful candidates were the Radicals McKean, 26 votes; Pettit and Bayard, 25 each; Findley, 2. Franklin received 10 votes, but Republicans claimed he was not seriously considered at this time because it was thought he would not serve.

25. Rush to Price, June 2, MHS *Proceed.,* 2 ser., XVII, p. 367. "Plan for a New Federal Government" in *Indep. Gaz.,* Oct. 25, 1786; "Rustick" in issue of May 31, 1787; "Sidney" in issue of June 6; see also July 5. "Nester" in *Mercury,* Nov. 24, 1786, attacked the unicameral legislature and the too frequent rotation of its members.

26. Oswald to Gates, June 4, NYPL *Bull.,* III, p. 41.

27. Geo. Fox to ————, June 9, Fox Letter Book, p. 11.

28. Redick to Irvine, Aug. 29, Irvine MSS., IX, p. 87. Redick was jealous of state rights and thought the states should be "niggardly" in surrending them; to Irvine, Sept. 10, 14, *ibid.,* IX, pp. 91-93. Editorial comment, "Tar and Feathers" and "Halter" in *Indep. Gaz.,* Aug. 8, 16, 30. "Z" in *Freeman's Journ.,* Aug. 22.

29. Lloyd, *Debates,* Sept. 28, I, pp. 115 ff.

30. *Ibid.* Coxe to Madison, Sept. 28, 29, *Doc. Hist. of Const.,* IV, pp. 304-306. Hiltzheimer, *Diary,* Sept. 28, p. 133. The Radical absentees were: Whitehill, Kennedy, Mitchell from Cumberland; Piper and Powell from Bedford; Antes and Dale from Northumberland; Findley and Barr from Westmoreland; Wright, McDowell, Flenniken, and Allison from Washington; Phillips and Gilchrist from Fayette; Smith and McCalmont from Cumberland; and Clarke and Miley from Dauphin. Antes had voted for calling a convention. Antes and Smith had been among the runaways of 1784.

31. Lloyd, *Debates,* Sept. 29. Unidentified letter, Oct. 11, *Doc. Hist. of Const.,* IV, pp. 324-327. McMaster and Stone, *Penna. and Fed. Const., passim.*

32. Montgomery to Irvine, Oct. 9, Irvine MSS., IX, p. 99. Unidentified letter, Oct. 11, *loc. cit. Indep. Gaz.,* Oct. 9. *Packet,* Oct. 10.

33. *JPA,* Oct. 25, Nov. 3, 14, pp. 5-6, 18, 56.

34. *Ibid.,* Oct. 24, 31, pp. 5, 14. Lloyd, *Debates,* Oct. 31.

35. Hiltzheimer, *Diary,* Nov. 8, p. 137. *JPA,* Nov. 13, p. 54. Lloyd, *Debates,* Nov. 13, II, p. 93. The unsuccessful candidates were Daniel Heister, John Bayard, and Samuel Miles.

36. *Packet,* Oct. 4. *Freeman's Journ.,* Oct. 10.

37. "Reply to Address" in *Packet,* Oct. 8. Webster's "Remarks on the Address of the Sixteen Members" in McMaster and Stone, *Penna. and Fed. Const.,* pp. 89-106. A representative selection of the newspaper literature is in *ibid.,* pp. 73-203.

38. Webster, "Diary," Sept. 15, Ford, *Webster,* I, pp. 219-220. Tench Coxe to Madison, Sept. 27, Oct. 21, *Doc. Hist. of Const.,* IV, pp. 296-297, 338-339.

39. Ford, *Harrisburg Convention,* p. 14n. Konkle, *Bryan,* p. 309n., thinks Samuel Bryan was the author with the connivance of his father. Rush to ————, Apr. 9, 1788, Rush MSS., vol. 42, p. 47, believed George Bryan to be the author. Francis Murray to John Nicholson, Nov. 1, Nicholson MSS., County Officials, Berks, Arch. Div. "From the Chronicles of Early Times: A Fragment" in *Freeman's Journ.,* Oct. 17.

40. *Packet,* Oct. 10. *Indep. Gaz.,* Nov. 1, 5, 6.

41. J. Duncan to Wm. Irvine, Oct. 3, Irvine MSS., IX, p. 98. Coxe to Madison, Sept. 28, 29, *Doc. Hist. of Const.,* IV, pp. 304-306. *Indep. Gaz.,* Oct. 11, 16.

42. R. Butler to Wm. Irvine, Oct. 11, Irvine MSS., IX, p. 100.

43. *Indep. Gaz.,* Oct. 16, 25, 26. The article in the issue of Oct. 25 stated that "Centinel's" abuse of Franklin and Washington was omitted when his writings were translated into German.

44. Bradford to Elias Boudinot, Oct. 2, Bradford Coll., Wallace Papers, I, p. 174.

45. G. Morris to Washington, Oct. 30, *Doc. Hist. of Const.,* IV, pp. 357-360. Grayson to Monroe, Oct. 22, *ibid.,* IV, p. 342. Carrington to Jefferson, Oct. 23, Bancroft, *Formation,* II, p. 446.

46. Powell to Washington, Nov. 13, *Doc. Hist. of Const.,* IV, pp. 378-379.

47. *JPA,* Nov. 19, pp. 36-37, 40-41. The pertinent documents are in McMaster and Stone, *Penna. and Fed. Const.,* pp. 204-211.

48. Harding, "Party Struggles over the First Pennsylvania Constitution," AHA *Annual Report* for 1894, falls into the error of assuming that the vote of Sept. 27 to call a convention was a strict party vote. This was not the case with at least half a dozen members. Four from Berks had voted consistently as Radicals but voted for the convention; the same was true of two members from Northampton, one from Northumberland, and perhaps Carson of Dauphin would fall into the same classification. This is an early indication of the split among the Radicals, the moderates being willing to call a convention.

49. *Indep. Gaz.,* Nov. 18.

50. Beard, *Econ. Interp. of Const.,* p. 274, based on records in Treasury Department at Washington. The nineteen were distributed thus: Philadelphia City 3, County of Philadelphia 2, Bucks 1, Chester 2, Lancaster 4, York 2, Northampton 3, Montgomery 1, Luzerne 1.

51. The eight members of the Cincinnati were Barclay, Boyd, Campbell, Chambers, Hartley, McKean, MacPherson, and Pickering; W. H. Egle's biographical sketches in McMaster and Stone, *Penna. and Fed. Const.* George Bryan, autobiographical fragment, Bryan MSS. In listing the groups favoring the Federalists, Bryan remarked: "The women—all admire Genl. Washington."

52. Biographical data prepared by the author from various sources. The average age of the Radicals in the Convention was over 46 years; that of the Republicans about 42 years. Forty-five per cent of the Republicans were in their thirties.

53. Hopkinson to Jefferson, Dec. 14, *Doc. Hist. of Const.,* IV, pp. 404-405. McMaster and Stone, *Penna. and Fed. Const.,* Ch. 1.

54. *Packet,* Dec. 14. McMaster and Stone, *op. cit.,* pp. 421-428. Thomas Scott from Washington County did not decide how to cast his vote until the last minute, according to the *Gazette,* Nov. 26, which declared that the day before the final vote he received an anonymous letter stating that he would lose his county office if he should vote for the Constitution. Next day he voted for adoption.

55. *Packet,* Dec. 13. *Indep. Gaz.,* Dec. 17. Sam. Powell to Washington, Dec. 12, *Doc. Hist. of Const.,* IV, p. 404. Muhlenberg to Pres. of Congress, Dec. 15, *ibid.,* II, p. 27.

56. "The Address and Reasons of Dissent . . ." in *Packet,* Dec. 18. The address is 10,000 words in length.

57. Hartley to Yeates, Dec. 26, Yeates MSS. *Gazette,* Jan. 2, 1788.

58. Report from Carlisle in *Indep. Gaz.,* Jan. 9. "One of the People" in *ibid.,* Feb. 7; see also issue of Jan. 12. Montgomery to Irvine, Jan. 9, Irvine MSS., X, p. 113.

59. Montgomery to Irvine, Jan. 19, Irvine MSS., IX, p. 114.

60. Bryan to John Ralston, Mar. 26, *Indep. Gaz.,* Apr. 9. Also see issues of Jan. 9, Feb. 14, 27. Montgomery to Irvine, Jan. 9; Stewart to Irvine, Feb. 20; Irvine MSS., IX, pp. 113, 120.

60a. Montgomery to Irvine, Apr. 27, X, p. 10. Wm. Bradford, Jr., to his wife, May 27, Bradford MSS., Wallace Papers, I, p. 183. "Theseus" in (York) *Penna. Chronicle,* Apr. 7. *Indep. Gaz.,* Mar. 14.

61. "Centinel" in *Freeman's Journ.,* Oct. 24, 1787; *Indep. Gaz.,* Oct. 5 through Apr. 9, 1788. Hopkinson to Jefferson, Apr. 6, 1788, *Doc. Hist. of Const.,* IV, p. 564.

62. Rush to Irvine, Dec. 21, 1787, Irvine MSS., IX, p. 107. Rush to Belknap, May 6, 1788, MHS *Colls.,* 6 ser., IV, pp. 403-405, asked to have his views published in Massachusetts. Coxe to Madison, Dec. 28, 1787; Jan. 16, 23, Feb. 6, 25, May 19, July 23; *Doc. Hist. of Const.,* IV, pp. 423, 444, 456-457, 522-523, 619, 812-814. He wrote over the signature of "An American," "A Freeman," and "A Pennsylvanian." *Packet,* Dec. 29, 1787.

63. Black to Rush, Feb. 13, Rush MSS., vol. 43, p. 120.

64. *Indep. Gaz.,* Feb. 19. The idea that the assembly could override the work done by the ratifying convention was in the air as early as December; Rush to Irvine, Dec. 21, Irvine MSS., IX, p. 107. Stewart to Irvine, Feb. 20; FitzSimons to Irvine, Feb. 22; *ibid.,* IV, pp. 120, 121. *JPA,* Mar. 1, 17, 22, 24, 29, pp. 119, 145, 155, 158-160, 179. Petition from Wayne township, Cumberland County, Mar. 1, McAllister MSS., 7312, f. 8. Rush to Hugh Williamson, Feb. 16, Ford, *Harrisburg Convention,* p. 12.

65. Scott to Rush, Mar. 3, Rush MSS., vol. 43, p. 121.

66. Findley to Irvine, Mar. 12, Irvine MSS., X, p. 2.

67. Duncan to Irvine, Mar. 23, *ibid.,* p. 4. This was doubtless Federalist propaganda for Findley's letter to Irvine does not give the least hint that he sponsored violent means.

68. Scott to Rush, Mar. 3, Rush MSS., 7260, f. 121. Ferguson, *Early West. Pa. Politics,* p. 95.

69. Account in Hazard, *Register,* Sept. 14, 1833.

70. Rush to ————, Apr. 9, Rush MSS., vol. 42 f. 47. Rush to Belknap, May 6, 29, MHS *Colls.*, 6 ser., IV, pp. 403-406. Bryan to John Ralston, Mar. 7, 12, *Gazette,* Apr. 2. *Indep. Gaz.*, Mar. 6, 24, Apr. 8. The account of the procession was issued as a broadside, July 8, 1788, Du Simitiere Coll. Hopkinson, who was chairman of the committee of arrangements of the procession, could not resist the temptation to write an account of an imaginary grand Anti-Federal procession in which the leading Radicals were delightfully satirized. This account was printed for the first time in Hastings, "Hopkinson and the Anti-federalists," *American Literature,* I, pp. 405-418.

71. Bryan to Gov. Clinton, Feb. 9, Ford, *Harrisburg Convention,* p. 13.

72. Arthur Campbell to Bryan, Mar. 9, Bryan MSS. Benj. Blyth to ————, July 3; Blyth to John Nicholson, July 3; resolutions adopted at the meeting; Ford, *Harrisburg Convention,* pp. 15-17. Circular letter signed by Blyth, July 3, Pa. Misc., box 11, LC. *Freeman's Journ.*, Sept. 24. *Journal,* Sept. 24. *Packet,* Sept. 2. "A Federal Centinel" in *Gazette,* Sept. 10. Ferguson, *op. cit.*, pp. 98-99. James Hanna to J. Vandergrift *et al.*, Aug. 15; proceedings of the meeting, Aug. 25; McMaster and Stone, *op. cit.*, pp. 553-557.

73. Gallatin's draft, Adams, *Gallatin,* p. 78. *Gazette,* Sept. 3, 10, 17. *Packet,* Sept. 15. The proposed amendments were: 1. Rights of sovereignty not vested expressly in Congress shall be deemed to remain in the states. 2. The ratio of representatives to population should be 1 to 20,000. 3. Legislatures should have the right to recall senators. 4. Congress should not have power to alter the conditions governing election of senators or representatives. 5. In place of direct taxes Congress should levy quotas on the states and have power to collect them if a state were delinquent. 6. There should be no standing armies in time of peace except by consent of two-thirds of both houses. 7. Exclusive legislation over the ten-mile area for seat of Congress should extend only to police power. 8. The militia should be practically under the control of each state. 9. Clause respecting vessels bound to or from any one of the states should be explained. 10. Except for admiralty cases Congress should set up no courts but the supreme court. 11. A further restriction of appellate jurisdiction. 12. No treaty should alter the laws of any state or of the United States unless assented to by the House of Representatives.

74. Bingham to Irvine, Sept. 1; Jas. McLene to Irvine, Sept. 12; Irvine MSS., X, pp. 3, 14. *Packet,* Sept. 19.

75. Mifflin to Gov. Randolph, Mar. 6, *Pa. Arch.*, XI, pp. 557-558. *JPA,* Oct. 4, 1788, pp. 276-277; Feb. 7, Mar. 3, 5, 1789, pp. 58-61, 112-113, 123-126; Mar. 1, 1790, pp. 157-158. E. P. Smith, "Movement towards a Second Constitutional Convention in 1788," in J. F. Jameson, ed., *Essays in Constitutional History.*

76. "A Federalist Centinel" and "A Freeman" in *Gazette,* Sept. 10, 17; also issue of Oct. 8. *Packet,* Oct. 15, and "A Federalist" in issue of Jan. 9, 1789.

77. Redick to Irvine, Oct. 23, Irvine MSS., X, p. 19. Hiltzheimer, *Diary,* Nov. 4, p. 147. *JPA,* Nov. 1, 5, pp. 5, 12.

78. Rush to Montgomery, Oct. 2, Rush MSS., vol. 42, p. 51. Jas. McLene to Irvine, Sept. 12; Eph. Blaine to Irvine, Oct. 2; Redick to Irvine, Oct. 2; Irvine MSS., X, pp. 14, 16, 17. *JPA,* Sept. 18, 23, 24, 30, pp. 242, 248-250, 259. Rush to Belknap, Oct. 7, MHS *Colls.,* 6 ser., IV, pp. 418-420, enthusiastically described Maclay as highly federal, possessing great talents for governmemnt, and independent in fortune and spirit.

79. *JPA,* Sept. 27, pp. 257-258; Nov. 5, p. 12. Rush to Belknap. Oct. 7, *loc. cit.*

80. "A Friend to Liberty and Union" in *Freeman's Journ.,* Nov. 12. Whether the Radicals formed their ticket at Harrisburg is not known. John Irwin to Wm. Irvine, Oct. 7, Irvine MSS., X, p. 18, would indicate that this was not the case, at least for all of the candidates. Geographically they were scattered thus: two from Philadelphia, two from Montgomery County, two from Cumberland, and one each from Westmoreland and Northumberland. Unsuccessful in carrying Irvine for state senator, his friends had him placed on the ticket for representative; John Irwin to Irvine, Oct. 7, *loc. cit.*

81. *Packet,* Oct. 23.

82. *Gazette,* Oct. 15, Nov. 12. *Freeman's Journ.,* Oct. 22, 29. Each county sent two representatives, except Bedford and Huntingdon, which sent one each, and four western counties which were represented by a total of two delegates. Over half the delegates from middle and western part of the state were men who had attained no political prominence, if any, beyond their own localities.

83. "Lucillus" in *Gazette,* Nov. 5, answered by "Centinel" XXII, *Indep. Gaz.,* Nov. 14. Wm. Bradford, Jr., to Boudinot, Nov. 14, Wallace MSS., Bradford Papers, I, p. 191, was sorry that Pettit had attended the Harrisburg convention for otherwise the public creditors would cast their votes for him. "Consistence" in *Packet,* Nov. 20. "A Manufacturer" in *Gazette,* Nov. 26, lamented that the Federalist ticket contained no men directly interested in manufacturing.

84. "To the German Inhabitants," a handbill translated in *Packet,* Nov. 19; "A German Federalist" in Nov. 24. "Sener" in *Gemein. Phil. Corr.,* Nov. 18, praised the Lancaster ticket as it was originally issued; "Ein Deutscher Wächter," in issue of Nov. 25.

85. *Gazette,* Dec. 17. A comparison of this vote with that in the ratifying convention of 1787, if it can be assumed that popular sentiment did not change greatly during the intervening year, indicates that the delegates of Northumberland, Franklin and Washington Counties who had voted eight to five for ratification now voted against the wishes of their constituents, for these three counties were overwhelmingly Radical in November, 1788.

An interesting situation developed when Scott resigned immediately after his election to the seat in the house of representatives. Neither

Council nor assembly believed they were empowered to accept his resignation. There was not sufficient time in which to hold another election. So the politicians planned to induce him to retain his seat with the understanding that he would not lose his county office of prothonotary; Wm. Bradford to ————, Feb. 7, Wallace MSS., Bradford Papers, I, p. 194; *JPA,* Feb. 13, p. 70.

86. Hamilton to Wilson, Jan. 25, 1789, *PMHB,* XXX, pp. 210-211. Wm. Bradford to ————, Feb. 7, Wallace MSS., Bradford Papers, I, p. 194. *JPA,* Feb. 6, p. 54. *Packet,* Jan. 7. Federalist ticket: James Wilson, Collinson Read, Laurence Keene, John Arndt, Edward Hand, James O'Hara, Samuel Potts, George Gibson, David Grier, and Alexander Graydon. Radical ticket: James Potter, Walter Stewart, James McLene, John Smiley, Edward Hand, Joseph Heister, Thomas Craig, David Rittenhouse, Philip Wager, and William Gibbons. Stewart and Hand were conservatives. "A Federalist" in *Packet,* Jan. 9. Returns from 13 counties are in issue of Jan. 9.

87. *PCR,* Nov. 12, 13, XV, pp. 592-593, 596. *JPA,* Nov. 13.

88. *JPA,* Nov. 14, p. 24.

89. Committee report in *Packet,* Nov. 13, 1788.

90. *JPA,* Nov. 14, 1787; Mar. 25, 1788; pp. 55, 58, 162-163; Nov. 20, 1788; Feb. 7, 11, 16, 28, Mar. 2, 1789; pp. 61, 66, 72, 106-111. Petition in *Gazette,* Feb. 15, 1789. *Packet,* Feb. 15; "Mentor" and "An Unprejudiced Spectator" in issue of Feb. 20.

91. "A Citizen" in *Indep. Gaz.,* Nov. 11, 1786; on increase in robberies, see issue of Nov. 21. *Packet,* Sept. 18, 1788; "O. T." in *ibid.,* Oct. 23. *JPA,* Mar. 26, 1789, pp. 189-190.

92. Rush to ————, Apr. 9, 1788, Rush MSS., vol. 42, p. 47.

93. *JPA,* Mar. 18, 27, 1788, pp. 149, 172-174; Feb. 17, 19, Mar. 4, 1789, pp. 80, 84-85, 114-115. Smith's letter in *Gazette,* Feb. 18, 1789. "A Federalist" in *Freeman's Journ.,* Nov. 12, 1788. The vote on restoring the College was 44 to 18. T. Coxe to Irvine, Mar. 13, Irvine MSS., X, p.24.

94. *JPA,* Nov. 5, 1788; Mar. 7, 1789; pp. 12, 127-131. *Gazette,* Feb. 4, Apr. 15, 22. *Packet,* Apr. 7, 9, 14. Hiltzheimer, *Diary,* Feb. 9, p. 150. T. Coxe to Irvine, Mar. 13, *loc. cit.*

95. *Gazette,* Feb. 4, Mar. 4, June 11, 1789. In the issue of Mar. 28 it was pointed out that seven sparsely settled counties containing only 13,000 electors would be able by the fourteen seats they would hold in the Censors to prevent any alterations to the Constitution; the rest of the state contained 56,000 electors.

96. Hiltzheimer, *Diary,* Mar. 19, p. 151.

97. Morris to Wilson, Sept. 21, Konkle, "Wilson," II, p. 381. Rush to Montgomery, Mar. 27, Rush MSS., vol. 42. f. 53. Morris to Peters, Aug. 9, Peters MSS., IX, p. 98.

98. Address in *Gazette,* Apr. 8.

99. "Friends of Harmony" in *Packet,* Apr. 29. The following articles in the *Gazette:* "A Pennsylvanian," Mar. 25, Apr. 29, July 1; "One of the People" and "A Freeman," Apr. 1; unsigned article and "A Commonwealth's Man," Apr. 15; "The Friends of Union" and "Just Government," Apr. 29; unsigned articles, Apr. 29, May 7, 27; "Observations," June 3, 10, 17, 24; "A Friend to Liberty and Society," July 15. Also issues of July 1, 15. *PCR,* Mar. 28.

100. *Gazette,* May 13, 20. "Cato" in issue of May 20 attacked these activities in Cumberland and Franklin Counties. In issues of June 3 the *Gazette* claimed that many Radicals of Montgomery County were signing petitions for a convention.

101. Morris to Peters, Aug. 9, Peters Papers, IX, p. 98. Wm. Bradford to Boudinot, July 24, Wallace MSS., Bradford Papers, I, p. 209, believed that both parties sincerely desired an alteration of the Constitution but that the principal agitation was over the mode of effecting it.

102. Clymer to Wilson, [Aug. 23?], Konkle, "Wilson," II, p. 380.

103. Rush to John Montgomery, Mar. 27, Rush MSS., vol. 42, p. 53. Wm. Bradford, Jr., to Boudinot, Sept. 6, Wallace MSS., Bradford Papers, II, p. 4.

104. *JPA,* Sept. 9, 12, 14, 15, pp. 241-242- 249-251, 254-255, 257, 261.

105. "Centinel Revived," XXXI, *Indep. Gaz.,* Sept. 12.

106. *Ibid.,* Sept. 9, *Packet,* Mar. 13, June 23. *Gazette,* Mar. 4. Hiltzheimer, *Diary,* Sept. 15, pp. 154-155.

107. Peters to Morris, Sept. 23, Peters Papers, IX, p. 105. Gallatin to Alex. Addison, Oct. 7, Adams, *Gallatin,* p. 80. James Marshall of Washington Co. to Gallatin, Oct. 9, quoted in Ferguson, *Early West. Pa. Politics,* pp. 102-103.

108. Wm. Bradford to Boudinot, Mar. 21, 1790, Wallace MSS., Bradford Papers, II, p. 18.

109. *JPA,* Nov. 2, 12, pp. 7, 26. Hiltzheimer, *Diary,* Nov. 11, p. 156.

110. Quoted in Adams, *Gallatin,* p. 83. Ferguson, *Early West. Pa. Politics,* p. 104, makes an overstatement when he says that practically every member had served in the assembly, Council, or Censors. Actually twenty-five members had served in none of these bodies since 1776, and if we add eight more who attended only the ratifying convention of 1787, there is a total of thirty-three who did not have public experience.

111. Wm. Findley, "The Fraud Detected" in Greensburg *Farmers' Register,* Sept. 25, 1799. Findley explains how this committee resulted from party and joint-party conferences held at the Bunch of Grapes Tavern. McKean declined to attend these private conferences because of his engagements as judge.

112. *Ibid.* Burd to Yeates, Dec. 3, Walker, *Burd Papers,* p. 153.

113. *Proceedings,* pp. 186-195. Ferguson, *op. cit.,* pp. 107-108. Adams, *Gallatin,* p. 81. Hiltzheimer, *Diary,* Dec. 31, p. 158. Hare and Pickering spoke against popular election of senators. On this point as well as many others Wilson and Lewis differed; Wm. Bradford, Jr., to Boudinot, Jan. 5, 1790, Wallace MSS., Bradford Papers, II, p. 9. In a letter of Jan. 10, *ibid.,* p. 10, to the same correspondent Bradford remarked on the "ingenious, solid, sublime" speeches made by Wilson on the topic of popular election, and added:

> . . . But as he was advocate for the choice being made by the people, he has disobliged many of his old friends—and very bitter feuds have taken place between him and Lewis who have been personally abusive of each other. Since the point has been settled the Convention begins to proceed with some rapidity thru' the report . . .

114. Burd to Yeates, Dec. 3, 10, 1789; January 17, 1790; Walker, *Burd Papers,* pp. 153, 154, 158. Schedule appended to Constitution of 1790.

115. Wm. Bradford to ————, Jan. 5, 1790, Wallace MSS., Bradford Papers, II, p. 9. Montgomery to Irvine, Aug. 3, Irvine MSS., X, p. 56. Montgomery was of the opinion that senators and perhaps the governor should be chosen by electors, or the latter by joint ballot of the two houses. The people at large, he thought, were not the best judges of the fittest men; furthermore, the senate should represent the landed property of the state. Address of the 56 in *JPA,* pp. 301-302. Lloyd to Pres. Mifflin, Sept. 20, *Pa. Arch.,* XI, pp. 728-729.

Bibliography

I. Guides

II. Contemporary Sources

1. Manuscript Material
2. Newspapers and Periodicals
3. Official Documents
4. Contemporary Writings
    a. General Collections
    b. Works of Individuals
    c. Other Contemporary Works

III. Secondary Sources

I. Guides

Beers, Henry P. *Bibliography of Bibliographies of American History.* N. Y., 1938.

Beers, Henry P. "Bibliographies of Pennsylvania History," *Pennsylvania History,* I-II (1934-1936).

Bining, Arthur C., comp. "A Selected Bibliography of Secondary Works on Pennsylvania History," *Pennsylvania Library Notes,* Oct., 1933.

Brigham, Clarence S. "Bibliography of American Newspapers, 1690-1820," American Antiquarian Society *Proceedings,* n. s., XXXII (1923), pt. 1, pp. 81-214.

Calendar of the Correspondence relating to the American Revolution . . . Phila., 1900. Describes the papers of Weedon, Richard Henry Lee, Arthur Lee, and Nathanael Greene in the American Philosophical Society.

Heartman, Charles F. *The Cradle of the United States, 1765-1789: A Collection of Contemporary Broadsides.* Metutchen, N. J., 1922, 1923. 2 vols.

Hildeburn, Charles R. *A Century of Printing. The Issues of the Press of Pennsylvania, 16851784.* Phila., 1886-1886. 2. vols.

Checklist of Philadelphia Newspapers Available in Philadelphia. Works Progress Administration, Historical Records Survey, Project 6102. Phila., 1937. Second edition. (mimeographed).

Griffiin, Grace Gardner, comp. *Writings on American History,* 1906-1933.

Ingram, John V. *Checklist of American Eighteenth Century Newspapers in the Library of Congress.* Washington, 1912.

New York Public Library *Bulletin.* 1897 to date.

Newlin, Claude M. *The Writings of Hugh Henry Brackenridge,* N. p., 1927.

Paltsits, Victor Hugo. *A Bibliography of the Separate and Collected Works of Philip Freneau together with an Account of his Newspapers.* N. Y., 1903.

Pennsylvania Bibliography. Bulletin number 2 of The Pennsylvania Historical Commission. Harrisburg, 1933.

Seidensticker, Oswald. "Die deutsch-amerikanische Zeitungspresse während des vorigen Jahrhunderts," *Deutsch-Amerikanisches Magazin,* I (1887), pp. 405-434, 568-588.

Shearer, Augustus Hunt. "Bibliographical and Descriptive Notes on the Issues of the Journal of the Pennsylvania Assembly, 1776-1790," *Pennsylvania Magazine of History and Biography,* XLI (1917), pp. 354-

364. Mr. Shearer was not familiar with the collection of the *Journals* in the State Library at Harrisburg.

Smyth, Albert H. *Philadelphia Magazines and their Contributors.* Phila., 1892.

II. Contemporary Sources

1. *Manuscript Material*

American Philosophical Society.

Fox, George. Letter Book.

Greene, Nathanael. Correspondence.

Lee, Richard Henry and Arthur. Correspondence.

Krauth Memorial Library, Lutheran Theological Seminary.

Muhlenberg, Frederick A. Manuscripts.

Library Company of Philadelphia.

McAllister Collection.

Rush, Benjamin. Manuscripts.

Smith Collection.

Historical Society of Pennsylvania.

Ashmead, Jacob. Manuscripts.

Balch Papers. Sub series: Shippen Papers. 2 vols.

Biddle, Charles. Autobiography.

Bryan, George. Manuscripts.

Cadwalader Papers. Vol. II on "Reed-Cadwalader Controversy" contains originals of material appearing in the Reed-Cadwalader pamphlets.

Clymer, Daniel C. Papers. 1 vol.

Colonial and Revolutionary Manuscripts.

Gardner, John. Papers.

Gratz Collection. Sub series: Members of Old Congress, Provincial Congress, Pennsylvania Convention of 1775, Pennsylvania Committee of Safety, Charles Thomson Papers, John Dickinson Papers, Winthrop Sergeant's *Loyalist Poetry of the Revolution* (interleaved with manuscripts), additional Gratz Manuscripts.

Hand, Edward. Papers. 2 vols.

Henderson, Robert. Letter Book, 1784-1790.

Henry, William. Manuscripts. 2 vols.

Hopkinson, Francis. Papers (photostats).

Hutchins, Thomas. Papers, 2 vols.

Irvine, William. Manuscripts. Vols. 1-10.

Lamberton Scotch-Irish Collection. 2 vols.

Logan, Maria Dickinson. Collection.

McKean, Thomas. Papers.

Marshall, Christopher. Remembrancer. 1774-1785.

Nead Papers.

Pemberton Papers.

Pennsylvania Petitions.

Peters Papers. Vols. VIII, IX, 1772-1791.

Provincial Delegates. 5 vols.

Rawle, William. Papers. Vol. 1, Journal, 1782-1826.

Society Collection.

Records of Pennsylvania Society for Promoting Abolition of Slavery.

Strettell Manuscripts.

Thomson, Charles. Letter Book, 1783-1784.

Wallace Papers. Sub series, William Bradford Papers. 3 vols.

Wilson, James. Papers.

Yeates, Jasper. Papers.

Wayne, Anthony. Papers. Vols. XII-XIX.

Transcripts of the Susquehanna Company Papers, in possession of Julian P. Boyd.

Library of Congress.

Atlee, Samuel J. and William. Manuscripts, 1759-1816. 1 box.

French Archives, Transcript of. Correspondence Politique, États-Unis.

Morris, Robert. Diary in the Office of Finance. 3 vols.

Pennsylvania Miscellaneous Manuscripts. 2 boxes.

Smith, J. Henley, Papers. Vol. I: Miscellaneous Papers of Jonathan Bayard Smith.

Thomson, Charles. Papers. 2 vols.

University of Pennsylvania.

Minutes of The Trustees of The College, Academy and Charitable Schools.

Minutes of the Trustees of The University of The State of Pennsylvania.

Rosengarten Collection.

Archives Division, Department of Public Instruction, Harrisburg, Pennsylvania.

Constitution of 1776.

Journal of the Council of Censors. Vols. 2, 3; Vol. 1 lacking.

Letters of Executive Council.

Minutes of the Fifth General Assembly of . . . Pennsylvania, 1780-1781.

Minutes of the First Session of the Eighth General Assembly.

Nicholson, John. Papers.

Philadelphia County Papers.

Post Revolutionary Papers.

Port of Philadelphia. Records, 1781-1783.

Revolutionary Papers.

Minutes and Proceedings of the Convention of the State of Pennsylvania held at Philadelphia, July 15th, 1776. Vol. 2 lacking.

Minutes of the Supreme Executive Council of the Commonwealth of Pennsylvania.

State Capitol, Harrisburg, Pennsylvania.

Nicholson, John. Letter Books.

Haverford College, Haverford, Pennsylvania.

Roberts Autograph Collection.

2. *Newspapers and Periodicals*

Carlisle Gazette & Western Depository of Knowledge. Carlisle, Penna.

Columbian Magazine.

Courier de l'Amérique.

Federal Gazette.

Freeman's Journal, or the North-American Intelligencer.

Gemeinnutzige Philadelphische Correspondenz.

Independent Gazetteer, or the Chronicle of Freedom.

Pennsylvania Chronicle, or the York Weekly Advertiser. York, Penna.

Pennsylvania Evening Post.

Pennsylvania Gazette.

Pennsylvania Herald and the American Monitor.

Pennsylvania Herald, and York General Advertiser. York, Penna.

Pennsylvania Journal and Weekly Advertiser.

Pennsylvania Ledger: or the Virginia, Maryland, Pennsylvania and New Jersey Weekly Advertiser.

Pennsylvania Mercury.

Pennsylvania Packet, or the General Advertiser.

United States Magazine.

Collection of Broadsides

Gilpin Collection, Historical Society of Pennsylvania.

Du Simitiere Collection, Library Company of Philadelphia.

Pennsylvania Broadsides, Library of Congress.

3. *Official Documents*

Journals of the House of Representatives of the Commonwealth of Pennsylvania Beginning the twenty-eighth Day of November, 1776, and Ending the Second Day of October, 1781. With the Proceedings of the several Committees and Conventions, Before and at the Commencement of the American Revolution. Vol. I. Phila., 1782.

Minutes of the . . . General Assembly of the Commonwealth of Pennsylvania . . . Phila., 1781-1790. Issued generally by sessions. Most complete collection is in Library Company of Philadelphia.

Minutes of the Convention of the Commonwealth of Pennsylvania, which commenced at Philadelphia, on Tuesday the twenty-fourth Day of November, in the Year of our Lord one Thousand Seven Hundred and Eighty-nine, for the purpose of Revising, and if they see Occasion, Altering and Amending, the Constitution of this State. Phila., 1789. With it is bound the *Minutes of the Grand Committee of the Whole Convention . . .*

Debates and Proceedings of the General Assembly of Pennsylvania on the Memorial Praying a Repeal or Suspension of the Law Anulling the

Charter of the Bank. Matthew Carey, ed. Phila., 1786. Covers the debates from Mar. 3 to April 1, 1786.

Proceedings and Debates of General Assembly of Pennsylvania, from September 4, 1787, to October 4, 1788. Taken in short-hand by Thomas Lloyd. Phila., n. d. 4 vols.

The Proceedings relative to Calling the Conventions of 1776 and 1790 . . . Harrisburg, 1825. Also contains the *Journal of the Council of Censors* but in a drastically abridged form.

The Statutes at Large of Pennsylvania from 1682 to 1809. N. p. 1896-1915. 17 vols. Compiled by James T. Mitchell and Henry Flanders. Vol. IX contains the proceedings of the Provincial Conference of 1776, the proceedings of the Constitutional Convention of 1776, and the Constitution of 1776.

The Pennsylvania Archives, Series I, 12 vols., Phila., 1852-1856. Series 11, 19 vols., Harrisburg, 1874-1890.

The Debate in the Several State Conventions on the . . . Federal Constitution . . . Washington, 1836. Jonathan Elliot, comp. Vol. II contains the debates of the Pennsylvania convention and the proceedings at Harrisburg.

Journals of the Continental Congress, 1774-1789. Washington, 1904-1937. 34 vols. Various editors. Often referred to as the Library of Congress edition of the Journals.

A Brief View of the Accounts of the Treasury of Pennsylvania . . . Phila., 1784. (John Nicholson, comp.) Covers years from beginning of the Revolution to Oct. 1, 1781, and the accounts from each county to Oct., 1782. The latter were issued separately with individual pagination.

A Statement of the Accounts of the United States of America . . . Phila., 1785. Robert Morris' account of his administration as superintendent of finance, 1781-1784. No pagination.

Documents Illustrative of the Formation of the Union of the American States. Washington, 1927.

Journal of the Council of Censors Convened, at Philadelphia . . . Phila., 1783.

Constitutions of Pennsylvania. Harrisburg, 1926. John H. Fertig, comp. The present author compared part of the original MS. Constitution of 1776 in Archives Division, Harrisburg, with the printed copy in this collection and found innumerable liberties taken with punctuation and capitalization in the printed copy; aside from these changes only one vital error was detected in the printed copy.

Minutes of the Supreme Executive Council of Pennsylvania, from its Organization to the Termination of the Revolution. Harrisburg, 1853. 6 vols. Binder's title reads *Colonial Records.*

American Archives . . . Peter Force, ed., 4th and 5th series. Washington, 1837-1853. 9 vols.

Diplomatic Correspondence of the United States, 1783-1789. 1833-1834. 7 vols.

4. *Contemporary Writings*

a. General Collections

(Allen, Andrew Hussey, ed.) *Documentary History of the Constitution of the United States of America, 1786-1870* . . . Washington, 1905. Vol. IV contains numerous significant letters.

(Balch, Thomas, ed.) *Letters and Papers Relating Chiefly to the Provincial History of Pennsylvania* . . . Phila., 1855. Selections from the Shippen Manuscripts.

Bancroft, George. *History of the Formation of the Constitution of the United States*. New York, 1882. 2 vols. Contains many letters of the period.

"Belknap Papers," *Collections* of the Massachusetts Historical Society. Fifth Series, vol. II (Binder's title: "Belknap Papers, Part I"), Boston, 1877. Correspondence between Jeremy Belknap and Ebenezer Hazard. Sixth Series, Vol. IV ("Belknap Papers, Part III"), Boston, 1891, contains letters from Benjamin Rush to Belknap.

Burnett, Edmund C., ed. *Letters of Members of the Continental Congress*. Washington, 1921-1936. 8 vols.

Durand, John, trans. and ed. *New Materials for the History of the American Revolution* . . . New York, 1889. Selections from the correspondence of Gerard and La Luzerne.

Henkels, Stan V., comp. and ed. Catalogues of auction sales. Occasional items were found in the following: nos. 677, 683, 694, 698, 738, 1078, 1092, 1183 (Robert Morris correspondence noted elsewhere), 1275, 1280, 1282, 1290, 1295, 1297, 1303, 1316, 1323, 1326, 1328, 1337, 1356, 1373. Phila., 1891-1924.

"Letters to Robert Morris," *Collections* of the New York Historical Society for the Year 1878. New York, 1879. Pp. 397-488.

"Letters to Robert Morris, 1716-1782," *Magazine of History with Notes and Queries,* XXIII (1916), pp. 247-267.

McMaster, John Bach, and Frederick D. Stone, eds. *Pennsylvania and the Federal Constitution, 1787-1788*. Phila., 1888. Collections of newspaper and pamphlet literature on the subject.

"Price Letters," Massachusetts Historical Society *Proceedings,* 1903. Second Series, XVII. Contains some letters from prominent Pennsylvanians to Richard Price.

1776. A Catalogue of Autograph Letters and Documents . . . Phila., 1926. Issued by the Rosenbach Company.

Sparks, Jared, ed. *Correspondence of the American Revolution, being Letters of Eminent Men to George Washington* . . . Boston, 1853. 4 vols.

Stevens, Benjamin Franklin, comp. *Facsimiles of Manuscripts in European Archives, relating to America, 1773-1783.* London, 1889-1898. 25 vols.

"Three Letters Written at Bethlehem, Pennsylvania, 1778," *Pennsylvania Magazine of History and Biography,* XXVI (1912), pp. 293-302.

b. Works of Individuals

Allen, James. "Diary," *Pennsylvania Magazine of History and Biography,* IX (1885), pp. 176-196, 278-296, 424-441.

Allen, William. *Extracts from William Allen's Letter Book.* L. B. Walker, ed. Pottsville, Penna., 1897.

Barbé-Marbois, Marquis de. *Our Revolutionary Forefathers: The Letters of Francois, Marquis de Barbe-Marbois during his Residence in the United States as Secretary of the French Legation, 1779-1785.* Eugene Parker Chase, trans. and ed. Duffield, N. Y., 1929.

Barbé-Marbois, Marquis de. "Marbois on the Fur Trade," *American Historical Review,* XXIX (1923-1924), pp. 725-740.

Biddle, Charles. *Autobiography of Charles Biddle, Vice-President of the Supreme Executive Council of Pennsylvania. 1745-1821.* (James S. Biddle, ed.) Phila., 1883.

Bond, Phineas. "Letters of Phineas Bond," American Historical Association *Annual Report* for 1896, I, pp. 513-659.

Boudinot, Elias. *Journal or Historical Recollections of American Events During the Revolutionary War* . . . Phila., 1894.

Brackenridge, Hugh Henry. *Gazette Publications.* Carlisle, 1806. Reprint of articles which appeared in *Pittsburgh Gazette.*

Burd, Edward. "Letters," *Pennsylvania Magazine of History and Biography,* XLII (1918), pp. 62-8, 141-155.

Burd, Edward. *The Burd Papers. Selections from Letters Written by Edward Burd. 1763-1828.* N. p. 1899. Lewis Burd Walker, ed.

(Cadwalader, John.) *A Reply to Joseph Reed's Remarks* . . . N. p., 1783. The manuscript of this pamphlet is in the Cadwalader Papers, II, pp. 6-28, HSP.

Chastellux, Marquis de. *Travels in North-America, in the Years 1780-81-82* . . . Translated from the French . . . London, 1787.

Clymer, Daniel. "Letters and Documents from the 'Clymer Papers'," *Pennsylvania Magazine of History and Biography,* XXXI (1907), pp. 43-47.

Conyngham, David Hayfield. "The Reminiscences of David Hayfield Conyngham, 1750-1834, of the Revolutionary House of Conyngham and Nesbitt, Philadelphia, Pa.," *Proceedings and Collections* of the Wyoming Historical and Geneological Society, for the Years 1902 and 1903. Wilkes-Barre, 1904. Horace Edwin Hayden, ed.

Coxe, Tench. *A View of the United States of America, in a Series of Papers. . .* .Phila., 1794. London, reprinted, 1795.

Cutler, Manasseh. *Life, Journals and Correspondence.* Cincinnati, 1888. 2 vols. William P. and Julia P. Cutler, eds.

Drinker, Elizabeth. *Extracts from the Journal of Elizabeth Drinker, from 1759 to 1807, A. D.* Phila., 1889. Henry D. Biddle, ed.

Findley, William. "William Findley of Westmoreland, Pa.," *Pennsylvania Magazine of History and Biography,* V (1881), pp. 440-450. An autobiographical letter to William Plummer, February 27, 1812.

Findley, William. "The Fraud Detected," Greensburg (Penna.), *Farmers' Register,* Sept. 28, 1799.

Fisher, Samuel Rowland. "Journal of Samuel Rowland Fisher, 1779-1781," *Pennsylvania Magazine of History and Biography,* XLI (1917), pp. 145-197, 274-333, 399-457.

Franklin, Benjamin. *Writings.* N. Y., 1905-1907. 10 vols. Albert Henry Smyth, ed.

Franklin, Benjamin. *Works.* N. Y., 1887-1889. 10 vols. John Bigelow, ed.

Frazer, Persifor. "Some Extracts from the Papers of General Persifor Frazer," *Pennsylvania Magazine of History and Biography,* XXXI (1907), *passim.*

Gérard, Conrad Alexandre. *Despatches and Instructions of Conrad Alexandre Gérard, 1778-1780.* Baltimore, 1939. John J. Meng, ed.

Gratz, B. and M. *B. and M. Gratz, Merchants in Philadelphia, 1754-1798. . . .* Jefferson City, Mo., 1916. William Vincent Byars, ed.

Graydon, Alexander. *Memoirs of a Life Chiefly Passed in Pennsylvania within the Last Sixty Years.* Edinburgh, 1822.

Hiltzheimer, Jacob. *Extracts from the Diary of Jacob Hiltzheimer, of Philadelphia. 1765-1798.* Phila., 1893. Jacob Cox Parsons, ed.

Hiltzheimer, Jacob. "Extracts from the Diary of Jacob Hiltzheimer, 1768-1798," *Pennsylvania Magazine of History and Biography,* XVI (1892), pp. 93-102, 160-177, 412-422.

Irvine, William. "Extracts from the Papers of General William Irvine," *Pennsylvania Magazine of History and Biography,* V (1881), pp. 259-275.

Lafayette, Marquis de. "Letters from Lafayette to Luzerne, 1780-1782," *American Historical Review,* XX (1915), pp. 341-376, 577-612. Waldo G. Leland and Edmund C. Burnett, eds. Selections from the archives of the French legation in the United States.

Lee, Richard Henry. *The Letters of Richard Henry Lee.* New York, 1914. 2 vols. James Curtis Ballagh, ed.

Logan, Deborah Norris. *Memoir of Dr. George Logan of Stenton by his Widow, Deborah Norris Logan with Selections from his Correspondence.* Phila., 1899. Frances A. Logan, ed.

La Luzerne, Chevalier de. "Rapport de chevalier de la Luzerne, ministre de France à Philadelphia, sur la situation politique, militaire et commerciale des États-Unis à la fin de l'année 1781," *Revue Historique Diplomatique,* V, (1891), pp. 431-436. Dispatch 203 from Correspondence politique, États-Unis, XIX, 131.

(Markoe, Peter.) *The Algerine Spy in Pennsylvania . . .* Phila., 1787.

Marshall, Christopher. *Extracts from the Diary of Christopher Marshall, Kept in Philadelphia and Lancaster, during the American Revolution, 1774-1781.* Albany, 1877. William Duane, ed.

Marshall, Christopher. "Letters of Christopher Marshall to Peter Miller, of Ephrata," *Pennsylvania Magazine of History and Biography,* XXVIII (1904).

(Morris, Gouverneur.) *Considerations on the Bank of North America.* Phila., 1785.

Morris, Robert. *The Confidential Correspondence of Robert Morris . . .* Stan V. Henkels, ed. Catalogue No. 1183. Phila., n. d.

Morton, Robert. "Diary," *Pennsylvania Magazine of History and Biography,* I (1877), pp. 1-35.

Moylan, Stephen. "Selections from the Correspondence of Col. Stephen Moylan, of the Continental Line," *Pennsylvania Magazine of History and Biography,* XXXVII (1913), pp. 341-360.

(Paine, Thomas.) *Public Good, Being an Examination Into the Claim of Virginia to the Vacant Western Territory . . .* Phila., 1780.

(Paine, Thomas.) *Dissertation on Government, the Affairs of the Bank and Paper Money. By the Author of Common Sense.* Phila., 1786. Also reprinted, Phila., 1838.

Thomas Paine to the Citizens of Pennsylvania . . . Phila., 1805.

Paine, Thomas. *Writings.* N. Y., 1894-1896. 4 vols. Moncure D. Conway, ed.

Penn, John. "John Penn's Journal of a Visit to Reading, Harrisburg, Carlisle, and Lancaster, in 1788," *Pennsylvania Magazine of History and Biography,* III (1879), pp. 284-295.

Rawle, Anna. "A Loyalist's Account of Certain Occurrences in Philadelphia after Cornwallis's Surrender at Yorktown," *Pennsylvania Magazine of History and Biography,* XVI (1892), pp. 103-107.

Rawle, William. "The Last General Assembly under the Pennsylvania Constitution of 1776. Extract from the Diary of William Rawle, Esq., one of the Members during its Final Session," *Pennsylvania Magazine of History and Biography,* XXV (1901), pp. 220-227.

Reed, Joseph. *Remarks on a Late Publication in the Independent Gazetteer. . . .* Phila., 1783.

(Reed, Joseph.) *A Reprint of the Reed and Cadwalader Pamphlets. With an Appendix.* N. p., 1863. The appendix contains additional letters on the controversy.

Robin, Abbé. *New Travels through North-America* . . . Phila., 1783.

Rodney, Caesar. *Letters to and from Caesar Rodney, 1756-1784. . . .* Phila., 1933. George Herbert Ryden, ed.

(Rush, Benjamin.) *Thoughts on Government: Applicable to the Present State of the American Colonies. In Letters from a Gentleman to a Friend.* Phila., 1776.

(Rush, Benjamin.) *Considerations Upon the Present Test-Law of Pennsylvania: addressed to the Legislature and Freemen of the State.* Phila., 1785. Second edition.

Rush, Benjamin. *A Memorial containing. . . . Sundry Incidents in the Life of Dr. Benjamin Rush. . . . Written by Himself. . . .* Lanorie, 1905. Louis Alexander Biddle, ed.

Schoepf, John D. *Travels in the Confederation, 1783-1784.* Phila., 1911. 2 vols.

Schoepf, John D. "Travels through Berks County in 1783," *Pennsylvania Magazine of History and Biography,* V (1881), pp. 74-81.

St. Clair, Arthur. *The St. Clair Papers. The Life and Public Services of Arthur St. Clair. . . . with his Correspondence and other Papers.* Cincinnati, 1882. 2 vols. William Henry Smith, ed.

Smyth, J. F. D. *A Tour of the United States of America* . . . London, 1784. 2 vols.

Thomson, Charles. "Papers of Charles Thomson," *Collections* of the New York Historical Society for the Year 1878, pp. 1-285.

Thomson, Charles. "Early Days of the Revolution in Philadelphia. Charles Thomson's Account of the Opposition to the Boston Port Bill. From the Sparks Manuscript in the Library of Harvard College," *Pennsylvania Magazine of History and Biography,* II (1878), pp. 411-423.

Warville, J. P. Brissot de. *New Travels in the United States of America. Performed in 1788. Translated from the French* . . . N. Y., 1792.

(Webster, Pelatiah.) *Reasons for Repealing the Act of . . . September 13, 1785, for repealing their acts . . . for Supporting and Incorporating the Bank of North America . . . By a Citizen of Philadelphia.* Phila., 1786.

(Webster, Pelatiah.) *An Essay on Credit, in which the Doctrine of Banks is Considered, and some Remarks Made on the present State of the Bank of North America. By a Citizen of Philadelphia.* Phila., 1786.

Webster, Pelatiah. *Political Essays on the Nature and Operation of Money, Public Finances, and Other Subjects.* Phila., 1781. These essays originally appeared in Philadelphia newspapers over the pseudonym, "A Citizen of Philadelphia."

(Wharton, Samuel.) *Plain Facts* . . . Phila., 1781.

Wilkinson, James. *Memoirs of My Own Times.* Phila., 1816. 3 vols.

Willing, Thomas. *Willing Letters and Papers* . . . Phila., 1922. Thomas Willing Balch, ed.

Wilson, James. *Works.* Phila., 1804. 3 vols. Bird Wilson, ed.

(Witherspoon, John.) *An Essay on Money as a Medium of Commerce; with Remarks on the Advantages and Disadvantages of Paper admitted into general Circulation. By a Citizen of the United States.* Phila., 1786.

c. Other Contemporary Publications

An Address to the Inhabitants of Pennsylvania by those Freemen of the City of Philadelphia Who are Now Confined in the Mason's Lodge . . . Phila., 1777. Statement by the Quaker exiles.

A Candid Examination of the Address of the Minority of the Council of Censors to the People of Pennsylvania: together with Remarks upon the Dangers and Inconveniences of the Principal Defects of the Constitution of Pennsylvania. By One of the Majority. Phila., 1784.

The Case of the Sloop Active. (Phila.), 1779.

An Essay on the Seat of the Federal Government . . . Phila., 1789.

"Observations of a London Merchant on American Trade, 1783," *American Historical Review,* XVIII (1913), pp. 769-780. E. C. Burnett, ed.

Proceedings of a Convention of . . . the New England States . . . August 3-9, 1780 . . . N. Y., 1867.

Proceedings of a General Court Martial for the Trial of Major General Arnold. N. Y., 1865. Reprinted from 1780 edition.

Proceedings of the General Town Meeting . . . Held July 26 and 27, 1779, in Philadelphia. Phila., 1779.

A Serious Address to . . . Quakers . . . By a Native of Pennsylvania. Phila., 1788. Second edition. Written before the British left Philadelphia in 1778.

The True Interests of the United States, and Particularly of Pennsylvania, Considered; with respect to advantages resulting from a State Paper-Money; . . . By an American. Phila., 1786.

III. Secondary Sources

Abernethy, Thomas Perkins. *Western Lands and the American Revolution.* N. Y., 1937.

Abraham, Evelyn. "Isaac Meason, the first Ironmaster west of the Alleghenies," *Western Pennsylvania Magazine of History,* XX (1937), pp. 41-50.

Alberger, John. "The Life and Character of Thomas Paine," *North American Review,* LVII, no. CXX (1843), pp. 1-58.

Albert, George Dallas, ed. *History of the County of Westmoreland, Pennsylvania. . . .* Phila., 1882.

Alexander, Edward P. *A Revolutionary Conservative: James Duane of New York.* N. Y., 1938.

Arnold, Isaac N. *Life of Benedict Arnold . . .* Boston, 1869.

Austin, James T. *The Life of Elbridge Gerry . . .* Boston, 1828. 2 vols.

Barthold, Allen J. "French Journalists in the United States, 1780-1800," *Franco-American Review,* Winter, 1937, pp. 215-230.

Beard, Charles A. *An Economic Interpretation of the Constitution of the United States.* N. Y., 1913.

Bell, Whitfield J., Jr. "Some Aspects of the Social History of Pennsylvania, 1760-1790," *Pennsylvania Magazine of History and Biography,* LXII (1938), pp. 281-308.

Boardman, Roger Sherman. *Roger Sherman, Signer and Statesman.* Phila., 1938.

Bolles, Albert S. *The Financial History of the United States from 1774 to 1789: Embracing the Period of the American Revolution.* N. Y., 1879.

Bolles, Albert S. *Pennsylvania, Province and State.* N. Y., 1899. 2 vols.

Boudinot, J. J., ed. *The Life, Public Services, Addresses and Letters of Elias Boudinot, LL.D., President of the Continental Congress.* Boston, 1896. 2 vols.

Breck, Samuel. *Historical Sketch of Continental Paper Money.* Phila., 1863.

Brownson, James I. *The Life and Times of Senator James Ross.* Washington, Penna., 1910.

Buell, R. C. "Constitutional Significance of Early Pennsylvania Price-Fixing Legislation," *Temple Law Quarterly,* XI (1937), pp. 314-329.

Cabeen, F. Von A. "The Society of the Sons of Saint Tammany of Philadelphia," *Pennsylvania Magazine of History and Biography,* XXV-XXVII (1901-1903), *passim.*

Campbell, Hugh C. *History of the Friendly Sons of Saint Patrick and of the Hibernian Society . . .* Phila., 1892.

Carson, Hampton L. "The Case of the Sloop 'Active'," *Pennsylvania Magazine of History and Biography,* XVI (1892), pp. 385-398.

Clarke, George L. *Silas Deane.* N. Y., 1913.

Clarke, William P. *Official History of the Militia and National Guard of the State of Pennsylvania. . . .* N. p., 1909. 3 vols.

Collins, Varnum L. *The Continental Congress at Princeton.* Princeton, 1908.

Conway, Moncure D. *The Life of Thomas Paine . . .* N. Y., 1892. 2 vols.

Craig, Neville B. *The History of Pittsburgh.* Pittsburgh, 1851.

Creigh, Alfred. *History of Washington County.* Harrisburg, Penna., 1871.

Crumrine, Boyd, ed. *History of Washington County, Pennsylvania.* Phila., 1882.

Dapp, Charles Frederick. "The Evolution of an American Patriot: John Henry Miller . . .," Pennsylvania-German Society, *Proceedings and Addresses,* XXXII (1924), pp. 1-68.

Davis, W. W. H. *History of Bucks County, Pennsylvania.* Doylestown, Pa., 1876.

Doniol, Henri. *Participation de la France à l'Établissement des États Unis d'Amérique*. Paris, 1886-1892. 6 vols.

Dunaway, Wayland Fuller. "The English Settlers in Colonial Pennsylvania," *Pennsylvania Magazine of History and Biography*, LII (1928), pp. 317-341.

Dunaway, Wayland Fuller. "French Racial Strain in Colonial Pennsylvania," *Pennsylvania Magazine of History and Biography*, LIII (1929), pp. 322-341.

Dunaway, Wayland Fuller. *A History of Pennsylvania*. N. Y., 1935.

East, Robert A. *Business Enterprise in the American Revolutionary Era*. N. Y., 1938.

Ellis, Franklin, and Samuel Evans. *History of Lancaster County, Pennsylvania*. Phila., 1883.

Ferguson, Russell J. *Early Western Pennsylvania Politics*. N. p., 1938.

Ford, Emily E. F., ed. *Notes on the Life of Noah Webster*. N. Y., 1912. 2 vols. Contains Webster's greater and lesser journals.

Ford, Paul Leicester. "The First Pennsylvania Constitution," *Political Science Quarterly*, X (1895).

Ford, Paul Leicester. *The Origin, Purpose and Result of the Harrisburg Convention of 1788: A Study in Popular Government*. Brooklyn, N. Y., 1890.

Forman, Samuel Egle. *The Political Activities of Philip Freneau*. Baltimore, 1902.

Graeff, Arthur D. *The Relations between the Pennsylvania Germans and the British Authorities (1750-1776)*. N. p., n. d. [Norristown, Penna., 1939.]

Goodman, Nathan. *Benjamin Rush, Physician and Citizen, 1746-1813*. Phila., 1934.

Greene, Evarts B., and Virginia D. Harrington. *American Population before the Federal Census of 1790*. N. Y., 1932.

Griffith, Ernst S. *History of American City Government: Colonial Period*. N. Y., 1938.

Harding, Samuel B. "Party Struggles over the Pennsylvania Constitution," American Historical Association *Annual Report* for 1894, pp. 371-402.

Harley, Lewis R. *Life of Charles Thomson*. Phila., 1900.

Harlow, R. V. "Aspects of Revolutionary Finance," *American Historical Review*, XXXV (1929), pp. 46-68.

Harris, Alex. *A Biographical History of Lancaster County*. Lancaster, 1872.

Hart, Charles Henry. "Robert Lettis Hooper," *Pennsylvania Magazine of History and Biography,* XXXVI (1912), pp. 60-91.

Hastings, George Everett. *The Life and Works of Francis Hopkinson.* Chicago, (1926).

Hastings, George E. "Francis Hopkinson and the Anti-Federalists," *American Literature,* I (1929-1930), pp. 405-418. Prints two hitherto unpublished articles by Hopkinson.

Hayes, R. G. "Business Regulation in Early Pennsylvania," *Temple Law Quarterly,* X (1936), pp. 155-178.

Hocker, Edward W. *The Fighting Parson of the American Revolution. A Biography of General Peter Muhlenberg.* N. p., 1936.

Hutcheson, Harold. *Tench Coxe: A Study in American Economic Development.* Baltimore, 1938.

Jenkins, H. M. *Pennsylvania, Colonial and Federal, 1608-1903.* Phila., 1903. 3 vols.

Johnson, Alvin W. *The Unicameral Legislature.* Minneapolis, 1938.

Jones, Matt Bushnell. *Vermont in the Making, 1750-1777.* Cambridge, Mass., 1939.

Jordan, Francis, Jr. *The Life of William Henry of Lancaster, Pennsylvania, 1729-1786.* Lancaster, 1910.

King, C. R. *Life and Correspondence of Rufus King.* N. Y., 1894-1900. 6 vols.

Knauss, James O. "Social Conditions among the Pennsylvania Germans in the Eighteenth Century, as Revealed in the German Newspapers Published in America," Pennsylvania German Society *Proceedings,* XXIX (1922).

Kohler, Max. *Haym Salomon.* N. Y., 1931.

Konkle, Burton Alva. *George Bryan and the Constitution of Pennsylvania, 1731-1791.* Phila., 1922.

Konkle, Burton Alva. *The Life and Times of Thomas Smith, 1745-1809.* Phila., 1904.

Konkle, Burton Alva. "The Life and Writings of James Wilson." 6 vols. Vol. II contains transcripts of letters to and from Wilson. In manuscript in American Philosophical Society.

Lee, Richard Henry. *Life of Arthur Lee.* Phila., 1825. 2 vols.

Lewis, Lawrence, Jr. "Edward Shippen, Chief Justice of Pennsylvania," *Pennsylvania Magazine of History and Biography,* VII (1883), pp. 11-34.

Lewis, Lawrence, Jr. *History of the Bank of North America.* Phila., 1889.

Libby, Orin Grant. *Geographical Distribution of the Vote of the Thirteen States on the Federal Constitution, 1787-8.* Madison, Wis., 1894.

Lincoln, Charles L. *The Revolutionary Movement in Pennsylvania, 1760-1776.* Phila., 1901.

Lombard, Mildred E. "James Searle, Radical Businessman of the Revolution," *Pennsylvania Magazine of History and Biography,* LIX (1935), pp. 285-294.

McLaughlin, Andrew Cunningham. *The Confederation and the Constitution.* N. Y., 1905.

Meader, Lewis H. "The Council of Censors," *Pennsylvania Magazine of History and Biography,* XXII (1898), pp. 265-300.

Miner, Charles. *History of Wyoming.* Phila., 1845.

Miner, Louise M. *Our Rude Forefathers: American Political Verse, 1783-1789.* Cedar Rapids, Iowa, 1937.

Minich, Michael R. *Memoir of the First Treasurer of the United States.* Phila., 1905. A biographical essay of Michael Hillegas.

Nevins, Allan. *The American States during and after the Revolution, 1775-1789.* N. Y., 1924.

Newlin, Claude Milton. *The Life and Writings of Hugh Henry Brackenridge.* Princeton, 1932.

Oberholtzer, Ellis Paxson. *Robert Morris: Patriot and Financier.* N. Y., 1903.

Peale, Albert Charles. *Charles Wilson Peale and his Public Services during the American Revolution.* N. p. (1896). Extensive quotations from Peale's autobiography.

Peeling, James Hedlay. The Public Life of Thomas McKean, 1734-1817. Ph. D. Thesis. Typewritten MS. in Library of University of Chicago.

Pennypacker, Samuel W. *Pennsylvania in American History.* Phila., 1910.

(Phillips, Henry, Jr.) *An Historical Sketch of the Paper Money Issued by Pennsylvania.* Phila., 1862.

Phillips, P. C. "American Opinion regarding the West, 1778-1783," Mississippi Valley Historical Association *Proceedings for 1913-1914,* VII, pp. 286-305.

Pickering, Octavius, and Charles W. Upham. *The Life of Timothy Pickering.* Boston, 1867-1873. 4 vols.

Potter, John E. "The Pennsylvania and Virginia Boundary Controversy," *Pennsylvania Magazine of History and Biography,* XXXVIII (1914), pp. 407-426.

Reed, William B. *Life and Correspondence of Joseph Reed.* Phila., 1847. 2 vols. Important for the numerous letters it contains.

Read, William Thompson. *Life and Correspondence of George Read.* Phila., 1870.

"Report of the Committee on Linguistic and National Stocks in the Population of the United States," American Historical Association *Annual Report* for 1931.

Richards, Louis. "Hon. James Wilson at Reading," *Pennsylvania Magazine of History and Biography,* XXXI (1907), pp. 48-52.

Rosenthal, Alfred. "The Marbois-Longchamps Affair," *Pennsylvania Magazine of History and Biography,* LXIII (1939), pp. 294-301.

(Rossiter, W. S.) *A Century of Population Growth.* Washington, 1909.

Scharf, J. Thomas, and Thompson Westcott. *History of Philadelphia, 1609-1884.* Phila., 1884. 3 vols.

Sellers, Charles Coleman. *The Artist of the Revolution:The Early Life of Charles Willson Peale.* Hebron, Conn., 1939.

Sellers, Horace Wells. "Charles Willson Peale, Artist-Soldier," *Pennsylvania Magazine of History and Biography,* XXXVIII (1914), pp. 256-286.

Selsam, J. Paul. *The Pennsylvania Constitution of 1776: A Study in Revolutionary Democracy.* Phila., 1935.

Selsam, J. Paul. "The Political Revolution in Pennsylvania in 1776," *Pennsylvania History,* I (1934), pp. 147-157.

Sharpless, Isaac. *A Quaker Experiment in Government: History of Quaker Government in Pennsylvania, 1682-1783.* Phila., 1902. 2 vols.

Siebert, Wilbur H. *Loyalists of Pennsylvania.* Columbus, O., 1920.

Seidensticker, Oswald. "Frederick Augustus Conrad Muhlenberg, Speaker of the House of Representatives, in the First Congress, 1789," *Pennsylvania Magazine of History and Biography,* XIII (1889), pp. 184-206.

Smith, E. P. "Movement for Second Convention of 1788," in *Essays in Constitutional History,* edited by James Franklin Jameson.

Smith, George. *History of Delaware County, Pennsylvania.* Phila., 1862.

Smith, Horace W. *Life and Correspondence of the Rev. William Smith, D. D. . . .* Phila., 1879. 2 vols.

Smith, William R. "Sectionalism in Pennsylvania during the Revolution," *Political Science Quarterly,* XXIV (1909), pp. 208-235.

Sparks, Jared. *The Life of Gouverneur Morris, with Selections from his Correspondence and Miscellaneous Papers.* Boston, 1832. 3 vols.

Stackhouse, A. M. *Col. Timothy Matlack, Patriot and Soldier.* N. p., 1908.

Staples, William R. *Rhode Island in the Continental Congress.* Providence, 1870.

Stillé, Charles J. *Life and Time of John Dickinson, 1732-1808.* Phila., 1891.

Stillé, Charles J. *Major-General Anthony Wayne and the Pennsylvania Line in the Continental Army.* Phila., 1893.

Sumner, William Graham. *The Financier and the Finances of the American Revolution.* N. Y., 1891. 2 vols.

Sutherland, Stella. *Population Distribution in Colonial America.* N. Y., 1936.

Thomas, E. Bruce. *Political Tendencies in Pennsylvania, 1783-1794.* Phila., 1938 (1939).

Van Tyne, Claude H. *The Loyalists in the American Revolution.* N. Y., 1929 (c. 1902).

Van Tyne, Claude H. *The War of Independence: American Phase.* Boston, 1929.

Walker, L. B. "Life of Margaret Shippen, the Wife of Benedict Arnold," *Pennsylvania Magazine of History and Biography,* XXIV-XXVI (1900-1902).

Westcott, Thompson. *Names of Persons Who Took the Oath of Allegiance to the State of Pennsylvania between the Years 1777 and 1789, with a History of the "Test Laws" of Pennsylvania.* Phila., 1865.

Wetherill, Charles. *History of the Religious Society of Friends Called by Some the Free Quakers in the City of Philadelphia.* N. p., 1894.

Wharton, Anna H. "Thomas Wharton, Junr. First Governor of Pennsylvania under the Constitution of '76," *Pennsylvania Magazine of History and Biography,* V, VI (1881-1882).

APPENDIX I

MAPS

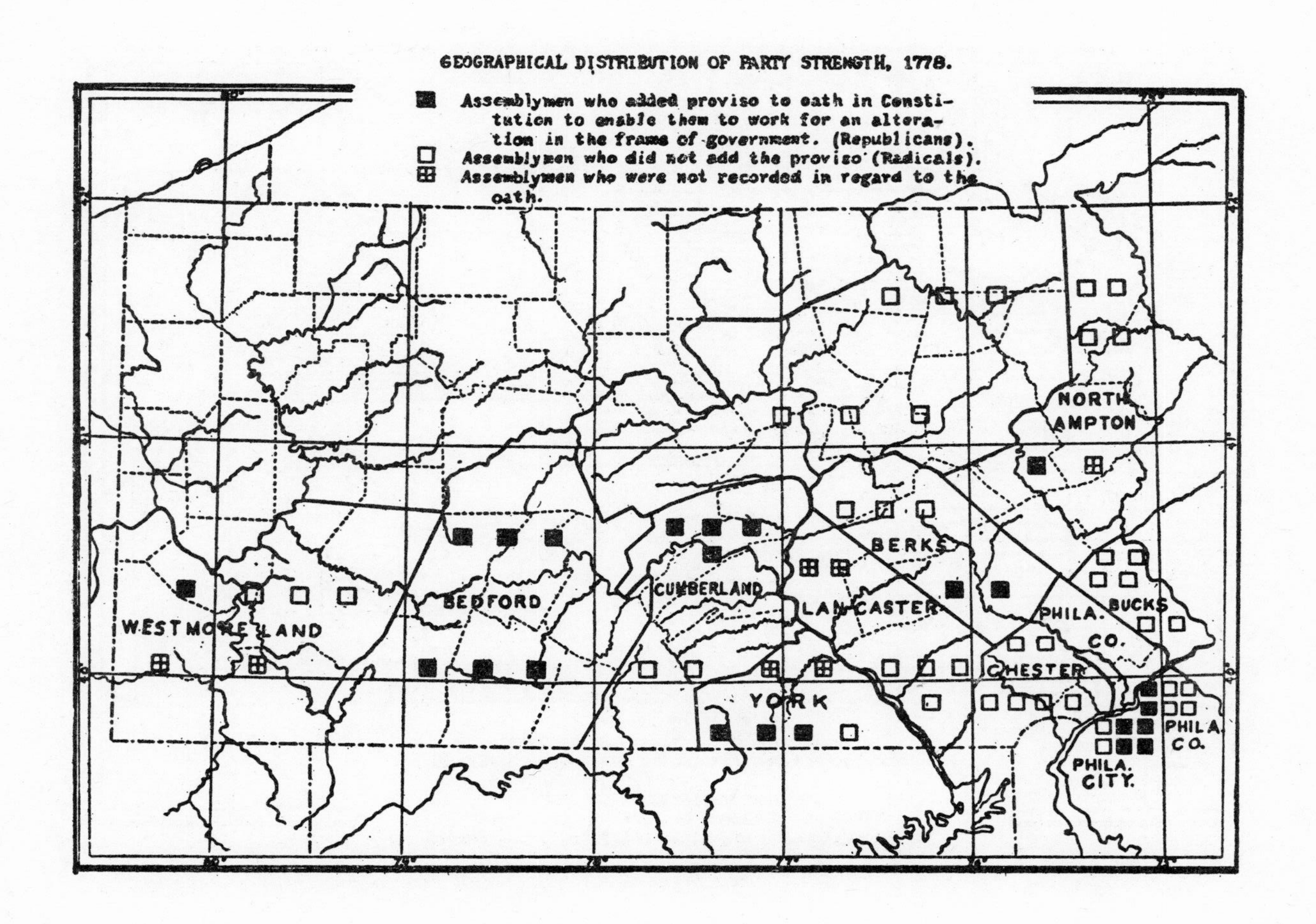
GEOGRAPHICAL DISTRIBUTION OF PARTY STRENGTH, 1778.
Assemblymen who added proviso to oath in Constitution to enable them to work for an alteration in the frame of government. (Republicans).
Assemblymen who did not add the proviso (Radicals).
Assemblymen who were not recorded in regard to the oath.
NORTH AMPTON
BERKS
BUCKS
PHILA. CO.
CHESTER
LANCASTER
CUMBERLAND
YORK
BEDFORD
WESTMORELAND
PHILA. CO.
PHILA. CITY.

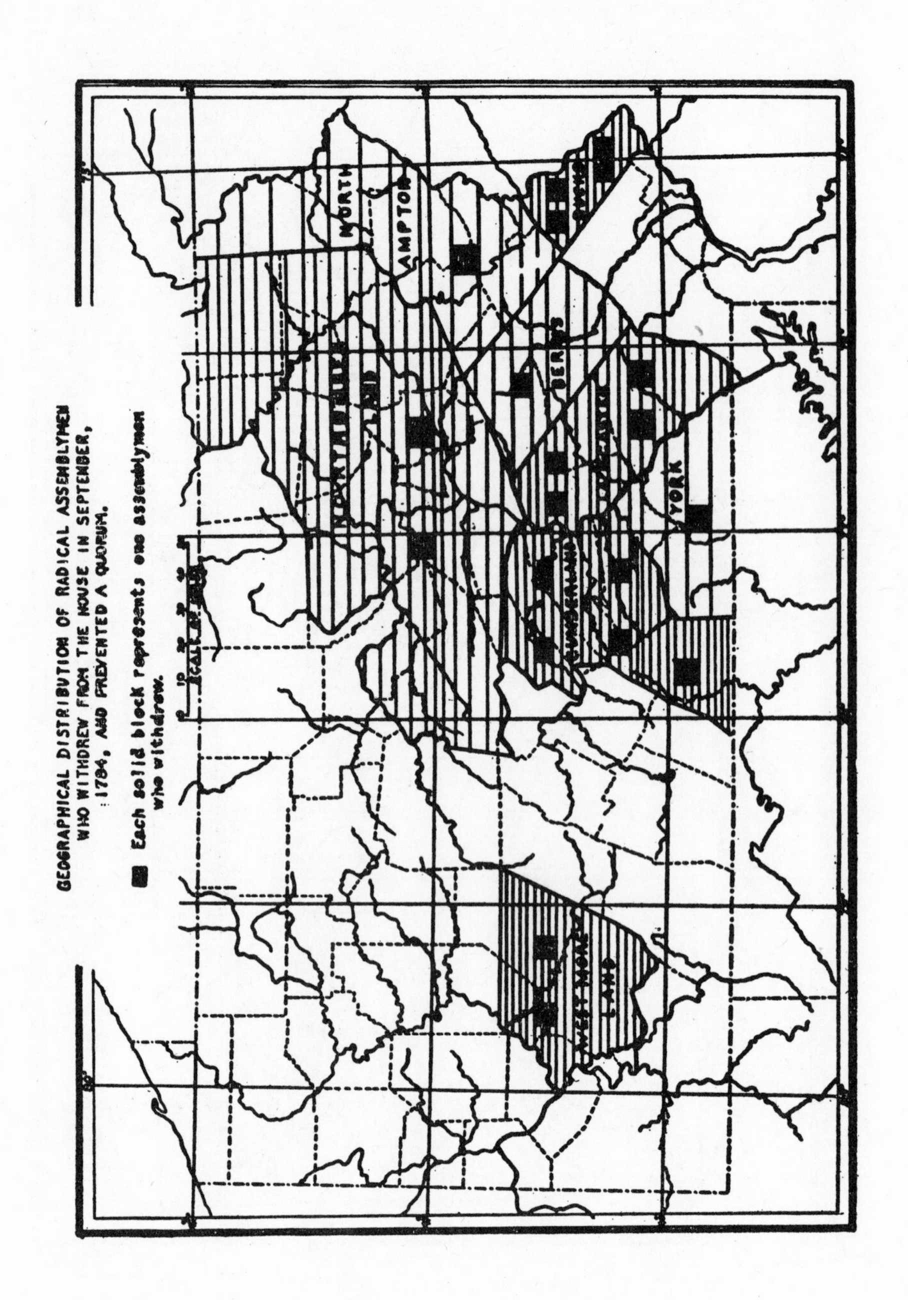
GEOGRAPHICAL DISTRIBUTION OF RADICAL ASSEMBLYMEN
WHO WITHDREW FROM THE HOUSE IN SEPTEMBER,
1784, AND PREVENTED A QUORUM.
Each solid block represents one assemblyman
who withdrew.
NORTH
AMPTON
BERKS
YORK
CUMBERLAND
WEST MORE
LAND

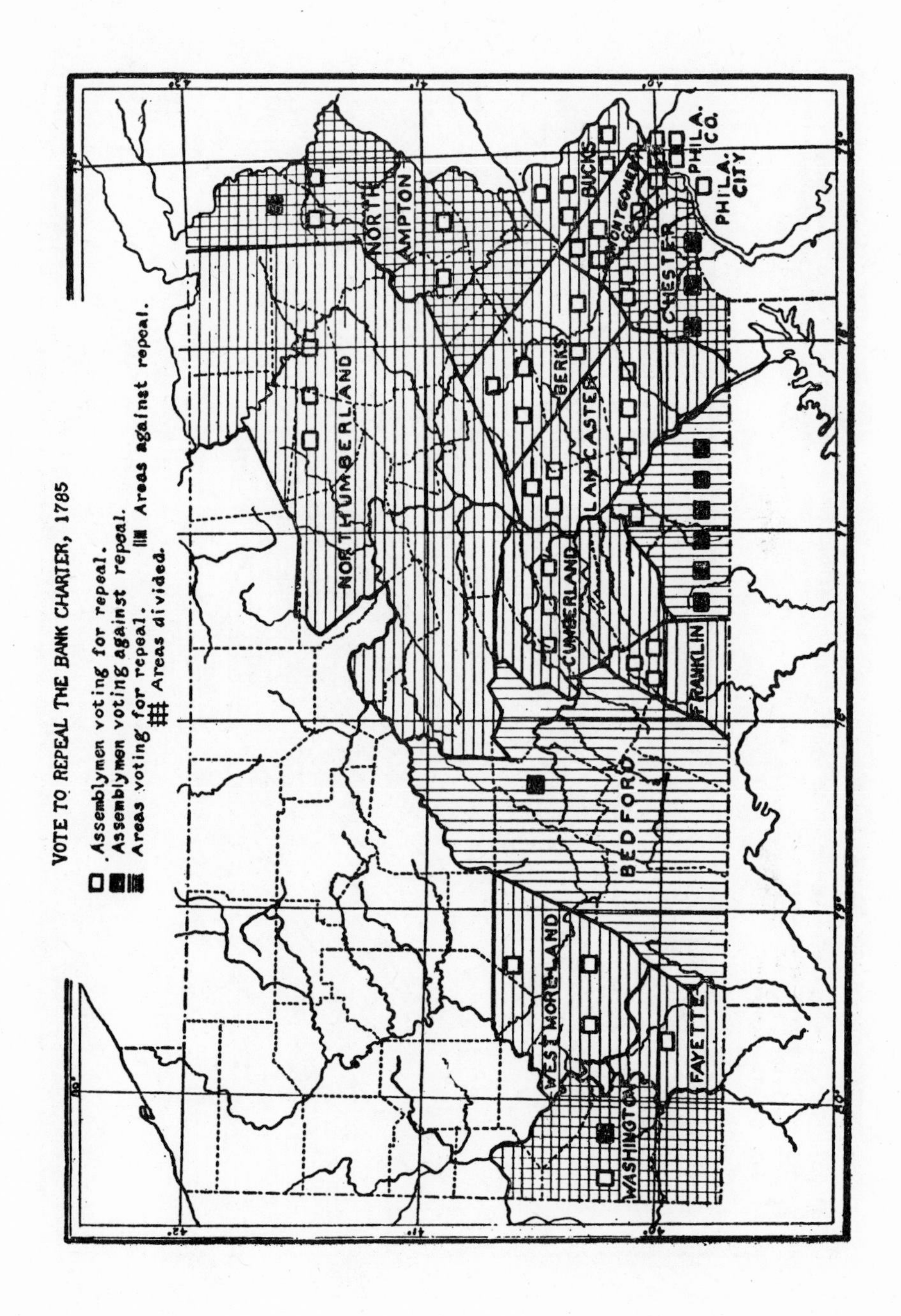

VOTE TO REPEAL THE BANK CHARTER, 1785

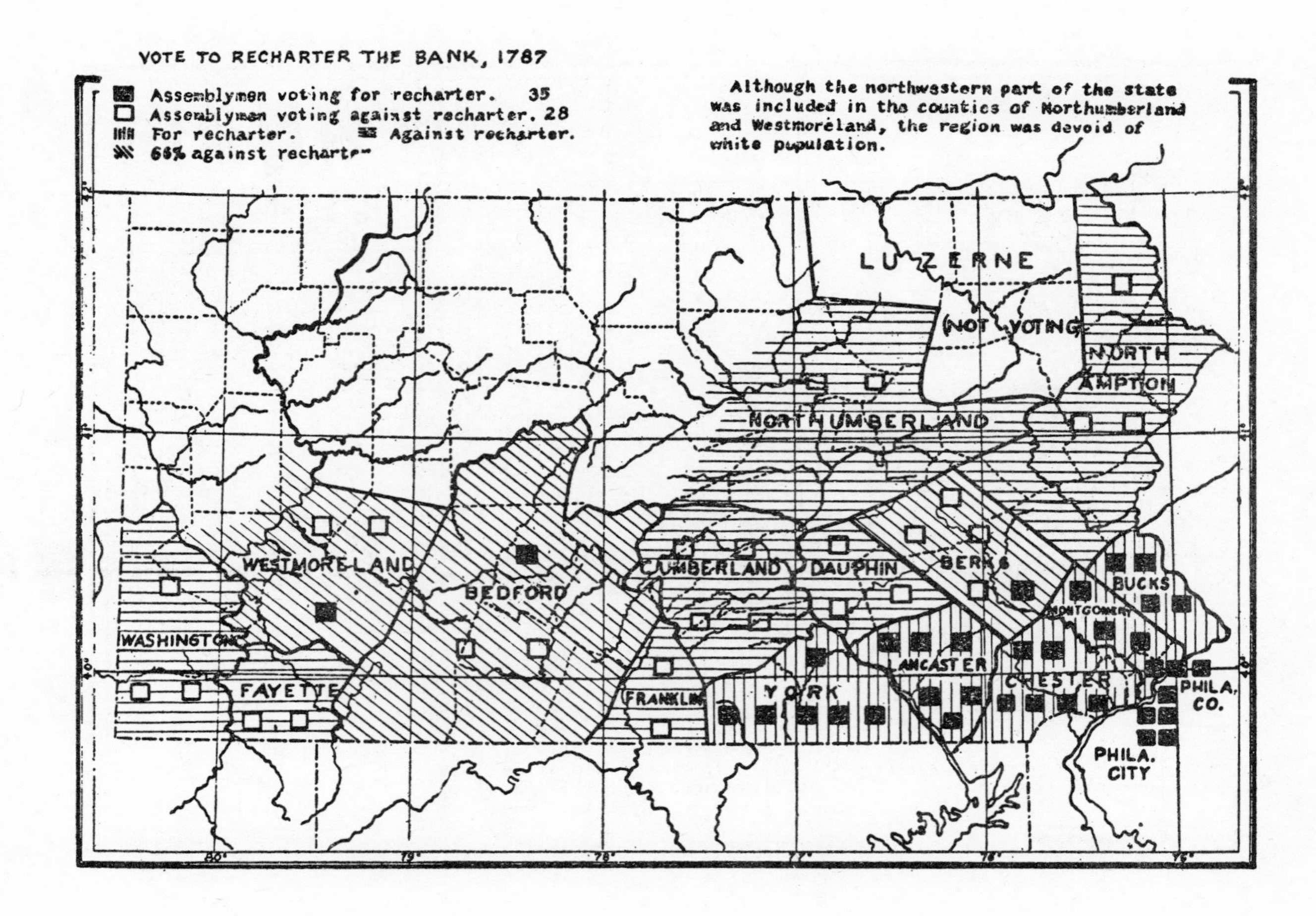
VOTE TO RECHARTER THE BANK, 1787
Assemblymen voting for recharter. 35
Assemblymen voting against recharter. 28
For recharter.
Against recharter.
66% against recharte
Although the northwestern part of the state was included in the counties of Northumberland and Westmoreland, the region was devoid of white population.
LUZERNE
NOT VOTING
NORTHAMPTON
NORTHUMBERLAND
WESTMORELAND
BEDFORD
CUMBERLAND
DAUPHIN
BERKS
BUCKS
MONTGOMERY
WASHINGTON
LANCASTER
FAYETTE
FRANKLIN
YORK
CHESTER
PHILA. CO.
PHILA. CITY
80°
79°
78°
77°
76°
75°

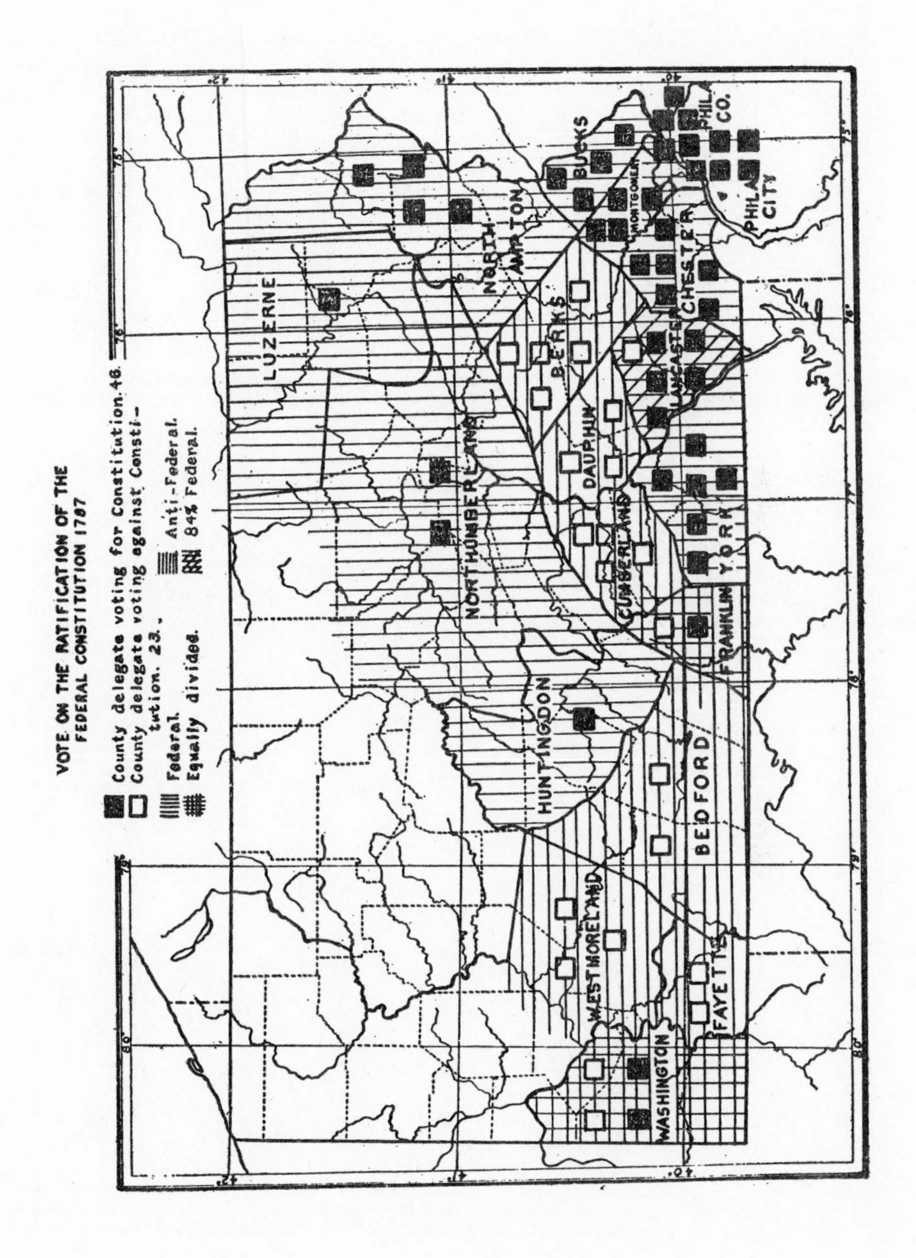
VOTE ON THE RATIFICATION OF THE
FEDERAL CONSTITUTION 1787
County delegate voting for Constitution. 46.
County delegate voting against Constitution. 23.
Federal.
Equally divided.
Anti-Federal.
84% Federal.
LUZERNE
NORTHAMPTON
BUCKS
PHILA. CO.
PHILA. CITY
MONTGOMERY
BERKS
CHESTER
LANCASTER
DAUPHIN
NORTHUMBERLAND
CUMBERLAND
YORK
FRANKLIN
HUNTINGDON
BEDFORD
WESTMORELAND
FAYETTE
WASHINGTON

APPENDIX II

Tabulation of Votes

The following data have been taken from *Pennsylvania Archives,* sixth series, XI, which gives the official election returns from the counties. The volume contains many lacunae. In some cases data have been found in newspapers and private letters; these sources are indicated at the proper places.

Usually the returns give only the votes for the successful candidates. Where votes for losing candidates have been available, the information is listed in parallel columns.

Tabulation of Votes

ALLEGHENY COUNTY			1789			
Councillor			Wilkins	1038		
BEDFORD COUNTY	1786		1789			
Councillor			Martin	600		
Assemblymen	Piper	529[a]	Moore	593[b]		
	Cannon	334	Husbands	589		
	Cable	289				
BERKS COUNTY	1776		1779		1782	
Councillor	Tea	90				
Assemblymen	Eckert	109	Heiser	555	Clymer	610
	Gehr	107	Levan	517	Lower	579
	Hunter	106	Eckert	477	Lincoln	505
	Spyker	94	Lower	436	Patton	374
	Gulden	80	Jones	321	Ludwig	307
	Levan	60			Ege	268
Councillor	1783		1784			
			Biddle	634		
Censors	Read	718				
	Gehr	629				
Assemblymen	Lincoln	733	Lutz	1135		
	Clymer	730	Lincoln	1135		
	Lollar	715	Lower	875		
	Lutz	690	Spyker	845		
	Bishop	445	Davis	744		
	Rice	401	Rhoads	553		

Bucks County	1777		1779		1780	
Councillor			Lacey	437	Fell	432
Assemblymen	Keller	183	Fell	481	Fell	432
	Cornell	125	G. Wynkoop	470	Savage	393
	Kirkbride	107	Scott	443	Scott	344
	Watts	105	Watts	382	G. Wynkoop	329
	Folwell	90	Savage	286	Morgan	280
	Grier	82				

	1782				1783			
Councillor	Wall	777	217	Wynkoop				
Censors					Smith	494	76	H. Wynkoop
					Hart	450	32	Chapmans
Assemblymen					Long	572	160	Hanna
					Savitz	540	82	McIlvaine
					Thomas	535	66	Craig
					Clark	514	63	Goforth
					Rue	213		

	1785		1786				1788	
Councillor	Dean	761					Gregg	1366
Assemblymen			Foulke	979	472	Smith[tt]		
			G. Wynkoop	975	455	Clark		
			Chapman	993	452	Irvine		
			Opp	937	421	Keller		

		1789		
BUCKS COUNTY (Cont.)				
Assemblymen	G. Wynkoop	1257	482	Smith
	Opp	1257	470	Brown
	Chapman	1241	468	Rodman
	Bryan	1224	405	Thomas
State Constitutional Convention	Ogden	1730	502	Benezet
	Jenks	1255	479	Backhouse
	Barclay	1237	477	Shewell
	Stout	1237		

	1777		1778		1779[d]	
CHESTER COUNTY						
Councillor	Mackey	284				
Assemblymen	Fulton	283	Fulton	375[c]		
	Cunningham	282	Anderson	342		
	Cochran	248	Culbertson	341		
	Gronow	239	Cochran	339		
	Culbertson	199	Gardner	337		
	Gardner	199	Fleming	245		

		1780			1781	
Assemblymen	Thomas	1293	630	McDowell	Frazer	839
	Hayes	1290	586	Hannum	Culbertson	521
	Harris	830	557	Pearson	Maffat	512
	Park	724	526	Harvard	Evans	472
	Boyd	708	498	Bell	Hannum	448
	Anderson	691	93	Moore	Moore	442
	Culbertson	688	36	Strawbridge	Anderson	389
	Evans	634	181	Others	Lindsey	387

	1784				1789	
CHESTER COUNTY (Cont.) *Councillor*					Ruston	1586
Assemblymen	Willing	1274	1003	Hannum	Thomas	2927 e
	Wayne	1258	998	Evans	James	2773
	Jones	1174	954	Fulton	Downing	2682
	Ralston	1157	952	Thomas	McDowell	2306
	Strawbridge	1078	941	Brannan		
	Frazer	1060	932	Moore		
	Potts	1038				
	Humphreys	1008				
Delegates to State Constitutional Convention					Gibbons	2869 e
					Bull	2359
					Ross	1956
					Boyd	1452

	1776		1777		1779	
CUMBERLAND COUNTY *Councillor*	Hoge	473			Whitehill	513
Assemblymen	McClean	483	Duffield	429	Smith	750f
	Duffield	478	McClean	428	Culbertson	674
	Clark	468	Clark	418	Hoge	661
	Alexander	453	Brown	412	Harris	656
	Brown	450	Whitehill	407	Watts	653
	Whitehill	447	Harris	243	McDowell	452
					Steel	243

CUMBERLAND COUNTY (Cont.)

		1782				1783		
Assemblymen	Duncan	1479	634	Montgomery	Brown	2210	1265	Dunlap
	Brown	1285	583	Allison	Watts	2066	1498	Allison
	Carothers	1181	565	Dunlap	Johnston	1936	1490	Bratton
	McClean	994	477	Smith	Carothers	1919	1338	Pawling
	Johnston	974	173	Rodgers	Brown, Esq.	1763	1239	Scott
	J. Hoge	862	99	D. Hoge	Smith	1763		
	Maxwell	637	51	Others	Whitehill	1711		
Censors					McClean	1762	1672	Harris
					Irvine	1705	1570	Maxwell

		1784			1786	
Councillor	Hoge	642	168	Duncan		
Assemblymen	Watts	642	169	Montgomery	Whitehill	2498[g]
	Harris	641	168	Irvine	Bales	1962
	Brown	638	165	Galbraith	Kennedy	1294
	Whitehill	636	165	Dunlap	Mitchell	1061

	1787		1789	
Councillor	Watts	1293		
Assemblymen	Mitchell	1507	Kennedy	2849[h]
	Beales	1230	Mitchell	2847
	Kennedy	1217	J. Hoge	2831
	Oliver	1115		
Delegates to State Constitutional Convention			Whitehill	1972[h]
			Power	1363
			Irvine	1358

	1785		1786				1787		1789	
DAUPHIN COUNTY										
Councillor	Brown	469					Kucher	282		
Assemblymen			Clark	542	368	Brodley[i]			Miley	1291[j]
			Miley	538	261	Orth			Carson	1004
			Carson	418					McCreight	811
Delegates to States Constitutional Convention									Gloniger	901[i]
									Brown	878
									Cook	843
DELAWARE COUNTY										
Assemblymen									Lloyd	1022[e]
									Riley	728
FRANKLIN COUNTY										
Councillor							Smith	938		
Assemblymen			Smith	317[k]						
			McCalmont	291						
HUNTINGDON COUNTY										
Councillor									Elliott	228

Lancaster County	1778		1783					
Councillor	Smith	1216	Atlee	1540				
Censors			Whitehill	1722				
			Chambers	1172				
Assemblymen	Gilchrist	676	Scott	2375				
	Grubb	673	Brown	2368				
	Lowery	665	Mercer	2344				
	Smiley	653	Craig	2342				
	Anderson	643	Slough	2274				
	Brown	607	Work	2216				
			Orth	2157				
			Hubley	1512				
			Cook	1314				
			Parr	1082				
			Coleman	1074				
	1785				1786			
Assemblymen	Hand	1384	720	Boyd[l]	Lowery	888	11	Craig[m]
	Hubley	1376	719	J. Craig	Carpenter	883	9	Boyd
	Lowery	1376	699	Illigh	Atlee	865	4	Jenkins
	Atlee	1371	697	R. Craig	Hubley	864	4	J. Porter
	Carpenter	1369	696	Potter	Ross	839	3	W. Porter
	Work	1368	692	Jenkins				
	Scott	1364	670	Smith				
	1787		1789					
Councillor	Ross	879						
Assemblymen			Miller	1336	1267	Clemson		
			Erb	1333	1172	Hopkins		
			Cunningham	1325				
			Dering	1320				

MIFFLIN COUNTY			1789			
Assemblymen			Harris	666[n]		
			Oliver	621		
MONTGOMERY COUNTY	1785		1786		1789	
Councillor	P. Muhlenberg	578				
Assemblymen			Reiff	1402[i]		
			Roberts	1294		
			Markeley	708		
			Vaux	546		
Delegates to the State Constitutional Convention					J. Morris	864[i]
					Potts	859
					Coats	741
					Shoemaker	680
NORTHAMPTON COUNTY	1778		1779			
Assemblymen	Rhoads	814	Rhoads	630	Depue	257
	Van Campen	679	Ralston	628	Sigfrid	123
	Driesbach	588	Wagner	583	Newcomer	70
	McFarren	499	Van Campen	355	Giger	59
	Wagner	425	Driesbach	285	Caston	64
					Stroud	45
	1780		1781		1782	
Councillor	Van Campen	330				
Assemblymen	Wagner	640	Hartzel	994	Hartzel	801
	McFarren	556	McFarren	881	Arndt	760
	Lattimer	496	Kohler	695	Stroud	742
	Kohler	415	Lattimer	592	Lattimer	452
	Rhoads	413	Stroud	429	Kohler	303

Northampton County (Cont.)	1783		1784			
Councillor	Balliot	363				
Censors	Jno. Arndt	808				
	Driesbach	589				
Assemblymen	Jac. Arndt	915	Mawhorter	902	558	Traill
	Stroud	894	Brown	879	492	Stroud
	Hartzel	592	Burkhalter	700	395	Arndt
	Brown	572	Hartzel	677	350	Schmyser
	Limbach	434	Ralston	577	525	Six Others

	1785		1786		1787	
Councillor			Traill	461		
Assemblymen	Mawhorter	551 o	Trexler	652	Trexler	1233
	Traill	496	Mawhorter	630	Mawhorter	1232
	Trexler	478	Brown	542	Burkhalter	1167
	Burkhalter	396	Burkhalter	441	Ealer	749
	Brown	375				

	1788		1789	
Councillor			Hertzel	551p
Assemblymen	Trexler	850	Ealer	602p
	Ealer	790	Balliott	562
	Ihrie	597	Ihrie	533
	Balliott	555	Lerch	477
Delegates to the State Constitutional Convention			Sitgraves	882p
			Mawhorter	565
			Rhoads	554
			Arndt	562

NORTHUMBERLAND COUNTY	1777		1778		1783			
Councillor					Boyd	266	279	Martin[r]
							34	Dale
Censors					Montgomery	317	274	Gray
					Hunter	288	265	Potter
							37	Others
Assemblymen	Deal	122	Dale	251	McClenaghan	304	295	F. Antes
	Fruit	119	Hemrod	250	Cook	288	240	Montgomery
	Murray	100	McKnight	247	Maclay	281	201	Weitzel
	Irvin	100	Martin	246			33	W. Antes
	Hemrod	100	Chambers	211			35	Fruit
	Flemming	72	White	201				

	1785				1786		1789	
Councillor					Maclay	413	Wilson	664[j]
Assemblymen	F. Antes	414	407	Maclay[s]	Antes	380[k]	Maclay	855[j]
	Dale	414	396	Weitzel	Dale	334	White	585
	D. Montgomery	410	297	Selling				

PHILADELPHIA CITY	1776				1780			
Councillor	No Councillor	406	211	Clymer				
			13	Moore				
Assemblymen	Parker	682	278	Rittenhouse	S. Morris	870	200	Hutchinson[t]
	Clymer	413	273	J. B. Smith	Muhlenberg	869	to	Gurney, and
	R. Morris	410	269	Shreiner	R. Morris	649	300	Kammerer
	S. Morris	407	268	Matlack	Delaney	615		
	Bayard	397	268	Wharton	Steinmetz	531		
	Shubart	393						

Philadelphia City (Cont.)		1781				1783		
Councillor	Bayard	604	425	Mifflin[u]				
			278	Dickinson				
Censors					Bryan	350	115	McKean[w]
							12	Lewis
							8	Patterson
Assemblymen	Muhlenberg	763	341	J. Reed[u]				
	S. Morris	760	326	Sergeant				
	Delaney	758	309	Schlosser				
	Steinmetz	751	303	Hutchinson				
	Meredith	751	303	Kammerer				
		1784				1785		
Councillor					Franklin	2347[x]		
Assemblymen	Pettit	1024	781	FitzSimons[v]	Will	2310	1135	Pettit
	Moore	1021	775	Nesbitt	Morris	1240	1115	Bayard
	Bayard	1014	767	Hall	FitzSimons	1232	1110	Kuhl
	Kuhl	1013	762	Sickle	Irvine	1230	1109	Moore
	Will	1002	730	Shields	Clymer	1224		
		1786				1787		
Assemblymen	Will	2432	1043	Pettit[t]	Clymer	1511		
	Morris	1604	998	Irvine	FitzSimons	1507		
	FitzSimons	1567	982	Kuhl	Hiltzheimer	1501		
	Clymer	1550	976	Adcock	Lewis	1483		
	Hiltzheimer	1539			Will	1480		
Members of Convention to Ratify Federal Constitution					Latimer	1215	235	Franklin[z]
					Rush	1211	150	Pettit
					Baker	1204	148	Rittenhouse
					Wilson	1203	137	Steinmetz
					McKean	1157	132	Irvine

PHILADELPHIA CITY (Cont.)	1788		1789	
Councillor	Miles	1487		
Assemblymen	Clymer	2017	Sickle	1197aa
	FitzSimons	2013	Hiltzheimer	1184
	Hiltzheimer	2011	Lewis	984
	Sickle	1990	Rawle	888
	Lewis	1850	Gurney	787
Delegates to the State Constitutional Convention			Wilson	1181aa
			Baker	1111
			Roberts	1102
			Lewis	1037
			McKean	708

PHILADELPHIA COUNTY	1776					July, 1777		
Councillor	No Councillor	370	133	Hill	Reed	84	2	R. Morris
			5	Bull				
			1	Antes				
Assemblymen	Knox	523	255	Hill				
	Dickinson	419	182	Bull				
	Gray	419	138	Lollar				
	Potts	407	136	Coates				
	Hughes	282	134	Neff				
	Antes	275	134	Currey				
			11	Others				

PHILADELPHIA COUNTY (Cont.)	1779		1781		1784			
Assemblymen	Knox	518	Holgate	1326	Engle	529	395	Robinson[v]
	Bayard	517	Heister	1311	Eyre	528	380	Mifflin
	Lollar	504	McClean	1311	Boyce	528	375	Ashmead
	McClean	487	Smith	1310	Vansant	527	375	Gray
	Heston	484	Gray	1160	Coates	510	373	Edwards
	Coates	450	Rees	830				
	Heister	422	Hill	691				
	Mecklin	344	Campbell	675				
	Thomson	302	Penrose	664				

	1786				1787	
Assemblymen	Mifflin	1462	549	Boyce[y]	Mifflin	777
	Gray	1461	545	Eyre	Robinson	775
	Salter	913	543	Nice	Salter	767
	Robinson	911			Logan	765
	Logan	910			Peters	750

	1788		1789	
Councillor	Mifflin	955		
			Peters	982[aa]
Assemblymen	Peters	956	Ashmead	819
	McPherson	956	Paul	788
	Salter	955	Britton	522
	Logan	955	Boyce	463
	Robinson	948		
Delegates to the State Constitutional Convention			Mifflin	786[aa]
			Gray	784
			Robinson	763
			Hare	545
			Edwards	476

Washington County	1784							
Assemblymen	Ritchie	776						
	Stevenson	756						
York County	1777		1778				1780	
Councillor	Edgar	333	Thompson	. . .	681	Ewing		
Assemblymen	Dixon	357	Hartley	680	183	Gossort	Ramsay	1496[bb]
	Agnew	356	Lilley	679	37	Dill	Mitchell	1482
	Dunwoody	354	Slagle	676	1	McClean	McClean	1479
	Dill	348	Edie	644	1	Hay	Smith	1434
	Orr	334	Schmyser	619			Dixon	1311
	Hahn	119	Ross	534			Lilley	1222
							Galbraith	1200
							Schmyser	1200
	1782		1783					
Censors			Hartley	2004	493	Swope		
			McAllister	1563				
Assemblymen	Hay	2072	McClean	2080	656	Scott		
	McGoffin	2023	Hay	2079	508	Albright		
	McPherson	1653	McPherson	2075	458	Mitchell		
	McClean	1447	McGoffin	2027	426	Dill		
	Schmyser	1372	Miller	1534				
	Hahn	1359	Gardner	1406				
	Scott	1356	Grier	1309				
	Lilley	1340	McConaughy	1178				

YORK COUNTY (Cont.)	1784		1785		1786	
Councillor	McAllister	880				
Assemblymen	McPherson	1130	Miller	768	Eichelberger	767
	Miller	939	McConaughy	763	Lilley	767
	Gardner	927	Schmyser	763	Tyson	763
	Hay	925	Gardner	755	McConaughy	763
	Ewing	917	Lilley	741	McClelland	762
	McConaughy	908	Tyson	630	Schmyser	760
	Tyson	874	McClean	587		
	Lilley	861	Eichelberger	566		

	1787				1788	
Councillor	Edie	1346	684	Eichelberger		
Assemblymen	Schmyser	1372	799	Tyson	McClelland	1505
	Mitchell	1360	678	Smith	Clingan	1463
	McClelland	1355	665	Jameson	Lilley	1379
	Lilley	1352	660	Edie	Schmyser	1179
	Reed	1332	647	Lewis	Tyson	1098
	Clingan	1241	458	Delap	Reed	704
			194	Dunlap		

	1789	
Assemblymen	Clingan	4222
	Reed	4177
	Schmyser	3678
	Stewart	3662
	Lilley	3416
	Godfrey	3055

VOTES FOR REPRESENTATIVES IN CONGRESS, 1788[cc]

	Thos Hartley	Henry Wynkoop	F A Muhlenberg	Geo Clymer	Thos Fitzsms	Thos Scott	Steph Chambers
Philadelphia	1726	1743	1774	1699	1714	1718	1217
Philadelphia County	776	786	812	769	764	766	593
Bucks	656	658	682	658	657	651	632
Chester	903	904	901	890	900	895	890
York	1497	1497	1492	1482	1488	1486	1475
Berks	24	27	187	26	7	5	24
Lancaster	655	656	771	642	652	649	651
Cumberland	285	283	285	287	268	281	271
Northampton	256	271	311	260	267	261	31
Montgomery	311	349	367	320	321	308	272
Dauphin	96	91	121	85	86	79	76
Northumberland	197	198	196	195	199	197	195
Franklin	374	375	373	363	363	365	364
Huntingdon	134	139	134	131	138	138	133
Bedford	91	92	97	93	92	90	51
Westmoreland	133	137	145	137	118	118	129
Luzerne	17	17	16	17	17	17	17
Total	8131	8223	8664	8054	8051	8024	7021
Washington[dd]	32	28	33	33	35	44	32
Fayette	28	29	29	29	30	28	27
Total	8191	8280	8726	8116	8116	8096	7080
Official return announced by Council[ee]	8163	8246	8707	8094	8086	8068	7050

VOTES FOR REPRESENTATIVES IN CONGRESS (Cont.)

	John Allison	P. Muhlenberg	Danl Heister	Wm Findley	Chas Pettit	Wm Irwin	Wm Montgy	Blair McClenachan	Robt Whitehill
Philadelphia	1214	821	796	376	357	333	309	286	272
Philadelphia County	600	495	495	346	333	337	329	289	293
Bucks	647	259	226	231	220	230	230	220	208
Chester	896	211	209	205	204	198	199	198	199
York	1489	205	203	209	201	205	193	195	198
Berks	28	450	458	442	440	437	435	430	275
Lancaster	647	320	348	347	347	344	343	342	223
Cumberland	271	1553	1559	1569	1563	1588	1560	1560	1562
Northampton	23	406	419	186	177	176	176	155	128
Montgomery	266	300	286	246	243	244	232	209	185
Dauphin	71	486	498	495	494	485	481	480	443
Northumberland	197	355	355	358	357	355	356	356	353
Franklin	380	545	541	555	551	552	554	549	545
Huntingdon	135	70	65	77	66	67	65	66	70
Bedford	50	214	212	175	173	173	172	172	168
Westmoreland	110	426	426	466	453	459	425	414	426
Luzerne	17	1	1	2	1	1	1	1	1
Total	7041	7117	7097	6285	6180	6184	6060	5922	5549
Washington[dd]	33	298	306	302	304	308	299	303	307
Fayette	24	50	52	51	53	54	50	52	52
Total	7098	7465	7455	6638	6537	6546	6409	6277	5908
Official return announced by Council[ee]	7067	7417	7403	6586	6481	6492	6348	6223	5850

Notes

a. Assembly debates, Nov. 2, 1786, in *Packet,* Nov. 3, 1786; also *JPA,* Dec. 9, pp. 69-70. Votes for Councillor are fragmentary.

b. *Freeman's Journ.,* Nov. 4, 1789.

c. *JPA,* Nov. 6, 1778, p. 233.

d. Conflicting returns. See *Pa. Arch.,* 6 ser., XI, pp. 130-135.

e. *Indep. Gaz.,* Oct. 17, 1789.

f. Fifth district did not vote.

g. *Indep. Gaz.,* Oct. 19, 1786.

h. *Ibid.,* Oct. 21, 1789.

i. *Ibid.,* Oct. 16, 1786.

j. *Ibid.,* Oct. 23, 1789.

k. *Ibid.,* Oct. 25, 1786.

l. *Ibid.,* Oct. 22, 1785.

m. *Ibid.,* Oct. 14, 1786.

n. *JPA,* Nov. 2, 1789, p. 5. Another return gave Oliver 611 and Harris 525.

o. For first three districts only.

p. *Indep. Gaz.,* Oct. 20, 1789.

q. *JPA,* Nov. 6, 1778, pp. 23ff. For another return, see *Pa. Arch.,* 6 ser., XI.

r. Disputed election. See documents in *Pa. Arch.,* 6 ser., XI, pp. 290-303.

s. *JPA,* Nov. 22, 1785, p. 53.

t. F. A. Muhlenberg to Henry Muhlenberg, Oct. 11, 1780, Muhlenberg MSS.

u. *Journal,* Oct. 13, 1781.

v. *Mercury,* Oct. 15, 1784.

w. Election of June 18. *Indep. Gaz.,* June 26, 1784.

x. *Mercury,* Oct. 14, 1785.

y. *Indep. Gaz.,* Oct. 12, 1786.

z. *Ibid.,* Nov. 18, 1787.

aa. *Ibid.,* Oct. 15, 1789.

bb. Fourth district not included. *Pa. Arch.,* 6 ser., XI, pp. 434-435.

cc. *Gazette,* Dec. 17, 1788.

dd. *Packet,* Dec. 20, 1788.

ee. *Ibid.,* Jan. 1, 1789.

tt. *Indep. Gaz.,* Oct. 13, 1786. The votes for Chapman are probably not quite accurate.

INDEX

B

F

I

J

K

L

M

N

T

Y

Z